CW00642206

PHILOSOPHY AND THE LANGUAGE OF THE PEOPLE

Which language should philosophers use: technical or common language? In a book as important for intellectual historians as it is for philosophers, Lodi Nauta addresses a vital question which still has resonance today: is the discipline of philosophy assisted or disadvantaged by employing a special vocabulary? By the Middle Ages, philosophy had become a highly technical discipline, with its own lexicon and methods. The Renaissance humanist critique of this specialized language has been dismissed as philosophically superficial, but the author demonstrates that it makes a crucial though controversial point: it is through the misuse of language that philosophical problems arise. He charts the influence of this critique on early modern philosophers, including Hobbes and Locke, and shows how it led to the downfall of medieval Aristotelianism and the gradual democratization of language and knowledge. This book will be essential reading for anyone interested in the transition from medieval to modern philosophy.

Lodi Nauta is Professor of Philosophy at the University of Groningen. He is author and editor of several monographs and essay collections, including the award-winning *In Defense of Common Sense: Lorenzo Valla's Humanist Critique of Scholastic Philosophy* (2009), and has written numerous journal articles and book chapters on medieval and early modern philosophy. He was a recipient of the Spinoza Award in 2016.

PHILOSOPHY AND THE LANGUAGE OF THE PEOPLE

The Claims of Common Speech from Petrarch to Locke

LODI NAUTA
University of Groningen

CAMBRIDGE
UNIVERSITY PRESS

University Printing House, Cambridge CB2 8BS, United Kingdom

One Liberty Plaza, 20th Floor, New York, NY 10006, USA

477 Williamstown Road, Port Melbourne, VIC 3207, Australia

314–321, 3rd Floor, Plot 3, Splendor Forum, Jasola District Centre,
New Delhi – 110025, India

79 Anson Road, #06–04/06, Singapore 079906

Cambridge University Press is part of the University of Cambridge.

It furthers the University's mission by disseminating knowledge in the pursuit of education, learning, and research at the highest international levels of excellence.

www.cambridge.org
Information on this title: www.cambridge.org/9781108845960
DOI: 10.1017/9781108991476

First published 2021

Printed in the United Kingdom by TJ Books Limited, Padstow Cornwall

A catalogue record for this publication is available from the British Library.

Library of Congress Cataloging-in-Publication Data
NAMES: Nauta, Lodi, author.
TITLE: Philosophy and the language of the people : the claims of common speech from Petrarch to Locke / Lodi Nauta, University of Groningen, The Netherlands.
DESCRIPTION: Cambridge, United Kingdom ; New York, NY, USA : Cambridge University Press, 2021. | Includes bibliographical references and index.
IDENTIFIERS: LCCN 2020052325 (print) | LCCN 2020052326 (ebook) | ISBN 9781108845960 (hardback) | ISBN 9781108994118 (paperback) | ISBN 9781108991476 (ebook)
SUBJECTS: LCSH: Philosophy – Terminology. | Philosophy – Language. | Philosophy, Medieval. | Philosophy, Modern. | Language and languages – Philosophy.
CLASSIFICATION: LCC B49 .N38 2021 (print) | LCC B49 (ebook) | DDC 101/.4–DC23
LC record available at https://lccn.loc.gov/2020052325
LC ebook record available at https://lccn.loc.gov/2020052326

ISBN 978-1-108-84596-0 Hardback

Contents

Acknowledgments

This book was written, for the most part, during my two terms as dean of the Faculty of Philosophy at the University of Groningen. To combine deaning, teaching, and research (not to mention birdwatching) remains a challenge, but I have been helped immensely by the fact that this faculty is not only a center of philosophical excellence but also a community where intellectual freedom and professional efficiency are matched only by a wonderfully collegial spirit, which even a nasty virus was not able to dispel. I am grateful to all my colleagues for making this place such an intellectually and socially inspiring environment.

For comments, suggestions, advice, and support of various kinds I am grateful to many of my colleagues and friends. In particular I should mention Han Thomas Adriaenssen, Michael Allen, Robert Black, Christopher Celenza, Alexandra Chadwick, Brian Copenhaver, Unn Falkeid, James Hankins, Jill Kraye, Martin Lenz, David Lines, Christoph Lüthy, Peter Mack, John Monfasani, Carla Rita Palmerino, Jan Papy, Matthias Roick, Andrea Robiglio, and Arthur Weststeijn. I thank Simone and our children Julia and Roeland for their love and delightful companionship.

The Dutch Research Council (NWO) did me an immense honor when it awarded me the Spinoza Prize in 2016. I would also like to thank the Royal Netherlands Institute in Rome (KNIR) for its hospitality on my usually brief visits, and its former director, Harald Hendrix, for inviting me to visit as a KNIR Fellow in the first three months of 2017.

Three chapters have been published before as articles, but they have been revised and in some cases expanded: Chapter 3 on Pontano in *The Journal of the History of Ideas* 72:4 (2011), 481–502; Chapter 4 on Vives in *The Journal of the History of Ideas* 76:3 (2015), 325–345; and Chapter 5 on Nizolio in *Renaissance Quarterly* 65:1 (2012), 31–66. Some sections of Chapter 2 on Valla are based on my article in *Renaissance Quarterly* 71:1 (2018), 1–32. I thank my publishers and editors for allowing me to reuse this material here.

Introduction

Throughout the ages philosophers have questioned our common-sense view of the world, claiming that the world is not as it appears to be.[1] This claim is almost the philosopher's *raison d'être*. Philosophy thrives on the idea that there is a deep structure – matter, atoms, substance, essences, powers, forms, faculties, the absolute spirit, hypostases, Platonic Ideas, or what have you – behind the phenomena we perceive and claim to know; it would amount to naive empiricism to think that what we see is all there is to know, or that it would be enough to justify our claims to knowledge. As a distinguished historian of philosophy has observed: "Over the centuries, it has been practically definitive of the philosopher's job to subject naive empiricism to a withering critique. Indeed, stages in the development of philosophy can be measured in terms of how far they depart, and in which direction, from our natural but naive pre-theoretical orientation toward empiricism."[2]

This departure from a so-called naive empiricism has often gone hand in hand with the development of a language that likewise departs from the way in which people commonly speak about the world. Like scientists, mathematicians, grammarians, lawyers, theologians, and practitioners of various professions, philosophers too developed their own technical language, sometimes staying fairly close to the common parlance of the time but often introducing a more technical, abstract, formal terminology, needed, so it was thought, to refer to and analyze these deeper (or higher) levels of reality, to bring clarity in our philosophical views, or to change our perspective on the world. Whatever it is that philosophers do, it usually comes with a terminology that for the non-initiated may look like mere

[1] "Common-sense view of the world" is of course a highly contested notion. The essentially contested nature of what is claimed to be "common" and "ordinary" when it comes to language use in philosophy is a central theme of this study; hence no attempt has been made in this general introduction to offer any kind of definition.

[2] Pasnau 2011, 115.

jargon, but for the philosophers in question is necessary to reach the rigor and precision that philosophical analysis requires. Hence, understanding philosophers often begins with learning their language; mastering the terminology of, for example, Spinoza, Kant, Hegel, or Heidegger, aided by books with titles such as *Le Vocabulaire de Spinoza*, *Kant Lexikon*, or *Hegel Dictionary*, is like learning a foreign language; and something similar is true of familiarizing oneself with the technical apparatus of analytical philosophy.

Dissonant voices have been heard over the centuries: Does ordinary language, in principle, not contain all the necessary terms, semantic nuances and distinctions, and pragmatic directions that we need for analyzing philosophical concepts? Do we not create rather than solve our philosophical problems by introducing all kinds of technical terminology? If technical terms can ultimately be translated into ordinary language, why not use the latter from the start? And if such a translation proves to be impossible, is that not a sign that we have been playing a game all by ourselves that has no longer any connection with the things we wanted to analyze or explain in the first place? Such questions have left most philosophers unperturbed, and they continued to believe that ordinary language is too imprecise, vague, and unstable for doing rigorous philosophy. Bertrand Russell spoke for many when he said: "Everybody admits that physics and chemistry and medicine each require a language which is not that of every day. I fail to see why philosophy, alone, should be forbidden to make a similar approach towards precision and accuracy."[3]

Such debates about the language of philosophy are well known, in particular, from the twentieth century when philosophical Idealism and the rise of formal logic led in some circles to a defense of the use of ordinary language. But we find appeals to common language or the common understanding of words also much earlier in history. One of the most prominent case studies is the critique by humanists and early-modern philosophers of the Aristotelian-scholastic language developed and practiced in the schools and universities of medieval and early-modern Europe.[4] It is the aim of this book to bring this critique into the narrative of Western philosophical history, showing that it reflected significant trends at that time that would ultimately effect a gradual erosion and demise of a paradigm that had ruled for hundreds of years. In several chapters devoted to a selective range of thinkers from this period, different aspects of this fascinating and highly complicated process will be studied.

[3] Russell 1959, 178. [4] Cf. Copenhaver and Schmitt 1992, 329–357.

This introduction serves to provide a general framework for the case studies that follow.

Aristotelian-scholastic philosophy was brimming with technical terminology. The reasons for this are too complex and too varied to discuss here, but the basic stages of its development are well known: Aristotle himself had already had to invent some technical vocabulary to express the central concepts of his philosophy and logic. Translators in antiquity from Cicero to Boethius struggled with his language and concepts, but succeeded in providing the Latin West with a corpus of writings that gradually became the curriculum in the schools and universities.[5] Translations of Aristotle from the Greek and Arabic as well as commentaries were added to the corpus in the twelfth and thirteenth centuries, and ever new forms of Latin vocabulary had to be coined to match the complexity of the logic, natural philosophy, and metaphysics and all the other parts of this growing edifice: *forma*, *intentio*, *species virtus*, *ens*, *entitas*, *esse*, *essentia*, *actus*, *potentia*, *haeceitas*, *perseitas*, *ubicatio*, *intensio et remissio formarum*, and *suppositio*, with all its all subdivisions and technical terminology such as *restrictio*, *ampliatio*, *distributivus*, *confusus*, *mobilis/immobilis*, *descensus*, *ascensus*, and a myriad of other terms. Building on this Aristotelian corpus, medieval scholars also initiated new developments, for instance, in what we might call the philosophy of language (e.g. the speculative grammar of the Modists), logic (e.g. terminist logic), natural philosophy (e.g. the semantic approaches by the so-called Calculatores), and theology, and many fresh problems in virtually every corner of the Aristotelian building were formulated and discussed throughout the period till the end of the seventeenth century. Also in the twilight of its existence Aristotelian scholasticism was certainly not the retarded, conservative force it is often portrayed to have been, but could challenge the new philosophy in interesting ways.[6]

The longevity, however, had perhaps taken its toll. Basic terminology had already been difficult enough to understand in all its complex uses and transmutations. But new terminology had to be coined to express ever new concepts and distinctions as specialization grew and debates intensified particularly in metaphysics and logic. What is true for almost any kind of theorizing is certainly true for the scholastic way of philosophizing: concepts require new concepts, and to clarify these new concepts still other concepts have to be introduced, and so on, till one might wonder whether

[5] Pasnau (ed.) 2014 contains state-of-the-art chapters on many aspects of the development of medieval philosophy.

[6] For a general discussion of the vitality and resilience of seventeenth-century scholastic Aristotelianism see Mercer 1993; Pasnau 2011 for a comprehensive treatment with full bibliography.

the gains of this ever-growing complexity are not subject to the law of diminishing returns; whether our philosophical systems, in the words of Francis Bacon, are not "but so many stage-plays, representing worlds of their own creation after an unreal and scenic fashion."[7] The higher we come in this conceptual building the more, it seems, we lose base with our initial object of study or question. It has become a game on its own, with new concepts or entities requiring new terms. Even a highly sympathetic interpreter of scholastic thought such as Robert Pasnau admits that "one risk this kind of analysis runs is that we will end up not just up to our necks in metaphysical parts, but positively drowning – that once we begin to postulate such entities, we will be forced to postulate infinitely many more."[8] We might think "that nothing of any explanatory value has been achieved by all this philosophizing." It is indeed "the timeless complaint made of all philosophy."

Whatever its truth-value, it was certainly a complaint made passionately by Renaissance humanists and early-modern philosophers alike. From the time of Petrarch onward humanists began to heap scorn on the so-called barbarous Latin of the scholastics, and this critique continued to be voiced by early-modern philosophers in various forms and in different contexts. Though a prominent feature of the humanist program of restoring classical Latin as the vehicle for learned communication and conversation, this critique of scholastic "jargon" has not attracted wide attention from historians of philosophy. While it is an exaggeration to say that the history of the critique of scholastic jargon is "virtually unexplored"[9] – one need only think of the age-old contest between philosophy and reason on the one hand and rhetoric and eloquence on the other – it seems fair to say that the slow and gradual demise of Aristotelian scholasticism has usually been analyzed with reference to metaphysics, natural philosophy, and psychology (the *scientia de anima*). Changes in metaphysical and physical concepts such as substantial form, substance, final cause, space, impetus, matter, and motion, have seemed more promising and more telling evidence for the new directions philosophy was taking in the sixteenth and seventeenth centuries. Less attention has been paid to the critique of language, though it is intrinsically connected to these changes. It is not difficult to understand the reasons for this relative neglect.

[7] Bacon 1857–1874, IV, 55 (*The New Organon*, I, 44).

[8] Pasnau 2011, 211 and 210 (on Scotus's analysis of the inherence of accidents in a substance).

[9] Burke 1995, 22. For some book-length studies on the debate between scholastics and humanists, in which criticisms of scholastic language play a significant role, see Moss 2003; Rummel 2000; Wels 2000; Nauta 2009; Schmidt 2009; Martin 2014; Celenza 2018.

First, the critique of language in this entire period often has the character of a topos, a highly repetitious litany that scholastic language is obscure, incomprehensible, ungrammatical, in short "barbarous." Without further explanation or justification, such a critique easily becomes monotonous, sterile, uninteresting, and philosophically shallow. At first sight, there does not seem to be much variation in these complaints during the period, and while in the beginning of the humanist movement there was at least a dominant paradigm to fight against, by the mid-seventeenth century one might get the impression that the critique had sometimes become something of a straw man, as other new and interesting developments, such as the rise of mathematics and the increasing use of experimental observation, began to occupy a much more prominent role.

Second, the critique seems to be not only monotonous and philosophically superficial, but also unfair. The claim then is that the humanists simply failed to understand the nature of philosophical and scientific analysis, which cannot do without a certain technical terminology. On this view, the humanist complaint that the Latin of the schools is unnatural, artificial, ugly, and ungrammatical only shows that humanists failed to see that a special language is needed to match the rigor of philosophical analysis. In addition to the revival of a classicized Latin, the humanist attempt to revive and emulate ancient rhetorical practice is likely only to deepen the philosopher's suspicion – as if rhetoric can replace the standards of exact, clear, and technical language that philosophy requires.

These sentiments are understandable, and yet historically there are good reasons to pay more attention to critics of scholastic language. First, mere repetition over the centuries might also be a sign that there was more at stake than some aesthetic preference. As already noted, Aristotelianism in all its variety remained a vigorous, resilient tradition, so that it remained, in the eyes of its opponents, a powerful paradigm worth attacking in the seventeenth century no less than in earlier times. Seen from this angle, the critique of language was not a by-product of a paradigm shift that took place elsewhere; it was a vital element in the critique of Aristotelian scholasticism as a whole. This leads to a second reason. We need not subscribe to a form of linguistic determinism to realize that language is deeply embedded in culture, giving expression to it and shaping it. We can therefore expect the language critique of this period to be more than just a critique of some barren expressions or some pieces of badly construed Latin. It could include the following items, starting with the critique of scholastic Latin itself:

- Scholastic Latin vocabulary and grammar (as opposed to "good" Latin following classical norms).
- The study of logic as an end in itself, a mere verbal art (as opposed to an examination of the things themselves, "*res*").[10]
- The Aristotelian ideal of demonstrative science, characterized by notions such as deduction, demonstration, definition, universality, certainty, and truth (as opposed to induction, observation, experience, particularity, and also to less stringent requirements of knowledge such as verisimilitude and probability).
- The study of artificially constructed fallacies and forms of argumentation (as opposed to an examination of arguments in practice or real life).
- Disputations and other scholastic methods, denounced as cavillations, quibbles, and sophistry, that aim at solely promoting one's own position (as opposed to collaborative efforts in the search for the truth).
- The *ipse dixit* attitude ("he has spoken"); that is, an appeal to the authority of Aristotle that was supposed to clinch the argument (as opposed to the *libertas philosophandi*, the freedom to philosophize).
- Scholastic terminology as quasi-precise but in fact "insignificant speech," devoid of any explanatory power.
- Scholastic language as the language of the Church and the university, used as a means to mystify, deceive, impress, or overpower the people (as opposed to the common language as an instrument of communication and bond of society).
- Technical language as a form of uncivilized behavior, and as pedantry (as opposed to civilized forms of conversation at court and in society at large).

We will meet these points in the chapters to come, but the point of listing them is simply to remind ourselves that the critique of language – again, whatever its historical plausibility – was a broad category, not limited to aesthetics or Latin philology. As an expression not only of thought but also of an entire approach and culture, creating identity and securing power, language was of course much more than a neutral verbalization of what went on in the mind. While humanists aimed at a reform of the language arts (the arts of the trivium: grammar, rhetoric, and dialectic) and the university curriculum based on the works of Aristotle, philosophers in the seventeenth century had sometimes different motives to criticize the

[10] The concept of *res* gradually changed from "subject matter" to "things" in the sense of material objects; Vickers 1987, 11. Cf. Eamon 1996, 292–296; Serjeantson 2006, 153–154.

language of the schools, but what many of them shared with their humanist predecessors was the conviction that the language of the schools was the expression of a culture that was hampering progress in the arts and sciences. Being more than just a critique of the barbarous concoction of a so-called unnatural and ungrammatical Latin, it could also target patterns of thinking and behavior that were deemed to be dangerously abstract or politically and religiously corrupt. Thomas Hobbes comes to mind of course, whose critique of the abstract nature of scholastic language went hand in hand with his rejection of a spiritual domain of souls of which the Church claimed to be the guardian and spokesman (see Chapter 7).

We can develop this point a bit more. Through the critique of language important notions, ideas, and attitudes were attacked that opponents had associated, rightly or wrongly, with Aristotelian scholasticism. This might look like a trivial point, for how else can one criticize a philosophical notion than by criticizing the linguistic expression used to speak about that notion? If one disagrees with the opponent's theory of free will, the argument is likely to start with the opponent's definition or use of the words "free" and "will." But while this is a valid point for any kind of (philosophical) debate, the critique of scholastic language often went further than the individual concept, rejecting an entire form of discourse because that discourse was believed to be intrinsically connected with a particular style of philosophizing. Because much of the rejected terminology referred to entities and distinctions of a metaphysical and logical kind, the language critique could easily lead, for instance, to a rejection of these entities and distinctions as well (see for example Chapter 5). Rejecting abstract entities is, of course, not an exclusively early-modern phenomenon; we need only think of a medieval nominalist such as William of Ockham, who was perfectly happy to use a technical, scholastic terminology himself, to realize that a critique of philosophical language exists in every philosophical tradition. It also does not mean that language critique inevitably led to a thoroughgoing nominalism or anti-essentialism. The point, however, is that certain philosophical and intellectual developments that are characteristic for this period were intrinsically linked to a critique of scholastic language: trimming scholastic ontology required trimming scholastic terminology, because the introduction of a new term, for example *haecceitas* (thisness) or *ubicatio* (being in a place) led to the postulation of a new entity, or vice versa. It could thereby easily become a critique that put a question mark over the existence or usefulness of various kinds of metaphysical and logical notions as well as distinctions such as the Aristotelian categories, transcendental terms, essence, act/

potency, matter/form, second intentions, common natures, universals, and so on. It is for this reason that language critique cannot be absent from a history of the gradual downfall of the Aristotelian-scholastic paradigm.

The questioning of abstract entities could also lead to a form of skepticism about the whole idea of reaching certainty and truth about essences, substantial forms, quiddities, haecceities, and the like. Scholars have detected skeptical tendencies in humanism, and the rise of forms of ancient skepticism has been seen as a hallmark of the early-modern period.[11] These are controversial claims, but it is not implausible to suggest that the critique of scholastic terminology referring to these entities went hand in hand with a growing awareness that such ideals of certainty and demonstrative truth, widely perceived at the time as essential ingredients of the Aristotelian system, are out of our reach. Again, we need to be cautious here. On the one hand, among scholastics we already find the idea that essences cannot be known and that we must be satisfied with probable knowledge; the conjectural status of natural philosophical knowledge was widely conceded among scholastic commentators in the sixteenth century, followed by Hobbes, Gassendi, and many others in the seventeenth century.[12] On the other hand, certainty was not given up *tout court* by early-modern thinkers, as testified by Descartes's search for indubitable truth, Hobbes's claim to have set the science of politics on a secure footing, Spinoza's philosophical system *more geometrico*, or Locke's attempt to show that morality is capable of deductive demonstration. But these seventeenth-century developments had been preceded by at least two centuries of a growing dissatisfaction with the demonstrative ideal of Aristotelian science; it was increasingly considered as a bookish and abstract affair that did not deliver the results its defenders had promised. Again, the rejection of (abstract) terms is of course not a sufficient condition for the rise of skepticism about the possibility of knowledge of the referents of those terms. But it seems plausible to suggest that the critique of scholastic language by self-professed outsiders of the Aristotelian paradigm facilitated or helped to create the possibility for skeptical tendencies and renewed attention to the notion of probability in knowledge and reasoning, thereby creating the intellectual space needed to explore new paths in science and scientific methodology.[13]

One development that is clearly linked to the critique of scholastic language – in this case the language and methods of the logicians – is

[11] For references and discussion see below, Chapter 6 on Sanches.
[12] Dear 1988, 29–30. Perler 2004, 2012, 2014; Adriaenssen 2017; Pasnau 2017.
[13] See Chapter 6 on Sanches.

what has been called the rhetoricization of dialectic.[14] Medieval logic was thought to be too abstract, too technical and far removed from the practice of speaking and arguing. In humanist writings medieval logic was often reduced to its bare essentials, but the more innovative efforts came from Valla and in particular Rudolph Agricola, who aimed at bringing together dialectic and rhetoric into one system of topical invention, showing how to find arguments by using a set of places or topics (*loci*) such as definition, genus, species, place, time, similars, and opposites. In Agricola's hands dialectic became a practical tool of argumentation that aided the student not only in organizing any type of discourse but also in analyzing a text in terms of its underlying questions and argumentative structure.[15] In the sixteenth century Peter Ramus launched an influential program of reorganizing the arts of dialectic and rhetoric, attacking Aristotelian logic and restricting rhetoric to style and delivery. Dialectic must be aimed at teaching what is of use in ordinary reasoning.[16] Whatever the merits of the humanist critique of medieval logic – and many historians of logic are likely to see in the humanist turn to a pragmatic and much less formal art of argumentation an aberration, and a regrettable interruption of the progress logic had made in the hands of medieval and late-scholastic logicians[17] – it is a critique that is an intrinsic part of the general erosion of the Aristotelian paradigm. And here too the critique resonated for a long time, as testified, for instance, by Gassendi's youthful invectives against Aristotelian philosophy or Locke's discussion of the syllogism.

These examples suggest that language critique can be seen as an expression of wider feelings of discontent with the language, methods, and style of argumentation as practiced by the scholastics. Language critique is thus a broad phenomenon, which is not surprising: it was the scholastic idiom that immediately stared the reader of any scholastic book in the face, whether it were a logical handbook, a commentary on Aristotle, a theological *summa*, or a treatise on a specialized metaphysical topic. It was the language that was often regarded as not only an unnecessarily abstract and artificial form of Latin, but also as infecting the thoughts that

[14] For references see Chapter 4 on Vives. [15] Mack 1993; Nauta 2009.

[16] Scholars are beginning to correct the view that Ramism was a vastly influential cultural and intellectual movement. See Raylor 2018, 152: "Ramism was a pedagogical technique – or, perhaps more accurately, a gimmick – rather than a philosophical position"; cf. also Hotson 2007 and Feingold 2001 for a corrective. Even the classic study by Ong already stressed the poor philosophical merits of Ramus's critique of Aristotle and medieval logic; Ong also commented on the limitations of Ramist influence (Ong 1958, 303–304). See also Mack 1993, 342 for a critical judgment about the philosophical merits of Ramus's program.

[17] Kneale and Kneale 1962, 298–316; Risse 1964; Broadie 1993, 197; Cf. Jardine 1988, 173–174.

it articulated and the social, religious, and political practices in which it was embedded.

So far we have given some reasons (illustrated by some examples) why, historically speaking, the study of language critique, in spite of its repetitious, sometimes superficial and polemical character, might be an interesting field of study. The focus so far has been on the destructive side of the critique. But the reasons are not exhausted by that, for there is also a constructive side to it, namely the formulation of an alternative to the rejected terminology of the schools. Given the broad character of the critique, which targeted not only particular "barbarous" words but also an approach, style, method, and even a wider culture that critics deemed pernicious for many different reasons, a study of alternatives can easily lead to an unwieldy field of research. Since everything has to do with language – whether one likes it or not, ideas have to be articulated in the first place – the formulation of alternatives to the scholastic language has necessarily a lot to do with changes in natural philosophy, metaphysics, logic, and argumentation, and many other fields that seem to transcend the critique of language as such. But without ignoring these wider dimensions, it is possible to focus on the conviction, widely felt though difficult to put into practice, that the language of the schools had to be replaced by something else, something more transparent, more comprehensible, and more common. The phrase "common" is a key word here, used by humanists and early-modern philosophers alike, and in the following paragraphs we will briefly look at some important points to be developed and discussed in the chapters on individual authors that follow.

The introduction of a so-called common language was only the start of the problem, for what exactly is a "common language"? What are its criteria? How broadly do we understand to take the word "common"? Who defines what "common" is? How can we stabilize and regulate common language? Such questions, which remind us of similar ones raised about the use of "ordinary language" in philosophy in the twentieth century, were often not posed in such explicit terms: it was always much easier to attack something else as unnatural and uncommon than to formulate one's own alternative. Though we can find pleas for the use of common language throughout the period, the answers and strategies obviously differed, if only because the intellectual landscape was constantly changing.

For the humanists, as we will see, the alternative was of course classical Latin, though they realized that Latin had seen its own internal development also in antiquity so that debates necessarily broke out as to whether only Ciceronian Latin was acceptable as a language for learned communication, conversation and scholarship, or if a Latin that was based on a wider range of authors was also permissible.[18] It was attractive for humanists in their fight against what they called the "barbarous" Latin of their opponents to present classical Latin as the common, natural language. But while it surely was a common language in the sense of the lingua franca of the learned and erudite, it was certainly not common in the sense of anyone's mother tongue, and not surprisingly tensions can be detected in their attempts to defend classical Latin as a common, natural language. Ironically, their efforts to recover classical Latin as a common language soon made people realize that it was a "dead language,"[19] an historical phenomenon of great importance and significance but also something of the past, or at least not a living organism anymore. While the core of the humanist program was the recovery, restoration, reappropriation, and emulation of the Latin of the ancients, it remained an uncomfortable truth that it was a language that had belonged to a particular culture and time, even though as a lingua franca it had survived that culture as an instrument of learning and token of civilization. In the end, the humanists' attack on the language of the schools was historically perhaps more successful than their promotion of classical Latin as the sole repository of learning and wisdom.

Some humanists made important contributions to the vernacular, for example Leonardo Bruni and Leon Battista Alberti, but many others ignored it or felt disdain for it; yet they could not stop its intrusion into domains where Latin had occupied a privileged position, such as the arts and sciences. In fact, as research in recent decades has shown, "scholarship in the quattrocento was not divided between Latin and vernacular humanism but thrived precisely because of its linguistic versatility and interaction."[20] Gradually, the vernacular began to occupy an every bigger role in the dissemination of knowledge, including Aristotelian philosophy

[18] See in particular Chapter 2 on Valla, with further bibliography.

[19] For some remarks on the notion of a "living/dead language" in the Renaissance, see Faithfull 1953.

[20] Rizzi and Del Soldato 2013, 232. On the vernacular translations of philosophical works such as those of Aristotle see Lines 2012 and 2015 with further bibliography. On humanism and the vernacular, see, e.g., Hankins 2006 (on Bruni); Celenza 2018, 120–137 (on Alberti and others); Maxson 2013; the contributions to Rizzi and Del Soldato 2013. In this study I will not deal with the rise of the vernacular in philosophy and science as such, even though its use could certainly be motivated by a dislike of scholastic Latin. The rise of the discourse of "facts" in opposition to the Aristotelian demonstrative ideal of science "should perhaps also be associated with the rapidly increasing tendency in the seventeenth century to write about natural philosophy in the vernacular and thereby escape the expectations about philosophical terminology and argument generated by the Latin of the schools" (Serjeantson 2006, 158–159).

and science. The institutional, societal, and economic developments underlying these changes need not detain us here, though, obviously, consideration of these developments will eventually result in a better understanding of the intellectual changes between 1300 and 1700. Though Latin continued to be the language of the Republic of Letters, the vernacular was clearly on the rise, and Galileo, Descartes, Hobbes and many others often used both Latin and the vernacular, dependent on the topic, their intended audience, or a variety of other considerations. But if "common" could no longer refer to the classical Latin so cherished by the humanists, what kind of language was supposed to be the ideal vehicle for philosophy and learning? As we will see, the rhetoric of common linguistic usage and common language remained a strong element in the ongoing attacks that early-modern philosophers felt necessary to launch against their scholastic opponents (whether made of straw or flesh and blood). In practice "common language" could either be Latin more or less loosely based on classical norms, or the vernacular, which could secure a more diversified readership. The variety remained immense, but what many authors shared was the conviction that philosophical language should be freed from scholastic terminology (even though this remained an ideal which many seventeenth-century philosophers including Descartes, Hobbes, and Spinoza could not live up to) but also from any rhetorical extravagance, metaphors, and all kinds of figurative language (here too, it was easy to fall short of the ideal).[21] A sober, plain, perspicuous style in science was championed by the Royal Society, at least if we are to believe the famous manifesto from 1667 of its first historian Thomas Sprat who spoke, in terms that frequently belied his own credo, of "a close, naked, natural way of speaking, positive expressions, clear senses, a native easiness bringing all things as near the mathematical plainness as they can; and preferring the language of artisans, countrymen, and merchants before that of wits or scholars."[22] In what may be called the democratization of

[21] Cf. Leijenhorst 2002a, 39: "Much of this [the language critique] is obviously a polemical construction that the *novatores* used so as to sell their own philosophy as the epitome of transparency. Perhaps the *novatores*' censure of 'insignificant speech' was precisely so vehement simply because they were frustrated by their relative inability to escape from it themselves."

[22] Sprat 1958, 113 (punctuation adapted). Vickers has forcefully argued that Sprat's recommendations were not meant to discard rhetoric or the use of metaphors in scientific writings per se, indeed scientific prose (including Sprat's manifesto) abounded with metaphors, similitudes, and rhetorical devices: "He is to be seen not so much as a reformer who brought about a change in prose style but rather as a symptom of a general distrust of language in circles connected with the new science" (Vickers 1987, 16). See also Shapiro 1983, 236–237, with references to Sprat, John Wilkins, Samuel Parker, Robert Hooke, and Robert Boyle; Vickers 1985; Gotti 1996, 13–40 on Boyle; Skouen and Stark 2017 with further bibliography. The basic picture of a gradual turn from a rich, abundant,

knowledge and learning that is, arguably, a feature of the period, "scholars" could easily be sneered at as pedants, and the association with a good, plain style, common sense, and the common people was never far away.[23]

What we clearly see here is the contested nature of the concept of a so-called plain, natural and common language. It was a notion that could take shape only in polemical debates and controversies, when it was gloriously held up against schoolmen, scholars, pedants, savants, and "wits," and opportunistically used to defend one's own position in philosophy and science, and also in political-religious controversies such as when, for instance, Royalists and Conformists in England usurped the ideal of stylistic plainness as a weapon to marginalize nonconformist sects.[24] Intended as descriptive terms, words such as "common," "ordinary," "natural," "plain," "pure," and "native" have a manifestly normative charge.[25] This obvious point makes it all the more intriguing to study how the notion of common language was pressed into service by humanists and early-modern philosophers alike.

The search for a viable linguistic alternative to the language of the schools – from the humanist restoration of classical Latin to the "plain," "native" speech of Sprat's "countrymen" – can thus be seen as the constructive side of the critique of language. But as said, it was not easy to develop the notion into something coherent, as we can already see from

Latinate style toward a style marked by brevity, clarity, perspicuity, and concreteness has been analyzed by many scholars working on English prose and rhetoric. On the stylistic ideal of perspicuity as against neo-Ciceronian elegance in Hobbes and others see Raylor 2018.

[23] Burke 1995, 35. Commenting on Descartes' dislike of the pedant and the professional scholar, France writes that Descartes "often compares the sound sense of the *honnête homme* with the twisted mind of the university teacher, appealing to the common sense of the former against the pedantic quibbles of the latter" (France 1972, 57).

[24] Vickers 1985. For the implications of what she called "the Latin language turn" (from scholastic to humanist Latin) for theology, see Moss 2003; Rummel 1995 and 2000; Cummings 2002; the literature is vast. The political-religious dimension of language use in this entire period deserves much more attention (and expertise) than I have given it in this book.

[25] "Plain," for instance, has the connotation of industrious, undeceiving, decent, grave, calm, and unaffected; Vickers 1993, 579. For an application of terms such as "plain," "easy," "natural," "immediate," "primary," and "universal" to the so-called common notions that we all share (such as quantity and place) see Digby 1644, 4–5: "we should acquiesce and be content with that natural and plain notion, which springs immediately and primarily from the thing itself, which when we do not the more we seem to excel in subtlety, the further we go from reality and truth." Just as common notions lie at the basis of every science, so common language, which is used to express our common notions, should be the starting point of every scientist: "the first work of scholars is to learn of the people, *quem penes arbitrium est et ius et norma loquendi*; what is the true meaning and signification of these primary names . . ." (8). While Horace's words, meaning "inasmuch as it is within the judgment, right and standard of speaking" (*Ars Poetica* 71), referred to usage as the prime criterion of correct speech, in early-modern times this quotation was frequently adapted to defend the language of the common people versus the artificial, technical language of the scholastics.

Sprat's close association of the language of the new science with "the language of the countrymen" and, at the same time, with the clarity and plainness of mathematics; for whatever language Sprat's "countrymen" spoke it would probably fall short of any "mathematical plainness" nor would it be always of much help to the scientist who was exploring fields such as astronomy, botany, medicine, hydraulics, optics, and the like: early member of the Royal Society Kenelm Digby, for instance, admitted that he had to borrow words "from the Latin school" in his *Two Treatises* (1644) because of the "scarcity of our language in subjects removed from common conversation."[26] Common language was an attractive notion if one sought to pretend to be unpretentious, but whether it was suited for the burgeoning domain of empirical science or the mechanistic philosophy that postulated a world of atoms and unobservable processes far removed from the world of "countrymen" and their "plain" speech was, of course, doubtful.

Indeed, was common language not inherently ambiguous, imprecise, and vague? (Again, all normative qualifications, this time with clearly pejorative undertones in contrast to positive ones such as pure, native, naked, natural.) This sentiment about common language being inherently ambiguous was widely shared during the period, but attempts to resolve it differed.[27] Geometry inspired many to stress the importance of definitions, though definitions too should be based, according to Thomas Hobbes, on the way in which a word "is most constantly used in common speech."[28] Authors of the Port Royal logic had less compunction about this: "the best way to avoid the confusion of words that one finds in ordinary language is to make up a new language and new words that are attached only to the ideas that we wish that they represent."[29] Still further on this road of banning all ambiguity and imprecision are the well-studied attempts to construct artificial, "universal," or symbolic languages, for example that of Royal Society member John Wilkins – attempts that other philosophers found attractive but unworkable (Descartes) or virtually impossible (John Locke).[30] These attempts to use, stabilize, revise, or go beyond common language, whatever it was, are a good measure of the challenge early-

[26] Digby 1644, 15. There were several scholars who voiced the same complaint about the scarcity or imperfection of English; see e.g. Charleton, quoted in Gotti 1996, 14 n. 1. Hence, scientific prose was often a hybrid of English and Latinate words; for some examples see Vickers 1987, 18–20.

[27] Cf. Shapiro 1983, 232. [28] Hobbes 1845a, 229 (*Six Lessons* 2); on Hobbes see Chapter 7.

[29] *Logique ou l'art de penser*, Arnauld and Nicole 1992, 79; trans. and quoted Laerke 2014, 537.

[30] His coworkers the naturalists John Ray and Francis Willughby had already realized that such a plan was infeasible; Raven 1942, 181–183, 343; Birkhead 2018, 44–46, 150–151 and 161–162. On these schemes, which will not be discussed in this book, see Lewis 2012; Shapiro 1983, 244–246, with further literature on Wilkins and his contemporaries; Subbiondo 1992. See also Salmon 1979 and

modern authors faced in finding an alternative for scholastic language. The challenge is well expressed by Francis Bacon in his famous description of the idol of the marketplace: "words are chosen to suit the understanding of the common people. And thus a poor and unskillful code of words incredibly obstructs the understanding"; but on the other hand, to embrace "the definitions and explanations with which learned men have been accustomed to protect and in some way liberate themselves do[es] not restore the situation at all. Plainly words do violence to the understanding, and confuse everything; and betray men into countless empty disputes and fictions."[31]

For all these reasons the critique of scholastic language and the challenges it posed to articulate alternatives need ideally to be studied as part of the wider history of the vicissitudes of Aristotelian scholasticism and its slow demise in the seventeenth century. By way of a critique of language much else came under attack, as the list above suggests. As already pointed out, much of this critique, arguably, aimed at self-promotion and served the critic's own rhetorical or philosophical agenda. Historians of philosophy, therefore, might well be justified in doubting the philosophical merits of this critique, arguing that Aristotelian-scholastic philosophy, certainly in its general outlines, aimed at doing precisely this, namely to do justice to a common-sense view of the world: to analyze the world in terms of real qualities and other features inhering in underlying substances, or to postulate a common nature of dogs by appealing to a substantial form "doghood" that explains not only its classification as a dog but also its individuation over time and at a time, are only two examples of attempts to offer an explanatory description of the world as perceived by us.[32] For this reason Descartes thought this "vulgar" picture could be debunked only by radically doubting everything we take for granted.[33] Historians with a sympathy for scholasticism are likely (and not without considerable justification) to regard the polemical skits by humanists and self-styled

Knowlson 1975. For Locke see Chapter 8. For Descartes see his letter to Mersenne from 1629 (Descartes 1985, 3:12); cf. Ricken 1994, 8–23 and Losonsky 2006, 69–71.

[31] Bacon 2000, 42 (*The New Organon* I, xliii). On Bacon's role, see Vickers 1968 and Jardine 1974.

[32] On the roles of substantial form see Pasnau 2011, 549–565.

[33] Garber 2001 is the classic statement that Descartes's *Meditations* aimed at undermining what Descartes called the "vulgar philosophy" of the schools: "What he objected to in Scholasticism was something he saw as common to all schools, a common conception of the makeup of the physical world together with a closely connected pattern of explanation in physics" (227). Scholastic language apart, Descartes also thinks that "ordinary ways of talking" can trick us into holding views that on closer inspection are not true, for example that we come to knowledge by sense perception; see the famous wax passage in *Meditations* II (Descartes 1984–1991, 2:21).

novatores as irrelevant, misguided, and untrue to the facts; but past thinkers' perceptions of their own times, even if illusionary and propagandistic, are no less part of history than less-partisan narratives, and they shaped the intellectual debates to come. In the end – whether one likes it or not – the building collapsed, and to explain and analyze this historical process means that one cannot ignore this tradition of critics.

But apart from these historical motivations there is also another reason why this critique is an interesting field of study, and here we come back to the point with which we started. Early-modern thinkers were of course not the first nor the last to criticize the language of their opponents. Indeed, philosophical jargon is of all times, and so are its defenders and detractors. We might therefore also see the critique of scholastic language as an example of the perennial question about the nature of philosophical language. Does philosophy require its own terminology – from technical terms to formal symbols – or does it have to use, as a rule, ordinary language (whatever that is), perhaps with some exceptions? Put in such general terms the question looks meaningless – as if one can settle the question or impose rules from the outside on the practice of philosophical activity, in fact on a myriad of practices that have gone on for thousands of years. Moreover, history shows that it is hardly ever a choice between the one or the other, with the exception perhaps of a formal proof in logic at one end of the spectrum and a popularizing piece for a wide public at the other. There are so many different styles and genres in philosophy, so many different ideas about what "good philosophy" is and how to practice it, that the question about the ideal or most suitable language in philosophy must indeed look overambitious, pretentious, if not downright silly.

This is not, however, how it has always been perceived as, for instance, the heated debates about ordinary language in the twentieth century already testify. Language is of prime importance to the modern philosopher who, as a rule, does not have recourse to empirical observation, experiments, or mathematical calculation, so it is not surprising that debates on this exclusive tool belong to the heart of philosophy itself.[34] What is lost if we become formal or technical, defining our notions by selecting some features while ignoring many others? What is lost if we use so-called ordinary language by which we tend to ignore subtle conceptual distinctions and logical categories? It might therefore be instructive to see the critique of scholastic language against the background of the perennial

[34] Superfluous to say that philosophy and science cannot be neatly distinguished for much of the time period under discussion.

question about the appropriate language to be used in philosophy. Such a broader perspective might help to tease out philosophically legitimate points in what often seem to be polemically charged debates without much philosophical depth.

The vastness of this territory – both historically and thematically – must seem to make any attempt to cover it in any detail a hopeless undertaking. There are simply too many interesting and relevant texts and authors from this period to cram into the space of one study. It can even be doubted whether such a protean theme as the status of language in this period can be told as a continuous, unbroken narrative. It is the familiar dilemma that faces every historian who is interested in tracing long-term developments without willing to sacrifice historical or textual detail for a bird's-eye view – in other words, a dilemma of whether to use a wide range of texts (or apt quotations from these texts) in a highly selective way to show these long-term developments, or to study a highly selective range of texts in such depth that these developments tend to disappear from sight. Most historians will probably try to combine the two approaches, ending up somewhere in the middle or perhaps more to the left or to the right of it, dependent on their themes, aims and research questions, and also on their interests and expertise. This book is a series of case studies that analyze some important figures from Petrarch to Locke as representatives of a tradition of critics of scholastic language and thought. Though the map can be drawn in many different ways, one "line" might be seen to run from Petrarch and Bruni to Valla, and from Valla to Pontano and to Vives, and from Valla and Vives to Nizolio.[35] This humanist critique of scholastic language was a source of influence – one out of many, to be sure – for early-modern thinkers such as Sanches, Hobbes, and Locke; there is much more continuity between the so-called Renaissance humanism and early-modern philosophy than is often suggested by modern scholars.[36] Many other critics could have been included, such as Salutati, Gianfrancesco Pico della Mirandola, Ramus, Patrizi, Bacon, Boyle, Descartes, and Gassendi – to mention just a few. But since observations on language and language critique are usually part of a much wider program of reform – as each of the case studies that follow hopes to illustrate – a choice has been made for

[35] For a different map, covering partly the same territory as this book, see Celenza 2018, which situates humanists' debates on language, philosophy, and culture in the wider context of societal and institutional developments in the Italian Renaissance from 1350 to 1525.

[36] See Levitin 2015. This continuity is the theme of several volumes, for example, Muratori and Paganini 2016. The first two pages of this Introduction borrow, with some changes, a few paragraphs from my contribution to this volume (Nauta 2016).

a somewhat more detailed study of a limited number of authors rather than a brief discussion of a greater number of texts and authors. And given the focus on the critique of scholastic language, other related and relevant themes do not feature prominently in this study, such as: the social context of humanism, societal and institutional developments and connection to language use; the rise of the vernacular; the debate on Ciceronianism; the *questione della lingua* (the debate on Latin versus the vernacular); the history of rhetoric; the history of logic or linguistic theories; later seventeenth-century attempts to construct a universal language (e.g. George Dalgarno and John Wilkins); and the development of English scientific prose. Relevant and interesting as they are, each theme would require a book in itself. Fortunately, there is already a wealth of scholarly studies on these themes.

Petrarch offers a natural starting point, being one of the founding figures of Renaissance humanism and the first serious critic of the language, thought, and culture of the scholastics. With Locke we have come to the end of this tradition and enter a new phase; he has rightly been called "a successor to the philosophy of language that defines Renaissance humanism," and his turn to language the "culmination of an intellectual development from Plato to Hobbes that steadily moved natural language to the center stage of philosophy," but his work also "begins the evolution of the philosophy of language and linguistics in the modern period" and its features "dramatically distinguish Locke's discussion of language from that of his predecessors."[37] Inspired by Locke, Enlightenment thinkers such as Condillac, Diderot, Helvétius, and Rousseau focused on the reciprocal development of language, thought, and society, paying increasing attention to the cognitive function and sociohistorical character of language. Societal and political reform was high on the agenda of these thinkers, hence linguistic and educational reform as well, since language was the instrument used to express and foster the interests of the ruling class who spread their own "distorted" meanings of political words such as "liberty," "aristocracy," "sovereignty," and "the people." Helvétius, for instance, observed that "the false philosophy of the previous century has caused our lack of knowledge of the true meanings of words. This philosophy consisted almost solely of the art of misusing words."[38] The main target of the Enlightenment critique of language was thus no longer the technical language of the scholastics, as Aristotelian scholasticism had by

[37] Losonsky 2006, respectively p. xiii, 22, xii, and 21.
[38] Quoted by Ricken 1994, 167 (*De l'esprit* I.iv).

now been overshadowed by new developments in science and philosophy in the preceding centuries; the dominant focus had shifted to the political and social vocabulary that was believed to keep people in enslavement. For this reason, Locke – as a bridge between old and new approaches toward language – will be the end point of this study.

CHAPTER I

Early Humanist Critics of Scholastic Language: Francesco Petrarch and Leonardo Bruni

Introduction

From the time of Petrarch (1304–1374) onward, humanists found the Latin language as used in the schools and universities ungrammatical, ugly, abstract, technical, in short barbarous. The language simply did not conform to the classical standards that had been so painstakingly rediscovered and held up for emulation by the humanists. Their target was, of course, not only scholastic language as such. The language was an expression of a way of doing philosophy that many humanists considered hopelessly abstract and out of tune with the way in which people actually talked, argued, believed, and thought. They were convinced, for instance, that many of the problems treated in logic and theology arose only because language had been used in an artificial way. The humanists thus criticized not only the grammatical constructions and individual words introduced and newly coined by the scholastics, but also their style and approaches and indeed the entire scholastic culture, which was often thought to be totally irrelevant for society or even dangerous to Christian faith (as in the case of Averroes's followers). Of course, humanism and scholasticism are not monolithic opposite entities, and it is better to imagine a spectrum with the two "-isms" at both ends with lots of intermediary ground where the two could and did meet. But this does not alter the fact that for many humanists scholastic language was a kind of jargon that was used to impress, but in fact served as a smoke screen to hide one's own ignorance. It was their use of good classical Latin and their study of the heritage of classical antiquity by which the humanists liked to distinguish themselves.

Perhaps more interesting than the precise wording of this critique are the premises from which humanists – often tacitly, sometimes openly – departed. Some of these premises have become so ingrained in the European historiography in which the classical tradition looms so large that it is easy to overlook the fact that they are not so straightforward at all. The first and most central premise is that classical Latin should be the alpha and omega in all intellectual pursuits. As the language of the Roman Empire, it had proven itself as the medium and vehicle of so much high culture and civilization that for the humanists it was axiomatic that we should return to this language for the recovery of arts and sciences as well as for conversation and communication for the benefit of society. While some humanists such as Leonardo Bruni and Leon Battista Alberti envisaged the vernacular as an equally powerful instrument with which to express ideas, thoughts, and beliefs, Latin remained for many, and for a long time, unquestionably *the* language, and any departure from it was seen as the beginning of the end.[1]

A second premise was the idea that the Latin to be emulated was the Latin of roughly 100 BC–AD 200. Some humanists famously restricted the chronological range to the life of one man, Cicero, whose eloquence and style were profound sources of inspiration for almost everyone, but this Ciceronianism was famously attacked by Erasmus in his *Ciceronianus*. Perhaps even more basic than these two premises was the belief that classical Latin should not be tampered with, since as a means for the expression of thought it could hardly be improved. It was a highly regimented language, an *ars*, and yet a natural, common language that had been the living tongue of a vast empire (even though discussion arose as to exactly what kind of Latin had been spoken in antiquity); it had served through the ages as a vehicle of higher learning, even though its existence had often been precarious. It should be studied and revived in its pristine, most glorious form, and breaches of the rules of grammar and the introduction of postclassical words were rejected or – as for instance in the case of biblical and ecclesiastical terminology – accepted with more or less reluctance. What these basic convictions also imply is the idea that the use of language matters. The critique of scholastic language seems to be founded on the belief that the choice of a language or a particular form of Latin had important repercussions for the way we think about the world, including ourselves; humanists were convinced that bad Latin leads to bad thinking and vice versa.

In the first chapters we will see how these convictions worked out in the thought of some major humanists. In this chapter we will set the stage by looking at two key figures in the humanist movement: Francesco Petrarch (1304–1374) and Leonardo Bruni (1369–1444), ignoring the contributions

[1] See Introduction, n. 20.

of many others, for example Coluccio Salutati, Poggio Bracciolini, and Flavio Biondo.[2] Petrarch was the most celebrated and influential humanist of his time, and the first to launch a serious attack on the culture of the schools and universities. Bruni was the first to attain a highly accomplished level of Latin prose style, as testified by his many translations from the Greek as well as his orations, treatises, letters, lives of famous men, and dialogues. Both humanists considered the revival and imitation of classical Latin as essential for the reform of learning, morals, education, and the arts.[3] It is impossible to do justice here to the multifaceted nature of their works nor is it necessary to study all the aspects of the revival of ancient learning they promoted in order to see on which basic assumptions this revival was based. This is not to say that they always clearly saw the implications of these basic assumptions and convictions. They famously preached the Ciceronian union of reason and eloquence, and of philosophy and rhetoric, but they were generally not interested in the more theoretical implications of their views. We must therefore be cautious in our interpretations while teasing out these implications to avoid foisting on them positions they did not hold or could not hold. Yet, it is not difficult to see that their views on language, translation, meaning, and Latin were anything but philosophically neutral.

Petrarch

Though he had his predecessors, Francesco Petrarch can be considered as the first serious critic of the language, thought, and culture of the scholastics. Petrarch's criticisms were voiced in a number of works and letters, setting the tone for later generations. The modern philosopher who is looking for serious argumentation about the use of language in philosophy will probably be disappointed by the invectives Petrarch heaped on the scholastics and "impious" philosophers from antiquity and his own time, but the ancient genre of invective, revived by him, required of course something other than tight reasoning or careful balancing of arguments pro and con. More importantly, it was practice rather than theory, "love" rather than "truth," "willing" rather than "knowing" that were the central coordinates in Petrarch's search for an alternative to the reigning paradigm of scholastic reasoning and teaching. A highly celebrated and influential

[2] Seigel 1968, 63–98; Witt 2000, 292–337; Celenza 2018; Hankins 2019.

[3] While the theme of this book is language, humanists should of course not be reduced to "language specialists."

man of letters and one of the greatest of Italian poets, Petrarch is a canonical figure in Renaissance humanism, and scholarship on his life, work, and influence is vast. For our purpose it will suffice to look at the basic convictions and assumptions of his humanist critique of the language and the culture of the schools – convictions that were often but not always shared by later humanists, some of whom we will study in the chapters to come.[4]

For Petrarch it was an article of faith that ancient Latin should be revived as the language of literary, moral, and religious reform, something that was the driving force behind much of what he wrote.[5] Linguistic and moral reform were two sides of the same coin: while he took great pains to create a classicizing style by immersing himself in the great writings of the ancient Romans, the study of antiquity was not something to pursue just for its own sake but also as a way to reform a culture that had failed, according to Petrarch, to address the intellectual, moral, and religious needs of the time. The reform was essentially a return to Christian virtue as preached by Augustine, who, like Petrarch, saw Cicero's eloquence as an ally for Christianity. Petrarch held a special devotion for Augustine, who was a Ciceronian before he became a Christian. Times had changed of course. As Stephen Menn comments: "The mature Augustine takes Cicero's ideal of the perfect philosopher-orator for granted; he is concerned to defend Christianity, not Ciceronianism. The humanists, however, finding a Christianity universally professed but scarcely felt, are moved to revive Ciceronianism as a means to reawakening Christianity."[6] Petrarch strongly believed that by studying and imitating the style of his ancient heroes, he could guide himself and his readers to Christian virtue. This was not a straightforward strategy of course. Cicero may have written beautiful Latin, but his thought remained essentially pagan, just as that of many other writers from classical antiquity. And while many humanists were happy to concentrate on literature and style, Petrarch's humanism had

[4] For instance, while Bruni never voiced any suspicion about rhetoric, Petrarch and Salutati, at certain points in their careers, were not so sure; for the latter the philosophical ideal could have an independence from rhetoric, an independence Bruni usually did not accept; Bruni's faith in the union of philosophy and eloquence remained strong and unabated. While for Bruni, as we will see, Aristotle was a highly eloquent writer, Petrarch had his doubts. And Christian piety played a prominent role in Petrarch while it was largely absent in Bruni. While in broad outlines similar, their humanist programs could show considerable differences on such points.

[5] Vasoli 1974; Trinkaus 1979, 52–89; Witt 2000, 230–291; Celenza 2018; Zak 2015; Hankins 2019. On Petrarch's influence see for example Rotondi Secchi Tarugi (ed.) 1997; Trapp 2003; Enenkel and Papy 2006; Hankins 2007–2008 (on Petrarch's shifting reputation between two generations of humanists, from Salutati to Bruni and Poggio); Kircher 2015 (a brief overview).

[6] Menn 1998, 43.

a Christian stamp, and at times he emphasized inner devotion and pious simplicity much more than eloquence and classical learning. He was a Christian after all:[7]

> If admiring Cicero is being a Ciceronian, then I am a Ciceronian. For certainly, I admire him, and I marvel at others who do not admire him. If this seems to be a new confession of my ignorance, I confess that it reflects my feelings and my wonder. But when it comes to pondering or discussing religion – that is, the highest truth, true happiness, and eternal salvation – then I am certainly neither a Ciceronian nor a Platonist, but a Christian.

Cicero, alas, did not know the true God, a fact even a counterfactual wish ("I feel certain that Cicero himself would have been a Christian if he had been able to see Christ or grasp his teaching") could not alter, even though he could come close to speaking like an Apostle.[8]

So the perennial question for Christian readers throughout the ages who felt uncomfortable in their love for a pagan culture was felt even more acutely by Petrarch: why on earth spend so much time studying classical antiquity while "unlearned" people such as fishermen and peasants could attain the same goal of living a devout Christian life without all this learning? After all, "Aristotle was a great man and a polymath" but, as Petrarch notices, "he was completely ignorant of true happiness that any devout old woman, or any faithful fisherman, shepherd, or peasant, is happier, if not more subtle, in recognizing it."[9] He had "failed to see this one great truth, which many unlearned people have seen and continue to see."[10] From this perspective, Ciceronian eloquence, for all its civilizing and saving qualities, could hardly be considered as a necessary, let alone a sufficient condition for the moral and religious reform that inspired Petrarch in his study of and attempt to emulate a classicizing style.

But, then, the reform was not aimed at pious "unlearned" people of course. What Petrarch had in mind was a union of eloquence and philosophy, where eloquence meant inflaming the mind toward love of virtue and where philosophy was roughly identified with moral philosophy, in much the same way that his great example Augustine had redefined classical philosophy in Christian terms.[11] Whatever did not contribute to virtue or the attainment of the blessed life – such as the study of the natural world – was rejected as pretty useless by Petrarch, at least in his more

[7] Petrarch 2003, 333 (*On His Own Ignorance* V). Almost all of the quotations that follow come from this text.

[8] Ibid.; cf. 275 (*On His Own Ignorance* IV). [9] Ibid., 265. [10] Ibid., 271.

[11] Rist 1994 for an analysis of Augustine's Christian reappropriation of ancient thought.

polemical moments (which were frequent): God "promises the knowledge of Himself. And if He grants this, it will appear superfluous to concern myself with the things He has created."[12] Central to Petrarch's critique was therefore not so much scholastic language as such but the anti-Christian tendencies he detected in Aristotelianism and in particular Averroism, notably doctrines such as the unity of the intellect, the preexistence of the soul, and the eternity of the world. And even if Aristotle's moral philosophy is not anti-Christian in itself – indeed, it contains something of value, even for Petrarch – it is too abstract and too theoretical for improving our moral lives:[13]

> I see how brilliantly he defines and distinguishes virtue, and how shrewdly he analyzes it together with the properties of vice and virtue. Having learned this, I know slightly more than I did before. But my mind is the same as it was; my will is the same; and I am the same. For it is one thing to know, and another to love; one thing to understand, and another to will. I don't deny that he teaches us the nature of virtue. But reading him offers us none of these exhortations, or only a very few, that goad and inflame our minds to love virtue and hate vice.

A certain anti-intellectualistic sentiment thus marks Petrarch's vision: "It is more prudent to strive for a good and devout will than a capacious and clear intellect. As wise men tell us, the object of the will is goodness, while the object of the intellect is truth. But it is better to will what is good than to know what is true."[14] Aristotle's philosophy is aimed at understanding and truth but it does not bring us closer to Christian virtue.

But much worse than Aristotle are his followers, who populate the schools and the universities, to Petrarch's great sorrow. They stupidly believe that Aristotle is the sole embodiment of timeless wisdom: his critics "are so captivated by their love of the mere name of Aristotle that they consider it a sacrilege to differ with whatever 'He' said on any subject."[15] Moreover, they had corrupted his works in their bad translations, for Petrarch had learned "from Greek witnesses and from Cicero's writings that Aristotle's personal style was sweet, copious, and ornate." Not daring to "write anything of their own," they often limit themselves to expounding the works of others, in particular the great master himself or Peter Lombard's *Sentences*.[16] Their disputes are "windy," their doctrines

[12] Petrarch 2003, 311 (*On His Own Ignorance* IV); cf. 239 (*On His Own Ignorance* II).
[13] Ibid., 315 (*On His Own Ignorance* IV); cf. Martin 2014, 29–30.
[14] Ibid., 319 (*On His Own Ignorance* IV). [15] Ibid., 313 for this and the following quotation.
[16] Ibid., 323.

"outlandish," their attitude "arrogant," their language "babyish and puzzled babbling," their dialectic "empty words and fleeting trifles."[17] It would, of course, be anachronistic to complain that Petrarch is exaggerating and that his critique is unfair. As already indicated, calling for a wholesale reform of the dominant culture requires something less subtle than a reasoned discourse or an argument; and the polemical attacks follow the literary conventions of the invective.[18]

As the expression of what Petrarch considers the impious, muddled, and confused thinking of "the mad and brawling mob of Scholastics,"[19] one would expect him to focus on their technical, abstract, and barbarous Latin, but his critique of language remains at a general level; he does not analyze it in the way a later humanist such as Lorenzo Valla would do. He duly denunciates dialectics, syllogisms, "crooked enthymeme" and so on, yet he seems at times willing to admit that scholastic language might be suited for certain philosophical pursuits such as "the intricate path of rational philosophy or the hidden one of natural philosophy";[20] but as soon as we are dealing with moral issues – which is also what is most important in life – it only leads to confusion; the jargon-ridden language encourages "outlandish fabrications," and vice versa: such fabrications cause this kind of language to be concocted as well.

A fundamental assumption here is the intimate connection between speech (or style) and thought:[21]

> Our speech is not a small indicator of our mind, nor is our mind a small controller of our speech. Each depends upon the other but while one remains in one's breast, the other emerges into the open. The one ornaments it as it is about to emerge and shapes it as it wants to; the other announces how it is as it emerges into the open.

Clarity of speech, as Petrarch repeatedly stresses, is a reflection of a clear mind:[22]

> clarity is the supreme proof of one's understanding and knowledge. Whatever is clearly understood can be clearly expressed, so that one person's inner thoughts can be transferred to the mind of his listeners . . . Such an art

[17] Ibid., 305; 233 (*On His Own Ignorance* II); ibid., 135 (*Against a Physician* III, 162).

[18] See Vasoli 1974, 143; Marsh 2015, 167–176. On invectives see Rutherford 2005; Helmrath 2010.

[19] Petrarch 2003, 322 (*On His Own Ignorance* IV).

[20] Quoted Witt 2000, 268 from Petrarch's *Familiar Letters* XIV.1. See especially *Against a Physician* III (in Petrarch 2003) for a highly polemical attack on dialectics, which led Trinkaus to observe that "it is easy to become lost in the labyrinth of his polemics" (Trinkaus 1979, 98).

[21] Petrarch, *Rerum familiarium* I.9 as quoted by Witt 2000, 241; cf. Seneca, Letter, 114.

[22] Petrarch 2003, 303 (*On His Own Ignorance* IV).

> [of teaching] must be based on clarity in one's intelligence and knowledge. Besides our knowledge, we need such an art to express our mental concepts [*conceptus*] and to impress them on others. But no art can produce clear speech from a clouded intellect.

Such passages as these might seem to mitigate the anti-intellectual attitude in Petrarch just mentioned. If a clear mind is essential for clear speech, and if clear speech is an important instrument in spurring the mind to virtuous action, then how could Petrarch also claim that "it is more prudent to strive for a good and devout will than a capacious and clear intellect"? Perhaps there is not much of a conflict here. Petrarch's Augustinian emphasis on will, love, pious devotion, virtuous action, and practical morality is meant to counteract what he sees as the theoretical, rationalist approach of the Aristotelian scholastics, including theologians who "make the greatest mistake of all by seeking to know God rather than loving him."[23] This does not mean that knowledge and a clear mind, filled with our mental concepts, are not important. Clarity of thinking and clarity of speech intrinsically belong to each other, and they both serve to instill the message of loving God and virtue. It depends on the immediate context which point Petrarch wants to emphasize. As so often, Petrarch's statements are not to be taken as steps in an argument but as polemical moves in an oratorical declamation that aims at persuasion and moral reform and reflection. Petrarch's statement about transferring one person's inner thoughts "to the mind of his listeners" has therefore a rhetorical rather than an epistemological background. The main task of the orator is to influence our beliefs and behavior, spurring us to virtue and the love of God. By contrast to Aristotle, "who barely arouses and excites our minds to virtue," the Latin authors "touch and pierce our vitals with the sharp, burning barbs of their eloquence," which in the end must inspire us to gaze upward, toward "lofty thoughts and noble desires."[24] For "speech" we must often read "style," as style for Petrarch is a reflection of one's individual personality:[25]

> I have read Vergil and Horace and Boethius and Cicero ... and these materials poured themselves into me so intimately and were attached not just to my memory but to my marrow itself and became one with my own nature.

[23] Ibid., 319. Petrarch's view seems to reflect Augustine's criticisms of philosophers in *Confessions* VII.
[24] Ibid., 317.
[25] Petrarch 2017, 341–343 (III.18 = *Rerum fam.* XXII.2) for this and the next quotation.

But from all this reading a personal style is confected that is an expression of one's own mind:

> I would much prefer my style be my own, however rough and unrefined, but well fitted like a robe, made to measure for my intellect, rather than another man's style decked with ambitious adornment but originating from a greater mind and overflowing on all sides in a way unfitted to a mind of humble stature.

This raises the question how Petrarch could reconcile the search for his own, distinctive Latin style with the desire to imitate and emulate ancient Latin. According to Ronald G. Witt, "Petrarch's idea of confecting his style from the most congenial aspects of pagan writing, however, militated against an in-depth inspection of individual styles."[26] And he continues:

> Petrarch had no conception of language as a developing constellation of verbal practices: style for him was solely a matter of individual achievement. While he had certain ingredients of a historical approach to language – he considered Cicero the acme of ancient eloquence and the Latin of the Middle Ages a great falling away from ancient standards – he had no idea of a "classical style" and tended to envisage a wide range of pagan authors and Christian writers at least down to Augustine as potential models for imitation.

This of course is only to be expected: Petrarch stands at the beginning of the humanist project to revive the language and styles of the ancients; as Latin still retains "an amorphous character" for him, his program must be considered as only a first stage in the process of entangling the various stages of the Latin language, a process Salutati was soon to take a step further.[27]

We cannot therefore expect a detailed analysis of the relationship between language and thought, or style and mind, or eloquence and philosophy. Petrarch crucially believed in the impact that classical style had on one's mind, emotions, and (virtuous) behavior, and thereby on one's personality. Hence, it had great potential for moral and religious reform. Much argumentation was not to be expected at a time when first and foremost an alternative to the scholastic culture had to be formulated in terms of a Christian reform based on the fusion of Augustinian

[26] Witt 2000, 270. Salutati had already recognized that Petrarch's style did not always meet classical standards; ibid., 326; Celenza 2018, 58; Hankins 2007–2008, 914 on *res* as the truth of things in Petrarch and Salutati. On the conflict between what Petrarch sees as the "weak," effeminate style of Ovid and the "strong" style of Cicero, Virgil, and Seneca, see Zak 2015.

[27] Witt 2000, 325–326, refers to Salutati as writing "the first literary history of Latin literature."

meditation and Ciceronian eloquence. Such tensions, as already mentioned, were inevitable: the admiration for antiquity versus the fact that it was a pagan antiquity, the admiration of a style that had been the vehicle of much pagan thought, the passionate defense of eloquence versus the need for an inner dialogue and meditation, the imitation of ancient Latin prose style versus the creation of one's own distinctive style, the belief in ancient style as a yardstick versus the need to accept and use later forms of Latin (e.g. ecclesiastical Latin), praise of knowledge and clarity of thinking versus extolling willing and loving over knowing and having a clear mind, and so on. But these inner conflicts are not something to be deplored: they show the meeting of different traditions, different allegiances and commitments, in one and the same mind that struggles to bring them all together into one vision. Petrarch's vision of an alternative culture to the predominant scholastic paradigm proved to be a powerful vision that exercised an immense impact on his contemporaries and future generations, even though later humanists such as Leonardo Bruni did not always have the same qualms about loving antiquity for its own sake as he did.

Leonardo Bruni

The humanist critique of scholastic language, as launched by Petrarch, was further developed by Bruni in his famous denunciation of the medieval translation of Aristotle's *Nicomachean Ethics*. Bruni thought that the translation was rendered in "such a puerile and unlearned fashion," full of transliterations of Greek words and unclassical Latin, that he decided to make a new translation in good classical Latin, which he published in 1416.[28] Aware that a new translation of such an important philosophical work that had been studied for almost two centuries in the universities would meet with suspicion or even downright hostility, he explained in his preface why he thought a new translation was necessary. Critics of Bruni's translation, however, were not slow to point out that philosophy should not be subordinated to rhetoric. On their view, philosophical arguments require precision and rigor in terminology, something which they thought was lost in a translation or work written in a Ciceronian style. Bruni responded to his critics in several letters and in an unfinished treatise *On the Correct Way to Translate*, "the first treatise on translation produced in western Europe since antiquity."[29]

[28] Bruni 1987, 213.

[29] Botley 2004, 42; Hankins in Bruni 1987, 210, where Hankins describes this as "the first treatise on translation ever." On this work see also Den Haan 2016, 103–108.

The debate has usually been depicted as a clash between two cultures, already announced in Petrarch's program of linguistic and moral reform of some decades earlier: the humanist culture in which the text of Aristotle – and indeed texts in general – are approached from a primarily linguistic, philological, and historical perspective versus a scholastic approach in which texts are treated as expressions of philosophical truths.[30] The clash has sometimes been described in even stronger terms, namely as opposing a humanist approach in which language is treated (often implicitly) as an active, creative, and formative power, against a scholastic-medieval approach that sees language as referring to and ideally mirroring a stable order of essences.[31] Humanists treated language as a social institution, shaped by the conventions and practices of its users, while scholastics used language primarily as a tool for approaching and describing the world of timeless essences. Such claims are often too general to do justice to the vast complexity and heterogeneity of both scholasticism and humanism, but in this particular case of Bruni's controversy they find support in some of the statements made by his main adversary, Bishop Alfonso of Cartagena. We find Alfonso, who had no Greek, saying things like "whatever is consonant with reason is what Aristotle must be considered to have said, and whatever our translation wisely expresses in Latin words, we may conclude was written in the Greek," and "we ought not to pay attention to what Aristotle says, but to what is consonant with moral philosophy."[32] Such statements indeed express a fundamentally different attitude from Bruni's historical and philological approach that starts from the Greek text of Aristotle.

In whatever terms we describe the clash, it is clear that some fundamental issues are at stake here. For our purposes the most important question, put in its most succinct and simple form, is: What are the requirements of philosophical language? Bruni's criticisms, while directed at the scholastic, postclassical terminology and transliterated Greek words in the medieval translation of Aristotle, are by extension a critique of the language and methods of medieval scholastics *tout court.* His conviction was that only classical Latin could render the thought and style of the ancients perspicuous, and perhaps – given the contours of his humanist program – this applied to thought in general. For him it was axiomatic that a classicizing style, which he so successfully imitated, was crucial for clear thinking: "The reading of clumsy and corrupt writers imbues the reader with their own vices, and infests his mind with similar corruptions."[33]

30 For example Harth 1968; Gerl 1981; Hankins in Bruni 1987, 204; Hankins 2003; Roick 2017, 109; Celenza 2018, 71–93.

31 Gerl 1981, 32–36, 93, and passim; Harth 1968, 49–52 and 56; Waswo 1979.

32 Alfonso in Birkenmajer 1922, 166; trans. Hankins in Bruni 1987, 204 and Hankins 2003, 201–202.

33 Bruni 1987, 241.

But if style is more than just the wrapping of the content, as Bruni's Ciceronian defense of a unity of reason and eloquence, or *res* (things, the subject matter) and *verba* (words), seems to imply, does translation not necessarily bring with it an alteration of the content? Languages are different in grammar, vocabulary, structure, and so on, and authors have their own different style, so that Bruni might have concluded from his own wide experience in translating not only from Greek into Latin but also from Latin into the vernacular, that a perfect match is impossible and that the meaning of the original text does not remain wholly intact in the process of being translated, something captured by the saying "traduttore, traditore" (translator, traitor).[34] And what does this word "meaning" (*sensus, significatio*) mean for Bruni? Is the meaning to be sought at the level of words or do we have to transcend the level of words and take larger textual unities (sentences, paragraphs, the entire text) as locations of meaning? As a humanist and practicing translator with no interest in such theoretical questions about meaning as such, Bruni did not raise this issue, yet implicit ideas about it are likely to influence the translator's approach to the text (word for word, sentence for sentence, etc.).[35] As we will see, Bruni's emphasis on the importance of an author's style might imply a position according to which meaning is not something beside the expression, as if it were a fixed entity indifferent to its linguistic expression, but something that emerges from an investigation into linguistic usage.

Bruni's criticisms of the thirteenth-century translator Robert Grosseteste, whose identity Bruni did not know, are basically twofold: the medieval translator was deficient in both Greek and Latin, and his knowledge of philosophy was insufficient in order to correctly render important philosophical terms such as good, moral worth, useful, pleasure, pain, and terms referring to the virtues. The two points are clearly related, and we have already seen Bruni claiming that "the reading of clumsy and corrupt writers imbues the reader with their own vices, and infests his mind with similar corruptions."[36] Without further elaborating on the connection between thinking and language, he accuses the translator of "making confusion of the subject matter as well as the vocabulary."[37] At the end of the preface he writes that he undertook his translation because he saw to his

[34] On Bruni's translations into the vernacular see Hankins 2006.

[35] Apel 1975, 182 warns not to overestimate the philosophical implications; see Gerl 1981, 92, 98, and 152 on Bruni's lack of theoretical interest; cf. Harth 1968, 55 and 58.

[36] Bruni 1987, 241.

[37] Ibid., 214–215; Latin in Bruni 1928, 79 (not in Bruni 2013): "ipsum res quoque simul cum nominibus confudentem." "Simul" seems to point to the close connection that Bruni sees between words and things.

dismay "how books that in Greek are utterly delightful are become harsh and hispid in Latin, with their vocabulary twisted, their matter obscured, and their doctrine undermined."[38]

Bruni's attack on the style of the translator is driven by his belief that Aristotle was a master of eloquence, something the scholastics in general had failed to recognize. Aristotle's copious and beautiful style should be matched in Latin so that Aristotle would recognize the Latin translations as his own, for "he would surely wish to appear among the Latins as he had made himself appear among the Greeks."[39] A similar point is made by Bruni in an early letter from 1400 addressed to Niccolò Niccoli where he spoke about his translation of Plato's *Phaedo*: "For those earlier translators followed Plato's words and idioms [*syllabas atque tropos*] whilst abandoning Plato himself, I, on the other hand, stay close to Plato; I imagine that he knows Latin, so that he can judge for himself; I will call him a witness to his own translation; and I translate as I think would please him best."[40]

Bruni's belief that Aristotle was an eloquent writer will probably puzzle the modern student of Aristotle. And also in Bruni's own time, as he tells us, there were "certain learned men" who had concluded from Aristotle's writings that "he is muddled, obscure, and awkward," to which Bruni replies that these texts are "simply the nonsense of the translations"; they are "*not* Aristotle's works – and if he were alive, he would himself repudiate them."[41] Bruni was convinced that Aristotle was a rhetorically skilled writer, whose style was ornate, polished, and beautifully crafted. In this he was probably inspired by Cicero, who had had access to the polished and ornate works of the early Aristotle that have since been lost. In the words of a modern scholar: Bruni was "the victim of a complicated trick of fate."[42] However, Bruni was not totally dependent on Cicero for his judgment, and forty years of engagement with Aristotle's works had made his conviction only stronger.[43] That conviction was not limited to Aristotle's *Ethics* and *Politics* but extended to the *Physics* and the *Metaphysics* – odd as that may seem to the modern student of these works. Further, the introduction in the fifteenth century, for example of the *Eudemian Ethics* and works attributed to Aristotle such as the *Rhetorica ad Alexandrum* and *De mundo*, may have fostered this belief in Aristotle's eloquence and concern about rhetoric; confirmation could also be found in another text that had recently become available, Diogenes Laertius' *Life of*

[38] Bruni 1987, 217; Latin in Bruni 1928, 81. [39] Bruni 1987, 213; Latin in Bruni 1928, 77.
[40] Trans. Botley 2004, 51–52.
[41] See his *Life of Aristotle* in Bruni 1987, 290; Latin in Bruni 1928, 46 and Bruni 2013, 340.
[42] Seigel 1968, 110; cf. Stinger 1977, 105–106. [43] Botley 2004, 44–51.

Aristotle. Moreover, Bruni's notion of eloquence seems to include also Aristotle's construction of arguments, the skillful disposition of the material, the frequent quotation from the poets, and the role of examples (e.g. in the *Politics*, believed by Bruni to be Aristotle's most rhetorical work).[44] Still, it is hard to avoid the impression that Bruni's belief could be held only because he was not well acquainted with the *Physics*, the *Metaphysics*, and the *Posterior Analytics*, possibly due to his own disinterest in the more theoretical parts of Aristotle's *oeuvre.* But Bruni could believe that even if Aristotle seems to lack eloquence in his theoretical writings (which, as we just saw, was something that Bruni denied) this was due only to mistreatment by Aristotle's medieval translators. What he, Bruni, had done for Aristotle in the field of practical philosophy was also possible for theoretical philosophy, which would then show Aristotle to be a master of eloquence in these disciplines too.

Another conviction, closely tied to Bruni's belief that Aristotle and Plato were highly rhetorically gifted authors, though each with their own distinctive features,[45] is that we need to transcend the level of individual words in order to do justice to their style. Words alone cannot convey a good sense of the overall effect, beauty, and expressiveness of the author's language. The whole seems more than the sum of its parts.[46] Word-for-word translation may be used when it does not lead to absurdity, but Bruni's emphasis on prose rhythm, sentence structure, literary polish, and everything that constitutes the author's style, requires a wider scope than word level, even though the majority of Bruni's examples of good and bad translations concern words. In order to replicate what Bruni's calls Plato's "majestic" style, its rhythmical qualities, its elegance, and its expressiveness, we cannot limit ourselves to jumping from one word to the next, connecting meanings of words as links in a chain. Rather, we must try to capture the spirit of the piece, or rather the spirit of the author. To do so we have to

[44] *Life of Aristotle* in Bruni 1987, 290–291. According to Bruni's older contemporary, Roberto Rossi, who produced a translation of the *Posterior Analytics*, Aristotle's eloquence "was due to his skillful disposition of his material" (Botley 2004, 49).

[45] For some qualifications of Plato's philosophy and style of philosophy see Bruni's *Life of Aristotle*, in Bruni 1987, 288–289 (Latin in Bruni 1928, 45 and Bruni 2013, 339), though he does not criticize Plato's literary style. See also Celenza 2018, 76–80 on Bruni's translation of Plato's *Phaedo*, stressing also the function it had for fifteenth-century readers on how to live well and die well.

[46] Copenhaver 1988, 87–88 mentions some obstacles to a consistent *ad verbum* method: (1) idiomatic expressions (e.g. *gero tibi morem*, I humor you); (2) the need to translate a word (e.g. *logos*) by using a variety of words in Latin; (3) to render a single Greek word by using a set of words (*aistheta* as *ea quae sensibus percipiuntur*, those things that are perceived by the senses).

recreate the text anew in our own language by summing up all the linguistic and stylistic powers available to us:[47]

> Just as men who copy a painting borrow the shape, attitude, stance and general appearance therefrom, not thinking what they themselves would do, but what another has done; so in translation the best translator will turn his whole mind, heart, and will to his original author, and in a sense transform him, considering how he may express the shape, attitude and stance of his speech, and all his lines and colors.

Bruni's conception of the translator as an artist was classical in inspiration, reflecting a period when translations could be considered as independent works of art, but it is also interesting to compare it with a modern view, according to which the act of translating is not just transferring wordless ideas, as if pouring the same wine from one bottle to another. With only expressions at his or her disposal, the translator creates expressions that match the original, that is, when there is a correspondence between their uses. As W. Haas has argued:[48]

> the translator chooses *what* units to translate, and he chooses such units as correspond or can be *made* to correspond to one another. He tries to keep the size of his translation units to a minimum. But he cannot, generally, avoid having to deal with units larger than the word.

But given the openness of the matching units, the translator

> is able to *create* expressions for his one-to-one mapping. This is how languages are fashioned and re-fashioned by translation. The translator, dealing with "free constructions," constructs freely. He is not changing vehicles or clothing. He is not transferring wine from one bottle into another. Language is no receptacle, and there is nothing to transfer. To produce a likeness is to follow a model's lines. The language he works in is the translator's clay.

At first sight, the similarities in formulation are striking. Both Bruni and Haas exploit the familiar notion of the translator as a kind of artist. A translation, if done well, is a new product, perhaps even a new work of art. In doing so, the translator will keep an open eye to what matches with what, not restricting him- or herself to the level of individual words. Bruni

[47] *On the Correct Way to Translate* in Bruni 1987, 220; cf. 218; Latin text in Bruni 1928, 86 and Bruni 2013, 111.

[48] Haas 1962, 228 for this and the following quotation. For the classical inspiration see Botley 2004, 53 referring to Pseudo-Cicero, *De optimo genere oratorum*. Salutati made some similar remarks about translation; Seigel 1968, 116–119, referring also to Eugenio Garin's conclusion that the humanist versions of Aristotle are often mere revisions of the medieval texts rather than wholly new renderings.

does not exclude word-for-word translation, when, for example, he writes that a good translator must have a thorough command of the target language: "he must have it completely within his power, so when he must render word for word, he will not beg or borrow or leave the word in Greek out of ignorance."[49] But the preservation of the author's style requires attention to much more than individual words. Bruni would therefore certainly agree with Haas's advice to the translator first "to determine the required 'style of speech.'"[50] While words form the basis of any text, Bruni's focus on style and rhetorical techniques leads to a focus on the matching of units broader than individual words.

The differences are as telling as these similarities, however. Bruni does not voice any skepsis about the notion of meaning; he would be puzzled by the phrase that "there is nothing to transfer." In Haas's view there is nothing to transfer because meanings are not the type of things that reside somewhere or can be moved, or can be attached to objects that they can be said "to denote" or "to refer to": "What an expression 'means' cannot be found as a separate entity beside the expression ... Meanings, we have learned, are the *uses* of expressions; they are the work expressions do."[51] On such a view, the meaning of a word is "a collection, an organised recollection, of many individual uses of it, i.e. of various occurrences of it: in verbal and non-verbal contexts, and in positions in which it contrasts with other words." Meaning is not a "pure idea," "which is supposed to be indifferent to its linguistic setting, and therefore transportable from one linguistic vehicle to another." Such a Wittgensteinian critique of meaning is of course wholly foreign to Bruni, indeed to virtually everybody up to the twentieth century. For Bruni it is quite unproblematic to say that words have meaning, and indeed to learn their meaning – as well as the meaning of idiomatic expressions, figures of speech and tropes – is the first step in becoming a good scholar and translator. Study of words involves an examination of their etymology and classical usage. Following grammatical tradition, Bruni frequently talks, quite traditionally, about words having "force and signification (*vim significataque*)," using very frequently words such as "to signify" (*significare*), "signification" (*significatum*), "sense" (*sensus*), and "meaning"/ "what the author has in mind" (*mens auctoris*).[52] What a classical Greek or Latin word means can be found only by carefully studying how it was used by the great authors of antiquity, but there is no

[49] *De interpretatione recta* in Bruni 1987, 220; Latin in Bruni 1928, 85 and Bruni 2013, 111.
[50] Haas 1962, 227. [51] Ibid., 212 and 213 for the next two quotations.
[52] Bruni 1987, 218, 220, 221, and 224 (Latin in Bruni 1928, 84, 85, 87, and 91, and in Bruni 2013, 110–112, 116); Bruni 1741, 207 and 208.

reason to think that Bruni would thereby identify the meaning of the word with its use, if only for the lack of any interest in such theoretical questions about meaning.

And yet it is not impossible to identify elements in his position that, if taken further beyond Bruni's own intellectual horizon, would go in a direction where meanings as entities, arguably, lose much of their identity as things (whether as mental concepts or as objects in the world, or both) independent of the linguistic expression: (a) Bruni's semantic investigations, in which words are explained by other words, and in which immersion in classical languages becomes an immersion in a web of words;[53] (b) his Ciceronian belief in the intrinsic connection between words and things (*verba* and *res*);[54] (c) his focus on style and larger textual unities which might render the search for a stable meaning that resides somewhere independent of the expression misguided; and (d) the focus on broad ethical and political concepts which are not objects "out there" like trees and dogs, something which makes it even more difficult to confront words with their meaning in the sense of comparing a word with a nonverbal object. Each of these points does not necessarily lead to a de-reification of meaning, and such a modern position is of course far from uncontroversial itself, but it would be out of place to enter into any discussion here. The point to stress is that Bruni's conception of the translator as an artist who has "to turn his whole mind, heart, and will to his original author" and to consider "how he may express the shape, attitude and stance of his speech, and all his lines and colors," might be said to favor a holistic approach to the text on the assumption that only such an approach can do justice to the style and broader intentions of the author.

This approach informs Bruni's list of requirements that a good translator must meet and that the medieval translator, according to Bruni, so

[53] Cf. Haas 1962, 215: "We do use expressions for the purpose of referring to things other than expressions. Our stock of significant expressions may be augmented by this operation; but only by assigning both the new expression and the new thing places among other expressions, never by merely referring one to the other." Moss 2003, 15–34 on Renaissance dictionaries in which webs of words proliferate, sometimes reflecting a "self-sufficient linguistic universe" as in the case of Perotti's *Cornu copiae* (published 1489): "a total culture is brought to life" (20). Stabilization of meaning was based on a careful examination of classical usage, summarized in increasing detail in dictionaries.

[54] Terence Cave, for example, sees a blending of word and thing in Erasmus' *De copia* (1512): "*Res* are neither prior to words as their 'origin,' nor are they a productive residue which remains after the words cease. *Res* and *verba* slide together to become 'word-things'; the notion of a single domain (language) having a double aspect replaces that of two distinct domains, language and thought" (1979, 21). For similar reasons, O'Rourke Boyle 1977 stresses the innovative character of Erasmus' view of language, an interpretation criticized by Waswo 1987, 218, who calls Erasmus's position "deliberately traditional." See also Harth 1970 on Erasmus's views on rhetoric and philosophy.

sadly lacked. The translator must possess "a wide and extensive knowledge of both languages," knowledge that is "wide, idiomatic, accurate, and detailed, acquired from a long reading of the philosophers and orators and poets and all other writers."[55] One must know the tropes and figures of speech with their idiomatic meanings as used by the authors, for often, "words mean one thing, the sense is another." The translator should also be thoroughly familiar with the literature of the author, and "he must possess a sound ear so that his translation does not disturb and destroy the fullness and rhythmical qualities of the original."[56] The translator must get under the skin of the author: "He cannot possibly preserve the sense to advantage unless he insinuates and twists himself into the original's word order and periodic structure with verbal propriety and stylistic faithfulness."[57] It is perhaps characteristic that only on a few occasions does Bruni mention knowledge of the things spoken of in the text to be translated, as a further requirement.[58]

All these qualities are lacking in the medieval translator, who is "deficient in both languages, and competent in neither."[59] Bruni gives several examples of mistranslations and Greek words which a translator had left untranslated, such as *eutrapelia*, *bomolochia*, and *agroikos*;[60]

> For all these expressions which out of ignorance he has left in Greek can be aptly and elegantly rendered in Latin. First of all, the expression "play" [*in ludo*] he uses I think would be much better rendered by the word "jesting" [*in ioco*]. We use "play" most often to refer to ball-games and games of dice; "jesting" is reserved for words. The laudable mean, which the Greeks call *eutrapelia*, we call sometimes "urbanity" [*urbanitatem*], sometimes "liveliness" [*festivitatem*], sometimes "affability" [*comitatem*] and sometimes "pleasantry" [*iocunditatem*] . . . All these words are recommended by their frequent use in the best authors.

Bomolochia can be translated as "buffoonery," and those trying and failing to fit into this category as "loutish." The medieval translator also uses the Latin word *bonum* (good) to translate the Greek *kalon*, while words such as *bonum*, *honestum*, and *utile* "are distinct terms among the Greeks, as they are among the Latins, and if he understood anything at all, he could never

[55] Bruni 1987, 218 for this and the following quotation; Latin in Bruni 1928, 84 and Bruni 2013, 110; cf. Pseudo-Cicero, *Ad Herennium* IV.17.
[56] Ibid., 220; Latin in Bruni 1928, 86 and Bruni 2013, 111.
[57] Ibid., 221; Latin in Bruni 1928, 87 and Bruni 2013, 112.
[58] Letter 18 in Bruni 1928, 140. In *De studiis et litteris* Bruni speaks of the combination of literary skill with the knowledge of things (Bruni 1928, 6; Bruni 2013, 175).
[59] Bruni 1987, 213; Latin in Bruni 1928, 77.
[60] Bruni 1987, 214; Latin in Bruni 1928, 79.

have confused them."[61] Further, he writes "delight" (*delectatio*) instead of "pleasure" (*voluptas*), and "sternness" (*tristitia*) for pain, departing "from the usage of Cicero, Seneca, Boethius, Lactantius, Jerome and other Latin authors." He had taken his words from the vulgar (*vulgus*), which is "hardly to be esteemed as a teacher of diction."[62]

Bruni's semantic investigations are also aimed at showing the richness of the Latin language. Latin is praised as "abundantly rich, acquainted not only with every form of expression, but with ample embellishments as well."[63] While not sharing the view of some of his contemporaries who, perhaps out of cultural rivalry, deplored the so-called verbosity of the Greeks versus the alleged conciseness of Latin, Bruni was convinced that Latin had all the resources to match whatever was written in (beautiful) Greek; hence there was no reason to leave Greek words untranslated in the text: "there has never been anything said in Greek that cannot be said in Latin."[64] We might expect Bruni, however, to have recognized the individuality of languages. As James Hankins notes:[65]

> It would have been natural for him, faced with the impossible task of preserving the propriety of his own language while rendering the most individual expressions of another, to have admitted its impossibility and to have realized that the forms of the expression native to a language are not simply a set of arbitrary signs standing for the unchanging objects of thought, as the medieval philosophers had held, but organic and individual expressions rooted in the historical experiences of a people.

This insight however was not fully grasped by Bruni, because he assumed "the cultural unity of Greece and Rome," and hence believed "that the Greek and Latin languages were, if not exactly interchangeable sets of signs for identical concepts, in any case fundamentally equivalent vehicles of expression." This cultural unity excluded the Jewish culture and the Hebrew language, which, according to Bruni, differs from Greek and Latin "in language and figures of speech so far from us that they even

[61] Bruni 1987, 215; Latin in Bruni 1928, 79.

[62] Ibid., 216; Latin in Bruni 1928, 80. The "vulgar" are the medieval translators with their poor linguistic skills.

[63] Ibid., 213; Latin in Bruni 1928, 78; cf. Cicero, *De finibus* 3.5.

[64] *On the Correct Way to Translate*, in Bruni 1987, 228; Latin in Bruni 1928, 95 and Bruni 2013, 119. On Poggio's rather negative perspective on Greek, see Botley 2004, 48: Poggio's views are related to "an ancient stereotype of Greekness: of Roman fears of the devious fluency of Odysseus and Sinon, and of a defeated nation corrupting the simple virtues of its conquerors with its sophistries."

[65] Hankins in Bruni 1987, 11 for this and the next quotation in the text.

write in the opposite direction."[66] There was nothing to be gained from studying Hebrew; "Greek is the language of philosophy, and for the sake of other disciplines, too, is worth learning. Together with Latin it offers the complete range of all branches of literature." It looks as if Bruni glimpsed the individuality of Hebrew here only to dismiss it as "barbarous."[67]

Bruni's conviction that Ciceronian Latin was perfectly capable of expressing all kinds of philosophical truths was of course controversial. Among contemporaries who were critical of Bruni's project were Archbishop Battista de' Giudici, a certain Demetrius, whose letter to Bruni is lost, and Bishop Alfonso of Cartagena, already mentioned, who wrote the most extensive critique. The criticisms come down to the essential point that philosophy and eloquence are not the same thing. According to Alfonso, we can already see this in Cicero, whose discussion of Aristotle's moral philosophy is not as detailed, precise, and thorough as that of the Greek philosopher himself. The elegant language comes at the expense of the subtle distinctions which Aristotle had made in his discussion of the virtues.[68] The same is true for Seneca, whose writings are praised for their moral appeal but whose philosophical discussion of the virtues is "cursory and unsuitable" (*summarie et improprie*). Further, Bruni's idea that moral discourse must be subject to eloquence goes against Cicero's own opinion that oratory and philosophy each have their own domain.[69] In short, the requirements of eloquence are not consistent with "the rigor of science" (*rigor scientiae*), which requires "strict technical language" (*sub restrictis et propriissimis verbis*) and "a strict propriety of words" (*simplicitatem rerum et restrictam proprietatem verborum*).[70]

The precise understanding apparently requires also leaving some technical terms untranslated. More in general, as Alfonso points out, Latin has always absorbed foreign words such as *grammatica*, *logica*, *rhetorica*, *philosophia*, and *theologia*, and in fact much of Latin vocabulary is rooted in Greek.[71] It would impoverish the language if we were to shut it up within fixed borders. We see this borrowing between languages all the time, not only in the sciences and arts but also in "common and forensic linguistic

[66] Bruni to Giovanni Cirignano of Lucca, 12 Sept. 1442, trans. in Bruni 1987, 335 for this and the next quotation.

[67] On medieval and early-modern polemics about the grammatical differences and the directions of writing between Latin and Hebrew, see Stein Kokin 2015.

[68] Alfonso in Birkenmajer 1922, 174 for this and the next quotation about Seneca.

[69] Ibid., 175. A later critic of Bruni, Battista de' Giudici made many similar points, referring also to Cicero's view that ornate language was inappropriate in philosophical discourse (*De officiis* III); see Hankins 2003, 213.

[70] Ibid.; trans. in Bruni 1987, 205–206. [71] Alfonso in Birkenmajer 1922, 168.

usage" (*communi ac forensi usu loquendi*).[72] Bruni himself uses terms such as *cola*, *commota*, *periodos*, *tropos*, and so on. A further advantage of transliterated Greek terms is that, as a modern commentator notes, "they brought no irrelevant semantic baggage with them; the words were empty tokens which could be filled with the philosopher's meaning. This practice was a familiar device to Latin audiences for whom Greek traditionally provided technical vocabularies."[73] It seems that Alfonso has such a point in mind when he criticizes Bruni for suggesting that Greek *eutrapelia* must be rendered sometimes by "urbanity," sometimes by "liveliness," sometimes by "affability," and sometimes by "pleasantry." These words do not mean the same thing, says Alfonso, and the translator was therefore right not to enter into semantic controversies (*contentiones*), which can be best settled in a commentary added to the translation.[74] Where the proper meaning of words cannot be rendered with equal brevity (*sub simili brevitate*), it is wise policy to leave the Greek word untranslated in the translation.[75] Alfonso fears that Bruni's translation confounds the conceptual distinctions which have been handed over by Aristotle, Boethius, and Augustine, and laid down for instance in a dictionary such as the *Catholicon*: "in philosophy words should not be loosened without restraint, since from the use of improper words error gradually adds to the things themselves."[76]

In the rest of his response Alfonso tries to meet Bruni on his own ground, offering explanations of the terms used by the medieval translator, sometimes giving Spanish equivalents (e.g. *alvardanus* for *scurra* and *corthesia* for *curialitas*) to make his point. Alfonso argues that in every instance the medieval translator's choice is better than Bruni's. He was right to opt for *delectatio* rather than *voluptas*, since it is a more general term; *tristitia* and *dolor* were used correctly by the medieval translator to make the point that it is sadness rather than pain we seek to restrain by moral virtue; also the distinction between several types of vicious actions was better rendered by the medieval translator, because vice (*vitium*) is not always the opposite of virtue, as Bruni's translation suggests. In his long excursions into the meaning of moral terms such as *bonus*, *honestus*, *delectatio*, *voluptas*, and *vitium* Alfonso frequently appeals to what a term "properly" means; for example, "pleasure," taken in its proper sense, means

[72] Alfonso in Birkenmajer 1922, 167; 168–169. [73] Botley 2004, 56; cf. Seigel 1968, 126.
[74] Alfonso in Birkenmajer 1922, 171 and 167. [75] Ibid., 169.
[76] Alfonso in Birkenmajer 1922, 169: "sine freno laxanda sunt."

solely bodily delights.[77] His concern in general is therefore not to check the adequateness of Bruni's translation but whether the translation makes sense philosophically speaking, that is, captures well the conceptual distinctions developed in the philosophical traditions.

Alfonso thus made some interesting and valuable points about philosophical terminology. Such terms are rich in content, having a whole philosophical tradition behind them, and to entangle all the semantic nuances requires a full understanding of the philosophical meanings of these terms, an understanding that comes with studying Aristotle, Boethius, the Church Fathers, and so on. In fact, a lack of philosophical understanding on Bruni's part had resulted in an absurd translation of *to agathon* as the highest good (*summum bonum*), thus implying that all objects tend to man's highest good, while Aristotle's teleology suggests something completely different, namely that all things tend to some end.[78] Translating a philosophical text requires not only a sound grasp of all the things Bruni had listed but also an understanding of philosophical concepts. An eloquent translation easily misses these subtleties and distinctions. Alfonso, however, undermines his own case by making resolute statements to the effect that reason dictates what we should read in the text: "whatever is consonant with reason is what Aristotle must be considered to have said, and whatever our translation wisely expresses in Latin words, we may conclude was written in the Greek."[79] In a debate on translation, this is of course not a strong position, even more so if ignorance of the source language (in this case Greek) makes it impossible to check the translation. And the conviction that Aristotle's text has *auctoritas* because Aristotle's philosophy is more or less the embodiment of reason and truth is also not a fruitful assumption for investigating the accurateness of a translation.

Alfonso's observations about the requirements of philosophical terminology, however, are not without their merits, and to some extent it is a pity that the issue of correct translation was mixed up with the issue of the proper standards for philosophical discourse, but of course they were

[77] Alfonso in Birkenmajer 1922, 181; cf. 179: "proprie sumpta." On the significance of *proprietas verborum* in fourteenth-century linguistic theory, see Harth 1968.

[78] Hankins 2003, 198–199. Bruni's translation of *tagathon* continued to arouse passionate responses, long after his death.

[79] Alfonso as translated by Hankins in Bruni 1987, 204. For Bruni's disappointing reactions to Alfonso, see Hankins 2003, 204–207, concluding that "his impatience and asperity of tone, his very lack of serious argument, and his evident expectation of general agreement show that the body of educated opinion was already on his side, and that the hermeneutical revolution of the humanists had already been victorious" (207).

closely related at a time when translation of philosophical texts, often recently rediscovered, presented a significant challenge.[80] Many philosophers then and now would agree with Alfonso about the need for a precise and exact terminology that expresses the conceptual distinctions in an accurate and precise way. (They might also want to point out that Bruni, too, had his own controversial assumptions, e.g. Aristotle's eloquence.[81]) But Bruni would respond by claiming that his Ciceronian Latin is as precise and exact as can be; eloquence, in the words of a later humanist, is "not a straining after refinement, but rather the ability to explain accurately and clearly the opinions and thoughts of our minds."[82] Such debates show that words such as "precise," "exact," and "faithful" are normative rather than descriptive terms. Of course, we are often able to distinguish between, for example, very loose (free) and literal translations, but following a very strict translation at the level of individual words might result in something that even the translator might not recognize, on second thought, as very faithful. Jonathan Barnes, for instance, believes that his revised translation of Aristotle's *Posterior Analytics* is "more faithful" to Aristotle's Greek than his first version from 1975, which betrayed "a profound misconception" of what he thought was "a stern fidelity to Aristotle's Greek" (word for word), while in fact it was written in a "sort of dog English: always inelegant and sometimes barbarous, it appeared here as comic or disgusting and there as merely incomprehensible."[83] There is no straightforward yardstick of fidelity or faithfulness, and how one understands the notion is, as we have seen, dependent on the translator's ideas about the language and style of the source text, about the author and his or her works and ideas, and the opportunities that the target language

[80] The trade-off between popular accessibility and philosophical precision was of course one of the recurrent issues in the battle between rhetoric and philosophy. The famous debate between Giovanni Pico and Barbaro from the 1480s readily comes to mind, with Pico playing the highly eloquent defender of scholastic thought and language against Barbaro who had criticized the "dull, rude, uncultured style" of the scholastics. One of the more interesting points in the debate is Pico's argument that, if language is conventional, "it may happen that a society of men agree on a word's meaning; if so, for each thing that word is among them the right one to use for the meaning agreed on." Hence, scholastics, like everybody else, may agree on a common norm of speaking. "There is no sense in saying that the one standard is wrong and yours is right, if this business of name-making is altogether arbitrary." Trans. in Breen 1968, 22 (originally published as Breen 1952); Moss 2003, 68–70; Kraye 2008; Hankins 2019, 21–23. There is a considerable literature on this debate; see MacPhail 2014, 21 n. 10.

[81] Cf. Seigel 1968, 125.

[82] Franz Burchard in 1558, as translated by Botley 2004, 60. Bruni's translation was criticized as too free by Johannes Argyropoulos, who made his own translation of the *Nicomachean Ethics*; Seigel 1968, 245–246. There were also humanists who continued to defend Bruni; see Botley 2004, 59–60.

[83] Barnes in Aristotle 1993, xxiv.

offers and the limitations that it seems to impose on the translator, as well as about the relation between style and content, word and meaning, rhetoric and philosophy.

The debate about translations and philosophical terminology continued among humanists who were producing ever more new translations of ever more works, and by the end of the fifteenth century almost all Greek literature as we know it today, including philosophical and scientific works, had become available. Seen from this broader perspective the debate sparked by Bruni's translation cannot be reduced to a controversy simply between humanists and scholastics. Translations always give rise to heated debates, and this was no different in the Renaissance from how it is now. But these debates were not directly aimed at scholastic language as such. To see how Bruni's critique of the so-called barbarous language of the scholastics was taken up and expanded into a comprehensive critique of scholastic language we must turn to his younger contemporary, Lorenzo Valla.

CHAPTER 2

From a Linguistic Point of View: Lorenzo Valla's Critique of Aristotelian-Scholastic Philosophy

Introduction

The humanist program was premised on the belief that the study and emulation of the Latin of the great authors in antiquity provided the key to clear thinking and elegant composition. The Latin the humanists encountered in the schools was regarded as a depraved and corrupted form of classical Latin. The study of the ancient language therefore went hand in hand with a critique of Latin as it had been developed in the schools and in particular the technical Latin of the theologians, philosophers, and grammarians. Why tamper with a beautiful and resourceful language in which so much wonderfully inspiring literature and philosophy had been written? The legacy of classical antiquity – the languages, rhetoric and style, literature and poetry, history, science, and much philosophical thinking on morals and politics – was believed to possess such great civilizing power and of such enduring value that contemporary culture and learning faded into nothing compared to this treasure house of beauty, culture, learning, and wisdom. Petrarch, Bruni, and other humanists argued that there was therefore no need to devise a technical language to express the deeper truths of philosophy. Such jargon could only mislead people in their search for moral virtue, Christian piety, literary accomplishment, civic virtue, or philosophical wisdom.

One of the underlying convictions therefore was that classical Latin, even though it had been the language of a culture long gone, could still (and could again) be treated as a living, natural vehicle to express people's thoughts and beliefs. From a modern point of view, this position – and thereby the humanist project as such – might seem to contain a deep tension, one already hinted at in the debate between Bruni and Alfonso in the previous chapter. A language is like a living organism, continuously changing, developing and adapting itself to ever new situations; so how could the humanists think that such an old language could be revived in a wholly different time and culture as a vehicle for all kinds of postclassical beliefs and thoughts? This tension, if ever very deeply felt, was greatly eased by the presence of an unbroken tradition of Latin as the language of learned culture throughout the ages, even though its existence had often been precarious in postclassical times. It was therefore a question of reviving or rekindling the language (and the styles, the genres, and so on), rather than inventing or constructing a new one. Moreover, the vernacular languages – including the Florentine *volgare* of Dante, Petrarch, and Boccaccio – had not yet come anywhere close to attaining the status of a stable, well-regulated and universally used language that Latin had obtained, though this was soon to change.

Whether such considerations of historical continuity and linguistic situation could have resolved that tension might, however, be doubted. It is one thing to promote classical Latin as a language for learned communication and literary composition; it is quite another to champion it as the only possible, or at least the only appropriate, vehicle for clear thinking, philosophical analysis, and in fact every kind of intellectual pursuit. To reject the language of the scholastics as artificial and unnatural requires a stronger argument for the naturalness of Latin, but a convincing argument for this is hard to produce; Latin was no longer any one's mother tongue, let alone the language of the masses. For a humanist it would have sounded heretical, but from a bird's-eye view classical Latin in the fifteenth century might be considered as no less artificial and esoteric than the Latin of the scholastics.

This very attempt to present Latin as such a natural, common language in opposition to the language of the Aristotelian scholastics is the focus of this chapter, in which we will examine one of the most important and influential humanists of his generation, Lorenzo Valla (ca. 1406–1457). While he shared many of the assumptions and convictions of his predecessors and contemporaries, Valla was undoubtedly more comprehensive, innovative and critical than they had been, not only in his studies of the legacy of classical antiquity but also in applying his expertise and methodological principles to other fields of learning than those we would now include as part of classical scholarship – fields such as theology, philosophy, dialectic, history, and law. Most relevant for this study is his critical engagement with Aristotelian-scholastic philosophy in his *Dialectical Disputations*, but the same critical attention to language informs his work on the New Testament that led in many places to emendations of St Jerome's canonical translation; his exposure as a forgery of the famous

Donation of Constantine, a pillar of papal claim to worldly power; and his most influential work, *The Elegances of the Latin Language* (*Elegantiae Linguae Latinae*, 1441) in which he criticizes, corrects, and expands on explanations of words, grammar, syntax, and morphology given by, mainly, late-classical grammarians. The six books of the *Elegantiae* contain prefaces that together read like a credo of the humanist program, giving it some of its most vigorous and combative formulations. These works – to which his controversial dialogue on the highest good (*De vero bono*), short treatises on free will and religious vows as well as translations and commentaries on classical works may be added – give Valla a preeminent place in Renaissance humanism.

Two Levels of Language Critique

Valla's critique of scholastic-Aristotelian philosophy was premised on the belief that classical Latin should be the norm for the language to be used in learned communication, the arts and sciences; any departure from this norm could only lead to misunderstanding, nonsense, and barbarity in speech, thought, and in the expression of the Christian faith (an important motivation for Valla). Valla's project can therefore be regarded, first and foremost, as the restoration of good, classical Latin. The notions that turn out to be central to this project are common linguistic usage, custom, and observation, and it will be necessary to study how Valla employed these notions in his critique of scholastic language. Knowledge of Latin, indeed of any language, is a matter of observing how people (the community of users of that language) actually use or have used that language. From the observation of the linguistic practice, grammatical rules and rules pertaining to the use of words can be deduced; rules are subsequent to practice, not vice versa. Linguistic practice, convention, and custom should sanction the rules of grammar and language use, and no philosopher or grammarian sitting in his or her armchair can prescribe any such rules or assign new meanings to words. Such a view sounds pretty modern, and Valla may indeed be credited with having developed an empirical, inductive approach to the study of Latin, and by extension to any kind of language. But at the same time his descriptive, empirical study had an essentially normative dimension: from the practice a norm was distilled that was consequently held up against all other forms of Latin.[1]

[1] Some modern scholars have emphasized the descriptive, empirical nature of Valla's study of Latin, while others have laid more stress on its normative and prescriptive dimension. For some voices in

The notions of linguistic usage, custom, and convention pertained therefore first and foremost to the practice of the great authors of antiquity, and in particular orators such as Cicero and Quintilian, who were Valla's principal sources of inspiration.[2] Common linguistic usage usually meant the usage of these authors, though the two are not identical, and here an interesting aspect of Valla's critical work emerges that is often overlooked. As will be suggested below, Valla sometimes combined or even fused two levels of criticisms: a critique of scholastic Latin as ungrammatical, barbarous and failing to meet classical standards, and a critique of that language as being out of tune with our allegedly normal, common, natural way of speaking, writing, and arguing. Unless "common" means "classical," and "common people" means "the users of classical Latin," these are two distinct types of critique. The language of the schools is held up against good, classical Latin, but also against the normal way of seeing and talking about things, and Valla sometimes invokes "the common people" (*vulgus, populus*) to make his point.

Valla's critique of Aristotelian doctrines and terminology, which will be examined below, is often supported by grammatical considerations. Yet, even though the linguistic context is Latin and Valla's criticism is voiced in Latin, the point is also often meant as an illustration of the supposedly artificial, unnatural nature of scholastic terminology, cut loose from daily practice and common-sense perception. Also, this makes Valla's language critique philosophically interesting: the idea that "common language," close to the way in which people are said to actually speak about things in a natural way, should be used in our philosophical and intellectual examinations clearly transcends the level of grammar, presupposing a particular view about the nature of philosophical language. In view of the theme of this book, this chapter will examine to what extent Valla was deliberately developing such a view, or whether he opportunistically

this debate see Camporeale 1972; Marsh 1979; Regoliosi 2000 and 2010; Kraye 2001; Rizzo 2002; Celenza 2018; Nauta 2018, with further bibliography. The two aspects are of course two facets of one and the same project: the expression that is found most in use among the authorities is the one to be preferred. Yet, as Cesarini Martinelli showed, Valla did not refrain from rationalizing or emending classical usage – even Ciceronian usage – if he thought that certain linguistic constructions could reflect the state of affairs in a more transparent way. Valla frequently attempted to reconstruct "la coerenza razionale del linguaggio" (58), showing at times a certain creativity in formulating rules and even inventing examples to get rid of ambiguities or contradictions in the Latin he was analyzing (Cesarini Martinelli 1980, 58, 69, 71, 75, 77).

[2] His vast learning and reading notwithstanding, many of his examples come from a rather limited range of authors, among whom – in spite of his professed predilection for Quintilian – Cicero takes pride of place in terms of sheer number of quotations, at least in the *Elegantiae*. Archaic writers, poets, and late-classical authors (including Christian ones) are discarded, while Seneca, Tacitus, and the two Plinys are rarely cited (and if so, often criticized); Cesarini Martinelli 1980, 66.

merged, if it suited his argument, the Latin perspective with that of the so-called common people.

The Grudge Against Aristotle and Other "Perverters" of Language

Before taking a closer look at Valla's critique of scholastic philosophy, one preliminary question must be asked: why did he hold such a grudge against Aristotle and his followers? His main sources of inspiration, Cicero and Quintilian, could not have been responsible for this rancor, nor could Leonardo Bruni, who, as seen in the previous chapter, held Aristotle in high regard. Valla's own personality might have something to do with it. He had an irascible temper and a highly polemical and oratorical style inspired by classical genres such as invective and oration. It had also something to do with the sometimes excessively competitive nature of humanist scholars, fighting for patronage and positions at the court or the papal chancery. Valla was eager to show off his learning, and he liked to use the tactic of shock and awe, sneering at others and downplaying their views and contributions. More importantly perhaps, Valla clearly regarded the Aristotelians as a sect that had claimed, so he thought, an exclusive right to wisdom, effectively usurping all institutional power. There had been many more schools in antiquity, but they had been outmaneuvered and eclipsed by Aristotle and his followers. Apart from the usual hyperbole, characteristic of the genre, Valla must have thought that the Philosopher could be dethroned only by a heavy onslaught not only on his thought but also his personality.[3] Aristotle is accused of impiety, arrogance, plagiarism, intellectual fraud and theft, unoriginality, obscurantism, inconstancy, and whatnot. This is not the most attractive side of the humanist anti-Aristotelian literature, but it is good to remember that some of these points ultimately led to a more serious engagement with the historical and philological aspects of Aristotle's *oeuvre* in the sixteenth and seventeenth centuries.[4] But it was in particular the allegedly abstract nature of (Aristotelian) philosophy that provoked Valla's

[3] Valla 2012, 1:3–13 (*Dialectical Disputations* [hereafter *DD*]1.proem.2–12). Cf. Francesco Patrizi's position, nicely summed up by Deitz (2007, 115–116): "whatever Aristotle had said that was true was not new, and that whatever he had said was new was not true." Another critic was Gianfrancesco Pico della Mirandola, who in his *Examen Vanitatis* (1520) cast doubt on the authenticity of Aristotle's writings, deplored his style, and argued that Aristotle was only one philosopher among many, unlike what the sect of Aristotelians might think. For these and other arguments (such as that Aristotle relied too much on sense experience), see Schmitt 1967, 63–83. For a comprehensive treatment of anti-Aristotelianism, see Martin 2014.

[4] Levitin 2015, 235–238.

anger: the Aristotelian scholastics analyzed things with the aid of a host of complicated concepts; their metaphysics was full of shady, unobservable entities that did not explain anything; their moral philosophy had nothing to do with how people actually acted and behaved; their logic was a theoretical construct cut loose from the way in which people talk, speak, and argue; and, most perniciously, they had defiled the Christian faith by their questions, distinctions, and bizarre attempts to subject the mysterious and the ineffable to rational explanation, using a terminology that was at once totally baroque and incredibly reductive.[5]

The Aristotelian philosopher was only one of Valla's many opponents – grammarians from late antiquity and the Middle Ages; lawyers and jurists with no skills that would enable them to understand Roman law; humanists who did not understand the importance of linguistic usage and custom in the field of classical studies; ecclesiastical authorities who had no Greek, and so on – they all could provoke Valla's wrath and scorn. But the serious message was not lost on later humanists, and even though many of them thought him much too aggressive and critical, they learned from him not only a wealth of insights into Latin grammar and vocabulary, but also a method of studying words and arguments in the context in which they occur, and how to apply this method not only to classical texts, but also to the Bible, patristic and medieval religious and philosophical texts, and historical documents. In his hands philology became a critical tool for sifting the spurious from the authentic, and for exposing all kinds of errors and misunderstandings (or what were considered as such), and hence a weapon for attacking established philosophical and theological dogmas and practices. Language was therefore the basis of all the arts and disciplines and the key to understanding the world, and though the revival of classical Latin was central to Valla's humanist outlook, his critique of abstract theory and speculation as well as of the language that fostered that way of doing philosophy and theology often transcended the level of Latin grammar and stylistic elegance. Some key passages will be discussed below.

Latin and Common Linguistic Usage

As already mentioned, the central notion to which Valla appeals time and again in his critique of scholastic philosophy is common linguistic usage, also referred to as popular custom (*consuetudo popularis*), the usual manner

[5] Cf. Celenza 2018, 178–227.

or custom of speaking (*mos loquendi*) and practice (*usus*). The Latin can be misleading here. The terms *communis, popularis,* and *vulgaris* (common, popular, ordinary) do not refer to the language of the streets, the vernacular language, let alone to what we would now call vulgar speech. Valla had borrowed the notion of usage from his classical sources, and in particular from his hero Quintilian, author of the *Institutio oratoria*, a vast rhetorical handbook, which was a kind of Bible for him.

As an orator Quintilian had defended the primacy of usage over grammatical strictness (*ratio*). To be sure, grammatical rules are important, but grammarians tend to overregulate a language, forgetting how people actually use it. These grammarians sometimes propose changing words by analogy to other words or word formations, even though the proposed words are not even in use. Quintilian was against such interventions, arguing that "speaking Latin is one thing, and speaking grammatically quite another."[6] This does not mean that any usage or any form of Latin is commendable. Just as certain practices such as "getting dead drunk in the bath" are not to be accepted in spite of their frequent occurrence, so the language of the masses or the uneducated, full of barbarisms and mistakes, should not be accepted.[7] In line with his idea of an orator as a good, wise man (female orators did not exist in Quintilian's world), Quintilian defines usage in speech as "the consensus of the educated, just as Usage in life is the consensus of the good."[8] He calls usage "the surest teacher of speaking" comparing it with money "marked with the public stamp," but this analogy must not be taken as a recommendation of the speech of the masses or of the uneducated people.[9] Next to grammatical strictness and usage, Quintilian lists antiquity (*vetustas*) and authority (*auctoritas*) as principles of correct speech: the first refers to the use of archaic words, which may give style a certain majesty and grandeur; the second refers to more or less the same thing, namely words from the best authors (in particular orators and historians), often from the past, but in both cases moderation is important: such words must be used sparingly.[10]

Fourteen hundreds years later Valla feels that these ideas have lost nothing of their value and relevance. Endorsing Quintilian's oratorical

6 Quintilian 2001, 1:173 (*Institutio oratoria* 1.6.27); 1:163 (1.6.3).

7 Quintilian 2001, 1:183–185 (*Institutio oratoria* 1.6.44).

8 Ibid. Walzer 2003 argues that Quintilian's aim is to fuse Stoic wisdom with Ciceronian eloquence.

9 Ibid., 1:163 (*Institutio oratoria* 1.6.3). The comparison of money and language, as conventional institutes, was already popular in antiquity; see Sluiter 2000, 117 n. 45 for some references. Cf. Casson 2016.

10 Valla 2012, 1: 181–183 (*DD* 1.6.39–42).

perspective, he agrees with the importance of usage and custom over grammatical strictness; linguistic usage and authority should govern our speech and writing. Like Quintilian, Valla defines this usage in terms of the language of the educated people – a usage based on the Latin of the best authors, in particular orators such as Cicero and Quintilian. As he writes in his *Dialectical Disputations*: "As for us, we must speak according to a grammatical standard, speaking not so much grammatically as in Latin – following not so much the rules of an art, in other words, as the usage of the educated and cultured people, which is the best art of all. And who does not know that speaking is based mainly on usage and authority?"[11] But it is not only the language of Quintilian that he regards as authoritative; also his oratorical perspective on the art of argumentation gives Quintilian's teachings an immense topicality in view of the abstract and technical approach of the dialecticians of Valla's own time. The over-regulation and systematization of rhetoric was already a thorn in Quintilian's side, and Valla applies this critique to grammar and dialectic in which he finds the same inclination to abstraction and systematization:[12]

> I have taken on his teachings as the best and most definitive not only because they are indispensable but also because they are suited not just to dialecticians and philosophers but also to the civil law and all the arts and to the everyday and communal practice of speaking [*quotidianae communique loquendi consuetudini*]. For when dialecticians teach about this topic and give their examples, they seem to be singing (if singing it is, and not croaking) to themselves.

According to Valla, the language of the scholastics is not only a depraved form of Latin but also an expression of an entirely misguided approach, viz. a theoretical logical approach instead of an oratorical and grammatical one that starts from the actual use of words and arguments. Whatever language people speak, they must always conform to the usage, custom, and conventions of their community, and for the Latin users this means the Latin of the orators and, more generally, "the educated people":[13]

> Anyone who abandons it [i.e., usage] must be hooted out of the company of educated people, no less than the scofflaw and scorner of custom must be expelled from the community. And just as nations and peoples have different customs and different laws, so do the natures of languages differ, each

[11] Ibid., 2:85 (*DD* 2.11.6).
[12] Ibid., 2:395 (*DD* 3.15.42). On Quintilian's skepticism regarding too great a reliance on rules, see Quintilian 2001, 2:427 (5.10.121) and 2:517–519 (5.14.31–32). Cf. Nauta 2009, 236–237 and 267–268.
[13] Ibid., 2:89 (*DD* 2.11.14).

> one sacred and unsullied among its own. Therefore we must rely on usage, as if it were a kind of established practice in the community [*tanquam quodam more civili*].

Interestingly, Valla moves smoothly from the sphere of Latin ("the educated people") to languages in general. He feels that his point is valid for any kind of language: it is usage that accounts for the structure of a language, creating a community of language users. That is also the reason why a general theory of grammar, here called by Valla "*ratio*," such as developed by medieval grammarians, the so-called Modists, must necessarily fail:[14]

> In fact, Greek, Hebrew, Latin, Punic, Dalmatian and other tongues differ not just in the words that are spoken, but in how speech is constructed, and this happens because of *practice* [*usu*], not theory [*ratione*], except in a few cases. We can no more give a theory for grammar (as some of those idiots do, including those who write about "modes of signifying") than for the different words that different peoples use.

Not only is it impossible to construct a general theory of grammar valid for all the different languages, but it is also futile to try to impose the use of any type of language or terminology that does not reflect the established practices of the community.

Valla's accusation is thus that the so-called barbarous, distorted, and technical language of the scholastics does not reflect the *mos civilis* (established practice in the community). By inventing their own language, the scholastics have placed themselves outside the community. Because their language is not in conformity to the linguistic usage of the community, it has been able to engender the strange puzzles, sophistries, sophisms, forms of unnatural argumentation, and artificial problems that give philosophers their *raison d'être*. In criticizing their *captiones* (sophistries), Valla condemns their philosophical practice and language again in terms of fraud and transgression of the law:[15]

> As long as I speak according to the usage of educated people, I cannot be rebuked, and if you attack me with sophistries, I shall appeal to the statutes and customs of language as a kind of civil law. In civil law there is no place for sophistry, in fact, and if anything is done with intent to defraud, the ruling will be to rescind it and make it null and void. But to oppose

[14] Ibid., 2:85 (*DD* 2.11.7). On Valla and medieval grammar, see Percival 1976; Gavinelli 1991; Codoñer Merino 2010; Lo Monaco 2010.

[15] Valla 2012, 2:355–357 (*DD* 3.14.5–6).

> sophistries we should examine them in detail and ponder the weight of their words.

Valla's remedy therefore is to consider "the weight of words."[16] It is only through a careful study of language as it has been used and ought to be used that sophistries and philosophical problems can be resolved, since these are the result only of a misunderstanding of language: these philosophers are "incapable of grasping any doctrine clearly, since they have too little skill in their own language – Latin, that is," let alone any skill in Greek, the language of their own master, Aristotle.[17] It is Valla's ambition, then, to show the linguistic roots of the philosophical problems; they often turn on the "meaning of words":[18]

> These dialecticians of yours, then, these philosophizers, should no longer wish to persevere in the ignorance of certain terms that they use, and they should turn back to speech that is natural, speech commonly used by educated people, especially since they will make no progress if they do otherwise, now that I have uncovered the truth about the many words that are the source of most mistakes.

Words and arguments should not be taken out of context, since this will easily change their normal, common meaning and, consequently, will give rise to philosophical problems where none existed. This is Valla's core conviction that drives his critique of Aristotelian-scholastic philosophy in his *Dialectical Disputations.*

The Critique of Scholastic-Aristotelian Philosophy and Language

In this work, Valla applies the general framework of common linguistic usage, convention, custom, and community to criticize a series of Aristotelian-scholastic doctrines and concepts such as the ten categories (substance, quality, quantity, relation, time, place, and so on), the transcendental terms (thing, good, one, true, etc.), and distinctions such as matter/form and act/potency, as well as several forms of syllogistic reasoning and other forms of argumentation. He also attacks some tenets of

[16] Ibid., 2:353 (*DD* 3.14).

[17] Ibid., 1:11 (*DD* 1.proem.17). Aristotle too is accused of having little skill in his own language, sometimes using Greek words and expressions in ways that do not reflect the linguistic custom. Valla does not say, however, which custom he has in mind.

[18] Ibid., 2:209–211 (*DD* 3.proem.3). Cf. ibid., 1:7 (*DD* 1.proem.9): "Even if they [Avicenna and Averroes] were great men, how much authority should they have when the meaning of words is in question, as in most problems in philosophy?"

Aristotelian ethics and natural philosophy. It is a bold attack on the foundations of Aristotelian philosophy, and Valla aptly calls a first version of this work the *repastinatio* of those foundations, a word which means retilling or reploughing but also cutting back and weeding out. Many arguments are based on grammatical considerations in line with Valla's aim, as just quoted, to have philosophers "turn back to speech that is natural, speech commonly used by educated people."[19] But as the discussion will show, the notion of linguistic usage not only refers to correct Latin but also to what Valla considers to be the normal, ordinary way in which people speak about things, regardless of the language they use.

The Aristotelian Categories

A central theme of the first book of the *Dialectical Disputations* is the reduction of the ten Aristotelian categories to three: substance, quality, and action.[20] Aristotle had developed the idea that there are ten supreme and irreducible genera of things: substance, and nine accidental categories such as quality, quantity, relation, time, and place. Valla was not the first to question the ontological status of these categories, but his approach is grammatical rather than ontological: he argues from a grammatical point of view that there is no need to have more than three categories: the world consists of things, which can be analyzed as substances qualified by qualities and actions. At the back of his mind are clearly the grammatical categories of noun, adjective, and verb, even though he realizes that there is no simple one-to-one correspondence between, for example, nouns and substances, or between verbs and actions. (A verb, for example, can also signify a quality.) Valla's aim therefore is to suggest that words that seem to refer to relation or quantity are in fact all terms that, from a grammatical point of view, are not different from qualitative terms: terms such as "bald," "two meters tall," and "father," are all terms of quality that qualify this particular man. Valla's reasons have often less to do with classical Latin than with what he thinks is a common-sense approach to the world of things, reflected by "how everyone talks" or "common linguistic usage." For instance, in reducing the category of having (of which Aristotle had given as examples: armed, clothed, having shoes on) to quality, Valla argues that being armed qualifies a person no less than being fat:

[19] Ibid., 2:209 (3.proem.3).

[20] For background and further analysis see Mack 1993, 42–51 and Nauta 2009, 82–125.

> For even though arms, clothing and shoes are bodily things, they still introduce a quality into the man since this is how everyone talks: "that one defenseless, and not the kind to go into battle armed." . . . Since things that are part of the body itself produce quality, why be surprised at things that come from the outside? When asked "what kind of man is that," we answer "stout, fat, plump and hairy."[21]

What does Valla mean by "everyone"? Only the educated people speaking the right kind of Latin, or indeed everyone, regardless of the language they use? In all likelihood, Valla thinks of the educated people, yet his point, while made in Latin, does not seem to be dependent on Latin. The ontological reduction would work equally well in another language. Valla's point seems to be conceptual: because things such as arms and shoes qualify a person, they must be considered as qualities, something which is reflected by the way "everyone speaks."

The same appeal to common linguistic usage is made to support the reduction of the Aristotelian category of quantity to that of quality. Valla first cites the usual authorities Cicero and Quintilian to support his position, and then states that "linguistic usage itself also confirms this" – namely, that "quantity is entirely a matter of quality."[22] In addition to quotations from classical authors, it is characteristic of Valla's approach to give self-invented examples, often of a rather homely nature, to make his point: "For when someone asks 'what kind of field did you buy,' you answer, 'oblong at the start, then wider, two furrows long and of varying width.'"[23] In other words, when someone asks how a thing is qualified, the answer may contain quantitative expressions, which shows according to Valla the subordination of quantity to quality. Later on he makes more or less the same point, taking over from Quintilian the distinction between authority, usage, and reason: "Mind you, it is not just me but the greatest authorities as well who say that this is quality, which linguistic usage itself – the best guide – affirms and reason does not resist."[24] He continues to show the dependence of quantity on quality by, again, giving examples of how "we" usually talk about things: "We speak" [*dicimus*] of a great heat, little coldness, long sound, and so on,[25] and we use quantitative predicates ("is big," "is two years old," "is five feet tall") to qualify a thing. Such a point is obvious "even to ordinary people [*vulgus*]": "For them, if someone asks 'what kind of voice did Stentor have,' you answer 'big,' 'large,' 'huge.'"[26]

[21] Valla 2012, 1:241 (*DD* 1.17.1). [22] Ibid., 1:245 (*DD* 1.17.7). [23] Ibid.
[24] Ibid., 1:247 (*DD* 1.17.9). [25] Ibid. 1:247 (*DD* 1.17.11); the examples are Valla's.
[26] Ibid., 1:255 (*DD* 1.17.19).

The same is true of quantitative terms such as "length," "width," and "depth," which differ, Valla says, only "by some sort of quality": "Because of this we usually say [*dicere solemus*] of certain plots of land that 'they are longer on the sides than at the ends,' which is also how geometers talk about the earth."[27]

Again, the pronoun "we" seems to refer to the educated people with good skills in Latin, and their usage is confirmed by what can be found in the great authors. The word *vulgus* apparently refers to the class of educated people, or at least users of (good) Latin. His self-invented examples of daily conversation between ordinary people must give the impression that classical Latin is a natural, common language that is a good reflection of how things stand in the world. But at the same time, the daily examples would work equally well in other languages; indeed this should be so, since Valla's claim that substances, qualities, and actions are the only really existing things is an ontological claim, which is supported by an analysis of Latin grammar but not dependent on it.

Valla also appeals to "the ordinary person" (*populus*) in his discussion of the Aristotelian category of place, which he seems to reduce to the thing that occupies that place. His arguments for this reduction are far from clear, but for our purposes it is enough to look at the way he appeals to common language. According to Valla, philosophers think that a barrel or a storehouse cannot be empty, because it still contains air even if everything has been removed:[28]

> But let us see who speaks better, the ordinary person or the philosopher. The ordinary person says that he calls the barrel "empty" when it lacks liquid ... Let the ordinary person respond that his is "the right to decide standards in language," and that he does not call such things "full" when there is nothing but air in them, except when the air itself is of some importance, as when the sails of ships or a ball or balloon for playing games are full.

Valla thus concludes that the "ordinary person speaks better than the philosopher, then, and all the best writers agree, calling the air above us sometimes 'empty,' sometimes 'void,' as in Vergil ... and Quintilian ... and Cicero ... ."[29] The quotations seem to imply that Valla's "common person" must be a speaker of Latin, for how else could the authorities

[27] Ibid. 1:255 (*DD* 1.17.21).

[28] Ibid., 1:267 (*DD* 1.17.38), with reference to Horace's *Ars Poetica* 70–72. The example derives from Cicero's *De Fato* 11.24; Cicero 1942, 2:221. The same example is used by Vives; see Chapter 4, n. 43.

[29] Ibid., 1:269 (*DD* 1.17.42).

confirm his or her talk? But the discussion does not seem to be about Latin (at least not primarily) but about the normal way in which people use words such as "empty" and "full." Addressing the scholastic philosopher (or the straw man that Valla creates), he writes:[30]

> For if you call a bowl without liquid "full" because there is still air in it, what need was there to boast about an astonishing fact unknown to ordinary people, declaring that "nothing empty is allowed in nature"? Don't children know that, especially those used to blowing into that balloon or bladder to inflate it?

It is a simple fact of life that an empty balloon can be filled with air, and this is also how children talk about it; to speak otherwise would be unnatural. It is a fact that can be expressed in other languages as well. The contrast between the philosopher and the ordinary person is between an unnatural and a natural way of using language. As in the other examples, it is not so much the ungrammaticality of the philosopher's language but its artificiality set up against the common, normal, and natural way of using words that is being criticized. But the support that the ordinary person can find in the Latin of the great authors, adduced by Valla, must suggest that Latin is a perfectly natural and "common" language. Valla's discussion combines and fuses these two types of criticisms – bad Latin and unnatural use of language – with the same goal in mind: to criticize the language of the philosophers.[31]

In his discussion of the Aristotelian category of passion/to be affected, something similar can be seen, but here the point is even more clearly conceptual and language-independent than in the previous examples. Valla's ontological commitments lead him to denying passion/being affected an independent status: being affected or undergoing something is no less an action than, for example, running:[32]

> I do not see how being affected is anything different than feeling an affect or passion, such as grieving, fearing or mourning . . . For how am I affected if

[30] ibid., 1:267 (*DD* 1.17.40).

[31] In some contexts, "the people" does not refer to educated people with skills in classical Latin. In criticizing the Aristotelian idea that the number one is not the beginning but the principle of number, he writes that when "mere women" (*mulierculae*) divide up eggs, "one" is of course considered to be a number, the first (uneven) number: "so mere women sometimes have a better sense about understanding words than mighty philosophers. Women actually put words to use [*ad usum*], while philosophers play games with them [*ad lusum*]." Ibid., 1:33 (*DD* 1.2.26). Cf. Petrarch quoted above, Chapter 1, n. 9.

[32] Ibid., 1:277 (*DD* 1.17.56).

> I am loved or feared or heard or even called – unless I am listening? But if I am listening, at that point it is an action.

The passive mood of a verb ("being loved" or "being called") does not mean that it signifies passive things; grammatical terms should not be taken literally: the accusative case, for example, has nothing to do with accusation. Valla concludes that being affected is an action, or, if it has become the passion (the affect) itself, a quality like being in love. It is therefore an abuse of the term "passion" to apply it to inanimate objects; these things cannot feel: "In things that cannot feel there is no affect because they are affected by nothing, as they act directly by their own nature."[33] Their "internal nature" is "an efficient cause because a mental intention is lacking." To this another point is added. Philosophers also abuse the term when they say that the senses are being affected by objects: "they abuse the proper meaning of the word."[34] Only when the senses are really being affected (that is, are suffering), for example, when my eyes suffer from too much light or my ears from too loud a noise can we speak of "being affected": "as long as the senses perform their functions, they *act*; they are not *affected* except when they suffer pain."

Valla's point about passion being an action is a philosophical claim, motivated by his ontological commitment to accept only substances, qualities, and actions as real things. Because the Latin perspective is so all-pervasive and self-evident for Valla, it is not always easy to determine whether his ontological convictions are shaped by Latin grammar or vice versa. His point is of course made in Latin, and the critique of the philosophical use of the term is supported by the meaning of the Latin term *pati* (to be affected) but the point about passion is a conceptual one that can easily be expressed in other languages as well.[35]

Transcendental Terms and Other Abstract Terms

Next to the Aristotelian categories there is another group of abstract words, the so-called transcendental terms. Here it is clearly grammar that shapes Valla's critique.[36] The transcendental terms – "being," "something," "one," "good," "true," and "thing" – were traditionally regarded as descriptions of

[33] Ibid., 1:277 (*DD* 1.17.57). [34] Ibid., 1:277–279 (*DD* 1.17.58–59).

[35] Valla's restriction of *pati*, however, does not seem to be in line with classical Latin. Moreover, an opponent might think that Valla is inconsistent when he argues that the senses must be said to "receive" (*recipere*) objects rather than being affected by them.

[36] Cf. Nauta 2009, 48–81. On the history of transcendentals, see Aertsen 1996.

being as such: whatever is a being, is also one, true, and so on. They were called transcendentals because they transcend the categories: the categories are supreme genera of being, but what they have in common, namely being (substance exists, quality exists, quantity exists, etc.), is not an eleventh Aristotelian category: the notion of being runs right through all the categories. A long tradition of thinking on the notion of being had given rise to a series of terms that distinguished various attributes of being. In long grammatical discussions of the use of these terms Valla argues that these can all be reduced to "thing" (*res*), because everything can be called a thing, including a good thing or the good, and one thing or the one. Valla is particularly scathing about the metaphysical notion of being (*ens*) itself. As he explains, what the philosophers forget is that the Latin word "*ens*" is a participle, meaning "that which is," just like the participle "walking" means "he/she/it that walks." Thus "being" (*ens*) can be analyzed as "that thing that is" (*ea res quae est*). Such an analysis makes it clear, Valla argues, how stupid it is to call something, for example a stone, a being, for this comes down to saying that a stone is a thing that is (*lapis est ens = lapis est ea res quae est*).[37] We can much better, and more simply, say: "a stone is a thing (*res*)." Grammatical analysis also leads Valla to reduce the other transcendental terms to "thing": the good or the one do not stand for something apart from things; they are just descriptions of things: the one means one thing, the good means a good thing. From a grammatical point of view, such terms as "good" and "true" are adjectives, and when used as substantives (the good, the one) they refer to qualities, hence there is nothing "transcendental" about them. Further, adjectives often signify the same as their abstract counterparts: "truth" and "true" do not differ in their significations, as can be observed from the way in which they are used; the same is true for "goodness" and "good."[38] Valla's message is that careful attention to the grammar of terms and the way in which they are used in linguistic practice demystifies such abstract entities.

Grammatical considerations also lead Valla to reject some notorious abstract terms often used by the scholastics: "entity (*entitas*)," "this-hood (*haecceitas*)," "identity (*identitas*)," "what-hood (*quiditas*)," and "perseity (*perseitas*)." As usual, Valla is not interested in the question of why philosophers had introduced these terms in the first place. Technical philosophical terminology – if not in line with good Latin – should be

[37] Valla 2012, 1:23–25 (*DD* 1.2.9–1.2.15).

[38] Ibid., 1:31–35 (*DD* 1.2.23–32). Grammatical considerations also lead Valla to reject the distinction between "to be" (*esse*) and "essence" (*essentia*), because "infinitives mean nothing different than their verbal forms when they are treated as nouns." Ibid., 1:67 (*DD* 1.5.5).

dismissed, as these terms do not conform to the rules of word formation. In Latin, substantives cannot be derived from participles such as "*ens*," from pronouns such as "*quid*" (what), and from adjectives, apart from some exceptions.[39] In all these discussions, of which only a few points have been highlighted here, Valla does not explicitly attack the ontological commitments that the use of abstract terms might imply; his aversion has a primarily linguistic motivation. Yet, his grammatical approach, which often critically engages not only with the scholastics but also with the late-classical grammarian Priscian, is aimed at making the whole domain of what his so-called opponents call "metaphysics" (*metaphysica*) less grand and less special; according to him, it is a domain full of poorly understood Latin terms.

The Distinction Between Act and Potency

Other important philosophical distinctions and concepts do not fare well either on Valla's grammatical account. What is the plus-value, he asks, of a standard philosophical distinction such as act/potency? It is a crucial distinction in Aristotle's philosophy used to explain, for instance, change, but Valla thinks it does not explain very much, though again he hardly tries to understand the philosophical questions that gave rise to the introduction of such terms and distinctions. Things can be turned or made into something else, as even a child knows, but what is the point of turning this simple fact of life into a metaphysical doctrine expressed in technical terminology? As Valla writes:[40]

> He [i.e., Aristotle] actually says that "this wood or this tree-trunk is a box not in act but in potency." Go ahead, Aristotle, make a box out of this wood. Will we say that "this wood is a box *in act*?" Has anyone ever talked that way? . . . What is the point of adding "in act"? Obviously, you reply, because for the wood to be a box is something else. Has anyone ever talked this way either, since reason does not even permit the locution? For it is one thing for wood to be *able* [*posse*] to be made into a box, another for it to be a box *in potency* [*potentia*]. In saying that it is "able to be made into a box," we already declare that it is not a box since, once it has been made that, it is not able to be made again into what it already was. How much better it would have

[39] Ibid., 1:55–63 (*DD* 1.4). Elsewhere, Valla also gives as reason that such words do not point to anything in the world: words such as *reitas* and *queitas* must be rejected because we do not find such things as thinghood in nature. Cf. Nauta 2009, 81.

[40] Ibid., 1:229–231 (*DD* 1.16.6–8). "Reason" (*ratio*) here seems to refer to internal consistency, implying that "to be a box in potency" is internally inconsistent: it is either a box or it is not.

been to keep the ordinary way of speaking [*communem loquendi consuetudinem*]: "this wood can be made into a box"! In other words, "the form and shape of this wood is change*able* into the form and shape of a box."

Words ending in "-able" like "changeable," "breakable," and "drinkable" sometimes signify "a potency" (*potentia*), "possibility" (*possibilitas*), or "aptitude" (*aptitudo*).[41] This aptitude or nature of a thing, however, is a quality rather than an action in spite of the word "act:" "What Aristotle should have said, then, is 'this tree-trunk is convertible into a box,' not that it 'is a box in potency.'" After a similar critique of "*entelecheia*," another term traditionally standing for action, act, or working, Valla waives "good-bye to these finicky and evasive terms of Aristotle's," admonishing us to turn to a description of things that is "simpler" and "better suited to natural meaning and ordinary usage."[42]

Valla's concern is thus to show the relationship between grammatical categories and the three categories that constitute the world of things. There is no need to follow Valla here in his analysis of a large group of verbs, verbal nouns, pronouns, and other type of words to see how his program, much inspired by Priscian and the grammatical tradition, is driven by his conviction that the ultimate categories into which things can be analyzed are substance, quality, and action, and that we must relate words and word classes to these three categories.[43] Grammatical analysis becomes thus a tool for downplaying the special status of many philosophical words and distinctions, or even for simply rejecting such words if they do not conform to common linguistic usage.

Dialectics and Natural Reasoning

After Valla's attack on what he calls the "foundations" (*fundamenta*) of Aristotelian-scholastic metaphysics and natural philosophy, he turns to dialectic in Books II and III of his *Dialectical Disputations*. To conclude our discussion of Valla's critique of scholastic language this section will briefly look at Valla's attempt to transform medieval logic toward a humanist dialectic, marked by a study of argumentation and forms of reasoning that are tailored to the practical goal of analyzing argumentative structures of classical texts.[44] The scope of the notion of common linguistic usage becomes wider, serving not only as a weapon to criticize the logicians'

[41] Ibid. (*DD* 1.16.8), for this and the following quotation.
[42] Ibid., 1:233 (*DD* 1.16.10–11): "ad naturalem sensum usumque communem accommodatius."
[43] Nauta 2009, 72–81. [44] See Mack 1993, 74–95; Nauta 2009, 212–268.

use of Latin words as technical terms in what Valla thinks is an ungrammatical and artificial way, but also as a tool to replace the formal approach in studying and analyzing forms of reasoning with an oratorical approach.

For the orator it is much more important that an argument *works*, which means whether it convinces one's adversary or public, than that it conforms to certain patterns of reasoning formalized by logicians. Hence, the form of the argument is less important. Valla's aim then is to deflate dialectic as the queen of arts – a title bestowed on it by medieval dialecticians; for Valla it is merely a component of invention, one of the five parts of rhetoric. Compared to rhetoric, dialectic is an easy subject, requiring not much time for mastering it, since it considers and uses only the syllogism "bare," as Valla puts it; that is, in isolation from its wider argumentative context; its sole aim is to teach.[45] The rhetorician, on the other hand, uses not only the syllogism, but also other forms of argumentation such as the enthymeme (incomplete syllogism), epicheireme (a kind of extended reasoning), and example. Orators have to clothe everything in persuasive arguments, since their task is not only to teach but also to please and to move. This leads Valla to downplay the importance of the Aristotelian syllogism and to consider forms of argumentation that are not easily forced into its straightjacket. Among these are captious forms of reasoning such as dilemma, paradox, and the heap argument (*sorites*), and Valla offers an interesting analysis of these forms in the last book of the *Dialectical Disputations*.

Without rejecting the syllogism *tout court*, Valla is scathing about its usefulness. He regards it as an artificial type of reasoning, unfit to be employed by orators since it is does not reflect the natural way of speaking and arguing. "Natural" is a recurrent word in this context. Valla thinks, for example, that some syllogistic forms (or parts of them) can be detected in the talk of all kinds of people:[46]

> But the form of the syllogism is not the clever thing cleverly disputed by me to describe the nature of the syllogism – you may gather how easy it is not only to understand but also to construct even when children talk among themselves, though they generally leave out the conclusion. I am talking about real syllogisms: for most of what is taught about syllogisms goes against nature and everyone's usage [*omnium usum*].

Some syllogistic patterns can therefore be accepted, since they can be observed in the speech of "even peasants, even women, even children."[47] In an earlier version of this passage Valla had made the same point, saying

[45] Valla 2012, 2:3–5 (*DD* 2.proem.1–7). [46] Ibid., 2:231 (*DD* 3.2.15).
[47] Ibid., 2:269 (*DD* 3.9.4).

that he had noted the syllogistic moods of which he approves, "not only in books and in the talk of the learned people but also in that of the uneducated (that is, those who speak in a natural way [*imperitorum idest naturaliter loquentium*])."[48] But to note and reconstruct syllogistic patterns in the speech of people is one thing, to insert fully fledged syllogisms in one's speech is another; at least, this is what Valla seems to mean when he explains – in apparent contradiction to what he had said in the passages just quoted – that "those who speak naturally [*naturaliter*], like orators, very rarely use the syllogism."[49] But while people naturally speak and argue in ways that show at times patterns of syllogistic reasoning, the art of dialectic that has arisen, so to speak, out of this fact is completely "against nature": "most of what is taught about syllogisms goes against nature and everyone's usage."[50] Nobody would argue, for instance, in accordance with the patterns as laid down in the third figure of the syllogism (every man is a substance; every man is an animal; therefore, some animal is a substance). Likewise, in criticizing examples such as "Plato is every animal" (*Plato est omne animal*) and "Plato is no animal" (*Plato est nullum animal*), Valla again appeals to what is "natural": "Let us speak naturally and in the way people speak."[51]

The syllogism not only often goes against nature but is also often useless. What is the use, for example, of concluding that Socrates is an animal if one has already stated that every man is an animal and that Socrates is a man? Valla concludes that this whole art of dialectic is a simple, puerile, and pedantic affair, hardly amounting to a real *ars* (art).[52] Valla's treatment of the syllogism clearly shows his oratorical perspective. Following Quintilian, he stresses that the nature of syllogistic reasoning is to establish proof.[53] One of the two premises contains what is to be proven, and the other offers the proof, while the conclusion gives the result of the proof. It is not always necessary, therefore, to have a fixed order (major, minor, conclusion). If it suits the occasion better, we can just as well start with the minor, or even with the conclusion. The order is merely a matter of convention and custom.

[48] Valla 1982, 2:548 (*Repastinatio* 3.12.8). Similarly, he criticizes Boethius for giving an example of an enthymeme "abhorrent to the orator's practice, or rather to ordinary human understanding [*a communi hominum intellectu*]": Valla 2012, 2:423 (*DD* 3.17.10).

[49] Valla 2012, 2:228 (*DD* 3.2.12). [50] Ibid., 2:231 (*DD* 3.2.16).

[51] Valla 1982, 2:485 (*Repastinatio* 2.12.15): "naturaliter atque hominum more." Cf. Valla 2012, 2:113 (*DD* 2.15.14).

[52] Valla 2012, 2:3 (*DD* 3.2.3). [53] Ibid., 2:217–231 (*DD* 3.2).

Valla's insistence on examining and assessing arguments in terms of persuasion and usefulness leads him to criticize not only the syllogism but also other less formal modes of argumentation. These modes usually involve interrogation, resulting in an unexpected or unwanted conclusion or an aporetic situation. Often, these arguments have something deceptive about them, and an important way of seeing through them is to consider the weight of words carefully. Valla considers the fallacies "collected by Aristotle in his *Sophistical Refutations* as for the most part a puerile art," quoting *Rhetorica ad Herennium* to the effect that "knowledge of ambiguities as taught by dialecticians is of no help at all but rather a most serious hindrance."[54] He refutes fallacies by examining the meaning and usage of words and the contexts in which they occur, but he is not interested in providing a comprehensive list of deceptive arguments and errors or in studying rules for resolving them. As he repeatedly states, what is required in order to disambiguate fallacies is not a deeper knowledge of the rules of logic but a recognition that arguments need to be evaluated within their wider linguistic and argumentative context. Such an examination of how words and arguments function will easily lay bare the artificial and sophistical nature of these forms of argumentation.

Careful attention to the meaning of words is also evident in Valla's analysis of a class of words that play an important role in logic, namely words such as "all/every," "some" and "no."[55] Syllogisms consist of propositions, and these propositions are traditionally divided according to quantity (universal or particular) and quality (affirmative or negative), for example "every horse is brown," "some horses are brown," "no horse is brown," and "some horses are not brown." Pronouns such as "every," "some," and "no/no one" determine the scope of the propositions. These types of propositions are important building blocks of syllogisms. Based on Latin translations of Aristotle's logical works, dialecticians used this highly selective set of words as technical terms with a specific role to play. For Valla, however, this does not mean that we can forget the fact that they are *Latin* words, the meaning and function of which can be studied only by carefully studying their occurrence in Latin. Grammarians and dialecticians often misunderstand the meaning and application or use of these words – errors that have consequences for the logical claims they make, for instance when they ignore the difference between the indefinite pronouns

[54] Valla 1982, 2:575 (*Repastinatio* 3.19.2); Pseudo-Cicero 1954, 86 (*Rhetorica ad Herennium* 2.11.16); Valla 2012, 2:287–369 (*DD* 3.11–14).

[55] Valla 2012, 2:31–90 (*DD* 2.5–11).

"some" (*aliquis*), "a certain" (*quidam*), and "any" (*ullus*). The difference is confirmed by "ordinary language," "authority," and "analysis" (*ratio*):[56]

> The difference between "a certain" [*quidam*] and "some" [*aliquis*] . . . becomes more apparent by negating them . . . "A certain one of you [*quidam vestrum*] did not call me," for example, is much different from "some one of you [*aliquis vestrum*] did not call me" . . . If what they want is ordinary language [*consuetudo loquendi*], I say the same thing about this as about other particulars, and here it is in everyday speech [*vulgaris sermo*]: "there is not someone luckier than me," . . . If they require authority, we find examples whenever these terms occur . . . Vergil writes . . . If analysis (*ratio*) is what you want, it is easy to produce: when I say "some one of you called me," I signify, while speaking in turn to each one, that either you, who are some one of these people, have called me, or else some other you, also some one of them.

While "ordinary language" often comes close to "authority," it is good to remember, as this passage makes clear, that Latin as commonly used is not identical to the Latin of Virgil or Cicero.

In addition, Valla also criticizes the dialecticians for severely limiting themselves to this highly selective group of words. Latin has many words to negate or deny something and many more words by which the quantity of a proposition is expressed. Valla embarks therefore on a study of these little words and how they determine the scope (universal, particular, singular) of a proposition. The possibilities turn out to be endless, especially if such a pronoun is combined with a negation: it makes a difference, for instance, whether the sign of negation comes before or after the verb, before or after the pronoun, and whether the pronoun occurs in the subject or the predicate position.[57]

These grammatical explorations lead then to a critique of the so-called square of contraries, which is a fourfold classification of statements in which the universal affirmative (e.g. every horse is brown) is contradictory to the particular negative (some horse is not brown), and the universal negative to the particular affirmative, while the universal affirmative is contrary to the universal negative, and the particular affirmative subcontrary to the particular negative; in addition the particular statements are called subalternates of their corresponding universal statements.[58] Logicians had made various claims about the truth values of these propositions, for example that contraries (e.g. "every horse is brown" and "no

[56] Ibid., 2:37 (DD 2.5.10); 2:59–63 (*DD* 2.8.1–2.8.6).
[57] Ibid., 2:31–95 (*DD* 2.5–2.12); Mack 1993, 74–76; Nauta 2009, 214–222.
[58] Ibid., 2:97–123 (*DD* 2.13–17); cf. Mack 1993, 58–66; Nauta 2009, 223–230.

horse is brown") cannot both be true but may both be false, and that contradictories ("every horse is brown" and "some horse is not brown") cannot both be true and cannot both be false (one must be true). Exploring the distribution of truth and falsity in such statements, Valla makes several critical points about these claims. To give just one example: he argues that the logician's use of "a certain" (*quidam*) as a sign of particular statements is inappropriate: my claim that "a certain one is wise" is not refuted by "a certain one is not wise": rather, true contrariety applies to proper names and pronouns ("Plato lives" versus "Plato does not live," or "This one is good" versus "This one is not good").[59] Valla's points about the truth values of these statements are not always consistent or easy to understand, but the general thrust of his critique is that terms and propositions should not be evaluated in isolation. Words, including terms of quantification and negation, derive their meaning from their context, and by context is meant a situation in which these propositions are used, that is in discussion, conversation, and oratory.

A similar critique of the rather arbitrary restriction to a limited set of words is applied to the notion of modality.[60] Scholastics usually treat only the following six terms as modals: "possible," "impossible," "true," "false," "necessary," and "contingent." Latin, however, is much more resourceful in expressing the modality of a proposition, for example "likely," "difficult," "certain," "useful," and "honorable," and their opposites. Again, it is Valla's oratorical perspective on words, propositions, and argumentations rather than the details of his discussion that is of relevance here.

Like his critique of metaphysical concepts, Valla's critique of scholastic-Aristotelian logic combines purely grammatical points about Latin words with conceptual claims about the truth values of propositions, the structure of arguments, and various forms of argumentation. But while the latter is often dependent on the former – Valla's Latin perspective is all-inclusive – these conceptual points often transcend the level of the discussion of Latin words and grammar. As noticed, Valla's critique is provoked not only by what he considers to be a deplorable ignorance of good Latin but also by the abstract and formal approach that takes words, propositions, and forms of argumentation out of their context. His claim, for instance, that universal propositions ("all horses are brown") can be a mixture of true and false is not a claim about Latin but a claim about the nature of a proposition, even though, obviously, it is made in Latin. Similarly, his claim that indefinite propositions without a mark of quantification (e.g. "elephant is black") must

[59] Ibid., 2:111 (*DD* 2.15.10). [60] Ibid., 2:127–143 (*DD* 2.19). Cf. Nauta 2009, 230–233.

be associated with universal propositions rather than with particular ones as the scholastics had done, is a conceptual claim rather than a point about Latin (though the lack of articles in Latin is relevant here).[61] And his analysis of forms of argumentation such as the heap argument, dilemma, induction, and enthymeme (treated by Valla as an imperfect syllogism) or even syllogism itself do not depend on Latin nor are they about Latin. This is wholly unsurprising of course, as the study of argumentation was older than Valla's Latin sources, and many of his examples, found in Cicero, Quintilian, and other classical or late-classical sources, ultimately derived from Aristotle's Greek works and the Greek rhetorical traditions. But that the two levels of critique – ungrammatical Latin and abstract use of language in general (e.g. in analyzing argumentations) – are frequently fused is not surprising either: Valla's universe is a Latin universe, and Latin is his point of departure, so conceptual claims often do depend on linguistic or grammatical observations, for instance about the use of pronouns such as "some" (*aliquis*), "a certain" (*quidam*), and "any" (*ullus*). To the question of whether quantification of propositions cuts across languages, transcending the vernacular use of words such as "all," "every," "any," and "a certain," Valla seems to reply: no, because quantification of propositions in Latin will depend on the meaning of the Latin words involved, while in German this might be different; he observes, for instance, that the place and use of the sign of negation is different in German.[62] Such a view might result in postulating a plurality of logics and logical rules: each language with its own logic – a view encouraged by the close connection that a humanist such as Valla sees between logic and grammar. On the other hand, Valla's revision of Aristotelian dialectic is aimed also at something more than presenting a new Latin logic (based on classical Latin, its grammar and vocabulary); it also wants to present a logic that is rooted in human practices of speaking, arguing, and reasoning.

Conclusion

Valla's critique of scholastic language is an interesting mixture of strategies, dependent on the theme and context of the discussion, though whether he was always conscious about the several levels of his critique may be doubted. As discussed above, the attack on the language of the scholastics and dialecticians could be launched from a primarily Latinate point of view, and this was surely Valla's main line of attack, given his overall humanist project to reinstall classical Latin (that is, the Latin that follows

[61] Ibid., 2:123 (*DD* 2.17.4). [62] Ibid., 2:87 (*DD* 2.11.8).

classical rules) as the language of learned communication, the arts, and sciences. Hence, one type of criticism is that scholastic language often fails to meet the rules of Latin grammar or uses words in an unusual, non-classical way. But the critique could easily transcend the level of Latin grammar when the target became the so-called abstract and unnatural way in which scholastics used concepts as opposed to the normal, ordinary way in which people use these concepts. The "ordinary way" was often still the Latin way, something that became clear from Valla's use of terms such as "the common linguistic usage" and "the ordinary person": while not identical to the Latin of the great authors, common linguistic usage referred to Latin, as Valla's discussion, for instance, of the Aristotelian categories showed: in this discussion, he frequently gives examples of what "we are used to saying" (*solemus dicere*) in such and such a situation. Though Latin is the springboard from which the attack is launched, in these cases it was not so much the ungrammatical Latin but the abstract use of language that was Valla's target. From here it was a short step – at least, this is the impression Valla perhaps unintentionally gave – to refer to ordinary people, regardless of the language they speak, the polemical claim being that uneducated people often speak better than philosophers: they put words to use (*ad usum*), while philosophers play games with them (*ad lusum*). Valla does not of course thereby champion the vernacular language of the uneducated people – the vernacular does not play any serious role in Valla's Latin universe – but in his critique of the unnatural way in which scholastics used concepts and language, he makes good use of the traditional topos of the folly of the learned versus the wisdom of the simple people; ordinary people use concepts or arguments in a natural way without using schemes like artificial syllogisms. In this respect they might even be said to come close to learned people such as orators who also "speak naturally." Depending on the context, the word "natural" may stand for the Latin of the educated people when opposed to the ungrammatical Latin of the scholastics, but it may also stand for the normal way in which educated and uneducated people alike use language and arguments against the artificial way in which words are used by the scholastics. In the first case, his admonition comes out like this: modern philosophers should "turn back to speech that is natural, speech commonly used by educated people"; in the second case, it comes out like this: "Let us speak naturally and in the way people speak," that is using speech and argument in a natural way, regardless of which language is used.[63]

[63] Ibid., 2:209–211 (*DD* 3.proem.3) and Valla 1982, 2:485 (*Repastinatio* 2.12.15), both quoted above.

Valla's treatment of classical Latin as a common, natural language to be used in theology and philosophy as well as in the language arts, is based on what might be called a sociolinguistic insight: language is a naturally evolving social practice, governed by conventions and a shared history: speakers should conform to the usage and conventions of their community on pain of becoming outcasts. As quoted above, Valla compares languages to customs and laws, each nation with its own language, law, and customs. For him, the community of Latin users are those who have used Latin that follows classical norms. This was of course the whole point of the humanist project, namely to restore Latin as the lingua franca to its pristine, glorious form, to be put into the service of a broader agenda of educational and societal reform. But it also created a tension right at the heart of this project, for in spite of the claim that Latin is a normal, natural, and common language, it also had a unique and privileged status as a literate, highly regimented, secondary, and artificial (from *ars*) language, the rules of which had been established (and canonized) long ago and, unlike those of other languages, were no longer subject to a continuous process of historical development, at least not a development that was accepted as positive; postclassical developments had led to a corruption of Latin. To group Latin with other languages such as German, "Punic, Dalmatian and other tongues" was perhaps a good tactic to chase the scholastics away from the linguistic community – defined as the group of educated people with good skills in the right kind of Latin – but the comparison, when pressed a bit further, also revealed the difference between Latin and living languages such as German that, arguably, were not defined in terms of rules established a long time ago by an elite group of people.

Valla might not have felt any tension, however. Latin had been the language of a vast Empire over a long period of time. It had been used by thousands or millions of people, and even though that situation had drastically changed after the fall of the Empire, he was now witnessing a restoration of classical Latin, to which he himself greatly contributed. Having immersed himself in the language and the heritage of classical antiquity, he could truly believe it was a natural, common language while at the same time a universal language providing a norm for correctness of speech, something the vernacular could not provide. It was a conviction that ignored the rise of the vernacular and the importance of specialized idioms in various disciplines. Moreover, in rejecting postclassical developments Valla refused to generalize his valuable sociolinguistic insight into the cultural and historical embeddedness of language. But it would be unfair to criticize him for not having realized all the implications of his own views. These views were the expression of a deep conviction that would inspire future generations of humanists to study and appropriate the riches of classical antiquity, thereby laying the foundations of modern historical and textual scholarship, while at the same time opening up crevices in the rocks of Aristotelian scholasticism. In the following three chapters we will study three humanists who, each in their own way, took Valla's program further.

CHAPTER 3

Giovanni Pontano on Language, Meaning, and Grammar

Introduction

Lorenzo Valla had given the humanist program some of its most combative formulations. He had also shown what this program entailed: an immersion into the language and the world of Latin (and Greek) letters. A language was a living thing, used by a community of speakers who had developed linguistic rules over time based on practice and convention. This community was defined by mastery of classical Latin, a language treated at once as a historical phenomenon and as a language that transcends time and place in being the storehouse of erudition and learning, a *sine qua non* for the development of the arts and sciences. The destructive side of this program was Valla's onslaught on later forms of Latin that did not meet the standards of common linguistic usage. Valla's primary target were the scholastics, and late-classical and medieval grammarians, but he also criticized, to the dismay of many humanists, Aristotle himself, as well as other ancient authorities and church fathers when, according to Valla, their use of language showed a misunderstanding of words or of the workings of language in general.

Many of these themes return in the work of the Neapolitan humanist and leading statesman in the Aragonese court Giovanni Pontano (1426–1503). One of the most elegant and distinguished poets of his time and the author of dialogues and treatises on moral, historical, grammatical, and astrological themes, Pontano was a humanist *pur sang*, whose approach was basically Vallian in spirit, though with substantial differences in his attitude toward the figure of Aristotle and ancient moral thought in general.[1]

[1] Gaisser, preface to Pontano 2012, ix: "arguably the best Latin poet of the Renaissance"; Kidwell 1991 on his poetry and life; Roick 2017 on his life and moral thought; Marsh 1980 on his dialogues; Monti Sabia and Monti 2010.

Though highly critical of Valla's irascible and disputatious temper, Pontano shared his conviction that discussing philosophical questions requires a deep familiarity with Latin (and Greek): "in discussing and reasoning nothing must be more entirely avoided than any confusion and uncertainty arising from words, and nothing is more to be sought than distinction and selection of words and things."[2] For Pontano, as for Valla, the basis of philosophy is language, and language meant, of course, Latin, with the notion of *consuetudo* (usage, convention) as a central parameter in settling questions of meaning. Hence, grammar – in its wide classical meaning – plays an important role in the discussions among the interlocutors in Pontano's dialogues. Like Valla and before him Petrarch and Bruni, Pontano also held medieval translators of Aristotle, dialecticians and scholastic theologians responsible for the demise of classical learning and knowledge of Latin. What Pontano called his own "Latin philosophy" was therefore in its essential outlines the humanist program of Petrarch, Bruni, and Valla. But we would do this versatile scholar-poet great injustice if we were to see him solely in the light of his predecessors. An enviable conversationalist and acute observer of human manners and conversation, Pontano not only studied, emended, and annotated the texts of ancient authors, he also used his wide knowledge of Latin vocabulary and moral discourse to give vignettes of social virtues and vices, and social intercourse in general; his book on speech (or conversation), *De sermone*, for instance, provides, in the words of one critic, "a social theory of language."[3] Inspired by his beloved ancient authors (in particular Aristotle and Cicero) and in critical dialogue with his contemporary fellow-humanists such as Valla, Pontano turned the study of Latin into a wide field that often transcended narrow philological boundaries. And precisely because for him language meant Latin, his acute observations on the social and emotive powers of language could easily go beyond a purely classical perspective. To see how Pontano developed his "Latin philosophy" as an elegant, refined, and semantically resourceful alternative to what he considered to be the abstract approach of scholastics and dialecticians, we will have to broaden our scope to some extent. Starting with his views on the origins of language, we will then move on to his observations on the

[2] Pontano 2019, 19 (*De Sermone* 1.9.1); for his opinion about Valla, whom Pontano had frequently visited in his own youth ("many very friendly meetings"), see ibid., 55–57 (1.18.6) and 387 (6.4.7).

[3] Marsh 1980, 135 n. 22; cf. Luck 1958, 121: it "is much more than a pale adaptation of ancient theories; it is, above all, a Renaissance book . . ." ; it "represents an important step in the formation of the ideal courtier." For a brief survey see Pigman's introduction and notes to Pontano 2019, with further literature (xxiv n. 13): "first and foremost a treatise of Aristotelian moral philosophy about the virtues and vices of speech," "providing an inventory of the kinds of speech in social situations" (xiii–xiv).

relationship between language, thought, and culture, ending with his "Latin philosophy."

The Origin of Language

In his *De inventione* Cicero famously credits the orator with the coming of civilization: a "great and wise man" assembled primitive men and "transformed them from wild savages into a kind and gentle folk through reason and eloquence."[4] But neither here nor elsewhere did Cicero become more specific about the early origins of language. Stimulated by the Ciceronian account, Pontano speculates on the question at several places in his work. As a humanist, who spoke and wrote Latin with a fluency that was greatly admired by Erasmus, Pontano was of course mainly interested in the development of Latin – a field of study that was still in its infancy – but his observations had an anthropological ring to them, with implications for language in general.

According to Pontano's account, the first users of language were primitive people, uncultivated farmers and workmen, who stood in direct contact with nature.[5] They were poor and their life was difficult. Accordingly, their language was poor as well: not only was their vocabulary limited to those words directly related to their simple life and work conditions, but the few words they did have were rough, unpolished, and uncultivated; primal man could care less when it came to well-structured and elegantly pronounced words. Indeed, "barbarous and savage people" are not to be considered as such because of "savagery" but because of their rude and rustic language.[6] In a remarkable passage from his work on grammar *De aspiratione*, Pontano writes that "in the beginning words did not drop from heaven but, because nature made men apt to speaking, they assigned names to themselves and to things."[7] As primitive people

[4] Cicero 1949, 5 (*De inventione* 1.2.2–3); a topos in the Greek rhetorical tradition. See also Wood 1988, 80–83. On ancient ideas on the early origins of language see Gera 2003.

[5] Pontano 1943, 205 (*Actius*): "Sermo coepit primum noster ab incultis et rusticanis, imo agrestibus ab hominibus; utque eorum erant res inopes, angustae, egenae, sic quoque sermo ipse inops minimeque affluens, verborumque perpaucorum ac sine ullo prorsus eorum excolendorum studio et cura." Cf. ibid., 207: "Sermo autem quo utimur ab agrestibus ac rudibus coepisse hominibus, illud declarat potissimum, quod pleraeque e primis illis impositionibus sunt rusticis incomptisque a rebus sumptae."

[6] Pontano 2019, 297 (*De sermone* 4.11.13). For the Virgilian inspiration see Marsh 1980, 107–110: "Pontano looks to an earlier age for the unspoiled propriety of a language in harmony with man and nature. He finds this harmony in the pristine setting of rural life and in the simple elegance of agricultural language in Virgil's *Georgics*."

[7] Pontano 1518–1519, 2:7v–8r; also in Germano 2005, 316. Pontano's words recall Valla's words that "analogy did not descend from heaven at man's creation" (*Apologus*, in Camporeale 1972, 524; cited from Marsh 1979, 105).

covered themselves with skins or leaves, they did not need (and hence did not have) words for clothes, weaver, or loom.[8] Interestingly, Pontano also gives a contemporary example of this practical basis of language. Acquainted with the recent explorations of new parts of the world, for example Columbus's discovery of the "New Indies," he mentions the inhabitants of the Canary Islands, recently discovered by Spanish pirates, who live almost naked but have an abundant vocabulary concerning those arts they practice.[9] Elsewhere he mentions the inhabitants of the Fortunate Islands, who live "according to the laws of nature" without any cultural, literary, or political life.[10] Language is a function of civilization. The invention of things requires new words, just as we now have words for all kinds of arms and weapons, which are recent inventions. Neither nature, nor some god, but only humans are the inventors of language.[11]

The same view is expressed at the beginning of *De sermone* where Pontano presupposes an analogy between a newborn individual and primitive man at the beginning of time. Again, the distinction between the earliest phase of Latin and the origins of language more in general cannot always be clearly drawn in Pontano's account. Starting on a clearly Aristotelian note, he asserts that people are social animals by nature, born to live in each other's company.[12] While living in very simple and primitive, conditions people began to develop language to give expression to feelings and thoughts, and to describe the world around them. The more developed speech is, the better man can cope with the necessities of life: "The greater and larger this [speech] is, the more abundant the supply of all those things that life requires, since want is given as a companion to men at birth."[13] Language was thus born in human interactions when primitive

[8] Ibid.: "Ante texturam enim inventam, cum homines pellibus aut librorum foliorumque tegumentis opirerentur, nec telae nec texturae nec ipsorum textorum extabant nomina . . . " (text as in Germano 2005, 316).

[9] Ibid., 317: "Contra vocabulis illi abundant apud quos plures artes disciplinesque exercentur: an non hodie videmus genera armorum, quibus nunc utimur, nova pleraque habere nomina." Monti Sabia 1993, 283–303, repr. in Monti Sabia and Monti 2010, 2:1135–1157, showing that Pontano was acquainted with these recent explorations, including that of Columbus.

[10] Text in Germano 2005, 200 n. 55 (from *De rebus coelestibus* XII).

[11] Ibid.: "non naturam aut deum aliquem, sed homines ipsos rerum nomina fuisse commentos," followed by the remark that the same thing is often referred to differently in different languages. In such passages Pontano seems to allude to the idea that the development of language is much dependent on the regional, physical, social, and historical circumstances of a people. Such conventionalism is also emphasized in *De sermone* (e.g. 2019, 11; 1.4.2).

[12] Aristotle, *Politics* 1253a1-29; cf. *Nicomachean Ethics* 1097b10.

[13] Pontano 2019, 7 (*De sermone* 1.1.3). For a similar expression see Pontano 1518–1519 1:151r (*De prudentia* 1.8), where Pontano talks about the helpless condition in which man starts life as a newborn baby and only slowly develops language skills and habits; cf. Roick 2017, 130–133 on Aristotle's metaphysical

men had to find names for their activities, crafts, and tools for simple communication. Speech was of course also used to express one's emotions and feelings. Without developing the point, Pontano hints at this aspect in *De aspiratione* where, based on the idea commonly taught by ancient grammarians that interjection reflects the speaker's emotion, he writes that "the most ancient Latins" hardly used aspiration except for words that directly expressed the speaker's "movements of the soul and emotions" as in exclamation words such as "Heu," "hei," and "heiulo."[14] Taken together with his other observations, it is not too far-fetched to say that Pontano locates the origin of language in the affective, emotive, and active sphere of human life.[15] At a time when the biblical episode of Adam giving all creatures a name fitting their natures was still an influential idea,[16] this emphasis on the affective, emotive, and active origins of language looks fresh and important. While the social, conventional nature of language is clearly a central idea in Valla, this emphasis is absent from his brief remarks on the origins of language.[17]

How did it develop from here, from this primitive stage? When life became more diversified, complicated, and civilized, language too – and Pontano now clearly has Latin in mind – grew in complexity and elegance. In some of his grammatical investigations Pontano views this process in a rather literal way: together with the products and crafts that ancient peasants brought into the villages and cities, they also introduced the words they used to refer to their rural products, activities, and life conditions, and these words were taken up and acquired new meanings or formed the basis of new words. Pontano explains that, for example, *cernere* was first used for selecting pulses and fruits, but gave rise later to words such as *certare* (fight) and *decernere* (distinguish) from which came *certamina* (fights) and *decreta*

notion of privation (as one of the three principles of generation), which Pontano turned into an anthropological description of the helpless condition in which man is born.

14 Pontano 1518–1519, 2:3r, and cf. 6v. On interjections see, for example Priscian 1855–1859, 2:90; on interjections in medieval grammar see Pinborg 1961, 117–138.

15 We are reminded of the Epicurean account of the origins of language in Lucretius' *De rerum natura*, a work often quoted by Pontano. Rejecting the hypothesis that "someone had distributed names amongst things and that from him men learnt their first word," Lucretius suggests that language grew out of man's natural inclination to utter various sounds to suit varying feelings, just as we see "wild beasts of all kinds are accustomed to utter sounds different and varying when they are in fear or pain, and when now joy begins to glow"; Lucretius 1982, 459–463 (*De rerum natura* 5.1028–90). As a humanist, of course, Pontano saw speech as something that separates humans from beasts; cf. Pontano 1518–1519, 1:1r (*De obedientia* 1, prol.): "duobus his, ratione atque oratione, a brutis maxime differimus."

16 Klein 1992.

17 Valla 2012, 1:219 (*DD* 1.14.22); cf. Nauta 2009, 53–58 on the question on the origin of language in Valla.

(decree).[18] *Pangere* (plant, e.g. of trees) came to be used, for example, in the sense of composing verse (and also to conclude, and to stipulate). *Serere* (sow) gave rise to series of all kinds of things, as can be seen in related words such as *sermo* (speech), *sermocinatio* (conversation), *disserere* (discuss), and *disertus* (well-spoken, skillful); *exarare* (plow) was later applied to writing letters and books. *Saepe* (often), *palam* (openly), and *e vestigio* (at once) also have rural origins. The first is related to *saepes* (hedge), the second to *pala* (spade), the third obviously to *vestigium* (foot).

Another cluster of words goes back to the primitive life conditions of the ancient inhabitants of Latium, who lived in holes (*in cavernis*), which gave them security (*cavere*), so that they felt safe (*caute*); from one form of the verb *cavere* (viz. "*cavisse*") was derived *causa* (*cavisse* > *caussa*, an old form of *causa*, testified by ancient inscriptions, as Pontano says). From *vehere* (bringing agricultural foods to the cities) was derived *vehestigo* (taking the same road), for *veha* is the old form of *via* (track), from which later derived *vestigium* (trace, vestige, etc.). Related to the pristine form *Am* meaning "around" are words that refer to things where the end curves or returns to its starting point, for example *hamus* (hook) and *annus* (year), *anus* (anus, and also, because of her bent figure, an old woman). From these words came, for example, *perannare* (to conserve things for a whole year – obviously, an important activity in rural, primitive communities) and *exanniculo* (> *exanclo,* to endure, in the sense of undertaking difficult activities as preserving and conserving food and wine). *Imbecillitas* (feebleness, weakness) is related to *baculum* (stick), which is derived from *viaculum*, a stick to help those who are elderly and have sore feet to walk along the road (*via*).

Pontano also attempted to trace the morphological form of words back to earlier, "cruder" forms. If a word did not sound nice, or if a word was rough on the ear or was difficult to spell, it was gradually simplified or made smoother by the omission of letters or syllables, often at the beginning or at the end of the word, but also sometimes in the middle. The examples are endless: *calcis* became *calcs*, and then *calx* (chalk); a similar pattern explains *grex* (flock), *dux* (leader), *adeps* (fat); *donicum* was simplified to *donec* (until), *tabulerna* led to *taverna* (tavern), *vehenter* gave *venter* (belly), and *voluntus* led to *vultus* (face); *fortuna* is derived from *ferentuna* (going back to *ferre*, to bring), and *sequeculum* led to *seculum* (century)

[18] The examples that follow come from Pontano 1943, 204–208 (*Actius*) and 190–192, where many more examples can be found. *Cernere* is mentioned by Quintilian as an example of a verb with different meanings, hence as a possible source for ambiguity; Quintilian 2001, 3:280 (*Institutio oratoria* 7.9.2).

without a diphthong, according to Pontano. Double letters got reduced to one (*redducit* > *reducit*; *refficit* > *reficit*). Pontano even devotes an entire treatise to the phenomenon of aspiration.

Without passing a verdict on the correctness of Pontano's observations, we can see that his systematic attempt to trace back words to the rural and simple life conditions of primitive man is an impressive example of what we may call his genealogical approach to language and its development in close connection to changing life conditions. But it is not only a description of how language grew in tandem with society, it also sets a norm: just as high society should never forget its origins in the simple rustic life of its ancestors, so correct language is that which shows its origins in the robust language of a time when humanity lived in harmony with nature, a time that is idealized in the bucolic setting of agricultural activities as portrayed by Virgil.[19] Pontano may be said to have appropriated here a typically Roman sentiment of a yearning for the innocent life of the rustic, far away from the cosmopolitan city with all its luxury and decadence.[20] This, however, is not an ideal that governs his thinking about the social virtues of language in his *De sermone*, in which the speech of the witty person is certainly not characterized by rusticity.[21]

After this primitive stage language not only became richer and more complex, but also more refined and more elegant, a process that was effected by, for example, "the shortening of syllables and letters." Poets were vital in this process: "they were the first among the learned that came forward."[22] Poetry must therefore be considered as a very early form of language. A gifted poet himself, it is not surprising to find Pontano underscoring the roles traditionally ascribed to poets in ancient society: poets were seers (*vates*), priests, the singers of tales, the promulgators of laws, and generally those who gave form to all kinds of knowledge and what was important to society. Hence, philosophers, physicists and orators alike, Pontano claims, took their precepts from Homer; Numa, king of the Romans, had his own verses on the gods frequently sung to the people,

[19] Cf. Marsh 1980, 109: "Correct usage is that which is closest to the ancient origins of language during the age of man's pristine harmony with nature."

[20] On Cicero's positive attitude toward agriculture, see Wood 1988, 115–119.

[21] For example Pontano 2019, 33 (1.12.2): someone who follows the customs of the country is called "agrestic and the vice, rusticity." In the formation of the "*vir facetus*" (the witty man), which is the main theme of *De sermone*, there is no place for the rustic speech of the countryman; the witty person shows "neither any sign of the country nor the overrefinement of the city" (ibid., 351; 6.1.1).

[22] Pontano 1943, 238, 205, and 208 (*Actius*) on shortening of letters and syllables; cf. 238–239: "expurgatis rudioribus illis vetustatis numeris," and 139: "Latinitatem musicarent." Cf. Cicero, *Orator*, esp. 140–174. Krostenko 2001, 118–119; Solmsen 1932, 151–154.

bringing "that very savage people to more human manners and a greater worship of God."[23] Empedocles sang about the natural world, and so on. For Pontano the poetical style is the most ancient one, "from which all later types of discourse have sprung," as comparison in particular with the two sister arts, oratory and history, shows.[24] Unlike Valla, who had claimed that history was superior to poetry, Pontano reverses the relationship. History, Pontano argues, is poetry in prose form, and rhetoric too borrows much from poetry for effective and persuasive speech.[25] Poetry stands historically at the beginning of civilization.

Language, Human Sociability, and the Passions

Pontano's emphasis on the affective, active, and social role of language in early times recurs when he turns his attention to the bond between language and human sociability. The social bond that speech forges was of course an age-old theme, which regained prominence in humanist thought. Humanists found a classic statement in Cicero's *De officiis*:[26]

> The first principle [among the principles of fellowship and society that Nature has established among men] is that which is found in the connection subsisting between all members of the human race; and that bond of connection is reason and speech, which by the processes of teaching and learning, of communicating, discussing, and reasoning associate men together and unite them in a sort of natural fraternity. In no other particular are we farther removed from the nature of beasts.

Against the background of this Ciceronian theme we must read one of Pontano's most programmatic statements, found at the beginning of *De sermone*.[27] It starts conventionally enough. Nature has endowed man with reason and language:

> And so, with reason men measure and order themselves and all their affairs, but with speech they preserve and protect the bond of union that has been engrafted by nature, and they explain and declare what reason itself dictates,

[23] Pontano 1943, 238 (*Actius*) and see also 233–234 where Pontano, apparently not thinking of this very early stage of poetry, says that the public of both the historian and the poet consists of learned men, unlike the orator who speaks to the common people and to judges; cf. Pontano 2019, 121 (*De sermone* 2.5.4: the sayings of the poets considered as oracles).

[24] Ibid., 238 (*Actius*).

[25] Ibid., 238; 199; 200. Valla's comparison is found in the preface to his *Gesta Fernandi Regis* (Valla 1973, 5). See below for Pontano's views of the art of history.

[26] Cicero 1913, 53–55 (*De officiis* 1.16.50).

[27] Pontano 2019, 4–6 (1.1) for what follows. For a brief paraphrase see Trinkaus 1983, 217; cf. Kahn 1983, 18.

> whether relating to the useful and serious or to jest and pleasure. Without speech reason is a maimed and completely weak thing, since man's life is particularly occupied with actions and with civil assemblies and meetings, of which speech itself is the foremost bond, as it is of all human society, and without which it is by no means possible to attain the highest good.

Speech, Pontano continues, is an essential condition for pursuing a virtuous and commodious life: "as reason itself is the leader and guide for the direction of every action, so speech is the minister of all those things that are conceived by the mind, considered by reasoning, and made public, since we are born sociable, as they say, and must live among the multitude." And he concludes:

> as reason is the leader and guide for directing actions and obtaining virtues, and speech is the interpreter of the mind and the instrument, as it were, of reason itself (since consultations, deliberations, and, finally, reasonings themselves consist of discourses [*dissertionibus*] and discourses in turn consist of words), so likewise speech itself provides to reason the instrument and also, so to speak, the material on which to act.

The same expressions recur frequently in other chapters, for example in chapter 13, where he writes that "speech itself and conversation are the most important bond holding society together, which we have been born and raised to care for."[28] This programmatic statement – Aristotelian and Ciceronian in spirit, to be sure[29] – contains at least two interesting elements that requires some discussion: the intrinsic connection between sociability and language, and the relationship between thought and language – each element has some wider implications. The rest of this section will discuss the first aspect, the next section the second aspect.

In the quoted passage we find Pontano recognizing and explicitly commenting on the intrinsic connection between sociability and language. One of the sources that must have inspired Pontano to postulate this bond is the classical description of oratorical "action," that is, the delivery of a speech. Central to successful oratory is the idea that people naturally recognize and instinctively respond to each other's emotions. As Cicero writes in *De oratore*: "action, which by its own powers displays the movements of the soul, affects all mankind; for the minds of all men are

[28] Ibid., 39 (1.13.1) Similar passages in Pontano 1518–1519, 1:157v and 160r (*De prudentia* 1.21 and 1.25), quoted by Roick 2017, 53.

[29] For example, Cicero 1913, 150 (*De officiis* 1.41.149: "totius generis hominum conciliationem et consociationem"). Cf. Garin 1951, 321 on the double tradition of Aristotle and Cicero in Renaissance thought.

excited by the same emotions which they recognize in others, and indicate in themselves by the same tokens."[30] Pontano was of course familiar with Cicero's account of *actio*, as his dialogue *Actius* in particular testifies,[31] but he saw this psychological mechanism of mutual recognition of emotions in a perspective wider than oratory, in line with his general aim in *De sermone* to deal with common speech (*oratio communis*) rather than formal oratory and rhetoric.[32] The mechanism is universal and based on what Pontano describes as our instinctive desire to be kind and benevolent to each other – a "natural inclination" (*naturalis commotio*).[33] The term "natural" indeed abounds in the works of Pontano: men are naturally inclined to socialize, to work together, to live in community. For Pontano this natural affinity is "a given," an irreducible aspect of human nature. Human passions are therefore not to be scorned; they arise out of "our natural movements and impulses," implanted in us to enable us to live a social life and work together.[34] Pontano does not restrict this natural affinity to human beings. In his astrological work *De rebus coelestibus* he speaks about "an agreement among the planets and (as I would say) a certain consensus and familiar affection, and (as the Greeks call it) a *sympathia. This also happens in civil life.*"[35]

Pontano thus combines the classical-humanist theme of the social bond between people, forged by (in the words of Cicero) reason and speech, with the astrological concept of natural or cosmological affinity. The concept of attraction, affinity, or (cosmic) harmony in the natural world found, as is well known, wide application in Renaissance astrology, magic, medicine, and natural philosophy, and from the seventeenth century onward the concept (or rather cluster of related concepts) was used in a wide variety of contexts, though in the new mechanical philosophy sympathy and antipathy began to be seen as obscure and obsolete powers that did not explain

[30] Cicero 1942, 2:179 (*De oratore* 3.59.223); cf. ibid., 2.44.189–190; Quintilian 2001, 3:59 (*Institutio oratoria* 6.2.26).

[31] Pontano 1943, 221, 232 and elsewhere (*Actius*); cf. Monti Sabia 1995, 4.

[32] Pontano 2019, 9 (*De sermone* 1.3.2).

[33] Ibid., 81 (1.26.2). The term *commotio* is used by Cicero in *De inventione* 2.19 and *De oratore* 2.53.216, but with different meanings.

[34] Pontano 1518–1519, 1:51v–52r (*De fortitudine*); Lupi 1955, 372; Tateo 1960, 170–171. Cf. Roick 2017, 136: "We have no inherent faculty or passion that would make us good or evil by nature," paraphrasing *De prudentia* (Pontano 1518–1519, 1:174v).

[35] Quoted in Trinkaus 1985, 455 (my italics). See also Pontano 1943, 143 (*Actius*) where Pontano uses the word to refer to the movements of the sky and stars: "sic a coeli ipsius siderumque commotionibus, per eam quae συμπάθεια Graece est, Latine *contagionem* fecit Cicero .... sic, inquam, a coeli stellarumque agitatu perpetuo animis nostra mens." See Soranzo 2014, 106 for the astrological context of this passage.

anything.[36] But it is interesting to see Pontano already using the classical word "sympathy," which was still rarely used in his own time, to allude to a universal and natural bond between people ("the civil life"). In stressing the natural, instinctive mechanism of the mutual recognition of emotions, Pontano might be said to hint at a core intuition that formed the basis of the eighteenth-century sentimentalist account of morality. Indeed, historians of Enlightenment thought have credited eighteenth-century philosophers with championing the essential role of fellow-feeling in human affairs.[37] Based on the classical rhetorical descriptions of "action" (delivery) that, as we have just seen, had also inspired Pontano, eighteenth-century philosophers such as Jean Baptiste Dubos, Condillac, David Hume, and Adam Smith underscored the sympathetic identification between orator and audience, and indeed between human beings in general.[38] The term "sympathy," often used by these authors, seems to have been introduced by Bernard Lamy (1640–1715). Whatever its origins, the concept was used by Hume and Smith to serve as the foundation of a naturalistic account of the development of morality. It would of course be anachronistic to see in Pontano's observations a clear anticipation of such a sentimentalist account. But it seems not too far-fetched to argue that from the same classical sources that inspired these eighteenth-century thinkers, Pontano had already derived a picture of fellow-feeling as an essential instinct in man's nature on which sociability grows.

The Impact of Language

Next to the socializing effects of language, the passage from *De sermone*, quoted above, raises another issue, namely the verbalization of what is going on in the mind of the individual speaker. The view of language as an instrument of thought is of course wholly traditional; it is the framework in which language had been regarded since antiquity, with Aristotle's

[36] See the contributions by Moyer (on Renaissance authors such as Ficino, Giovanni Pico della Mirandola, Fracastoro, and Paracelsus), and Mercer (on Conway and Leibniz) in Schliesser (ed.) 2015.

[37] Aarsleff in Condillac 2001, xii–xiv. For views of language in the Enlightenment see Ricken 1994 *passim*, and p. 101 on Condillac's language of action; Gordon 1994, 43–85 on the rise of the notion of sociability in the eighteenth century.

[38] Hume 1978, 575–576 (*Treatise* III.1); Adam Smith 1982, 11 (*The Theory of Moral Sentiments* I.1.1). On the rhetorical background of Hume's notion of sympathy see Potkay 1994, 46, who notes that the "Ciceronian-Demosthenic ideal of sympathetic identification between orator and audience is a commonplace of eighteenth-century rhetoric." See also Jones 1982 on the Ciceronian and French contexts of Hume's moral thinking. On the history of the concept see Schliesser (ed.) 2015.

distinction between natural concepts and conventional words at the beginning of *De interpretatione* as *locus classicus*.[39] It is therefore hardly surprising that Pontano uses such images as instrument, minister, and interpreter for language, calling reason its leader, master, and guide. This implies a rather passive, dependent, and purely executive role for language; language is here regarded as a mere conveyer of ready-made prior thoughts, an outward manifestation of what is going on inside.

Pontano's words, however, can also be read as containing the germ of a different, much more active view of language. When Pontano states that "reasonings consist of discourses (*dissertionibus*) and discourses in turn consist of words" and hence that "speech provides reason the material on which to act," it is tempting to interpret him as believing that thinking is done with and in words, and that speech penetrates into the inner workings of the mind. Although reason is called the leader (or master) and speech its servant, the implication of Pontano's statement that "without speech reason is a maimed and completely weak thing" points in a different direction: it is the servant who actually rules the master. It is as if Pontano endorses what the modern philosopher Max Black once called "the model of the melody" (language as intrinsically bound with thought and constitutive of it) in opposition to "the model of the garment" (language as a mere container of thought) that, as we have just seen, is present in the very same passage.[40] This was, however, not Pontano's intention. He surely did not want to suggest that thinking would come to a full stop when it lacked speech as its *interpres* and *instrumentum* (its mouthpiece, spokesman, vehicle, instrument). In his *De rebus coelestibus*, for instance, he gives an astrological explanation of the phenomenon of stuttering and lisping, without suggesting (and rightly so, of course) that such impediments in speech are signs of a lack of cognitive powers.[41] In general, his account presupposes the traditional distinction between thinking and expressing one's thought, and such a distinction is also implied in Pontano's observation that we sometimes speak quicker than we think – an important asset in witty conversation, which is a major theme of *De sermone*.[42]

[39] Cf. Hall 1936, 98 n. 12, referring to Cinquecento authors such as J. C. Scaliger, Bembo, Varchi, and Tolomei. On the predominance of the Aristotelian paradigm see Demonet 1992 and Maclean 1998.

[40] Black 1972, 86–91. On the debate whether such ideas can be ascribed to humanists such as Valla, see Nauta 2009, 269–291.

[41] Pontano 1518–1519, 3:251r–252r (*De rebus coelestibus* X), where Pontano explains stuttering as a result of too much bodily dryness or too much humidity, ultimately caused by planetary constellations.

[42] Pontano 1943, 227–228 (*Actius*); cf. 269 (*Aegidius*): "cogitatione tantum concepta post voce enuntietur." Cf. Pontano 2019, 233 and 235 (*De sermone* 3.19.3; 3.20.4) and Pontano 1518–1519, 1:164v (*De prudentia* 1.31).

For Pontano it was quite natural to think of language both in terms of an instrument for thought and as an active, shaping force with a considerable degree of autonomy. Standing in the rhetorical tradition of Cicero and Quintilian, and a brilliant writer and poet himself, Pontano shares with his classical authorities, and the humanists we have discussed in the previous chapters, the basic conviction that reason and eloquence, or thought and language, are intimately interwoven. Cicero had famously said in *De oratore*: "eloquence is one of the supreme virtues . . ., which, after compassing a knowledge of facts, gives verbal expression to the thoughts and purposes of the mind in such a manner as to have the power of driving the hearers forward in any direction in which it has applied its weight."[43] And in the next sentence he speaks of "this method of attaining and of expressing thought, this faculty of speaking," that "was designated wisdom by the ancient Greeks." We see here several functions that a modern philosopher might want to distinguish being mentioned in the same breath: the expression of one's thought, the communication of it to the public, and the intention of being understood in such and such a way, aiming at a particular effect in the audience. Cicero does not spell out the basic assumption on which his plea for a union of wisdom and eloquence is based, namely that clear language is essential for clear thinking, probably because it seems such an intuitively plausible assumption. The models of "the garment" and "the melody" seemingly fuse together in one account of a seamless interrelation between thinking and verbal expression.

As we have seen in the previous chapters, this conviction was central to the humanist program, and found influential formulations, for example in Petrarch, Bruni, and Valla. As Bruni wrote in his *On the Study of Literature* from 1424: "The reading of clumsy and corrupt writers imbues the reader with their own vices, and infests his mind with similar corruptions."[44] Valla was often quite explicit about the causal connection, stating at various places in his works that a lack of knowledge of classical Latin leads to muddled thinking, incorrect reasoning, and abstruse theorizing.[45] Similarly, this humanist conviction informed much of what Pontano says about language and grammar – whether it is about the impact of language on our emotional life, about the union of eloquence and philosophy, the relationship between Greek and Latin, the adequacy of *verba* to express the *res*, literary style of historians and poets, or the

[43] Cicero 1942, 2:43–45 (*De oratore* 3.14.55). Cf. Fantham 2004, esp. 237–286.
[44] In Bruni 1987, 241; see Chapter 1, n. 33.
[45] Valla 2012, 1:7; 1:260; 2:208 (*DD* 1.proem.9; 1.17.30; 3.proem.3), and elsewhere. See Chapter 2.

importance of grammatical investigations. All these discussions are premised on the belief – not always explicitly articulated – that language does more than just register preexistent thoughts and things, but influences the way in which we describe and perhaps think about the world. This is of course not to ascribe any form of linguistic idealism to Pontano – that is, the idea that language constitutes the world or that the world exists in so far as it is spoken about (rather vague claims, to say the least) – but it is to say that for Pontano, as for his source of inspiration Valla, elegance and semantic precision are essential aids in making aspects of the world "visible," something which an allegedly less precise language than Latin would not be able to do.

Perhaps the most direct way in which we feel the impact of language on our life is at the level of emotions. To move one's audience was of course one of the three official functions of the orator, and being a poet himself Pontano hardly needed the classical accounts in Cicero and Quintilian to recognize the immense power words can have over human life.[46] Words, he says, can evoke all kinds of emotions in us, and can become so great that they seem even "to dominate our very minds" (*dominari in animis ipsis nostris*).[47] In the dialogue *Aegidius*, he even compares the effect of human speech with God's creative act.[48] Solely by his Word God had created the world and man ("let there be light," etc.), and later, "when mankind was on the road to perdition," God sent his Son – again, his Word – to save mankind. Hence, it should not surprise us, Pontano concludes, that human words too can produce astonishing effects such as bringing people back to life who are already standing with one foot in the grave or – from the opposite side – causing people to commit suicide. Indeed, "there is no greater power and strength in man than that which consists of words." Because this power is potentially so strong, it is vitally important that eloquence is closely connected to wisdom, otherwise we shall have put, as Cicero had said, "weapons into the hands of madmen."[49]

This leads us directly to a second theme: the plea for a reunion of eloquence and philosophy. Whereas Cicero had attributed the severance between the tongue and the brain to the rise of philosophical sects after

[46] Cicero 1942, 1:22–24; 2:42 (*De oratore* 1.8.30–33; 3.14.55), and elsewhere.

[47] Pontano 1518–1519, 3:198v (*De rebus coelestibus* XIII).

[48] Pontano 1943, 271 (*Aegidius*) for this and the following quotations; ibid., 221 (*Actius*); cf. Kappl 2006, 52–53.

[49] Cicero 1942, 2:42 (*De oratore* 3.14.55). In *Aegidius* Pontano praises eloquence as the art which enables a whole civilization to communicate the most profound wisdom; this will be discussed later in the chapter.

Socrates, Pontano follows Bruni and Valla in situating the start of this process after the fall of the Roman Empire, when in particular "the pursuit of eloquence died out completely, and hardly a trace of grammar itself remained."[50] The contentious philosophers are to blame: "dialectic has been corrupted first by Germans and Gauls, then also by our own people, and they are now making a hash of it."[51] In an analysis that owes much to Bruni's *Dialogues*, Valla's *Elegantiae*, and other humanist works of the earlier Quattrocento, Pontano attributes the decline of philosophy to faulty translations and interpretations of Aristotle, and to a general sloppiness about words.[52] This negligence has resulted in the belief that Latin, rather than being the "abundantly rich language" that it is, is a poor language, at least for doing philosophy, and that we cannot render the force and meaning of Greek words into Latin or in a meaningful way (*nec Latine . . . nec significanter*).[53] But of course we can, Pontano says, endorsing a position already forcefully argued by his predecessors: whatever can be said in Greek can be said in Latin, and sometimes even better.[54] As Pontano frequently says, words can be more or less "adequate," "appropriate," "proper," "fitting," "significant" (in the sense of a word covering its meaning), and he also speaks of the "nature of a word," by which he means its proper meaning.[55]

The whole point of hitting on the right word, however, presupposes that there is a preexistent referent (a person, a quality, a concept, a past event, etc.) that can be captured more or less adequately by the linguistic expression. But this does not mean that language is merely registering what is already there. In his important discussion of history and the historian's style, to which we have already alluded earlier in this chapter, Pontano shows how style is all-important in bringing to light the connections between things, and hence, albeit implicitly, in how language structures the way we see the past, making it "visible." Following Cicero, Pontano states that *historia* consists of *res* and *verba*, things and words. It is not that the words bring order to a chaotic and formless matter, for things themselves, Pontano says, exhibit order and disposition: they follow each other in succession, being connected by causes and effects, by motives and aims,

[50] Pontano 1943, 259–260 (*Aegidius*); cf. 231 (*Aegidius*); Valla 1962, 1:3–5 (*Elegantiae*, preface to Book I).

[51] Pontano 2012, 37 (Charon); cf. Marsh 1980, 115. For Valla's critique see Chapter 2.

[52] Pontano 2012, 37.

[53] Pontano 1943, 283–284 (*Aegidius*).

[54] Pontano 1943, 281–282 (*Aegidius*). Cicero, *De finibus* 3.5. For Bruni's position, see Chapter 1, n. 64; cf. Valla 2012, 1:7 (*DD* 1.proem.8): "most translations of Aristotle's works are bad."

[55] Pontano 1943, 271 (*Aegidius*): "quae vox, [i.e. *privatus*] suapte natura adversatur *publico*"; Pontano frequently says that a word can express a thing "recte," "proprie," "Latine" (or "Romane"), and "significanter."

and so forth.[56] The ontological status of this order is not entirely clear in Pontano's account: sometimes he refers to the order of events as they occurred in the past and links such an order with the order of nature (*natura*), but at other times he writes as if this order is the product of the historian who shows the connections between the individual events by describing their causes and effects as well as the motives of the historical agents, the wars, the lands, cities, and all the other elements that make up the historical narrative.[57] In spite of some ambiguity in terminology – he speaks of *ordo, enarratio, dispositio, series*[58] – the basic idea seems clear enough: the historian's task is to bring order to his material, by clearly conceiving how all the events fit together into a coherent whole, offering explanations of historical events, distributing praise and blame, using such words that are fitting, and employing a style that is varied and elegant but never forced or artificial.[59] Pontano stresses the affinity between the style of the poet and that of the historian, following Quintilian in speaking of history as *carmen solutum*,[60] but history is of course also closely related to the art of oratory, in which arguments are found, and the material is ordered and expressed in an elegant and persuasive verbal account. Both the rhetorician and the historian must know how to describe things so vividly – by conjuring up vivid mental images – that the audience or readers feel they were witness to the scene or events. In his detailed analyses of the writings of Livy and Sallust, Pontano's main point is that language is the cement of the historical narrative and that without the right words and stylistic features such as *celeritas* (readiness, wittiness), *brevitas* (succinctness), and *elegantia* (elegance), the past cannot come to life and cannot be put "before our eyes" (*ponere ante oculos*), that is, the mind's eye – a traditional expression that Pontano borrows from Cicero and Quintilian.[61]

Language thus takes an active role in the way in which reality – past or present – is presented. As already said, it would go too far to argue that

[56] Pontano 1943, 217 (*Actius*); cf. ibid., 229 and elsewhere.

[57] Pontano 1943, 212, 215, 217, 229–230, and 212–213, 227, 229 (*Actius*). Cf. Cotroneo 1971, 87–120, without recognizing such a tension.

[58] For example Pontano 1943, 217 (*Actius*). [59] Ibid., 212.

[60] Ibid., 199: "historiam censeant poeticam quasi quandam solutam" and 194. On Pontano's indebtness to George of Trebizond's *Rhetoric*, see Ferraù 1983, 73–105; Monti Sabia 1995, 7. But in stressing the close affinity between the historian and the poet, Pontano follows Quintilian (*Inst. orat.* 10.1.31) more than Cicero (and George of Trebizond); Cicero considered history an *opus oratorium* (*De legibus* 1.5, *De oratore* 2.9.36).

[61] For example Pontano 1943, 193, 219 (twice) and 221 (*Actius*). See Cicero 1942, 2:17 (*De oratore* 3.5.19) and Quintilian 2001, 3:60 and 4:378 (*Institutio oratoria* 6.2.32 and 10.7.15); for George of Trebizond see Monti Sabia 1995, 5.

Pontano actually conflates the levels of things and linguistic description; his discussion presupposes such a distinction, yet it also emphasizes time and again the formative role of the historian in creating historical reality by describing the connections between historical events – a task that requires all the semantic precision and elegance of the Latin language. Indeed, *res* and *verba* are intimately related to each other: "the individual words almost completely encompass or comprehend the things."[62]

"Our Latin Philosophy": Grammar and Semantic Precision

To use the right word, the right construction, and the right style requires a thorough familiarity with the Latin language. It is of course axiomatic for Pontano that Latin is such a semantically precise and elegant language that we do not need, for instance, to leave Greek words untransliterated or use inept Latin terminology in our moral and scholarly disquisitions. As noted, Pontano followed Bruni and Valla in seeing the decline of philosophical learning to be the result of the absence of the study of eloquence and the neglect of Latin. In particular dialectic and grammar had suffered from the philosophers' lack of attention to language – a major theme, as we have seen, in the work of Valla. Fortunately, in his own time scholars have begun to turn their backs on these faulty translations, Pontano says, and he expresses the hope that, before he departs from this world, he may see "our Latin philosophy expounding its topics with a more refined style and elegance, and that abandoning this contentious manner of debating it may adopt a more tranquil form of speech and discussion, using its own proper and purely Roman vocabulary."[63] What Pontano in effect is saying is not just that Latin is a beautiful language and that for aesthetic reasons we should stick to the usage of the venerable, ancient authorities – this, of course, is true as well – but that it is an exceptionally rich and precise language for describing, or even evoking, reality, whether that concerns our systems of beliefs, ethical maxims, or scientific and philosophical ideas. For Pontano the numerous and subtle distinctions embodied in Latin had not just been made arbitrarily but were drawn because men found them worth drawing. Its stock of words and grammatical distinctions had developed over a long period of time, and they should not be tampered with; at least,

[62] As the interlocutor in *Actius* comments on a passage in Sallust: "singula verba res pene complectuntur singulas" (Pontano 1943, 212).

[63] Pontano 1943, 280 (*Aegidius*), trans. in Marsh 1980, 107.

not when there is no clear reason for doing so, for Pontano felt no qualms about coining a word or two himself.

The study of grammar is therefore a vital aspect of what Pontano called his "Latin philosophy." Investigations of words and grammatical distinctions are essential for clarifying things or concepts. The examples that follow will convey an impression of his method and aims. These methods and aims are certainly not original with Pontano. Valla showed in his *Elegantiae* how to carry out such investigations. This program however had to be defended, modified (if necessary), and expanded, and this is what Pontano tried to do, agreeing with Valla's methodology but also correcting him on his own terms.[64] Moreover, Pontano also opens up new themes to which the Vallian method is applied, such as a subtle examination of the language of social discourse in his *De sermone*, to which we shall come in a moment. We will first look at his observations about the translation of some important philosophical concepts.

In the dialogue *Aegidius* the interlocutors discuss mistranslations of some philosophical terms.[65] The term *privatio* (privation), for instance, which is the third principle of generation (along with form and matter) that Aristotle had distinguished, is criticized as not being an appropriate word to express the corresponding concept; *carentia* (lacking) would be better, but that word was hardly known or understood by early users of the term. *Privatio* is derived from *privatus,* the opposite of *publicus*. It often has the meaning of "deprived of"; physicists use it in the sense of emptiness or void (*vacuitas*). It belongs to the class of verbal nouns such as *vectatio* (carrying), *legatio* (embassy), and *verberatio* (beating), but since these words indicate "merely something either passive or something active while the physicists need a term that indicates the nature of what is in question," the term *privatio* is not an appropriate word to indicate that the matter is prepared to accept a form, and is longing for it, since it suggests the absence of something that was taken away from it. According to Cicero, *carere* (and *carentia*) fulfill this role much better. *Carere* indicates that something is missing in the sense of something that is needed for completion, as matter stands in need of a form. In spite of Cicero's authority, however, *privatio* has come into use, and we may therefore accept it, heedful of Horace's dictum that "in usage's hands lies the

[64] Cf. Marsh 1979, 113.

[65] For the examples in this paragraph see Pontano 1943, 271–273 (*privatio, carentia*), 280–282 (*hexis, habitus*), 282–284 (*krasis, complexio*).

judgment, the right and the rule of speech," even though the semantic associations might take us in the wrong direction.[66]

Next, Pontano discusses *habitus* as a translation of the Aristotelian concept *hexis,* meaning inclination, inner state, or attitude. According to Pontano, *habitus* is derived from *habere* (to have), just as *hexis* is from Greek *echō*, but unfortunately *dispositio* rather than *habitus* has become the usual word, for reason of structural similarity: *dispositio* structurally corresponds to Greek *diathesis,* which refers to the same concept of inner state or attitude. *Dispositio*, however, is a wholly inadequate translation, since in Latin it means ordering and setting things in order (such as soldiers), which has nothing to do with such an inner state or inclination (e.g. being inclined to be courageous or generous). An extensive survey of the semantic contexts in which these and related words are being used must show that Latin has all the resources to make the necessary fine distinctions in meaning. A third example concerns Greek *krasis* (mixing, blending), which was erroneously translated as *complexio*. The Latin word means embracing, encompassing, comprising rather than mixing. Again, Pontano makes an impressive survey of related Latin words meaning mixing, blending, uniting, and so on to show how subtle differences in things (or aspects of things) can be expressed only if one knows the nuances of words.[67]

Though particularly known for its "theory of wit," Pontano's *De sermone* also offers perhaps the best example of his "Latin philosophy." Here he examines in detail, with Aristotle's *Nicomachean Ethics* and other classical texts at his elbow, the social virtues and vices as they manifest themselves in conversation and social intercourse. Without going into much detail, we may note that Aristotle had distinguished three virtues of sociability: truthfulness (between boastfulness and mock modesty), pleasantness in the giving of amusement (between buffoonery and boorishness), and pleasantness as exhibited in life in general (between obsequiousness and quarrelsomeness). At a later point in his discussion, Aristotle calls this last mean "a laudable state – that in virtue of which a man will put up with, and will resent, the right things and in the right way; but no name has been assigned to it, though it most resembles friendship." Being "concerned with the pleasures and pains of social life," this person responds

[66] *Ars Poetica*, 70–72, often alluded to by humanists and early modern philosophers, for example Valla 2012, 1:267 (*DD* 1.17.40); Sanches 1988, 176–177; Digby 1644, 8; Leibniz 1969, 126.

[67] On the related term medical term *eukrasia* (*bene constitutus*), see Pontano 1518–1519, 1:153v (*De prudentia* 1.17), discussed by Roick 2017, 52. See also Ferraù 1983, 84 n. 1, which shows that Pontano is referring to George of Trebizond.

in the right way in accordance to the situation and the company, "rendering to each class what is befitting."[68] But Aristotle does not come up with a name for this virtue ("the mean is without a name"). Based on Aristotle and other classical authorities who had developed a rich vocabulary of approbative terms meaning "elegant," "witty," "charming," "urbane," and the like, Pontano seizes the opportunity to give this unnamed virtue a name: wittiness or facetiousness, for which he coins a new noun *facetudo*, which comes close to but is not identical to positive qualities such as being affable (*comis*), urbane (*urbanus*), charming (*lepidus*), mirthful (*festivus*), and pungent (*salsus*).[69] The witty man brings relaxation, and his witty conversation is soothing, restful, and helpful; his goal is to provide social entertainment at the right moment, in the right way, in the right tone (which may be sharp but never detrimental to his fellow human beings), keeping the right balance in speech and behavior.[70]

> Thus the witty man I am now training will be pleasant and cheerful when telling jokes, and will have a calm face composed to refresh, pleasing and elegant, when responding, with a voice neither languid nor coarse but virile and glad, urbane in motion as one who shows neither any sign of the country nor the overrefinement of the city. He will shrink from buffoonishness as if from a cliff and relegate obscenity to parasites and mimes. He will use caustic and mordant sayings in such a way that, unless provoked and irritated, he does not bite or taunt back, yet never moves away from the honorable and that composure of mind characteristic of a freeborn man.

As Luck comments: "It is this 'goodness' or 'kindness' of the *vir facetus* that justifies his role as a social ideal. His wit is not just an exuberant outpouring of his temperament or mood; it is controlled by *ratio* and directed by a sense of measure (*mensura*). His *facetudo* is both an aesthetic and a moral quality."[71] The witty man "is a true artist, not only an 'artist of life,' but an artist *par excellence*."

It goes without saying that language plays a vital role here. Without semantic precision it would be difficult to give an exact idea of the social

[68] Aristotle 1984, 2:1750–1751 (*Nicomachean Ethics* II.7, 1108a10–1108b10) and 2:1778 (IV.6, 1126b12–1127a12).

[69] Pontano 2019, 37 (*De sermone* 1.12.10); the word and related words such as *urbanus* occur very frequently. Luck 1958, 118 n. 39 argued, however, that the etymology Pontano gives derives from Donatus's commentary to Terence, *Eunuchus*, 427. Luck calls it a "new social and aesthetic ideal" (118), stressing Pontano's "ability to think through independently and critically an accepted ancient theory, and to modify it in an essential point" (117).

[70] Pontano 2019, 351 (6.1.1). Gender-neutral language would mask here the fact that women – witty or not – were absent from Aristotle's and Pontano's account of witty conversation.

[71] Luck 1958, 120 for this and the following quotation.

performance of the witty person and all the qualities closely associated with it. As said, in defining this virtue Pontano discusses a number of related terms which are aspects of it or are somehow related to it, yet not identical with it: *amicitia* (friendship), *comitas* (courtesy, affability), *lepidus* (charming, witty), *salsus* (salty, witty, pungent), *festivus* (humorous, mirthful), *humanus* (humane, cultured), *urbanus* (urbane, elegant, polished, witty), *verus* (true), and so forth.[72] Without discussing Pontano's arguments, the following gives an idea of the semantic precision he tries to achieve by, for instance, arguing that *humanitas* is not quite the same as *comitas*, *popularitas* (courting of popular favor) not quite the same as *comitas*, *festivus* more restrictive in scope than *urbanus*; *urbanus* being (slightly) different from *facetus*, that *verus* (true) and *verax* (truthful) are not the same, and so forth. The corresponding vices also receive detailed attention, and subtle differences between various kinds of flattery, garrulity or prolixity, and verbosity are explained. Thus, there are many species of flatterers (*adulatores*), and several types of *captatores* (people reaching eagerly after something); *verbosus* (verbose) is not quite the same as *loquax* (talkative, loquacious), and such a talkative person is close to but not identical with a *nugator* (trifler, jester, braggart); *litigiosus* (quarrelsome, disputatious) is not quite the same as *contentiosus* (contentious); *arrogantia* (presumption, arrogance) is similar to but not identical with *ostentatio* (ostentation), and the latter is close to but not identical to *iactatio* (boasting). It is important to make these distinctions, Pontano frequently says, to make things appear "more clearly" (*distinctius*), more "lucidly" or "to understand things better," so that we avoid talking at cross-purposes, for "confusion and uncertainty arise from words."[73] He therefore frequently looks for the term that characterizes (a) the thing itself, (b) the corresponding virtue/vice, and (c) the person who exhibits the virtue/vice, for example, *contentio*, *contentiositas*, *contentiosus* or *veritas*, *veracitas*, *verax*. Pontano is eager to coin a word if none seems to be available; for example *rixatio* (brawlery) of which the corresponding term is in use (*rixator*), and *facetudo* (or *faceties*) itself.[74] Sometimes, however, no term is suggested, and then Pontano is content to note, as Aristotle himself sometimes did too, that we do not

[72] The following paragraph is based esp. on *De sermone*, book I; the titles of the chapters clearly indicate the virtues and vices under discussion. On these approbative terms in Cicero and Catullus, see Krostenko 2001, who calls this the language of social performance. Pontano is indebted to Cicero's account of wit (*De oratore* 2.219–290, on which see, e.g., Rabbie 1986, 216–290).

[73] Ibid., 19 (1.9.2: "ne confusio incertitudoque exoriatur e verbis aliqua"); cf. ibid. 41 (1.13.2: "distinctius intelligatur"); 37 (1.12.10: "ut aperte magis intelligatur"); and so on.

[74] Ibid., 52 (1.18.2) (*rixatio*) and 37 (1.12.7) (*facetudo*).

have a word for it; for example, for excessive taciturnity or for the mean between quarrelsome (*contentiosus*) and flattering (*adulans*).[75] And in his search for the important virtue of *mediocritas*, for which Aristotle had not provided a name, Pontano suggests *comitas* (courtesy, affability) but notices that some might prefer to leave it unnamed. However, as long as we see the what and how (*quae* and *qualis*) of the virtue, Pontano does not want to insist on this point.[76]

Building on, and also at times correcting Valla's findings, Pontano's explorations testify to the high level of semantic precision at which he aims. His semantic surveys take on an enhanced significance when he writes:[77]

> Both poets and writers about things human and natural add expression to things, and from this adding the words are called "adjectives," and with them they declare, explain, and even define [*finiunt*] properties and terms. For when they say that man is a rational, mortal animal, they define man himself and declare what his substance is. What about when poets speak of "peaceful rest," "bristling arms," and "fertile Ausonia" – aren't they indicating the quality of arms and rest and fields? And when they speak of "low-lying Italy," "extending fields," and "sloping hills," aren't they intimating the situation and position? And where they speak of "huge limbs" and "wide seas," what do they wish to designate if not the amplitude of the members and the magnitude of the sea? In the same way those who write about character need to define [*terminent*] our actions, which constitute character and virtues, by adding words.

Pontano's point is not the trivial or tautological one that we require words to describe the natural or human world. The underlying assumption is clearly that in marking the boundaries (*terminare*) of things (including human actions), words enable us to distinguish aspects of reality in the first place.[78] Only a full grasp of the nuances of words enables us to describe people's multifaceted experience of the world. Such a view is founded on

[75] On Pontano's indebtedness to Aristotle, see Luck 1958, and especially Roick 2017, 135: "Throughout his works, Pontano kept to the threefold scheme of middle, defect, and excess and corroborated it on a linguistic level by giving a name to those virtues and vices that Aristotle had not labelled." Cf. Lupi 1955, esp. 377. In *De sermone*, however, the triad of mean, excess, and deficiency is not always so clear; cf. Pigman in Pontano 2019, xiv.

[76] For example, ibid., 93 (1.28.11); 81 (1.26.1).

[77] Ibid., 65 (1.23.1); see Roick 2017, 82–91 and Marsh 1979, 111–115 on Pontano's emendations of some of Valla's grammatical observations.

[78] Pontano does not have the Aristotelian categories in mind, but it is worth noting that the passage seems to bring home a point that was central to Valla's reductive account of the nine accidental categories to quality and action. As we have seen in Chapter 2, for Valla there is no need to have separate categories apart from substance, quality, and action; words indicating position, relation, quantity, place, and time indicate a quality of a thing no less than quality-words such as "red" or "round" do. Grammatically, all these terms are adjectives indicating how a thing is qualified.

the belief – surely questionable – that an allegedly "impoverished" language lacking sufficient resources to make the subtle differences between, for example, different moral qualities or actions would easily lead to a blurring of such differences and distinctions.[79] For Pontano, a speaker who uses *arrogantia* for *ostentatio* or *verbositas* for *loquacitas* will find it difficult to make the conceptual distinction in the first place.

Conclusion

While critical of the man and some of his grammatical explanations, Pontano thus follows, to some extent, in the footsteps of Lorenzo Valla. His "Latin philosophy" is in its essential outlines the typically humanist program of a careful study of Latin vocabulary, grammar, and other aspects of the language, based on a wide reading of classical works. Semantic precision and elegant phrasing can be achieved only by delving into all this literature; only such a study can provide one with a full grasp of the norms of speaking and writing that the humanist wants to attain. For Pontano, as for Valla, common linguistic usage means Latin as used by classical authorities but, unlike Valla, Pontano is not overly preoccupied with arguing that Latin is a common language as opposed to the language of the schools. Since his interests do not lie in the Aristotelian Organon or Aristotelian-scholastic logic, we do not find arguments to the effect that scholastic Latin is not only ungrammatical but also unnatural, going against the way in which ordinary people speak and argue regardless of the language they use – a strategy that we found Valla using in his critique of the categories, the transcendental terms, the syllogism, and other fundamental tenets of Aristotelian philosophy.

This does not mean that Pontano would have disagreed with Valla's judgment of the allegedly abstract nature of scholastic language, and indeed Pontano duly criticizes the medieval translations of Aristotle's works and scholastic vocabulary, deploring, with Petrarch, Bruni, and other humanists, post-Boethian developments in the study of Latin, literature, and eloquence. But the constructive side of Pontano's "Latin philosophy" is much more developed than the destructive side, since his aim is to offer a reformulation of classical moral thought, based on a careful semantic inquiry into the meaning of terms. Without a detailed study of grammar in all its aspects we cannot attain the semantic precision that an analysis of the virtues and reason requires. The study of grammar is

[79] See Nauta 2006b, and Chapter 8, n. 51.

therefore not an antiquarian exercise but serves the goal of providing his contemporaries with an updated version of Aristotelian virtue ethics, brought from Athens to Naples, from classical antiquity to the fifteenth-century court and society. In this respect, Pontano's "Latin philosophy" is not only a grammatical study of semantic discriminations but also a practical program of understanding and, accordingly, acting on the lessons to be learned from Aristotle, Cicero, and other classical authorities. To act virtuously, prudently, and rationally, or to speak wittily, we must first learn to distinguish and categorize various types of moral behavior both in acting and speech, but we can make such conceptual categorizations only if we have learned the semantically rich resources of the Latin language – "its proper and purely Roman vocabulary."[80] Petrarch had complained about the distinctions which Aristotle thought were needed to analyze the virtues: "I see how brilliantly he defines and distinguishes virtue, and how shrewdly he analyzes it together with the properties of vice and virtue. Having learned this, I know slightly more than I did before."[81] This is not Pontano's perspective: we know definitively more after having made the necessary distinctions. As masters of the distinction, the scholastics would agree of course, but they would not see these distinctions as crucially embedded in the "common usage" of the ancient authorities. Such an intrinsic connection between the semantic resources of Latin and the analysis of moral concepts was a conviction so deeply ingrained in the humanist mind that it was almost impossible to question it, in particular when faced with the medieval translations that, in the eyes of Bruni and his followers, had badly translated Greek terms, conflated terms, or left words untranslated. But it was a conviction that gradually became less and less self-evident, in spite of the humanist defense of Latin as the language of culture, the arts, and sciences. Glimpses of this can be detected in the work of the humanist Juan Luis Vives, the subject of the next chapter.

[80] See above n. 63. [81] Petrarch 2003, 315 (*On His Own Ignorance* IV); see Chapter 1.

CHAPTER 4

Juan Luis Vives on Language, Knowledge, and the Topics

Introduction

Friend of Erasmus and Thomas More, the Spanish humanist Juan Luis Vives (1492–1540) was a prominent voice in sixteenth-century debates between humanists and scholastics on language and learning . Though he had harsh words to say about Lorenzo Valla, whom he accuses of having made many errors in dialectic and philosophy, and even "in the rules of the Latin language,"[1] Vives was clearly indebted to Valla, taking up several themes we have already met in the latter's work: the importance of common linguistic usage as the surest guide in speaking and writing; the crucial role of language in human society and culture, and in the acquisition of knowledge; the story of the downfall of the arts and sciences due to a neglect of linguistic and literary studies; scholastics as linguistic outcasts; the critique of the art of dialectic, and of the language of scholasticism in general. However, Vives developed these arguments in his own way as part of his program of educational and linguistic reform, laid down in his massive encyclopedia of the arts, *De disciplinis*, in twenty books, consisting of the treatise *On the Causes of the Corruption of the Arts* and a treatise on education, *De tradendis disciplinis*. This work was complemented by his youthful diatribe *Against the Pseudodialecticians*, a major treatise on rhetoric entitled *De ratione dicendi*, and a series of smaller treatises on rhetoric and dialectic. His arguments on common language, though clearly indebted to Valla, can be understood only against the background of his wider view of language, its origins and development, its functions, and its

[1] *De causis corruptarum artium* III, 7 (M III:151); Valla's arguments "neither rest on sound reasoning nor are they accepted by anyone as tenets of this art." Vives could also be positive on Valla; see the references in Waswo 1987, 121 n. 48. Unless otherwise stated all references are to Gregorio Mayans y Siscar's edition, J. L. Vives, *Opera Omnia* (8 vols., Valencia, 1782–1790; repr. London, 1964), henceforth abbreviated as M.

connection with thought and culture. In this chapter we will therefore have to zoom out, examining Vives's positions on these themes and assessing their originality and place in the more long-term developments with which this study deals. Before we turn to Vives's ideas, we must briefly set this chapter in the context of scholarly debates on their originality.

Vives exercised considerable influence on his contemporaries and later Renaissance authors such as Ramus and Gassendi. He was read by authors such as Francisco Suárez, Francisco Sanches, and Descartes. According to Carlos Noreña, his impact on Scottish common-sense philosophy was considerable, as he was read and praised by Thomas Reid, Dugald Stewart, and William Hamilton. In the nineteenth century he received renewed attention as an educational theorist and as a critic of Aristotelianism from Ernest Renan, Wilhelm Dilthey, Pierre Duhem, Ernst Cassirer, and others.[2]

Modern scholars, however, have disagreed about the originality and significance of his contributions to the field of language studies. For some he is "one of the most original philosophers of language" of the Renaissance, who even comes close to anticipating modern logical achievements such as Bertrand Russell's type theory or John Lyons's semantics.[3] For others he is a timid, half-hearted follower of Lorenzo Valla, whose views on language and knowledge were congenial to Vives, yet apparently too radical for him to endorse.[4] Other scholars, too, agree that Vives was not very innovative in dialectics but nevertheless think that his work embodies "an original, unified and distinctively sixteenth-century account of the art of thinking and composition, articulated in a set of related moves," pointing especially to Vives's original observations on rhetorical topics such as style, decorum, emotional manipulation, and forms of writing.[5] And while historians of logic and medieval philosophy are generally negative about the contributions to dialectic by humanists such as Vives, who has thrown out "the good with the bad,"[6] historians of Renaissance humanism, on the other hand, have praised him for what they see as a radical break with scholasticism, and his insistence on the historical embeddedness of language and human culture.[7]

It is not surprising that scholars have interpreted Vives's position in different ways. Standing as he did between medieval and modern times, between old and new modes of thinking and writing, and living at a time

[2] Guerlac 1979, 2. Casini 2006, 16–18. Noreña 1970, 5 and 283.
[3] Coseriu 1971, 234 and 254; Brekle 1985, 109, n. 127. [4] Waswo 1987, 113–133.
[5] Mack 2008, 242. [6] Broadie 1993, 197. Cf. Kneale and Kneale 1962, 298–316.
[7] See several contributions to Fantazzi (ed.) 2008, with full bibliography; Del Nero 1991; Noreña 1970.

when Aristotelian scholasticism had come under attack but the new science and philosophy had not yet crystallized, it is only to be expected that we find a certain ambivalence between traditional and more innovative expressions of Vives's philosophical ideas. For instance, his formulations sometimes suggest a passive role for language, but the rhetorician in Vives realized that language can take on an active role, perhaps shaping the way we think, feel, and hence respond to the world. And while some of his formulations suggest a belief in a stable order of essences, independent of human categorization, other formulations seem to give priority to the shaping power of the human mind, governed by the topics (*loci*). At times Vives can sound like a realist, while he also sometimes endorses a nominalist position.

In this chapter we will locate these philosophical "tensions" against the background of his critique of what he regarded as the useless and misleading abstractions of scholastic-Aristotelian thought. As we will see, Vives follows Valla closely in believing that the scholastic metaphysical and logical apparatus, expressed in abstract and technical language, had blocked our view of the world of concrete individual things. For him linguistic and philosophical abstraction mutually reinforced each other, and his program of educational and linguistic reform, much inspired by classical rhetoric and his predecessors Valla and Rudolph Agricola (1444–1485), was aimed at clearing away what he (rightly or not) regarded as scholastic abstractions in order to return to the world of concrete things (*res*), described in a language that matches our experience of the world. Vives presents himself as a defender of "the common language," "the common speech which everyone uses," or "the common language and the common method of understanding," but, like Valla, he seems to exploit the ambiguous notion of "common, natural language," usually meaning Latin but sometimes also the natural language of the people versus the unnatural, artificial language of the scholastics. We will discuss and analyze such tensions as emerge from Vives's account in what follows.

From a more general point of view, Vives's ideas on language, knowledge, and the role which the topics play as organizing principles of knowledge, can be taken as an illustration of a wider trend that characterizes the period: a move away, often antimetaphysical in spirit, from the abstract and the general toward the concrete, the singular, and the empirical.[8]

[8] For example Kondylis 1990; Ogilvie 2006; Kessler 1979, 141–157.

Knowledge and Language as Functions of Man's Natural Condition

A central feature of Vives's views of language and knowledge is his insistence that they are functions of man's biological nature. In several places in his works Vives starts therefore with a brief sketch of the early origins of human civilization to show how acquisition of knowledge, and the development of language to communicate that knowledge, are grounded in people's natural condition, governed by the principle that they seek the good and avoid the harmful. From distinguishing harmful from beneficial food to the invention of crafts and arts, man's *ingenium* – as Vives stresses – was crucial in securing a safe place in a dangerous world and in building up social communities when humans left their caves. Though speaking here only of human beings, Vives generally follows common teaching that all living creatures have a natural inclination toward self-preservation, and that the emotions – in themselves neither good nor bad – play a vital role in avoiding the harmful and seeking the beneficial.[9] But it was man who was given a higher rational faculty by God, by which man was able to transcend the here and now, using reason to inquire into things, to gaze over past, present, and future, to "examine all things, to collect, to compare, and to roam through the universe of nature as if it were his own possessions."[10]

From these early beginnings man began to build up knowledge, and this gradual development of knowledge, crafts, the arts and sciences is a recurrent theme in Vives's works. Probably inspired by Aristotle's *Politics* and Cicero's *De inventione*, Vives then tells the story of socialization, from closely knit families to larger communities that started to build villages and cities, which required the introduction of laws and government. Obviously, speech is a crucial element in this story, also grounded in man's natural condition.[11] Without suggesting that human speech developed out of animal sounds, as Lucretius did in his *De rerum natura* (book V, 1028–1090), Vives does link the two together: man shares with animals the uttering of sounds for expressing feelings and desires (*motus quosdam animi et affectiones*), and some animals who live in communities such as bees and ants "emit signs (*signa*) somewhat similar to human speech."[12] These natural sounds are what grammarians traditionally called "interjections," and elsewhere Vives refers

[9] *De anima et vita* III (M III:422–436); a modern edition is Vives 1974. Cf. Noreña 1989; Casini 2006, 138–159.

[10] *De tradendis disciplinis* I, 1 (M VI:243; Vives 1971, 11; 2011, 3); cf. ibid. (VI:298, Vives 1971; 2011, 73).

[11] Ibid.; cf. *De causis corruptarum artium* IV, 1 (M VI:152: justice and language).

[12] *De ratione dicendi*, I, 1 (M II:93). For a modern edition, with Spanish translation, see Vives 2000.

to this category, stating that while sounds in animals are signs of their emotions, in man they are signs of their "entire mental life (*animi universi*): mind, imagination, emotions, intelligence and the will."[13]

Vives does not offer much speculation on the details of this gradual development from simple to more complicated forms of language, but he observes that languages naturally developed from simple to more complicated systems of signs:[14]

> By the help of speech, their minds, which had been hidden by concentration on bodily needs, began to reveal themselves; single words [*verba singula*] were attended to, then phrases and modes of speaking [*phrases ac loquendi modi*], as they were appropriate for use, i.e. as they were marked by public agreement of opinion, which is, as it were, what a mint is to current coin.

Primitive languages are thus characterized by a simple structure, being almost concatenations of nouns referring to concrete objects, without syncategorematic words such as "all," "if," "and," "unless," "only," and "except." They also generally lacked words that refer to grammatical and logical categories such as "noun," "verb," "syllable," and "syllogism," for which Vives uses the traditional name of secondary words (*secundaria*) or words of words (*nominum nomina*). Stylistic refinements were also not on the mind of early speakers: they spoke in a manner that was "rambling or disconnected (*dissolute*) nor did they connect parts of a sentence rhythmically (*alligabant numeris*)."[15] As the analogy between the early stage of mankind and that of an individual was never far away from such thinking, Vives too compares this early language with the language of children, who likewise do not yet make well-connected sentences; they use separate words for individual things, without having yet formed abstract concepts, nor do they use syncategorematic and higher-order words.[16]

How the process went on Vives does not tell. Like other humanists he recognizes different forms of Latin in antiquity and he suggests that "from Greek discourse came the Latin; from the Latin, the Italian, Spanish, French were derived," but knowledge of the earliest stages that preceded the Greek language was a field of speculation into which Vives did not

[13] *De anima et vita* II, 7 (M III:372) and *De censura veri* I (M III:143) where Vives adds that some interjections in Latin and Greek may transcend the level of purely natural sounds and may be regarded as parts of speech. Cf. Pontano, above Chapter 3, n. 14.

[14] *De tradendis disciplinis* I, 1 (M VI:245; Vives 1971, 14; 2011, 5–6); cf. Cicero, *De oratore* 2.38.159 (Cicero 1942, 1: 313); Quintilian, *Institutio oratoria* 1.6.3 (Quintilian 2001, 1:163).

[15] *De ratione dicendi* I, 6 (M II:116–117).

[16] *De censura veri* I (M III:144–145); *De anima et vita* II, 7 (M III:369–370; Vives 1974, 302); ibid., II, 8 (III:372; 312).

enter.[17] At one point in the *De tradendis disciplinis*, he refers to "that original language in which Adam attached the names to things" and to the diversity of languages as a punishment of sin, but this is an isolated remark and is not followed up by an attempt to trace words back to a pre-Babylonian language – an attempt that his contemporary Luther would have deemed fruitless anyway after the radical dispersion of languages after Babel.[18]

Usually, Vives emphasizes the natural growth of language, knowledge, culture, and the arts from their early origins to later times, and though he does not develop it explicitly, his view, not unlike Pontano's (studied in the previous chapter), is that the early rise of language must be located in the small communities of primitive people who started using groans, grunts, cries and other sounds for communicating their feelings, desires, and perhaps, at a higher level, their plans, beliefs, and ideas. Just as the acquisition of knowledge started as a necessary consequence of man's natural condition but developed gradually into systems of arts and sciences, so speech as something that is natural to us (*loqui naturale est nobis*) developed into systems of signs, governed by art and convention.[19]

Signification

It is this notion of convention that plays a central role in Vives's critique of the language of the late-medieval scholastics. But before we discuss this critique in more detail, we must briefly look at Vives's general remarks on *significatio*, a notion notoriously difficult to correlate with such modern notions as signification and meaning.[20] His account seems to vacillate between two different approaches: on the one hand, he repeatedly stresses that words derive their meaning from the usage of the linguistic community; on the other hand he defines *significatio* in terms of the relationship of

[17] *De ratione dicendi* I, 1 (M II: 95–96); *De tradendis disciplinis* III, 1 (M VI:300–301; Vives 1971, 94; 2011, 77) on derivation of languages. Cf. Valla who had stated that Italian, French, and Spanish "have a certain affinity," claiming that Spanish derived from Italian; Valla 1962, 1:388 (*Apologus* 2); Tavoni 1984, 272; Valla 1962, 1:29 (*Elegantiae* 1.29).

[18] *De tradendis disciplinis* III, 1 (M VI:299; Vives 1971, 92; 2011, 74). See Coseriu 1971, 238, rightly calling the passage a *Fremdkörper*. Luther, *In primum librum Mosis enarrationes*, f. 169, cited by Dubois 1970, 53.

[19] *De tradendis disciplinis* III, 1 (M VI:298; Vives 1971, 90; Watson's translation, unlike Del Nero's (Vives 2011, 73), overlooks the distinction between speech, which is natural, and language, which is an art: "loqui naturale est nobis, hanc vero linguam, aut illam artis").

[20] Ashworth 1981, 310. I will use these terms interchangeably. Vives himself talks of *significatio*, *sensus*, *notatio*, and so on without seemingly distinguishing between them. The same is true for Valla; see Nauta 2009, 311 n. 48 with references.

the word with the concept.[21] But for Vives there does not seem to be any incompatibility here. Speakers must conform to the linguistic practice of their society if they want to be understood; as a rule they cannot invent new words just by themselves or use existing words in wholly new ways, on pain of exclusion from their community. But this does not mean that the meaning of the word "tree" cannot be identified with the idea or concept *tree* that the speaker has in mind. Thus we find Vives adopting the traditional notion of signifying as "making a sign, that is, indicating something to someone,"[22] and a signifying word as "a common token by which people display (unfold) to others their thoughts (that is what they conceive in their minds): and so usage is the ruler of what is signified." Three aspects are involved: (a) signification is always a process which concerns a receiver; hence Vives states that "we cannot treat signification in the abstract but is always in respect to someone (*significare non vero simpliciter sumendum est aut universaliter, sed semper respectu et ratione alicuius*)." (b) The speaker's mind is involved since it is the speaker who uses a sign that stands for the idea he or she wants to communicate. And this immediately introduces a third aspect: (c) if communication is to be successful the word must be used in accordance with its common usage; a self-invented word or an existing word with a new meaning will result only in misunderstanding and miscommunication. Hence we find Vives repeatedly saying that usage is "the ruler of what is signified (*usus est dominus significatuum*)."[23]

A sign has thus a twofold function: it stands for an idea or concept (Vives does not develop this point) in the speaker's mind, and it is a common token by which communication of that idea becomes possible. Vives can thus write that the meaning of words "regards the mind" (*vocum significatio, hoc est notatio, animum spectat*), while usage – that is, knowing how these ideas are commonly expressed in the language of the community – is

[21] On late-scholastic ideas about signification see Ashworth 1981, 310–311; see also Spade 1982, 188. Waswo 1987, 122–130 sees a fundamental tension between a potentially radical view of the "cognitively constitutive function of language" and a traditional semantics according to which words refer to things or concepts.

[22] *De censura veri* I (M III:142). Cf. Ashworth 1981, 310: "By the late fifteenth and early sixteenth centuries the standard definition of *significare* was 'to represent something or some things or in some way to the cognitive power.'" Vives does not think there is a one-to-one correspondence between words and concepts. Criticizing the distinction between simple and complex concepts, he writes: "For our mind often understands composite words simply, and simple ones compositely" (*De causis corruptarum artium* III, 5; M VI:121).

[23] *De censura veri* I (M III:143).

essential for successful communication.[24] The fact that we can think of – and speak about – fictive things or things that no longer exist such as "Hector," "chimera," or "the Punic war" (Vives's examples) leads him to think that meaning "regards the mind, not things." Even though such a thing is not (or no longer) to be found in nature, "it survives in the mind and lives as long as it is understood by the intellect (*intelligentia*)." Vives does not make it clear whether this principle applies only to notions of which the thing does not exist or no longer exists, for he adds, rather confusingly, that "some words will be said to signify something that is only in the mind, other words [will be said to signify] what is in the nature of things."[25] Since Vives had just said that the signifying word is a token by which the speaker makes his or her notion clear to someone else, he seems to think that words do not directly refer to things but are tokens of what goes on inside the mind.

So while the word is a sign of the speaker's idea, it is of course not up to the speaker to choose or invent a word to express the idea. The three aspects mentioned above hang intrinsically together, preventing a solipsistic process of privately assigning meaning to words by an individual. Signs are always signs for someone within a particular social context: as examples Vives gives signs understood only by horses, or only by dogs; particular languages such as Spanish, Latin, and Greek, and some special languages, clearly governed by conventions or tacit mutual understanding (*conventu vel tacito consensu*), such as the speech used among blind people in Spain, among swindlers and crooks, among diplomats, or between individuals such as Cicero and Atticus.[26] While signifying (that is, standing for) the speaker's idea or concept, the word as sign must be used in accordance with the common usage of the community: the people's usage is the ruler (*dominus est usus populi*). That usage and conventions, which govern the meaning of words, are always conventions of a particular group or nation underlies his diatribe against the dialecticians of his time. When dialecticians defend their newly invented terminology by saying that "words take their meaning by convention," Vives answers: "Perfectly true, but still we must understand from whose will and convention they take their meaning. For Roman words do not mean what Parthians or Indians decide, nor do Parthian or Indian words take their meaning at the Romans' will, but

[24] *De censura veri* I (M III:143) for this and the following quotation. This dual aspect brings to mind Locke's theory, which will be the subject of Chapter 8. Vives's account, however, is too brief to make much of such a superficial similarity.

[25] For the late-scholastic debates on whether words signify words, things, or both, see Ashworth 1981.

[26] *De censura veri* I (M III:143).

Roman words from Roman authority and Parthian words from Parthian."[27] What counts as Roman authority or the common people, is however not a simple question for Vives to answer, as we will see now.

Linguistic Custom and Common Language: The Critique of the Scholastic Dialecticians

Vives uses the notion of linguistic custom to great polemical ends in his critique of scholastic dialectic and philosophy more generally. Having studied at the feet of scholastic dialecticians such as John Dullaert and Gaspar Lax in Paris, Vives had more knowledge of late-medieval developments of this art than his predecessors, but the majority of his points clearly remind us of Valla's criticisms.[28] They all boil down to the charge that late-medieval logicians, while using a semblance of Latin (*aliqua specie sermonis latini*),[29] do not follow the rules of that language – the common usage as testified by classical authors from antiquity – in writing, speaking, or in analyzing language and argumentation. In going against common linguistic usage, they completely ignore the conventions of the Latin community, inventing their own jargon or giving new meanings to old words, and more generally place themselves outside the community of people with common sense (*sensus communis*). The examples that must support this accusation often derive from late-medieval sources, though Vives often makes the examples more bizarre than they were, ignoring or simply rejecting their purpose, which was, namely to study terms, propositions and forms of argumentation in order to establish their properties, truth conditions, and rules of inference.[30] It is not only the abstract character of all these rules and distinctions that infuriates Vives but also the idea that these dialecticians, in his opinion, want to prescribe rules to a linguistic community to which, in fact, they themselves hardly belong.

In developing this critique, Vives often made the same points as Valla. These points include:[31] the idea that usage is more important than

[27] *Adversus Pseudodialecticos* (M III:47, Vives 1979, 67).

[28] For a brief account of Vives's early education at the College of Montaigu, see Guerlac 1979, 17–24.

[29] *Adversus Pseudodialecticos* (M III:41, Vives 1979, 55).

[30] See esp. *Adversus Pseudodialecticos* (M III:43–44, Vives 1979, 59–61); Broadie 1993, 197–206, shows that these apparently bizarre examples mentioned by Vives such as "A head no man has, but no man lacks a head" made perfectly good sense in the context of late-medieval logic.

[31] They can be found throughout *Adversus pseudodialecticos* and *De causis corruptarum artium* III. The latter work also contains Vives's criticisms of the Aristotelian corpus: the *Categories* belong to metaphysics (*prima philosophia*) (VI:337); the contents of *De interpretatione* belong to grammar (341); the *Prior Analytics* contains much superfluous material that is also useless for practical

grammar or reason (in the sense of a set of highly regular patterns of word formation); the revulsion against the use of letters in dialectic; the rejection of the standard routine of reducing every statement into subject, predicate, and copula ("Plato reads" into "Plato is reading"); the rejection of the unnatural order of some syllogistic modes, and the rejection of the elaborate refinements of supposition theory of terministic logic (ascent, descent, ampliations, restrictions, confused, and distributive, merely confused, mobile/immobile, and so on); a critique of the arbitrary restriction to certain words in logic and philosophy (e.g. transcendental terms, hypotheticals, exponibles, quantifiers such as "all" and "every"); the critique of words such as *incipit/desinit*; the admonition not to spend too much time on dialectic; the emphasis on the varieties among languages, for instance in the use of negatives; and the equivalence (in some contexts) of "impossible"/"never," "necessary"/"always," "possible"/"occasionally." Vives's harsh words about the quality of Valla's arguments, referred to at the start of this chapter, therefore ring somewhat insincere. But what is more interesting is to see the same tensions arising that we detected in Valla's account when it comes to the notions of common language, common sense, and the common people. Let us therefore look in more detail at how Vives builds up his case.

As said, the core of Vives's argument is that the dialecticians should adapt themselves to the established rules of the Latin language rather than inventing their own rules and terminology: "A dialectician should use words and propositions that no one can fail to understand who knows the language he speaks, Latin, or Greek, in Greek."[32] Vives thinks – rather implausibly – that even Aristotle had used a language that everybody used at that time. In words that would certainly not have found favor with Valla, he writes: "Aristotle did not define even the smallest rule in his entire dialectic so that it would not conform to the same meaning of Greek speech that scholars and children and women and all the common people used."[33] In fashioning his art of dialectic, Aristotle did not use a self-invented language but "the common Greek that all the people spoke."[34]

application (117–118); the doctrine of demonstration in the *Posterior Analytics* is rather useless (347); the *Topics* is not without merit but also without much practical use (349). In the end Vives praises Aristotle in moderate terms even though he does "not agree with him" (124).

[32] *Adversus pseudodialecticos* (M III:40, Vives 1979, 53).

[33] Ibid. (M III:53, Vives 1979, 79). For Valla's opinion on this, see Chapter 2, n. 17.

[34] Ibid. (M III:41): "ad vulgarem illum Graecum, quem totus populus loquebatur"; Vives 1979, 55; cf. *De causis corruptarum artium* III, 6 (M VI:141).

The dialecticians, however, did not follow Aristotle's example, and conjured up their own words:[35]

> if we all profess a Latin logic, words will have the meaning established by Latin practice and usage, not our own. It is unbecoming and foolish in Latin logic to use Getic or Sarmatian words, or not even those, but words belonging to no nation, which we have conjured up ourselves. Indeed, I should very much like to hear from these men: if they were to teach dialectic in Spanish or French, which is as feasible as in Latin or Greek, would they make up rules as they please rather than take them from the structure of the language itself?

The situation is even worse, for not only are these dialecticians not understood by the common people, they often do not even understand each other, because they disagree among themselves about their dialectical rules. Alluding to his teachers at the College of Montaigu in Paris where he had studied, he writes:[36]

> If I were to profess a Vivist logic, you a Fortist, he a Laxean and another a Dullardian one, it is certain that words would then mean to us whatever we please. But if we all profess a Latin logic, words will have the meanings established by Latin practice and usage, not our own.

Vives seems to think, then, that dialectic must follow the rules of the language in which it is formulated. To a modern logician this is a rather bizarre position, but for Vives dialectic was closely tied to language ("it concerns itself with speech"), setting rules, for example, for the use of the negative and quantity words like "all" and "some" – rules which according to him could only be gleaned from linguistic practice.[37] In any case, Vives thinks his conclusion that we should conform ourselves to "common use in speaking" (*usum loquendi communem*) is true no less for grammar than for dialectic and rhetoric: "For first there were the Latin and Greek languages, and then in these the rules of grammar, of rhetoric, of dialectic were observed; language was not twisted to adapt to them, but the rules followed the language and accommodated themselves to it."[38] The formulation of rules should follow from an observation of practice:

> We do not speak Latin in this manner because Latin grammar bids us to speak so, but on the contrary, grammar bids us to speak so because the

[35] Ibid. (M III:47, Vives 1979, 67).
[36] Ibid. (III:47, Vives 1979, 67); cf. III:5, Vives 1979, 76: "every man travels his own road wherever it leads, at his own pleasure, and thinks he has finally reached a glorious goal when he differs widely in every respect from everyone else . . . ."
[37] Ibid., 141 (Vives 1979, 133). [38] Ibid. (M III:41, Vives 1979, 55), also for the next quotation.

> Latins speak this way. The same holds true in rhetoric and dialectic, each of which depends upon the same language as grammar ... And so dialectic discovers what is true, or false, or probable in this common speech which everyone uses [*in hoc vulgari, et qui est omnium in ore sermo*].

Just as Aristotle's Greek is used by the "entire populace (*totus populus*)," so the Latin of the classical authors is a language that "everyone uses." This claim is of course only true if Vives restricts the notion of "populace" to the educated people who have mastered the Latin as canonized by Cicero and other authoritative writers. This however would make his argument against the scholastics much weaker, and his rhetoric of "all people" (*vulgus, populus, omnes homines*) seems to point to a much wider category, as the reference to the "free Roman people" suggests:[39]

> But if they would not be willing to accept rules from conventional discourse to teach logic in other languages, why do they want to exercise this tyranny over the language of the free Roman people, and force it to accept rules of speech from men as uncultivated and barbarian as themselves?

So while he clearly wants to establish the Latin of Cicero and other authoritative writers as the medium of learned communication through the ages, if it suits his polemical aims he is happy to broaden that category by talking about "all users," "the entire populace," and "the free Roman people," as if there were just one linguistic community. This indeed might have been his view, for elsewhere he states that Latin was learned "from popular usage" (*ex populi usu*): "the Latin tongue, formerly, as all others also, was learned from popular usage, but after the state [or city: *in civitate*] became corrupted, it began to be sought in the writers, those, that is, who wrote from the time when Cato was censor to the time when Hadrian was Emperor."[40] In his attacks on the language of the scholastics he is therefore happy to blur the distinction between popular usage and the learned Latin of the great authorities. And when he refers to other languages such as Spanish or French, he also seems to have a broad, all-inclusive scope of the entire linguistic community in mind: "I should very much like to hear from these men: if they were to teach dialectic in Spanish or French, which is as feasible as in Latin or Greek, would they make up the rules as they please rather than take them from the structure of the language itself?"[41]

[39] Ibid. (M III:47–48, Vives 1979, 67–69).

[40] *De tradendis disciplinis* III, 6 (M VI:325; Vives 1971, 132; Vives 2011, 108). Cf. Valla, 2012, 1:9 (*Dialectical Disputations* 1.proem.12).

[41] Ibid. (M III:47, Vives 1979, 67).

We find the same ambiguous scope of "the people" in the continuation of this passage. The scholastics used the notion of "rigor" to defend themselves. To the question of why they think they can depart from common usage, their answer is that they speak "rigorously" (*de rigore*): in making a distinction between "good," "common," or "everyday sense" and an "exact," "rigorous," or "philosophical" sense, they create room for themselves to uphold the truth of those of their claims (mainly in logic) that in everyday speech would be false, for example, "You are not a man," which might be true within a particular logical context, but false in daily, common usage. Vives thinks this self-acclaimed freedom is false; we have to follow the rules and conventions of the language we use:[42]

> Every language has its own appropriateness of speech, which the Greeks call *idioma*. Words have their own meaning, their own force, which the uneducated masses sometimes misuse. The better educated make some concessions to the common people in the use of language; among themselves they think and speak in a different manner, though not to any great extent and mostly on abstruse and philosophical subjects which the people would not be in a position to know as precisely as the philosophers understand them.

Vives thus admits that common, uneducated people sometimes misuse language, but in the examples from Cicero which he proceeds to quote, it becomes clear that there is nothing wrong with the claim of common people that, for instance, the vessel is empty, while strictly speaking this is not true (because it still contains air). Vives now thinks he can reply to the logicians with an explanation of what true rigor is:[43]

> it is plain that rigorously, that is in the true and real sense of the word, the sentence, "This vessel is empty," is false; and so is this one, "You wish something for no reason"; but in the everyday sense these are often true. This rigor, then, is an exact and inflexible pattern of speech . . . To state it more plainly, rigor is this very appropriateness, this distinct, innate, and genuine force, the right and true meaning of Latin discourse.

This Latin rigor can be learned only from good Latin authors. But in applying Cicero's distinction of the common manner of speaking and the philosophical manner to the notion of rigor, Vives seems to get himself into trouble. On the one hand he accepts the identification of rigor with good classical Latin (the common language, as he frequently calls it); on the other hand he identifies it with the true, real (philosophical) sense. And

[42] Ibid. (M III:48, Vives 1979, 69); cf. *De causis corruptarum artium* III, 6 (M III:142).

[43] Ibid. (M III:48, Vives 1979, 69); also used by Valla (see Chapter 2, n. 28); it derives from Cicero's *De Fato* 11.24 (Cicero 1942, 2:221).

while he first speaks of a misuse of language by the uneducated people, he then says that a sentence such as "the vessel is empty" is true in the everyday sense. Two issues seem to be conflated here: (a) the language of the common people (in the wide sense of everybody who follows the *idioma* of their language) versus the artificial, unnatural language of the logicians (who do not follow the *idioma* of that particular language); (b) the common manner of speaking (the common people who say "the vessel is empty") versus the more exact manner of speaking ("natural philosophers" who say "the vessel is not empty"). While the first issue turns on language, the second issue is language-independent.[44] Like Valla, Vives blurs these two senses of "the common people" (those who use *Latin* in a grammatically correct way and those who use language in a natural way) to make his point about what he sees as the unnatural, artificial nature of the language of his opponents.

This conflation makes it possible for Vives to criticize the scholastics for departing from common usage, while "the educated people" are allowed to use language in a different way from the common people, especially "on abstruse and philosophical subjects which the people would not be in a position to know as precisely as the philosophers understand them" (quoted above). In the first case, the issue concerns a particular language, Latin; in the second case, the issue seems to concern the broader issue of a slightly more exact way of speaking, though the Ciceronian example of the empty vessel can hardly count as an "abstruse subject."

Vives's attempt to redefine the notion of rigor as the *idioma* of a particular language – as "an exact and inflexible pattern of speech" – is also unsuccessful in another way: in his attempt to turn this notion against his opponents, Vives must stress the "rigorous" nature of good classical Latin, but this gives the misleading idea that linguistic usage was fixed once and for all, as if there had been no development of Latin in classical antiquity. Vives knows better of course, as his discussion of Latin in *De tradendis disciplinis* and *De ratione dicendi* shows.[45] But in spite of his recognition, not unique to him of course, that Latin had developed over the centuries, the primary role he sees for Latin is to be a storehouse of erudition and learning, and a shared international medium. Such a role requires stability and a certain fixed character and identity. Like Valla, Vives must try to reconcile two pictures of Latin: Latin as a timeless tool of

[44] On the distinction between the exact and common manner of speaking in Valla, see Chapter 2, n. 28.

[45] *De ratione dicendi* I, 2 (M II:95); *De tradendis disciplinis* III, 6 (M VI:325; Vives 1971, 132).

expression and communication, transcending boundaries of time and space, and Latin as a natural, historical phenomenon that evolved over time. Vives does not seem to feel any tension. For him Latin can be considered natural and "artificial" (from *ars*) at the same time: natural in the sense that it was a language in use by people for whom it was more or less their mother tongue; artificial in the sense that it is no longer anyone's mother tongue but an acquired language, an ideal distilled from the flux of time.

We may doubt, however, whether this would solve the tension. While the former aspect of Latin as a natural language is developed by treating Latin on a par with other languages such as French and Spanish – each with its own *idioma*, its own users, conventions, history, practices, and usage – the latter aspect of Latin as a timeless *ars* underscores the unique position of Latin vis-à-vis the vernacular languages, which do not have "the rigor" defined by Vives as "an exact and inflexible pattern of speech." To put it bluntly, the more Latin is treated on a par with the other languages – a strategy Vives pursues in his attacks on the so-called unnatural language of the scholastics – the less unique its position becomes, and the more difficult it might be to defend one particular version of it as canonical; and if one does select one version and christens that as canonical, might we not ask the same for French or Spanish? Which version of Spanish can be considered as an analogue to the common linguistic usage of the great Latin authors? If on the other hand we stress the sacramental nature of (one particular version of) Latin as a timeless instrument for higher learning, one loses this strategy of defending Latin as a common, natural language against one's opponents. This dilemma was created by the humanists themselves in their rejection of the scholastic language as something artificial and unnatural.

Functions and Purposes of Language

Vives's critique, however, was not limited to the Latin used by the scholastics. His educational and linguistic reform – shared by many of his humanist contemporaries – aimed at a thorough transformation of the language arts and of knowledge and science in general. It would be out of place here to try to discuss this program in any detail, but in view of the fact that the critique of language is part of a wider movement away from scholastic modes and thoughts, we will consider in what follows an important aspect of this program. Vives's views on argumentation. While not against traditional logical forms of argumentation, which he rather perfunctorily discussed, Vives believed that the art of argumentation should be based more closely on how people actually argue (or have argued), just as the analysis of language should be based on linguistic usage and practice. Invention of arguments is as important as judging their validity. A great source of inspiration was Rudolph Agricola, whose *De inventione dialectica* had brought together rhetoric and dialectic into one system of topical invention, thereby helping to bring about a pragmatic turn in dialectics. Agricola's work contains an innovative treatment of the topics and it also explores a whole range of issues concerning what we would now call communication and information. These ideas had a substantial impact on later thinkers including Vives, Erasmus, Latomus, Melanchthon, Ramus, and Nizolio, and Agricola's account of the topics was required reading for almost any sixteenth-century author of dialectic books. To understand Vives's contribution we need to take a few steps back, starting with a brief discussion of the functions and purposes that Vives assigns to language and argumentation, which will connect us to his epistemology, his view of the role of language and of the topics as seats of argumentation in expressing our knowledge of the world.

From the discussion so far we can distill a variety of functions that Vives assigns to language. Its main function is to be an instrument for thought, that is, an expression of what goes on inside the mind – a wholly traditional idea, of course. Without language our thoughts, "shut in by the grossness and density of the body," remain hidden.[46] To describe this primary function Vives employs several metaphors of a rather traditional kind: language as a river that flows from its source or as water from its fountain, that is, the mind; or words as the body, and thought as the soul and hence as the "life of words"; language as the seat (*sedes*) of thought or its "image" (*imago*), or its servant.[47] These metaphors suggest that the direction of influence is unilateral: words are used for expressing what has been thought out by the mind. Vives's views on signification, already discussed above, confirm this basic idea: "The signification of words, that is, the meaning, regards the mind."

But like Pontano, Vives realizes that language is not so much a neutral verbalization but exercises considerable influence on our mental life, indeed on all aspects of life: "No course of life whatever, and no human

[46] *De tradendis disciplinis* III, 1 (M VI:298; Vives 1971, 90).

[47] For example *De ratione dicendi* I,1; II,1; III, 12 (M II:94, 130, 236); *De anima et vita* II, 7 (M III:371; Vives 1974, 308). *De tradendis disciplinis* III, 1 (M VI:298; Vives 1971, 90; 2011, 73). Cf. Pontano as discussed in Chapter 3.

activity can continue without speech."[48] In words that echo ancient rhetoricians but also contemporary humanists such as Agricola and Giovanni Pontano, Vives writes that "emotions of the mind are enflamed by the sparks of speech, and so too reason is impelled and moved by speech," and thus "in the whole kingdom of the activities of man, speech holds in its possession a mighty strength which it continually manifests." The power of language also affects our judgment: "It should have the capacity to explain most aptly what they think. By its means much power of judgment should be developed." Language is therefore not the neutral instrument that some traditional metaphors suggest (such as a servant that serves reason as its master, or as clothing for the body) but can "leave stings in the minds of the audience (*in animis audientium*)." Language can be an active, shaping force on our mental and emotional life.[49]

From the perspective of the community, language is not just the expression of the thoughts of an individual but the social bond that ties people together. As a humanist with a more than solid grounding in ancient rhetoric, Vives frequently underscores the social as well as the socializing effect of language as praised, for example, by Cicero. The close link between language and civilization is a running theme throughout Vives's *De disciplinis* (and in humanist thought generally), which also voices the typically humanist sentiment that ignorance and corruption of the Latin language is an important cause of the downfall of the arts and sciences in the postclassical era. But while the *De disciplinis* focuses on Latin as the storehouse of learning and language of the Church, Vives realizes full well that the socializing effects of language are marked features of any language, even of what he regards as the gibberish of his scholastic teachers in Paris, whose identity as a social group is formed by the bond of their technical terminology. Hence, his treatise on rhetoric is introduced not as a work on Latin rhetoric but on rules for effective and sound communication in any language (*non unius modo vel alterius linguae sed in commune omnium*), even though obviously Latin is his model and source of inspiration and examples.[50]

[48] *De tradendis disciplinis* IV, 3 (M VI:356; Vives 1971, 181; 2011, 155). Next quotations IV, 3 and III, 1 (M VI:356 and 298; Vives 1971, 180, 91; 2011, 154–155; 74).

[49] *De ratione dicendi* II, 5 (M II: 146). Cf. Cicero, *De oratore* 1.8.30–33; 3.14.53 (Cicero 1942, 1:23–25, and 2:43). For Vives on emotions, see n. 9 and 13. Language can of course also hurt and harm, as Vives was well aware (III, 12; M II:237: language should obey our mind rather than our emotions). Cf. also *De tradendis disciplinis* IV, 3 (M VI:357, Vives 1971, 181). Such metaphors as vessel/content and clothing/body were frequently used to indicate the relationship between words and things; see, for example, Pontano, Chapter 3, n. 27, or Erasmus at various places in his work.

[50] *De ratione dicendi* II, 2 (M II:94). Cf. Pontano, whose aim in *De sermone* is to deal with common speech (*oratio communis*) rather than formal oratory and rhetoric. See Chapter 3, n. 32.

For Vives the notion of language as *instrumentum societatis humanae* implies that we get to know a culture and its learned traditions by studying its language, and this gives us a third purpose of language. Language is the gate to the treasury (*sacrarium*) of culture and learning, hence students should "gain as much of the language as will enable them to penetrate to those facts and ideas, which are contained in these languages, like beautiful and valuable things are locked up in treasuries."[51] Vives does not develop this insight in any anthropological way, let alone arrives at a notion of linguistic relativism, yet he often refers to the fact, well known to translators, that every language has "its own appropriateness of speech, called *idioma* by the Greeks"[52] not to mention its own meaning and charm (*vis et gratia*); and that languages obviously have their own rules, customs and conventions, for example in the use of negatives, in the composition of words, and in countless other linguistic phenomena.[53] Vives's view of language as a social binding force is the background of his emphasis on linguistic custom, and we have seen him developing this point in his critique of scholastic language.

We should of course not distinguish too sharply between these functions of language – language as expression of thought, as instrument of the social bond, as treasure house of learning and culture – as for Vives these are clearly aspects of one and the same picture. This picture he elucidates in *De ratione dicendi* by analyzing four purposes of speech, namely to explain, to prove, to move, and to please, derived from the classical three aims: to teach, to move, and to please.[54] Interestingly, these functions of language are presented as a consequence of man's postlapsarian condition. In the pristine, ideal situation about which Vives remains vague, communication was a completely transparent process: speakers expressed themselves in the clearest terms, listeners understood them perfectly, and there was no weak link nor manipulation or deceit in the communication of thoughts.[55] In the pristine situation, the natural purpose of this God-given gift was just to express one's thought. The "natural purpose" (*naturalis finis*) of language, then, is explanation. But "explanation no longer sufficed" after sin (*delictum*) had darkened the human mind, and proving and persuading became

[51] *De tradendis disciplinis* III, 1 and IV, 1 (M VI:298 and 345, Vives 1971, 91 and 163; 2011, 74, 139).

[52] *In Pseudodialecticos* (M III:48; Vives 1979, 68).

[53] *De causis corruptarum artium* III, 6 (M VI:143); *In Pseudodialecticos* (M III:47, Vives 1979, 67). In *De tradendis disciplinis* he writes that the study of rhetoric should include "a general account of philology; in what manner languages arose, developed and decayed; how the power, nature, riches, elegance, dignity, beauty and other special virtues for discourse of each language should be estimated" (Vives 1971, 183).

[54] *De ratione dicendi* II, 11–15 (M II:155–158).

[55] *De ratione dicendi*, II, 11 (M II:156).

necessary tools as ignorance, deceit, partisanship, and confusion entered human relations. But this does not mean that for Vives language is a necessary evil: it can be used for evil purposes, but just as the emotions are neutral in themselves (*neutri*), so language too is something that can be used in evil and good ways – a traditional defense of rhetoric that dated back to antiquity.[56] Indeed, the ideal situation seems just that: an ideal, almost hypothetical situation, as humans are not spiritual angels that can just read each other's minds. This means that even more moral weight is put on the use of language than is usually done, language being a vital element in the moral education of children: just as human behavior should be ruled by reasonableness, prudence, modesty, piety, a love for truth, and a regard for the social and moral well-being of fellow humans, so the use of language should be geared to these ends and exercised by the same virtues.[57]

So in itself (*in re ipsa*) language has just one purpose – to explain – but related to us (*nostri*) three: "to prove, to move and to keep the attention of the audience (*pascere*) by speech."[58] Inspired by Agricola, Vives divides explanation into teaching and proving, describing these functions in terms often derived from Agricola, whose work he knew well.[59] Just like Agricola, Vives has a keen eye for all the elements that go into effective communication: "we have to consider the personality of the speaker and of the listener, and the nature of the particular business in hand, to decide what are the means suitable to produce a particular effect in relation to a particular place and time, having regard to the particular speaker and listener."[60] This is true for any kind of situation, but in particular in the case of the emotional appeal of a speech:[61]

> Before everything else we must consider who we are and who are the people whose emotions we wish to arouse or placate, what is their judgment of the matter in question, what do they value greatly, what very little, which emotions are they liable to, which immune from, out of which emotions do they move easily to which ones . . . We must put on their mind and their whole character while we are thinking about what would benefit our case and we must put ourselves in their place, that is, we must consider diligently,

[56] Cf. *De tradendis disciplinis* IV, 3 (M VI:357, Vives 1971, 181; 2011, 155). On emotions being "neutral" (*neutri*), see *De ratione dicendi* II, 11 (M II:156).
[57] *De causis corruptarum artium* IV, 1 (M VI:152).
[58] *De ratione dicendi* II, 11 (M II:157); cf. *De tradendis disciplinis* IV, 3 (M VI:357; Vives 1971, 181; 2011, 155).
[59] For Vives's debt to Agricola, see Mack 1993, 314–319.
[60] *De tradendis disciplinis* IV, 3 (M VI:357, Vives 1971, 182; 2011, 155).
[61] *De ratione dicendi* II, 60 (M II:165–166); trans. in Mack 2005, 81.

> supposing we were them, that is, if we have the same convictions about things as them, by what means we would now be moved (or placated) in the present business. This act of imagining [*phantasia*] is wonderfully adapted for finding out what we must do.

Like humanists such as Agricola and Pontano, Vives develops here ideas that were pivotal elements in ancient rhetoric. The psychological mechanism by which we can recognize mutual emotions and hence can put ourselves in someone else's place was well known to ancient orators and philosophers.[62] Vives's observations are acute here, testifying to his great sensitivity to the varied use of language depending on context.

The Order of Knowing and the Order of the World

But while moving and persuading are important in contexts where a speaker wants to get his or her audience to believe, accept, or deny a position, explaining is important in many other contexts where we just want to make ourselves understood without aiming primarily to create belief in an audience: "the aim of this kind of speech is to be understood: of the speaker truly to explain what he conceives in his mind and convey to the hearer."[63] This might suggest a rather unproblematic correspondence between man's cognitive powers, finely adapted to their function, and the world that man has to get to know. But Vives's optimism about the cognitive process is at times qualified by his belief that postlapsarian man cannot know the true essences of things. Before we can discuss Vives's solution to bridging the gap between the essential structure of the world and the human mind, we must therefore briefly look at his epistemology, which is a natural outcome of his view of the early origins of man's cognitive powers.

Vives accepts the Aristotelian picture of knowledge-acquisition as a combination of sense perception and reason: based on a careful and repeated observation of a whole range of phenomena, reason has to make an inductive step from these observations to general conclusions:[64]

> In the beginning, first one, then another experience, through wonder at its novelty, was noted down for use in life; from a number of separate experiments the mind gathered a universal law, which, after support and confirmation by many experiments was considered certain and established.

[62] Cicero 1942, 2:179 (*De oratore* 3.59.223); cf. 2.44.189–190; Quintilian, *Institutio oratoria* 6.2.26 (Quintilian 2001, 3:59). For Pontano, see Chapter 3, n. 33.

[63] *De ratione dicendi* II, 47 (M II:158); trans. in Mack 2005, 80.

[64] *De tradendis disciplinis* I, 2 (M VI:250, Vives 1971, 20; 2011, 11).

But if the experiments (that is, observations) do not agree with the general pattern or rule, we (or later generations) should continue the search:[65]

> in teaching the arts, we shall collect many experiments and observe the experience of many teachers, so that from them general rules may be formed. If some of the experiments do not agree with the rule, then the reason why this happens must be noted down. If there are more deviations than agreements or an equal number, a dogma must not be established from the fact, but the facts must be transmitted to the astonishment of posterity, so that from astonishment . . . philosophy may grow.

As already noted, Vives thinks the growth of knowledge is the result of a natural, inborn inclination of man to seek out the beneficial and avoid the harmful. This principle also explains why we have an inborn sense of good and bad, and an inner conscience that praises and blames ourselves and others, and why all people have a notion of a god (*Deum esse*).[66] Indeed the mind has a "natural kinship," also called "affinity," "friendship," or "affection," with "the first principles from which, as from seeds, other truths proceed."[67]

This Stoic notion of innateness, popularized for instance by Boethius in his *Consolation of Philosophy*, had always been a good answer to the Platonic idea that knowledge is recollection of things that the soul already knew before birth. But this optimism is toned down by Vives's Christian picture of fallen man. Though duly invoking the prelapsarian condition of man in which perfect knowledge was possible, Vives does not elaborate on it, and seems to regard the fallen condition of man as a given, that is, as the natural situation in which we find ourselves. This condition sets limits to what we can know, and Vives repeatedly states that we cannot know the inner essences of things but only sensible qualities. In his early *De initiis, sectis et laudibus philosophiae* from 1518, he writes, for instance, that the New Academy under leadership of Lacydes and Carneades argued "that things could not be understood and accordingly that nobody could rightly affirm or know anything, both because of the inherent difficulty of the things being studied and because of the frailty and obscurity of the human mind."[68] Like his predecessor Agricola, who thought that there are many things about which we do not have certainty, Vives thinks that we can reach only probable knowledge: "What knowledge we have gained can

[65] *De tradendis disciplinis* II, 4 (M VI:296, Vives 1971, 87–88; 2011, 70).
[66] *De prima philosophia* I (M III:186).
[67] *De instrumento probabilitatis* (M III:82); Mack 2008, 245; Noreña 1970, 249; Casini 2006, 40–41, referring to Cicero, *Academica* II.31 and *De natura deorum* III.17.
[68] Vives 1987, 39; *De prima philosophia* I (M III:194); cf. Casini 2006, 36.

only be reckoned as probable and not assumed as absolutely true."[69] In short, knowledge of essences is at best a well-informed guess or conjecture on the basis of sense perception, and at worst a sheer impossibility. Investigations of nature can never result in indubitable knowledge and absolute certainty but are always approximations, the quality of which depends on our data and our reasoning process.

How far does this skeptical sentiment go? Here we come to an important theme in Vives's thought. Is there such an order of essences "deep down," unavailable for the human mind, or is the order as we see it all there is? If the human mind can reach no deeper than the outer surface of what we see, it seems to follow that reality is dependent on our epistemic categorizations. And indeed we find Vives frequently stating – in line, again, with Valla – that knowledge is always dependent on how we see things and think about them, and on how we judge things to be; how things are in themselves we cannot know.[70]

Topics as a Bridge Between Mind and Reality

However, our epistemic categories cannot simply be of our own making; they must ultimately be grounded in reality. Here is where the topics come in. Because Vives's treatment of the topics can be regarded as an illustration of wider trends, here discussed under the umbrella of a critique of language and argumentation, we will end this chapter by looking at his discussion of this important theme. The topics, as we know, were a set of places (*loci*) such as definition, genus, species, place, time, whole/part, and so on, for inventing arguments. They had a long and complicated history behind them when Agricola composed his *De inventione dialectica* in the late 1470s (published posthumously only in 1515). While his direct predecessor Lorenzo Valla had been content to give a long extract from Quintilian's account on the use of the topics in oratory, Agricola renewed the field by organizing the rhetorical and dialectical sets into one system of topical invention, based on the lists of Cicero and Boethius (who had used that of the Aristotelian Themistius).[71] Agricola thus departed from Boethius, who

[69] *De tradendis disciplinis* IV, 1 (M VI:347–348, Vives 1971, 166–167; 2011, 142), but in *De prima philosophia* Vives rejects Protagorean relativism (M III:194). Agricola, *De inventione dialectica*, with Alardus's commentary (Agricola 1539; repr. Nieuwkoop, 1967), 2.

[70] *De prima philosophia* I (M III:194): "ex sententia animi nostri censemus, non ex rebus ipsis"; cf. Valla's *Dialectical Disputations*, in Valla 2012, 1:32–34; cf. Nauta 2009, 68–71 on Valla's position on truth, knowledge, and belief.

[71] Mack 1993, 117–167; Cogan 1984, 163–194; Moss 1996, 77–80. For Quintilian's account, see *Institutio oratoria* 5.10.94; Valla 2012, 2:163–207.

had emphasized the difference between rhetoric and dialectic, each with its own system of topics, and returned to Cicero's more flexible, pragmatic use of the topics. For Agricola the topics formed a logic of inquiry rather than a system in which the topics as universal propositions should guarantee the validity of assertions made in an argument. The differences between Agricola and late-medieval logicians, which cannot be discussed in detail here, are therefore considerable: in Agricola there is no attempt to reduce topical argument to syllogisms (though the force of the syllogism remains an ideal even for informal arguments[72]) in the way in which, for example, William of Sherwood and Peter of Spain tried to do, nor do we find a theory of consequences of a late-terminist kind (as we find, e.g. in Ockham). Indeed, Agricola rejects Boethius's topical maxims, whereas these maxims, whose function it was to lend power to syllogisms or to complete imperfect syllogisms, formed an important ingredient in medieval dialectic.[73] From the treatments of Cicero, Quintilian, Boethius, and others, Agricola built his own system, geared toward finding effective arguments and laying bare the argumentative structure of texts. It thus enabled the student to organize any type of discourse and analyze texts in terms of underlying questions and argumentative structure. The vast impact of the *De inventione dialectica* is telling evidence of changing intellectual circumstances in the sixteenth century.[74]

For both Agricola and Vives the topics were thus primarily labels for arguments that we can use concerning a particular subject matter.[75] But the topics as labels of arguments are derived from a consideration of things and the aspects they have in common such as substance, quality, action, cause, and effect; indeed many of the topics are presented as reflecting the things themselves. Agricola's topics, for instance, are divided into "internal" topics, which are "within the substance of a thing" (e.g. genus, species, property/ difference, whole, part) or "bring a certain manner or disposition to it" (adjacents, actions, subject); and "external" topics, which refer to "necessarily joined aspects" (e.g. causes, effects, place, time), or "accidents which can exist with or without a thing" (e.g. contingents, similar/dissimilars) and those that are joined to the thing "without necessity" (e.g. opposites). Topics thus refer

[72] Mack 1993, 141–142.

[73] See Bird 1962, 307–323, on 313. Stump 1989, 135–156 (terminist logicians, esp. Peter of Spain), 253–258 (Ockham). For Boethius's theory, see Stump's translations with studies: Boethius 1978 and 1988; Green-Pedersen 1984, 330 writes that "probably we must credit Agricola with a rather original achievement," but his conclusion that "Agricola is thinking in terms of rhetoric and not logic when he writes about dialectic" must hence be qualified.

[74] Mack 1993, 257–374.

[75] Vives, *De instrumento probabilitatis* (M III, 86–115).

to aspects of a thing or describe aspects "around" it; they show us the way "into the nature of things," or even "the intimate and hidden nature of things."[76] As Peter Mack writes: Agricola seems to believe that "connections between the terms of propositions" are grounded in "similar connections really existing in the world": "The implication that the connections named by the topics exist in the world appears to suit some topics (such as causes) better than others (such as similitudes)."[77] We might expect therefore to find a rather fluid transition from speaking about the world to speaking about the human mind that notices common aspects of things. Indeed Agricola's formulations sometimes show such a fluid transition from speaking about the things themselves to the topics that are based on them; genus and species, for example, are more than just concepts or general headings under which to review a thing or case; they seem real aspects of that thing. Agricola also talks frequently about "the nature of things" or "the inner essence of a thing," even though, as he admits, this often eludes us: the true nature of things often "remains hidden from us," and hence arguments directly based on the substance or causes of things are often very hard to find.[78]

What Vives learned from Agricola (and the Ciceronian–Boethian tradition on which the latter was standing) was to see the topics not just as places of argumentation but as grounded in reality, though this applied to some topics more directly than others. We can see this bridge-function at work in his treatises that deal with the topics: *De instrumento probabilitatis* on topical invention, and a neglected but interesting treatise on the predicables and definition, entitled *De explanatione cuiusque essentiae*. In these works Vives explains how the topics are the material that brings order into our investigations by collecting and noticing what things have in common. The investigation into this method of inquiry (*ratio inquirendi*) is the invention and disposition of topics (*ars de inveniendo*).[79] In *De explanatione cuiusque essentiae* he starts with a metaphor of nature as a pharmacist – a metaphor that we find being used also in other contexts:

[76] Agricola 1539, 22–24; 72, 93, 146 (*De inventione dialectica*); cf. ibid., 24 where Agricola writes that his treatment of the topics follows the "nature and order of things." A similar position is defended by Ramus, on whom see Patey 1984, 22.

[77] Mack 1993, 140–141. For Agricola's view see also Nauta 2012b.

[78] Ibid., 171; cf. ibid., 44 for an apparently fluid transition from topics as saying something about real aspects of things to topics as signs. Agricola stresses the limits of human understanding, e.g. in ibid., 2 (Academy), 26 (lack of true differentiae), 35 (idem), 43 (difficulty of finding true differentiae), 72, 163, 207 (Academy). Mack 1993, 177–181 argues that Agricola was not a sceptic, at least not in the strict sense, "in that, although he believed that most things are not certain, for him the *probabile* included the certain," *pace* Jardine 1977, 143–163.

[79] *De instrumento probabilitatis* (M III, 86).

just as a pharmacist or a perfumer who has a box full of phials, flasks, and bottles with labels attached to them describing what they contain, so nature "divides everything in small boxes (*pixides*) as it were with a name attached to them, what they have in common: man, horse, adamant, pear, whiteness, blackness, virtue, vice."[80] Changing the metaphor, Vives then compares nature with a city. Just as there are families living in a big city, so things that belong together (apples, horses) can be distinguished in nature. We group things together on the basis of their similarity: "this essential similitude is called a universal in the schools (*in schola*)."[81] While Vives follows common tradition, it is significant that he uses the same metaphor of the pharmacist's or perfumer's classification in *De instrumento probabilitatis*, but this time in order to refer to the topics rather than to the things themselves: it is now the topics that are compared with labeled phials and bottles.[82] Though the use of the same metaphor might suggest an identification between topics and the real aspects of things, this is of course not Vives's intention. But because the topics as labels or headings under which we are invited to view and discuss things are based on their common aspects as noticed by the mind (e.g. essence, quality, cause, effect, and so on), the association of things and topics facilitates an easy transition from reality to the mind. Hence, the topics can be seen to some extent as a reflection of the ontological order and, as such, an instrument and heuristic aid for the human mind. In searching for similitudes between things, the mind detects common patterns on the basis of which it groups things in categories. This is of course essential for argumentation, as Boethius had already taught: to argue – to put it in its most rudimentary form – that A is B (or not B) requires listing features of A and features of B, and comparing the lists, finding a medium between A and B. Arguments thus connect what is known with what is in doubt and needs proof. The same list of topics can be used in every art and science, and be of use to a lawyer, physician, mathematician, or orator.[83]

This transition from the order of being to the order of knowing is perhaps eased by Vives's ambiguous use of the traditional word "similitude," an ambiguity that we find in his predecessor Agricola as well, and

80 *De explanatione cuiusque essentiae* (M III:121). In Konrad Gesner we find the same image (and many other ones) to illustrate the commonplace book as systematic storage: "an apothecary's shop with medicinal ingredients neatly stowed in separate containers" (Moss 1996, 191).

81 *De explanatione cuiusque essentiae* (M III:121).

82 *De instrumento probabilitatis* (M III:86). Cf. *De causis corruptarum artium* III, 3 (M III:120: "pixidum indices").

83 *De instrumento probabilitatis* (M III:86); on argument as a medium of argumentation see Agricola 1539, 7–8 (*De inventione dialectica*).

also, arguably, in many thinkers who were indebted to the classical account by Boethius. In Boethius's discussion, universals seem to have a double existence: they exist both in particular things and as concepts in our mind.[84] The mind abstracts doghood after observing many dogs, noticing the similitude between them, and forming the concept of doghood. The concept would be null and void if there were nothing in extramental reality that corresponded to that concept. But Boethius does not want to give up the Aristotelian principle that primary, particular substances are the building blocks of reality. Hence, universals must be said to be particular as sensed in particular things – they might be identified with the "likenesses" between things – but universal as grasped in thought.

Vives's position comes close to the Boethian account but is probably directly indebted to Agricola. Thus, on the one hand Vives, following tradition, equates similitudes with the inner essences of things, calling them "universals," and saying that similitudes between things exist in reality, independent of our thinking and linguistic expression (*extra nomina atque intelligentias nostras*) "since the similitude is in the things themselves, or rather the things themselves are similar and conforming to each other."[85] This similitude can be called a "nature, manner, reason, form, or sign (*natura seu conditio seu ratio seu forma seu nota*)" and "genus for wider groups and species for smaller more limited groups." On the other hand, similitude also refers to what these essences, unknown to the human mind, effect at the level of what *is* visible and knowable to the human mind: qualities and actions. The similarities are what things have in common, and these common features are ultimately caused by the inner essences.

Now for Vives this noticing of similarities is aided and structured by the topics. The topics as "common headings" refer to the common condition of things: each thing belongs a certain genus, has a certain substance, is caused by something, has a certain effect, is at a certain place, and so on. Thus, although the nature of individual things eludes us, we can observe the similarities and disagreements between things: "there is nothing in nature which is not joined to something else by the bond of comparison (*similitudinis nodo*)."[86] Inspired by Agricola, Vives thus sees the topics as a set of universal aspects of things that help to bring order to the immense variety of nature. But he is also taking over a certain ambiguity from

[84] For a convenient text see Spade 1994, 20–25; cf. Marenbon 2003, 23–32.

[85] *De explanatione* (M III:124): " . . . genus hoc aut species non modo in nominibus vel nostris intelligentiis est situm, sed in natura rerum est ea similitudo ac communio, etiam extra nomina atque intelligentias nostras; est enim in ipsis rebus seu potius res ipsae similes conformesque."

[86] *De instrumento probabilitatis* (M III:104).

Agricola's account, an account that he had helped to edit after Agricola's death:[87] topics are based on the condition of things, yet they are not identical with them. The genus animal in a horse, for instance, is not identical with the topic *genus* that has led the mind to look for the type of genus in that horse to be used in argument. The yellowness that two things have in common is not the same as the topic of *contingent* that has led the mind to look for common accidents in these things. This close connection between topics and things is also what causes the ambiguity in Vives's account: as similitudes, topics are called the essences of things while they are also the set of categories that organize the features we see.

It is now possible to understand why modern scholars have found it difficult to characterize Vives's ontological position. On the one hand, he admits that the agreements between things must be based on something that is independent of human thinking and linguistic expression, "since the similitude is in the things themselves, or rather the things themselves are similar and conforming to each other"; species and genus are not dependent on our categorization.[88] As we have seen, Vives often speaks in terms of essences as hidden cores or natures of things. But he also states that the world consists of individual substances and individual accidents, and that generality in nature can be defined only in terms of what we see as common elements in different things. In his *Against the Pseudodialecticians*, he criticizes realists for confusing the metaphysical and the physical order, and in the *De anima et vita* he also seems to side explicitly with the nominalists when he writes that "there is no universal in the imagination nor in nature; but it is only attained through discursive reason (*ratione discurrente*) under a very confused and very thin image when the mind strips itself off, as best as it can, from the attributes of fantasy."[89] Thus universal concepts are formed after careful and repeated observation, guided by the grid of the topics, and yet they have a foundation in reality. But this does not mean that the essence of a thing must be a "common" entity as if one and the same form doghood were instantiated in many individual dogs. The dog Bello has a unique essence that – through its effects in sensible qualities and actions – can be grouped together with the dog Freddie, which has its own singular essence revealing qualities and actions similar to those of Bello. Such a position comes close to the Boethian account, which was certainly not without its own ambiguities.

[87] See Alardus's statement in the preface to Agricola's little treatise on universals, in Agricola 1539, 36. On the ambiguity in Agricola, see Nauta 2012b, 213.

[88] *De explanatione* (M III:124): "non modo in nominibus vel nostris intelligentiis."

[89] *De anima et vita* II, 1 (M III:344; Vives 1974, 222); cf. Casini 2006, 22–23.

The topics thus aid us in categorizing things or aspects of things, but – to add a further layer – they are also used by Vives to suggest a division of *words*: the way in which we carve up reality is reflected by a division of words (*distinctio nominum*), for example, words taken from the essence such as "man," and "rationable"; words pointing to qualities such as "whiteness" and "blackness," and so on. Vives realizes that the immense variety of words does not allow for any neat categorization. It might not be impossible to put things "in certain boxes" or "assign to them certain seats" (*in certas sedes tribuere*), but with words this does seem impossible, given "the immense variety of words and languages."[90] Yet, from Vives's list it is not difficult to recognize the topics, which turn out to be not only aids in thinking but also in making linguistic categories.

That such a linguistic division also reflects the workings of the topics is not surprising; for if the topics structure what we consign to thought (*verbis sensa consignantur*) – and we have seen that they indeed prompt us to look for, for instance, causes, effects, or parts and whole, attributes, so on – it is likely that they are also reflected in language, which is "the expression of thought." In some places Vives even suggests that "the power of almost all knowing and understanding lies in words; for in words are perceptions (*sensa*) registered, and all that takes place in the mind and in thought is expressed in words."[91] Again, this does not mean that Vives endorses a view that holds that language determines thought, but he is willing to see the topics as an important grid that guides our knowledge and speech about the world. What Peter Mack says of Agricola is true for Vives too: "All that can be said about something, and all that something is, is to emerge from a consideration of the topics," and this "provides an explanation for the ways in which the topics are to be used for discovering material and for thought."[92]

Conclusion

Vives's ideas of language, knowledge, and argumentation, which testify to his wider views on human culture, and his ideas on how this culture should be reformed by education and learning, are clearly the product of his wide reading of Cicero, Quintilian, Boethius, and many other classical sources, and also his direct predecessors Valla and Agricola. From these sources he distilled and developed some of the key ideas that we have discussed in this

[90] *De explanatione* (M III:127): "in tanta licentia sermonis et tanta varietate linguarum."
[91] *De prima philosophia* I (M III:193). [92] Mack 1993, 140–141.

chapter. Like Valla he presents himself as a defender of "the common language," "the common speech which everyone uses (*in hoc vulgari, et qui est omnium in ore sermo*)," the "common sense and normal human speech," or "the common language and the common method of understanding."[93] The notion of "common" however is ambiguous, and we have met the same kind of tension in Vives's account that we found in Valla's. In most contexts the common language is of course Latin, the language of learned Europe throughout the ages, but in Vives's attack on what he considered the linguistic and dialectical aberrations of his scholastic opponents, common language could also mean the usage and conventions of any linguistic community. Though his critique focuses on the Latin of his opponents, the point is sometimes phrased in terms that go beyond this particular language: "One must consider, with respect to all words, what the mind habitually and ordinarily understands by them (*mens soleat communiter intelligere*)."[94] For Vives, the language and argumentation of the scholastics are an expression not only of bad Latin but also of an entire attitude or mentality that runs against common understanding and common sense, something hardly surprising since these people "have left the natural world that they inhabit," being "ignorant of practical life and common sense."[95]

The critique of scholastic language thus went hand in hand with a rejection of what Vives saw as the abstractions of his opponents, "those useless sophistical discourses on the 'intension' and 'remission' of qualities, or uniform motion, or motion uniformly deformed and deformedly deformed," as he puts it in a youthful work.[96] And in his chapter on the study of nature in his *De disciplinis* he writes: "He is not a philosopher, who talks subtly about instants (*instantibus*), and *de motu enormi aut conformi*,[97] but he is one, who knows the origin and nature of plants and animals, and the reasons why, as well as the way in which, natural events happen."[98] Having listed books to be read by the student, Vives continues: "He who would advance still further must study outward nature by close observation."[99] Rather than engaging in typically scholastic altercations and quarrels

[93] *Adversus Pseudodialecticos* (M III:41, Vives 1979, 55): "in communi lingua observata . . . per communem modum intelligendi"; *De causis corruptarum artium* III, 6 (M VI:141), and elsewhere.

[94] *Adversus pseudodialecticos* (M III:139, Vives 1979, 129). Cf. *De causis corruptarum artium* III, 6 (M VI:141).

[95] *De causis corruptarum artium* III, 6 (M VI:149).

[96] "Praelectio in *Convivia Philelphi*," quoted by Del Nero 2008, 197.

[97] "Enormi" is probably a corrupt reading for "difformi."

[98] *De tradendis disciplinis* IV, 1 (M VI:348, Vives 1971,167).

[99] Ibid., IV, 1 (M VI:350, Vives 1971, 170 for this and the next quotation).

> he will observe the nature of things in the heavens, in cloudy and in clear weather, in the plains, on the mountains, in the woods. Hence he will seek out, and get to know, many things from those who inhabit those spots. Let him have recourse, for instance, to gardeners, husbandmen, shepherds and hunters, for this is what Pliny and other great authors undoubtedly did.

Such a student requires "great and exact concentration" in observing "every part of nature, in its seasons, and in the essence and strength of each object of nature."[100] And Vives gives similar advice to the student of the practical and mechanical arts, suggesting that they enter "shops and factories to ask questions from craftsmen, and get to know about the details of their work."[101] He speaks of "a great delectation" that the pursuit of the study of nature brings; it "stimulates the desire of knowledge, which for every human mind is the keenest of all pleasures. Therefore whilst attention is given to observation of nature, no other recreation need be sought."[102]

Already in Agricola we find this emphasis on the study of concrete things. In several places in his *De inventione dialectica* and also in his famous letter to Jacques Barbireau containing an extensive plan of study, he champions empirical observation of all aspects of things. Empirical observation enables us to bring the phenomena under groups, general laws, general rules and precepts, which make up the arts and sciences: "I would recommend you attack the things themselves (*res ipsas*). You have gotten to the stage of needing to examine the geography and nature of lands, seas, mountains and rivers; the customs, borders and circumstances of nations that live on earth; the empires in their historical or extended forms; you have now got to look into the medicinal properties of trees and herbs . . . ."[103]

These recommendations, however, do not turn these humanists into empirical natural philosophers. Though there is an inquisitive spirit running through Vives's works, learning remains essentially a bookish affair: his vast encyclopedia of the arts lays down, first and foremost, a curriculum of reading. And it would go too far to see in him, as some scholars have done, a precursor of Francis Bacon.[104] It is also not surprising that the pious Christian that Vives was frequently states that learning and also the study of nature is only justifiable if it serves human society and religion: "Thus the contemplation of nature is unnecessary and even harmful unless

[100] Ibid., 171. [101] Ibid., IV, 6 (M VI:374, Vives 1971, 209; 2011, 176).
[102] Ibid., IV, 1 (M VI:348, Vives 1971, 167).
[103] Agricola 1539, 62–65; 70–71; 75–76; 209; letter no. 38 in Agricola 2002, 207, with two minimal changes to the translation offered there.
[104] Cf. Watson 1971, ciii–cxi; Crescini 1965, 77–78; Vasoli 1968, 635.

it serves the useful arts of life, or raises us from a knowledge of His works to a knowledge, admiration and love of the Author of these works."[105] So the pragmatic and practical overtones of his educational reform seem to be meant to curb the vainglorious scientist or philosopher who pursues learning only for its own sake, though it must be said that Vives seems to have in mind the abstract philosophical studies, which he had pursued himself as a young student in Paris.

Vives was therefore not someone who contributed directly to a program of natural study or empirical observation of nature. But perhaps one may view his ideas on language and knowledge as an indirect contribution to the creation of an intellectual climate that fostered such explorations. Our discussion has pointed to what we may call a de-essentialization of universals, that is, a move away from universals as entities that are one and many at the same time, to be dug up by a process of abstraction, and toward topics as ordering principles that guide human cognition and argumentation. As they had for Agricola and his sources, for Vives, too, the topics reflect similarities in nature in a more or less direct way. As a system they may be said to form a grid through which knowledge can be acquired and arguments be formulated. It would be far from the humanist's mind to deny that there is a stable order of essences, independent of human categorization, yet our knowledge of it can be had only by way of inference on the basis of our seeing connections, and this process of collecting and comparing data is guided (though not determined) by the topics.[106] As we have seen, the topics are a much broader group than the traditional universals of genus, species, difference, and property, and hence constitute a much more flexible set of categories, partly directly reflecting the essential and accidental nature of a thing, partly less directly reflecting them, when we define a thing or have an opinion about it. They enable Vives to suggest what we may call a horizontal ontology in which concrete things, grouped in classes on the basis of what we empirically observe, take center stage, rather than hierarchies of universals such as genus and species somehow residing in individual things though never identical with them – a line of thinking developed by Mario Nizolio (1488–1567), whom often mentions Vives and whose *De veris principiis* will be the subject of the next chapter. We see a similar shift in Vives's ideas on the soul. Here too the drift of his

[105] *De tradendis disciplinis* IV, 1 (M VI:348, Vives 1971, 167).

[106] *De instrumento probabilitatis* (M III:86): "optimum factu est visum eam ipsam inquirendi rationem et colligendi probabilia, quam omnes communiter usurparent, observare, annotare, in praecepta redigere, et artem conficere, quam de inveniendo nominarunt."

argument moves away from a metaphysical consideration of the real nature of the soul toward a description of its phenomenological manifestations.[107]

This is of course not an entirely new phenomenon in the sixteenth century. Already in the later Middle Ages we see scholastic thinkers turning away from substance and essence and moving toward an examination of sensible qualities – or at least a defense of such an approach.[108] But what we can see in humanists such as Valla, Agricola, and Vives is that a critique of philosophical abstraction goes hand in hand with a critique of linguistic abstraction. They were of course not alone nor the first to warn against reification and hypostatization, but equipped with their linguistic and rhetorical training they could argue that such reification and hence a belief in abstract entities were caused by a misunderstanding of language. A philosopher should have a good knowledge of language, for it is the "common meaning of words" rather than the technical terminology of the scholastics that should be followed (*communis verborum usus*; *sensus communis*; *verbis de vulgo sumtis*).[109] Even metaphysics is a discipline that must take its starting point from common usage, laying bare (*enucleare*) the meaning of individual words, since "the rise and disappearance of nearly all problems in the disciplines are dependent on the way we phrase them in language."[110] Vives's appeal to common language is at the same time a plea for the observation of the world of things.

[107] Already noticed by Wilhelm Dilthey; see Casini 2006, 16, with further literature.

[108] Pasnau 2011, 634–635. [109] *De prima philosophia* I (M III:193).

[110] Ibid.: "itaque diligenter communis verborum usus est animadvertendus, ex quo plurimae in omnibus disciplinis et existunt quaestiones, et profligantur."

CHAPTER 5

Anti-Essentialism and the Rhetoricization of Knowledge: Mario Nizolio's Humanist Attack on Universals

Introduction

In the previous chapters we have studied the critique of scholastic language as part of a wider program of reform of the arts and sciences, in particular the trivial arts (grammar, dialectic, rhetoric). Just as abstract, technical Latin had to be replaced by Latin that followed the common linguistic usage of the classical authorities, so the abstract topics discussed by the scholastics had to be replaced by an examination of concrete things, *res*, whether they be linguistic phenomena to be gleaned from the study of texts, things from the natural world, or the religious experience of people. The reform was often framed as a thorough transformation of the Aristotelian corpus of texts and the scholastic modes of thought centered around this corpus. Not all humanists were, however, virulent anti-Aristotelians: unlike Valla, humanists such as Bruni, Pontano, Agricola, and Vives were – each in their own way – moderate in their critique or even praised the master himself. Rather than speaking of one tradition of humanist anti-Aristotelianism it is better to speak of "varieties of anti-Aristotelianism" that could range from the virulent attacks on anything to do with Aristotle and his followers to moderate proposals to transform themes, approaches, and methods, without discarding the good things Aristotle and Aristotelian traditions had brought.[1]

In this chapter we will study a humanist who adds a new element to the critique of the language and conceptual apparatus of the scholastics: Mario Nizolio (1488–1567), who explicitly places himself in the humanist tradition, referring frequently to Valla, Agricola, Vives, and others. Focusing on his interesting but undervalued work – the 1553 *De veris principiis et vera ratione philosophandi contra pseudophilosophos* (*On the true principles and true way of philosophizing against the pseudo-philosophers*), edited by Leibniz

[1] Cf. Menn 1998, 47; Martin 2014.

in 1670 – we will show that his critique involves a radical de-ontologization of the conceptual armory of the scholastics, a turn toward the world of empirical things, a recognition of the central role that the human mind plays in our categorization of the world, and a plea for a clear, transparent language in doing philosophy and communication in general.[2] Rejecting universals as essences as well as Aristotelian categories and transcendentals, Nizolio wanted to defend a horizontal ontology in which concrete things, grouped in classes by a creative act of the human mind, take center stage.

Famous in his own time for his *Observationes in M. T. Ciceronem* (1535), which had already gone through more than fifty editions in the sixteenth century, Nizolio's philosophical work was given serious attention only much later, thanks to Leibniz's catholic philosophical interests. The name of Nizolio thus duly features in general accounts of Renaissance humanism and philosophy.[3] In a few perceptive pages Ernst Cassirer praises Nizolio for his emphasis on the concrete world of empirical things and their qualities as the subject matter of scientific investigation, arguing that Nizolio completed "the empirical critique of Aristotelianism" started by his predecessors, and thus "prepared the turn [*Wendung*] of physical science and theory of knowledge" as developed in the dissident natural philosophy of Telesio and others.[4] Recently, Erika Rummel has suggested that Nizolio's work is important "because his emphasis on experience and sense perception marks the transition from the scholastic method and its humanistic alternatives . . . to a more critical scientific method."[5] Building on this scholarship, this chapter will offer a more comprehensive analysis and evaluation of Nizolio's ideas. We will start by looking at Nizolio's humanist credo, which forms the background of his attack on universals. The central part will be an analysis of Nizolio's criticisms of the traditional five predicables (genus, species, *differentia*, property, accident) by which things were allotted a place in the Tree of Porphyry, and his account of the process of abstraction that led to the formation of these universals. After a brief discussion of proof and demonstration, and the relationship between dialectic and rhetoric, as well as between rhetoric and philosophy, we will be able to evaluate Nizolio's program and assess the claim that it can

[2] Leibniz 1966, 408, thinks Nizolio's title too grand and prefers a title such as "Logica quaedam reformata et ad puram propriamque loquendi rationem revocata," a logic reformed and brought back to a pure and proper account of speech.

[3] For example, Rossi 1953; Vasoli 1968, 606–632; Copenhaver and Schmitt 1992, 207–209; Breen's introduction to Nizolio 1956.

[4] Cassirer 1906–1957, 1:145–147. In the same spirit, see Kondylis 1990, 115–129, a brief but excellent discussion.

[5] Rummel 1995, 159; cf. 162–164, 175–177, 182–183, 188–190; cf. Wesseler 1974.

be considered as a preparatory step in the slow and gradual downfall of an old paradigm and the emergence of a new one.

From a Linguistic Point of View: Nizolio's Humanist Credo

The humanist credo with which Nizolio opened his attack on scholastic philosophy was the expression of a life devoted to the study of classical authors, in particular, Cicero. Born in Boretto in Reggio Emilia in 1488, Nizolio became tutor in the household of the noble family of the Gambara, and it was to Count Giovanni Francesco Gambara that he dedicated his first work, the *Observationes in M. T. Ciceronem* in 1535.[6] Around 1540 he tried to get a post at the University of Milan but lost to Marco Antonio Maioragio, a much younger scholar with whom he exchanged bitter polemics on Cicero between 1546 and 1548. He was almost sixty when, in 1547, he became professor at the University of Parma, and was thus well into his sixties when his *De veris principiis* appeared in 1553. In 1562, already seventy-four years old, he was appointed head of the gymnasium in Sabbioneta by Vespasiano Gonzaga, and died four years later in 1566.

Nizolio's output is not impressive. Apart from the two principal works, the *Observationes* and *De veris principiis*, he wrote only a few short polemical works against Maioragio and Celio Calcagnini. As his modern editor, Quirinus Breen, has remarked: "All these writings have a common bond of Ciceronianism."[7] However, Nizolio's reputation as arch-Ciceronian should perhaps be modified. In his style he was no slavish imitator of Cicero.[8] Erasmus's *Ciceronianus* (1528) and the controversies that it and other works sparked may have exercised a "moderating" influence on Nizolio's own Ciceronianism.[9] Unlike J. C. Scaliger and Stephen Dolet, Nizolio did not attack Erasmus, though he must surely have been angered by the *Ciceronianus*, since in his preface to the *Observationes* he already spoke of (unnamed) "detractors" (*obtrectatoribus istis*) of Cicero.[10] His real

[6] The work was supplemented by new word lists of Nizolio and others; the 1548 edition was entitled *Nizolius sive Thesaurus Ciceronianus*: see Breen's introduction to Nizolio 1956, xxiii–xxvi. I have used the 1613 edition, printed in Frankfurt.

[7] Breen's introduction to ibid., xv. Nizolio also published a translation of a lexicon of obsolete words in the Hippocratic writings of Galen. For a good summary of the polemics see Breen's introduction (Nizolio 1956); cf. Copenhaver and Schmitt 1992, 207–209.

[8] Breen's introduction to Nizolio 1956, xxi, xlvii n. 151. See Schmitt 1972, 15: "one cannot unequivocally speak of a neat division of Ciceronians and anti-Ciceronians in the Renaissance." See also n. 21 below.

[9] Breen's introduction to Nizolio 1956, xxii–xxiii.

[10] Nizolio 1613, dedicatory page to Giovanni Francesco Gambara (no page number). Nizolio can also be positive about Erasmus (on trees and plants having no souls); Nizolio 1956, 1:201–202 (2.9).

bête noire, however, became Maioragio, whom he had admired earlier in Milan. When Maioragio published his *Antiparadoxa* in 1546 – in which he criticizes Cicero for believing that the Stoic paradoxes are Socratic and for arguing as an orator rather than as a real philosopher – Nizolio felt deeply offended and started what soon became a vitriolic and unedifying series of polemics, in which the late Calcagnini also became a target. These polemics address a number of issues that recur in the *De veris principiis*. As has been noted by Breen, Nizolio's attack on universals was occasioned by the controversy about the title of Cicero's *De officiis*, a title criticized by Calcagnini, who thought that Cicero should have written *De officio* in the singular.[11] Nizolio defended Cicero by distinguishing between literal and figurative speech. The point seems utterly trivial, but it made Nizolio realize an important point; namely, that a failure to recognize the figure of speech of synecdoche (to use the singular for the plural or part for the whole) had given rise to the errors not only of Calcagnini and the like but also of the many philosophers who believed in the existence of universals. This brings us to his major work, *De veris principiis*.

One of the assumptions in Nizolio's attack on scholastic philosophy is that the scholastics endorsed, almost *tout court*, a realist interpretation of the universals. With the exception of the nominalists, almost all philosophers from the time of Plato and Aristotle onward believed in the existence of universals – whether located in the external world or in the human mind – in a way that, in Nizolio's view, is fundamentally mistaken. This belief has wrought so much havoc in philosophy – universals being the foundation of metaphysics and dialectics – that Nizolio sees it as his principal task to eradicate universals once and for all. A discussion of the various scholastic positions is clearly not part of Nizolio's brief. Medieval authors such as Albert the Great, Thomas Aquinas, Duns Scotus, and William of Ockham are mentioned but never discussed.[12] For Nizolio it is enough to bring the scholastic authors under the suitably vague and contemptuous name of "pseudo-philosophers," reminding us of Vives's "pseudodialecticians." His main targets are the old authorities Aristotle, Boethius, and Porphyry, and also some modern authors such as Joachim Périon (1499–1559), Johannes Rivius (1500–1553), Chrysostom Javellus (ca. 1470–1538), Rudolph Agricola (1444–1485), and J. L. Vives (1492–1540). The latter two are duly praised for their learning and for their critical attitude toward the Aristotelian tradition, yet Nizolio thinks they were still

[11] Breen's introduction to Nizolio 1956, liii. On Maioragio, see also Breen 1958.

[12] Nizolio 1956, 1:65 (1.6).

too much under the sway of a belief in universals.[13] Only Lorenzo Valla comes close to Nizolio's own position. Valla had reduced the ten Aristotelian categories to three: substance, quality, and action. He had also reduced the six transcendental terms – being, something, thing, true, good, one – to just one: thing (*res*).[14] And while Valla continued to use the predicable terms, he heavily criticized the Tree of Porphyry for not squaring with reality.[15] Moreover, rhetoric, rather than dialectic, was the queen of arts, and metaphysics was to be dismissed, in particular because of its nefarious influence on theology. According to Nizolio, however, Valla had not eradicated the Aristotelian-scholastic system root and branch, and had lopped off only some branches and leaves.[16] It is left to Nizolio, as he likes to present it, to let the Aristotelian edifice crumble at last by destroying its foundations, that is, universals – and, in their wake, other basic notions such as transcendentals and categories. His radicalism seems unsurpassed: "no other sixteenth-century authors with similar views have so far been identified."[17]

Indeed, Nizolio's aversion to universals does not seem to have been shared by many humanists, who were often able to combine a critical attitude toward traditional philosophy with a belief in universals as a stable structure of essences.[18] We find Nizolio's motivation at the beginning of his work, where he formulates his humanist credo in the form of five principles of "correct philosophizing," much in the spirit of Valla and Vives.[19] Next to having a profound knowledge of the classical languages and their literatures, as well as a sound grasp of rhetoric and grammar, we should avoid senseless questions and use clear language, introducing new expressions and words only if absolutely necessary. And we should follow "the five senses, reason, thought, memory, experience and observation," rather than Plato, Aristotle, or any other ancient or more recent author.[20]

This last principle – number four on Nizolio's list – might seem difficult to square with his reverence for classical authorities, Cicero in particular. The reverence, however, is not absolute, even though Cicero is Nizolio's most important source of inspiration. Cicero himself, as Nizolio does not fail to point out, championed the *libertas philosophandi*. Seeing a matter

[13] Nizolio 1956, 1:92 (1.8).
[14] On Valla's program of ontological reduction, see Chapter 1; on Valla and Nizolio, see Monfasani 1988, 209–210; Mack 1993, 116.
[15] Valla 2012, 1:84–88 (*DD* 1.7). [16] Nizolio 1956, 1:35 (1.2). [17] Mack 1993, 116.
[18] Agricola 1539, 37–41, on whom see above Chapter 3, and also Friedrich 2002; Nauta 2012b. On Vives see Chapter 3. Melanchthon 1846, 520; cf. Frank 1995, 33–37. For Peter Ramus's indecisive position on universals, see Ong 1958, 208–209.
[19] Nizolio 1956, 1:21–30 (1.1). [20] Ibid., 27 (1.1).

from various angles, without committing oneself to one particular philosophical school, was essential to Cicero's Academic outlook. Although Nizolio might have felt slightly uncomfortable about Cicero's endorsement of Academic skepticism,[21] he had no doubts about the importance of the *libertas philosophandi*, formulating it in similar terms as "the freedom and true independence to think and judge about all things just as the truth itself and the nature of things require," and rejecting the ancient schools as well as the more recent ones, such as the Albertists, the Thomists, the Scotists, and the Averroists.[22]

Nizolio's humanist credo clearly forms the background of his campaign against universals, and is reflected by the title: *De veris principiis et vera ratione philosophandi contra pseudophilosophos*. Universals cannot be seen or observed with the senses, being but the product of philosophical abstraction. Together with the categories and transcendentals and a host of other technical scholastic concepts, they form a theoretical superstructure that, according to Nizolio, prevents a clear view of the world of concrete things. As we will see below, this belief in universals is the result of a misunderstanding of language. To be sure, the Ciceronian Nizolio was convinced of the beauty and expressive power of classical Latin (and Greek), and thus an essential part of his program aims at replacing dialectic with rhetoric and at a defense of the Ciceronian union of eloquence and philosophy, but it also contains a philosophical point that goes beyond merely aesthetic preferences. As Nizolio wants us to believe, the language of the great authors of antiquity – and he speaks of both Latin and Greek – is presented as a language that reflects common sense (*ad communem omnium sensum*) and the habits and customs of the people, and the only true path to knowledge of the world;[23] at one point he even says that knowledge of these languages should be combined with careful attention to how ordinary people speak, and elsewhere he defends a particular thesis with words that remind us of Valla's strategy of justifying a position "not only because Cicero and the other ancient authors show that this is so but also because common linguistic usage of all the people confirms it") – without explaining who all these people are.[24] Thus while Nizolio's notion of common linguistic usage is usually determined by what we learn from "the grammarians and the orators," for Nizolio, as for his sources of inspiration Valla and Vives, it was tempting to blur the distinction between learned Latin

[21] Schmitt 1972, 72–73, referring to Nizolio 1956, 2:190, where Nizolio makes a critical remark on the "*Sceptica sive Ephectica et Academica nova*, to which also Cicero belonged, that had confused things greatly and had rendered things uncertain"; on Cicero's skepticism, see Görler 1995.

[22] Ibid., 26–27. [23] 1:147 (2.2). [24] Ibid., 1:26 (1.1); 1:202 (2.9). Cf. 2:80 (3.7).

and the language of the common people, particularly when such an elision aided in his critique of scholastic language. Given his intention to bring science into direct contact with the world of concrete things, it was natural for him to view classical Latin as the common and natural vehicle for expressing our view of the world. The full implication of this conviction becomes clear only later, but already at the start the basic assumption that drives Nizolio's program, just like that of his sources of inspiration, is that linguistic abstraction and philosophical abstraction are intrinsically connected: both lead us away from the world of individual, concrete things.

Classes of Words and Things

The attack therefore starts on a linguistic note. General terms such as "man" and "animal" and also terms such as "genus" and "species" themselves are collective terms.[25] The general term *cat* does not refer to a substantial form cat-hood, let alone a Platonic Idea Cat, but to the class of individual cats, which means no more than all individual cats taken together. Nizolio's argument goes basically as follows. Since words, Nizolio says, were invented to refer to things, we must look at words and word classes to see what there is, ontologically speaking. His presentation, however, follows a different order: since reality "comes first," he starts with dividing things into four classes with corresponding ways of being, and then introduces four word classes that exactly correspond with these four categories of things.[26] Things can be divided into substances and qualities, and these can either be singular or a multitude (*multitudo*). The four ways of being that correspond to these four classes of things are: independent existence; to exist in something else; to exist on one's own; and to exist in a composite way, that is, to consist of more than one thing.

From an ontological point of view, this is a remarkable categorization for someone who wants to do away with any kind of abstract entity. One would expect Nizolio to have limited his ontology to individual things – that is, individual substances and individual qualities – for unless he erroneously thinks a heap of stones to be of the same ontological order as the class of stones, he willy-nilly introduces an abstract entity: a set or class is not the same as a random collection of individuals. As we will see, this

[25] Nizolio 1956, 1:41–53 (1.4).

[26] Ibid., 37–40 (1.3). Cf. 59 (1.6) where the classes of things, created by "god or nature" ("a Deo sive a natura") are said to be exactly the same in number as "the names and appellations imposed by grammarians and inventors of words" ("linguarum Authores et vocabulorum inventores nomina atque appellationes imposuerunt").

ambiguity between groups as multitudes and classes runs right through Nizolio's account. What is clear, however, is that Nizolio's inspiration for coming up with this fourfold ontological division is linguistic. There are also four word classes, with corresponding modes of signification: substantives, adjectives, proper names, and appellative names; and each word class refers to an ontological class, for example, substantives to individual things, and so on. The clear aim of these divisions is to categorize universal terms as collective terms.

To develop this point Nizolio accepts the traditional distinction between proper names and appellative names. Proper names always refer to a concrete individual, even though we can sometimes use the plural to refer to just one individual. An appellative name is defined as a word that is common to many individual things and is said of these things in many statements.[27] Appellative names can be divided into collective names such as "army," "party," "folk," "nation," "group," "genus," and "species," which always refer to a multitude of individual things, and what Nizolio calls "simple" appellative names, such as "animal," "human being," "tree," and "plant." The incorporation of *genus* and *species* among the collective names is supported by examples from classical authors who use these words always to refer to groups or classes; for example, Seneca, "everything we suffer as a mortal genus [*mortale genus*]." The second category of simple appellative names stands in between collective names and proper names, because these words can refer sometimes to individuals and sometimes to groups.[28] For example, "human being" (*homo*) in "Socrates is a human being" refers just to Socrates, when said of Socrates only, but when taken in a nonliteral sense (*figurate*), the singular *human being* can also stand for the whole class of human beings. In this case terms such as "animal," "human being," and "tree" are collective names.[29] Nizolio singles out three features of this use of simple appellative names: a singular is used instead of the plural, the word is used in a nonliteral sense, and such a word is used more than once and in more than one statement.[30] Thus, if used in its literal sense, "living being" (*animal*) in "Plato is a living being" refers to this one individual and is not a collective name. But when used in a series of

[27] Ibid., 41–53, esp. 52 (1.4). [28] Ibid., 42 (1.4).

[29] Nizolio's scheme at the end of *De principiis* (Nizolio 1956, 2:196) is therefore somewhat misleading, because appellative names seem to be strictly divided into collective and simple names, while many simple names can become collective ones in the way explained by Nizolio in the text. For the same reason, it is confusing that he frequently refers to this category as "simple, non-collective [names]" ("simplicia sive non collectiva"); for example, see ibid., 42 (1.4).

[30] Ibid., 50 (1.4).

statements – "man is a living being," "cow is a living being," "lion is a living being" – and when used in a nonliteral sense, the word is a collective name, referring to the whole class of living beings.[31] Nizolio thus wants terms to refer either to one singular or to a group as a whole – *singillatim aut universe sive in universum*. There is nothing in between: "animal" does not refer to a universal that is one and common at the same time.

Nizolio's account is hardly satisfactory. He suggests that "genus" and "army" are collective names in much the same way: just as an individual soldier is part of a cohort, the cohort part of a legion, and the legion part of an army, so an individual is part of a group of people such as Trojans, this group is part of a wider group, human beings, and this group again part of a still wider group, living beings.[32] Now the term "genus" itself may be a collective name as used by classical authors, but a genus term such as "animal" is clearly different from "army" or "nation," for while we can say "Socrates is a living being," we cannot say "the soldier is the army." Nizolio mentions the objection, but flatly rejects it: "genus" or "species" cannot truly (*vere*) be predicated in the nominative of its species or individuals.[33] Thus, in "Socrates is a human being," the term "human being" is not the species when the term is used in its literal sense; it refers just to this one individual. If used metaphorically and in many different statements, it refers to the species.[34] However, the cases remain different, and Nizolio frequently acknowledges this: an army is not a genus, he admits, and yet they are both collective names.[35]

These and other difficulties apart, Nizolio's basic idea is clear: terms refer either to one singular or to a group as a whole, as the world consists of things (being the highest class) that can be divided in groups, and these groups further subdivided in groups, down to the level of individuals.[36] Language can easily mislead us into postulating common essences, but with a correct understanding of the use of words – singular/plural, literal/metaphorical, and so on – we can recognize the root of this error.

[31] Ibid., 51 (1.4).

[32] Ibid., 105 (1.10); 42–43 (2.2); see also 93 (1.8): "Both [Socrates and Plato] agree in having the same name 'man' and in belonging to the same genus, just as two soldiers belong to the same army."

[33] Ibid., 44 (1.4); 84 (1.7). [34] Ibid., 43–44 (1.4).

[35] Ibid., 119–120 (2.1). Moreover, Nizolio is not always clear about the criteria for distinguishing the literal from the nonliteral use of a term. How do we know whether "animal" refers just to Socrates and not to the whole class of human beings? See Nauta 2012a, 42–43.

[36] For example, ibid., 190 (2.8): following Valla ("ut recte inquit Laurentius Valla in primo Dialecticae suae libro Cap. II"), Nizolio maintains that there is only one true transcendental: *thing* (*res*); *being* (*ens*) can be reduced to *thing*, just like the other traditional transcendental terms. Everything is a subgroup of *thing*, which is the widest possible class, containing all things. Cf. Valla 2012, 18–36 (*DD* 1.2) and Chapter 2, n. 36.

Predicables

But if there are no essences that divide reality at its joints, is any categorization possible and as real as any other? What are the criteria according to which we carve up reality in the way we do? Sometimes Nizolio gives the impression that he considers any categorization as good as any other. To be sure, we tend to group humans with humans, and ants with ants, but we can also group the two together – to use Nizolio's own example – if we take as our criterion "taking precautions for the future," since this is what ants and humans have in common.[37] Whatever common trait we happen to notice among things is sufficient to form a group, a class. On closer inspection of Nizolio's argument, however, it seems that all classes are equal, but some classes are more equal than others. He finds himself speaking of "substantial" and "essential" species.[38] Let's see how.

One strand in Nizolio's thought is to do justice to the basic ontological picture with which he had started. There is just one universal or type of universal: genus, that is, a collection of individual things.[39] We can use the term "species" for a smaller collection as part of its genus, but ontologically speaking there are only collections, made up of individual things. Nizolio has to admit, however, that not every collection is a genus. A collection is a genus only when it comprises all the species and individuals that are subordinate to it: the genus tree consists of all species of trees (oak, elm, etc.) and their individuals. Just as genus is defined in terms of its species, so is species defined in terms of its genus, that is, as part of a bigger collection, but it is denied the status of universal, because it is always oriented toward its higher genus.[40] As soon as it is predicated of something subordinate to it, it loses its character of species and becomes a genus, for example, the predicate "man" in "John is a man." Likewise, man and horse are species of the genus animal, that is, parts of the collection of things that are animal, but as soon as we predicate "man" of "Trojan" or "Theban" – Nizolio's example borrowed from Cicero's *De inventione* – it becomes a genus.[41] This also applies to the level of individuals: as soon as "Trojan" is

[37] For example, Nizolio 1956, 1:98 (1.9). [38] Ibid., 141 (2.2); and also 122 (2.1); 139 (2.2).

[39] Ibid., 97 (1.9); 115–134 (2.1).

[40] Ibid., 144 (2.2). Cf. Agricola 1539, 54. Nizolio often quotes from and discusses Agricola, something overlooked in Mack's otherwise excellent survey of Agricola's influence in the sixteenth century: Mack 1993, 280–372. Nizolio 1956, 2:109–110 (4.1), writes about the significance of Agricola's work when he himself was still a boy (*puer*).

[41] Cicero 1949, 65 (*De inventione* 1.32): "Often the same thing is a genus in relation to one thing and a species in relation to another. For example, man is a species of animal, but a genus of which Thebans or Trojans are species."

predicated of Koriskos, Trojan is the genus and the individual Koriskos its species. Indeed, the *species specialissimae* are not man and horse, as in Porphyry's tree, but individuals.[42] Nizolio thus seems to de-ontologize genus and species: they seem to be no more than convenient labels for indicating groups and subgroups.

Strange as this position may seem, it is interesting to note that a similar move can be detected in the work of Peter Ramus. As Walter J. Ong suggested a long time ago, Ramus saw, perhaps unconsciously, the world as consisting of little corporeal units, or "simples," which can be grouped into clusters, and these combined with other clusters, and so forth: "Ramus thus tends to view all intellectual operations as a spatial grouping of a number of these corpuscles into a kind of cluster, or as a breaking down of clusters into their corpuscular units."[43] All these clusters or groupings are called genera, which leads Ramus to conclude that individuals and species are exactly the same thing.[44] Nizolio does not quote Ramus in his work, but since he frequently refers to Périon's *Dialecticae libri*, a work that also included Périon's two orations against Ramus, it is highly likely that he was acquainted with Ramus's Aristotelian critique. (Ramus's *Dialecticae institutiones* and his *Aristotelicae animadversiones* were published in 1543.)[45]

A certain affinity is further visible in Nizolio's argument that man and woman are two different species of the genus human being (*homo*), just as Trojan and Theban are different species of that same genus – a position Ramus also defended. This was a highly unconventional position, the defense of which helped to outlaw Ramism in late-sixteenth-century Leipzig.[46] For Nizolio, however, it was a logical outcome of his position that species are parts of genus. He heavily criticizes Vives, who had argued against Cicero that woman and man, just like Trojan and Theban, are only accidental, nonessential qualifications of the species human being; man and woman do not contribute to the essential form, but only concern the "matter." In a remarkable reference to transsexuality Vives had written that people who had changed their sex did not receive thereby a different

[42] Nizolio 1956, 1:140 (2.2). [43] Ong 1958, 203. [44] Ramus 1543, 14.

[45] In particular, Nizolio's discussion of the authenticity of Aristotle's works in the last book of his *De principiis* suggests an acquaintance with Ramus's *Aristotelicae animadversiones* from 1543; see Breen's note in Nizolio 1956: 2, 177 n. 37, for some possible links, concluding that it was "praticamente impossibile ch'egli non abbia conosciuto le *Animadversiones* di Ramus." On Périon, see Vasoli 1968, 406 n. 4.

[46] Ong 1958, 203, and n. 20, from which it appears that this opinion was not yet present in the 1543 edition of Ramus's work, but it can be found from 1552 onwards.

essence.[47] Nizolio replies that, even though we can make a difference between, on the one hand, nonessential, accidental, or "external" species – such as man/woman and Theban/Trojan of their genus human being – and, on the other hand, essential, "inner and natural" species – such as human being and horse of their genus animal – the former are no less species than the latter, because they can all be considered as subgroups of a larger group, the genus. The relationship between genus and species can thus be "essential" or "accidental": a white wall and a white cloth belong to the genus of white things, yet their inclusion is of an accidental kind since their whiteness is something accidental. But his reply to Vives becomes inconsistent when he says that someone who belonged to the genus human being goes over to the *genus* woman on changing his sex, for he had started his argument stating that man and woman were two *species* of the genus human being.[48] It is the same kind of double talk that Ong ascribed to Ramus, and "which drove Ramus's opponents frantic."[49]

The admittance of essential versus accidental species looks like a fatal blow to his nominalist program, but Nizolio does not see it that way. He tries to handle all subordinations of species under genus in purely extensional terms.[50] Horse is an "essential" species of animal because there is no horse that is not an animal, while a white wall belongs only accidentally to the genus white because there are walls that are not white. And a Theban belongs, as human being, essentially to the genus man, but as a Theban only accidentally so. But of course this suggests that all horses (or all humans, etc.) have something in common, which is the reason why we put them in one species subordinated to the genus animal in the first place. Does this not imply the existence of an essence or an essential quality, in other words, a universal? Nizolio does not think so, claiming that the universal simply is the collection of, say, horses or white things. But can we not say then that an army is a genus after all, with the soldiers as individual species? Nizolio must explain what the criteria are to categorize things. This would require, however, a revision of the traditional predicables.

This is indeed what he tries to do. The intention seems to de-ontologize the predicables by suggesting that there are more criteria to categorize things than the traditional five predicables, and that all these criteria are reducible to genera. The *differentia* rational is the class, or *genus differens*, of rational beings.[51] The property (*proprium*) sensation is the class or *genus proprium* of

[47] Vives 1782–1790, 3:124 (*De explanatione cuiusque essentiae* I), quoted by Nizolio 1956, 1:140 (2.2): "non migrabant ab effectione essentiali in diversam."
[48] Nizolio 1956, 1:141 (2.2). [49] Ong 1958, 204. [50] Nizolio 1956, 1:138 (2.2).
[51] Ibid., 115–135 (2.1).

things that have sensation, and so on. The criteria that Nizolio adds are difficult to distinguish from the traditional ones: we can group things because they have something in common (*communia*), for example, having a body, which gives the class of living and nonliving things. We can also group things because they are similar, giving the class *genus simile* – for example, ants and humans, which both take precautions for the future – or group things because they are contrary to each other, such as vice and virtue. More problematic is Nizolio's introduction of "substantial" as a criterion, giving the class *genus substantiale*, for example, animal for man, since "animal resides [*insitum*] in the substance of man, without which man cannot exist at all."[52]

Nizolio's attempt to blur the line between the criteria by which we group things and the class that we get as a result is, of course, highly problematic, but it was perhaps a natural reading of traditional authorities, such as Porphyry and Boethius, which latter writes that "to animal are subordinated the *species* rational and non-rational."[53] Also, the difficulty of distinguishing clearly between different types of accidents was something that Nizolio inherited from tradition. In Porphyry's *Isagoge*, for instance, it is left unclear how property differs from *differentia* and also from nonseparable qualities such as the Ethiopian's blackness, mentioned by Porphyry in his chapter on accidents.[54] Property was defined as what occurs in the entire species, in that species only, and always, such as the capacity to laugh in man, but the *differentia* rationality would fit this definition equally well.[55] This was, however, a difficulty that Nizolio put to his own advantage in his fight against what he saw as a rigid and hierarchical system of fixed and essentialist predicables.[56] In claiming that all predicables are genera, he denies that there are basic differences between them: they are all the same and only differ, as he states in one of his more polemical moments, "in their relation to what is subordinated or superordinated to them."[57] Having sensation is a *differentia* dividing plants from animals, but a property when related to the class of living beings, that is, a property shared by rational and nonrational beings.[58]

[52] Ibid., 121 (2.1). [53] Boethius, quoted in Nizolio 1956, 1:152 (2.3). [54] Porphyry 1966, 20.

[55] Warren in Porphyry 1975, 57 n. 52: "The relations between difference, property, and accident were subject to ambiguity and confusion." See also Marenbon 1997, 130–131.

[56] Nizolio 1956, 1:216 (2.11); 160 (2.3). [57] Ibid., 160 (2.3).

[58] According to Nizolio, definition consists of genus and property rather than genus and *differentia*, implying that there is a clear difference between the two; elsewhere (for example, ibid., 195–205 [2.9]), he accepts the traditional account, which provokes a critical comment from Leibniz (ibid., 162 n. 9 [2.3]): "This is nothing but sophistry" ("Hic nihil aliud quam logomachei"). Parenthetically, Leibniz uses the same word *logomachia* (sophistry, playing with words) to denounce some of Spinoza's artificial and obscure terminology; see Laerke 2009, 950.

Evidently, there are some deep tensions in Nizolio's program as analyzed so far, tensions that suggest that it was not easy to employ consistently a purely extensional approach of groups and the individuals out of which they exist. We may note the following points.

(1) On the one hand, Nizolio singles out "seven or eight" predicables, which, as we have seen, he identifies with genera (using the traditional Porphyrian term *genera subalterna*), thereby suitably conflating the criteria by which we group things and the groups themselves. But if white is a genus to which, for example, the wall and the cloth belong because they are (accidentally) white, then we can have many more classes; in fact, just as many as there are qualities. Nizolio seems thus to heap together not only groups and criteria – such as having something in common or being contradictory to each other – but also qualities such as whiteness. Indeed, the class of qualities is very broad: not only can we make a genus of, for example, white things, but also one consisting, to give Nizolio's own example, of ants and human beings.

(2) This raises the question of the precise ontological status of classes. On the one hand, Nizolio defends a horizontal picture of the world: there are only individual things that can be grouped in broader or narrower classes, but they are all at the same ontological level; there is no hierarchy of essences. On the other hand, he clearly distinguishes between individuals and groups, a distinction that seems to give groups their own ontological status, irreducible to the individuals out of which they exist: genera are "eternal" and "immortal."[59]

This leads to a further tension:

(3) Nizolio argues that the genus is the only universal: as a class it is called a thing, that is, a thing of things.[60] Classes are real things in the world. But we also find Nizolio often saying that only words can be general, and neither things nor concepts can be.[61] What he means is that universals cannot be those mysterious entities that he thinks scholastic philosophers operate with – entities that are not one (for they are predicated of many things), nor many (for it is the same predicate said of different

[59] Nizolio 1956, 1:43–44 (1.4), where Nizolio says that if one takes away all individuals of a genus the genus vanishes – a traditional point also made by Porphyry, but difficult to square with the view that genera are "eternal" and "immortal": Nizolio 1956, 1:75 (1.7). For Leibniz's response to this, see the last section of this chapter.

[60] Ibid., 129 (2.1): "For genera of things are things, not notions" ("Genera enim rerum res sunt, non notiones"). And ibid.: "both species and genera of things are true things, not notions" ("tam species quam genera rerum, non notiones sint, sed res verae").

[61] Ibid., 118 (2.1, criticisms of what Nizolio calls the "Stoic" attempt to define genus in terms of concepts).

individuals) – but that only words can be general, that is, used to refer to a group of things. He therefore seems to apply the term "universal" to things (that is, genera) but also to words, while he himself repeatedly accuses the "pseudo-philosophers" of confusing things and words that refer to things.

(4) The last point is closely related to the previous one. While Nizolio claims to follow the nominalists in stating that only words can be universal,[62] his treatment does not follow the terminist approach of Ockham at all. Ockham had argued that "genus," "species," and other universals are nothing but terms of second intention, that is, logical terms.[63] The predicamental order consists not of things but of our mental concepts, which are ordered according to the scope of their predication. Nizolio, however, equates universals with the genera, that is, with things, because he believes only words – and neither things *nor concepts* – can be general in the sense of referring to many things. What he does not seem to realize is that for a nominalist, concepts, being certain intentions of the mind, are singular entities that can stand for many things. It is not surprising, therefore, to find nothing equivalent to Ockham's mental language of our concepts in Nizolio's scheme.[64]

Comprehensio versus Abstraction

But if universals are to be equated with collections of individuals, how do we make these collections? How do we arrive at our categorizations? For Nizolio the central question in the debate on universals becomes all the more pressing: are groups or genera simply a product of the individual human mind, or are they somehow out there in reality, to be reflected in our mind? Nizolio's convictions lead him to embrace – hardly consciously – both positions at the same time. On the one hand, his whole project is aimed at reestablishing a direct contact between the human mind and the world of concrete things. The abstract entities that we are supposed to find hidden in things and then abstract from them are merely the product of the philosopher's imagination and have led us away from the world of concrete

[62] Ibid., 65 (1.6); 82 (1.7).

[63] For example, William of Ockham 1978, 36; William of Ockham 1974, 67–71. See also Panaccio 2004, 151–152.

[64] Interestingly, Nizolio's source of inspiration, Valla 2012, 1:85 wrote that "species and genus are just part and whole," just as head and torso as parts of a body. Strictly speaking, this is even less Ockhamist than Nizolio's account; cf. Nauta 2009, 37–41.

things.[65] He must claim that his universals, his genera, constitute reality itself, and indeed we often find him doing so: they are made by nature (*a natura facta*).[66] On the other hand, his de-essentializing program, flattening out the hierarchical picture of his so-called opponents, brings with it a major role for the human mind, which has the capacity to group individuals in many different ways. Such relativism, however, should not be taken too far. Analyzed as substances with their qualities, things are out there, and even though they can be grouped in many different ways, the qualities picked out by the human mind are real aspects of the world and not invented.

Nizolio's solution is to substitute abstraction with *comprehensio*, an act of the human mind that gathers together all the individuals of a genus "simultaneously and at once" (*simul et semel*): such genera, taken together, are the subject matter of the sciences and scientific propositions and argumentation. It is a "philosophical and oratorical act," he says, by which he means an act of comparing things and seeing the similarities between them.[67] It is a "*philosophical* act," since it plays an important role in philosophy, where definitions are based on similarities between things: when we define a human being as a rational, mortal animal we thereby define the whole class of human beings, that is, all men and women, on account of their similarities. In spite of his professed hostility to everything Aristotelian, Nizolio is indebted to Aristotle for this crucial notion, and he approvingly quotes from Aristotle's *Topics*, where the importance of an examination of likeness for deductions, inductions, and definitions is stressed.[68] What is said of one member of a class applies to all of them on account of the similarities noticed, or "comprehended."[69] It is an "*oratorical* act" because we find the trope of using the singular instead of the plural – or part instead of the whole, or one thing instead of a plurality or the entire group – often used by orators, poets, and prose writers. It is what rhetoricians call *intellectio*, or synecdoche, but it is not something limited, Nizolio stresses, to refined literate language or orations.[70] Also in daily speech (*sermo quotidianus*), common people (*populus, vulgus*) use this figure, when they use singular for plural, part for whole, or one thing for a multitude or an entire class (or vice versa).[71] Synecdoche seems to be the

[65] Nizolio 1956, 2:79–90 (3.7). [66] Ibid., 1:78 (1.7). [67] Ibid., 2:80 (3.7).
[68] Aristotle 1984, 1:180–181 (*Topics* 108a37–b31). [69] Nizolio 1956, 2:80 (3.7).
[70] Ibid., 1:46 (1.4).
[71] Ibid. Cf. 41 (1.4): "a Scriptoribus atque etiam a vulgo"; Quintilian 2001, 3:435–437 (*Institutio oratoria* 8.6.19–20).

linguistic expression of *comprehensio*: in order to talk about a class or group of things one must be able to gather mentally all its individuals.[72]

Nizolio does not give us much detail about this notion of *comprehensio*, however. It does not seem to be a process but rather an instantaneous grasp of a group, as he compares it to seeing a herd.[73] The idea seems to be that when, for example, a biologist speaks about bats, she or he is talking about the entire class of bats, taking all bats simultaneously together, all at once. Science is not about essences or universals that must first be abstracted from the concrete objects, but it is about these objects themselves, or rather about the genera in which they are grouped.[74] Knowledge is primarily to be had of groups or classes. But here too Nizolio's account is not wholly nominalist, in spite of his claim to follow the *nominales*. According to Ockham, a universal such as *dog* is produced in the mind on seeing a dog and noting its essential features.[75] This similitude can then stand for all the objects resembling each other and this concept. Though it is a particular act of the mind it can stand universally for all its referents, by virtue of its resemblance to each of them. Nizolio, however, does not accept any kind of abstractionist account of knowledge, and places universals outside the mind: they are the genera out there, comprehensively understood by the scientist, the orator, or whoever speaks about the world, making categorizations and statements about them and about their mutual relations.[76]

But does Nizolio not simply beg the central issue? To claim something about bats is to talk about the class of bats, about all individual bats taken together. But on the basis of what do we take them together? It is tempting to give an answer along Ockhamist lines: we take them together because we have gone through a process of abstraction before, abstracting the essential feature of bats and using that feature as our mental concept and as a natural sign to stand for each individual bat. Nizolio's revolt against abstraction

[72] Nizolio 1956, 2:80 (3.7); Cicero 1942, 2:85 (*De oratore* 3.27.106) and 1:295–297 (*De oratore* 2.31.135), quoted by Nizolio 1956, 1:74 (1.7).

[73] Nizolio 1956, 1:72 (1.7). [74] Ibid., 2:82–84 (3.7).

[75] William of Ockham 1974, 57–65; see also Panaccio 2004, 119–143. A very simplified version is presented by Melanchthon 1846, 520: species are called "acts of cognizing, portraying an image in the mind, which we call common because it can be applied to many individuals" ("revera actus intelligendi, pingens illam imaginem in mente, quae ideo dicitur communis, quia applicari ad multa individua potest"). Melanchthon then equates Aristotle's species with Plato's Ideas, and they are said to be perpetual, "because the knowledge or definition of a rose remains in the mind, even in wintertime . . . and this one definition is true and perpetual" ("quia rosae noticia seu definitio manet in mente, etiam in hyeme . . . et una est uera ac perpetua definitio").

[76] Also, Nizolio's notion of *comprehensio* is wholly different from Ockham's notion of intuitive cognition. Intuitive cognition gives us direct and correct information about the existence of an object, while Nizolio's *comprehensio* is a mental act by which we grasp individual things as a group.

makes such an answer impossible, and though he assigns an important role to the mind in comprehending the genus *simul et semel*, he avoids talking about mental concepts. Yet he does not deny that we consider things in separation from each other, for example, a quality from its substance, a quality from other qualities, a line from its surface or subject, and so forth.[77] This is indeed what the mind does in comprehending *simul et semel* all individual qualities without their substances, or all individual lines without their matter. We do not abstract or separate things but simply grasp things under a particular aspect, ignoring other aspects. In his edition of Nizolio's work, Leibniz writes here that such a position – abstracting is nothing but considering an object without considering other objects – "has lately been inculcated in many by Thomas Hobbes."[78]

We thus see Nizolio tackling both horns of the dilemma at once. Are categorizations the product of our mind, or are they already out there, waiting as it were to be "comprehended" by an act of the mind? Redefining universals in terms of genera – that is, identifying universals with the classes of objects themselves rather than with mysterious essences that have to be dug up through a laborious process of abstraction – Nizolio thinks he can claim that we can categorize things in many different ways. To use a modern example, we may group bats with bats (one sort) but also with birds (aspect of flying), or, alternatively, with whales and dolphins (making use of echolocation), depending on our questions and interests, but the classes, constructed by the human mind, are always part of reality. It looks like a shrewd alternative to the mind-world identity as defended by moderate realists such as Thomas Aquinas, according to whom the mind and the world are structurally identical.[79] Nizolio simply skips the whole process of transforming bodily information into an immaterial state by way of sensible and intelligible species; nor does he offer an Ockhamist account in terms of intuitive and abstract cognition. But without further explanation, his notion of mental comprehension seems a lot more mysterious than the scholastic process of abstraction, in spite of his claim that his account does not introduce mysterious entities such as universals.

Science, Proof, and Argumentation

As explained, one of Nizolio's aims is to bring science in direct contact with the world of concrete things by lifting the veil of scholastic categories,

[77] Nizolio 1956, 2:84 (3.7).
[78] Ibid., 90 (3.7): "Quod abstrahere, si sano sensu accipiatur nihil aliud sit, quam considerare unam rem, alia non considerata, pluribus hodie inculcavit Thomas Hobbes."
[79] On this position see Pasnau 1997, 295–305; Perler 2006, 135–153.

transcendentals, and universals that had blocked, so he thinks, our view of the world.[80] One of the reasons why universals had been postulated, Nizolio writes, was the idea that science could not be about individuals since they are corruptible;[81] hence, the need for a stable, eternal structure of essences. But if science is about collections of individual objects, does that not make scientific truth dependent on their actual existence here and now? Indeed, one of Nizolio's principal sources, Agricola in his *De inventione dialectica*, said that in order for knowledge and definitions to be possible, things must exist now or in the future.[82] Nizolio must argue that his universals, the genera as classes of things, can be the object of statements that for their truth are not dependent on the actual existence of individual members of the classes, and indeed we find him making the claim that classes themselves are "eternal and immortal."[83] Classes comprise not only actual members of a class here and now but also those of the past and the future. It is not easy to reconcile this claim with other strands in his thinking as analyzed above, such as the flexibility in the mind's grasp of universals and the equation of a class or a genus with its individuals. Leibniz therefore seems correct in remarking that Nizolio cannot get out of this so easily.[84] Nizolio must either admit that induction never gives us certain knowledge (we have experience only of a limited number of cases) or that the mind's *comprehensio* of the universal is not based on individual cases at all. Nizolio was not yet ready to take the first horn of the dilemma, but the other horn would come close to reifying the genus, something which, of course, would go against the spirit of his reform. One way out of the dilemma would perhaps be to view universals as meanings that can be fixed by definition. Arguably, such an approach, by which the extension of a universal or general idea is defined by its content, was developed by Locke, but this is clearly not a feasible option for Nizolio.[85]

A further consequence of his extensional approach is to redefine the nature of syllogisms. In arguing syllogistically, Nizolio says, we move from wholes to parts, rather than from universals to particulars, and – in the case

[80] Nizolio 1956, 1:189–193 (2.8). [81] Ibid., 75–76 (1.7).

[82] Agricola 1539 (*De inventione dialectica* 2.8), quoted by Nizolio 1956, 1:131 (2.1).

[83] Nizolio 1956, 1:76 (1.7).

[84] Ibid., 87 n. 5 (1.7). For more on Leibniz's response, see the last section of this chapter.

[85] Locke 1975, 419–420 (*Essay* 3.3.19): "so the essences of those species are preserved whole and undestroyed, whatever changes happen to any or all of the individuals of those species." Locke, too, had problems accommodating the more traditional view of essences as being ingenerable and incorruptible with a conventionalist and, as Jolley calls it, "deflationary" view; see Jolley 1999, 143–168, at 153: Aaron 1967, 21–41, also points to such strands in Locke (see esp. at 32); see also Newman 2007, esp. 343–346. For Locke's position, see Chapter 8.

of induction – from parts to wholes rather than vice versa.[86] Proving something is basically showing that a part (an individual, a class) is part of a bigger group, rather than showing that a genus can be predicated of each of its members. One proves that Socrates is a living being by taking as premises that the class of living beings contains the class of human beings, and the class of Socrates (just one member) is part of the class of human beings, as if one were drawing increasingly smaller concentric circles. Perhaps Nizolio thought (erroneously) that such a terminology of classes *containing* other classes or *being contained* in other classes would suppress a belief in universals – although, of course, one can be a nominalist concerning universals but still defend the attribution of essential predicates to things.[87] In general, Nizolio does not show any interest in syllogistics as such, and, unlike his fellow anti-Aristotelian Valla, does not review the different figures and moods.[88] His point is that syllogistic reasoning is based on a comparison of classes of wider or smaller scope rather than predicating universal features of all individuals of a class.

Rhetoric: *Res* and *Verba*

Having rejected universals, Nizolio thinks he has put dialectic and metaphysics, in which universals play a central role, in their place. Rhetoric, if properly defined, is the queen of arts. Again, Nizolio is more radical here than his humanist predecessors. Valla had subordinated dialectic to rhetoric, but still conceded a small preparatory stage to the former. Agricola had defined dialectic as the art of speaking convincingly or plausibly (*probabiliter*) about any subject, as suitably as possible.[89] Most humanists tried to erode the boundary between dialectic and rhetoric, but did not aim at completely dissolving it. Nizolio wants to go further, broadening the scope of both logic and rhetoric such that they come down to much the same thing. Once this is established, the way would be clear to argue, as many humanists had already done, that philosophy is essentially a rhetorical subject, and that we must return to the fusion of rhetoric and philosophy, of eloquence and reason, as defended and propagated by

[86] Nizolio 1956, 1:78 (1.7). [87] A good example is Buridan, on whom see Klima 2005.

[88] Valla 2012, 2:210–271 (*DD* 3.1–3.9); see Nauta 2009, 239–268; Mack 1993, 84–92; Vives briefly discusses the syllogisms, alongside other forms of argumentation in *De censura veri*; Vives 1782–1790, 3:169–184 (on which, see Mack 2008, 233). On Valla and Vives see Chapters 2 and 4.

[89] Valla 2012, 2:2–6 (*DD* 2.proem.); Agricola 1539, 206 (and cf. 193). On the meaning of *probabiliter* in Agricola, see Mack 1993, 169–173; see also above Chapter 3 on Vives; cf. Rummel 1995, 169–177; Wels 2000, 187–194.

Cicero. With this aim in mind, Nizolio distinguishes the "false logic" of the pseudo-philosophers from the "true logic," which he defines as the art of speaking well about whatever kind of subject. It is the art that concerns all kinds of communication: discussing, disputing, speaking, and discoursing on all types of questions and about all kinds of subjects, written or spoken.[90] It is then a short step to identify this true logic with rhetoric, which Nizolio claims is broader than the specialized field of forensic oratory. Following Cicero and Quintilian, Nizolio defines rhetoric as the art of speaking well.[91] Having broadened both disciplines in this way, Nizolio equates logic (or dialectic) with rhetoric. The two disciplines do not essentially differ in their subject matter (they treat all subjects); their questions (they both treat general and more specific questions, that is, theses and hypotheses); means of argumentation (both use syllogisms, induction, enthymemes, and example); and techniques (they both use the question-and-answer technique) and their tasks.[92]

With this equation between dialectic and rhetoric in place, it must have been tempting for Nizolio to equate rhetoric with philosophy *tout court*, but he sticks to the Ciceronian distinction between philosophy as knowledge and wisdom, and rhetoric as the verbal expression of this knowledge. The two, however, are intimately connected. "The science of wise thinking" and "elegant speaking" are two sides of the same coin, and Nizolio ardently defends this union of brain and tongue, of reason and eloquence, of philosophy and rhetoric.[93] The two are not separate areas, but one organic whole, just "as body and soul constituting one living being." In Cicero's own words, duly quoted by Nizolio: "Every speech consists of matter and words, and the words cannot fall into place if you remove the matter, nor can the matter have clarity if you withdraw the words."[94] The assumption is that clear and transparent language is essential for clear thinking: indeed, the assumption, as we have seen above, was explicitly formulated by Nizolio as one of the essential conditions for "true and correct philosophizing," alongside a profound knowledge of the classical languages and their literature, as well as of grammar and rhetoric.[95]

[90] Nizolio 1956, 2:91 (3.8). [91] Ibid., 50 (3.5); cf. ibid., 38 (3.3). [92] Ibid., 50 (3.5).

[93] Cicero 1942, 2:45–47 (*De oratore* 3.15.57), 47–49 (16.59–61), 57 (19.69), 59 (19.72–73), 113 (35.142–143), all cited by Nizolio, much aided by his own *Observations in M. T. Ciceronem*; cf. Wesseler 1974, 27–29; Rummel 1995, 175.

[94] Nizolio 1956, 2:31–33 (3.3); 1:82 (1.7) (quotation from Cicero 1942, 2:17 [*De oratore* 3.5.19]). For a good discussion of Cicero's view on *res* and *verba*, see Fantham 2004, 237–266.

[95] Nizolio 1956, 1:22–23 (1.1).

Does such a position result in what some scholars have called, in a rather grand phrase, "the verbalization of the world"?[96] For if things can only be grasped and brought to light and understood if we use the right language – which is the language of the common people, developed and refined by the great authors of classical antiquity – does this not imply that our view of the world is somehow shaped by language? If knowledge and reasoning are based on the way we comprehend individuals as members of groups, and if this act of *comprehensio* is also an oratorical act, as Nizolio explicitly argues, then language seems to determine the ways in which we categorize the world. Such an intimate connection between words and things may render it difficult to distinguish between *res* and *verba*. And, indeed, scholars have argued that the line between the two becomes blurred in many a humanistic text.[97]

In a similar vein some scholars, particularly in the German-speaking world, have interpreted Nizolio's position in terms of a "verbalization or linguification of the world [*Versprachlichung der Welt*]," "a unity of word and thing," and "a comprehensive speech act [*Sprechakt*]" that has an essentially cognitive function and aim, or perhaps a "pre-cognitive" function: in comprehending things *semel et simul* we first form groups of things in a kind of intuitive act, and only at a second stage do we use these groups or categorizations in our discourses, definitions, and proofs.[98] This interpretation, however, is too far-fetched. Admittedly, Nizolio gives cause for such a reading, as he does not explain how our grasp or comprehension of things as one group or class relates to the rhetorical figure of synecdoche or *intellectio*: does the latter shape the way in which we make our categorizations, or is it merely an outer verbalization of the inner mental act of comprehension? But it goes too far to suggest or to imply that he equates the act of thinking with its linguistic expression. Indeed, it would be very strange to say that our capacity to grasp the whole class of individual dogs when we recognize, for example, that Bello is a dog, is the same as the linguistic expression "Bello is a dog," or is constituted by it. In general, Nizolio assumes that words refer to things. Indeed, he makes it quite clear that we should not mix up words and things, for it was precisely mistaking

[96] See n. 98 for references.

[97] See Cave 1979, 21 on Erasmus, quoted Chapter 1, n. 54. Cf. Frank 1995, 77: "kein äusserliches Denominationsverhältnis, sondern eine innere Beziehungsrelation"; "die Rhetorisierung der aristotelischen Kategorienlehre als neues, durch die Sprache vermitteltes Wirklichkeitsverständnis."

[98] Otto 1983, 509–511; Wesseler 1974, 124–147, and esp. at 143; Thieme, preface to Nizolio 1980, 15–16; Hidalgo-Serna 1990.

words for things that led to the postulation of universals by the "pseudo-philosophers."

This would still leave open the possibility that *comprehensio* precedes discursive reasoning, but there is no textual evidence in Nizolio for a distinction between, on the one hand, the creative, rhetorical act of *comprehensio* – in which "word and thing are unified" and in which "the world is grasped in its historicity and contingency" – and, on the other hand, the "rational, scientific and logical" thought that would follow upon such an intuitive understanding.[99] Indeed, Nizolio explicitly argues that synecdoche is used in definitions, syllogisms, proofs, and arguments, as well as in other kinds of forms of language.[100] This suggests that there is no two-step process of (1) a prerational comprehension-synecdoche and (2) a rational-logical processing of the intuitive insights gained in step 1. What such a statement does imply, however, is that the mental grasping and the verbal expression of what we grasp are interlinked. While it goes too far to ascribe to Nizolio a verbalization of thought, we might call it a rhetoricization of knowledge.

Concluding Remarks: Leibniz on Nizolio

What is the significance of Nizolio's attempt to replace the doctrine of universals and the concomitant notion of abstraction with an extensional approach in which classes are groups of individuals grasped simultaneously and comprehensively by the mind? Historically, the attempt failed, as Nizolio's philosophy – to paraphrase Leibniz – suffered "suffocation" almost as soon as it saw the light.[101] While Nizolio's humanist work on Cicero enjoyed immense popularity, his attack in *De principiis* on universals and other basic tenets of Aristotelian-scholastic philosophy elicited little response, unlike the even-more-virulent attacks by Peter Ramus, which would soon provoke widespread controversy.

It would therefore seem too much to claim, as Cassirer did, that Nizolio was "the culmination of the empirical criticisms of Aristotelian philosophy," since Nizolio did not directly contribute to natural philosophy

99 Such a picture is presented by Wesseler 1974, 59–147. He uses the same crude dichotomy to characterize scholastic thought versus humanist rhetoric. Ibid., 105–123, also argues that *exemplum* plays an important role in Nizolio's account of *comprehensio*, but this goes against Nizolio's own account, according to which example and enthymeme are not independent forms of argumentation: see Nizolio 1956, 2:137–138 (4.2).

100 Ibid., 80 (3.7).

101 Leibniz 1966, 405: "Philosophia Nizoliana prope in ipso partu suffocationem aegre effugit."

himself.[102] Yet, standing in a longer tradition of anti-Aristotelianism, Nizolio's criticism of universals, essences, and abstraction may be regarded as a necessary preparatory step in the slow demise of the Aristotelian paradigm. In taking individuals to be grouped in classes on the basis of similarity grasped by the human mind, Nizolio thinks he has no use for substantial forms and essences, let alone divine archetypes. In this he is even more radical than Valla – who still referred, though incidentally, to the Augustinian notion of divine illumination and was ambiguous about universals – and certainly more radical than Agricola (a realist of some sort), Vives, and Melanchthon.[103] Nizolio is wholly secular in his approach, omitting any reference to a divine mind whose ideas would function as eternal archetypes; and equates God with nature (*a Deo sive a natura opifice*), stating that God and all divine things are truly *res naturales*.[104]

His horizontal, lean ontology of only individual substances and qualities, grouped in classes, has clear affinities with Ockhamist nominalism, and this brings us to a second point. It may be tempting to associate his idea – that the real universals are genera that the human mind forms in a comprehensive act – with Ockham's theory of concepts as intellectual acts in which the act itself stands for a thing known. However, as we have seen, many of his claims do not fit in with the Ockhamist program of establishing a mental language of concepts as grounding spoken and written language. Nizolio himself invokes consistently the rhetorical notion of *comprehensio* rather than Ockham's theory. Nizolio does not speak about concepts in the mind that have meaning by nature – an important Aristotelian idea that undergirds Ockham's account – or about concepts as singular entities.[105] Thus, while for Nizolio universals are out there in the form of individuals collected in groups, for Ockham universals are concepts, singular entities that can stand for the individuals resembling the concept and each other. But as we have seen, Nizolio's notion of universal is ambiguous, for while he clearly wants to de-essentialize Aristotelian philosophy by defining universals in terms of classes, the cognitive act by which the individuals are grasped as a class might also be assigned the role of universal. And in spite of his rejection of any kind of reification or hypostatization, he also speaks of universals as being "eternal" and "immortal." His basic conviction remains firm, however: individuals and groups (*singillatim aut universe sive in universum*)

[102] Cassirer 1906–1957, 1:149. [103] Valla 2012, 1:33 (DD 2.2).
[104] Nizolio 1956, 1:59 (1.6); 2:45 (3.4). Nature as a divine creator was a traditional topos, which Nizolio could have taken from, for example, Cicero or Galen.
[105] William of Ockham 1990, 41–45; Panaccio 2004, 119–143.

should be the object of knowledge and scientific statements, rather than forms and predicables being reified or hypostatized. It is therefore not surprising that Nizolio puts experience and sense perception on his list of the true principles of "correct philosophizing."

Thus, Nizolio's basic conviction is that hypostatization and reification, rooted in a misunderstanding of common language, have bedeviled philosophy, and have impeded a fresh look at the world of concrete, empirical things. This has led scholars to link him not only with Ockham, to whom Nizolio himself refers, but also with modern philosophers such as Gilbert Ryle (1900–1976), who thought that universals are the product of a misunderstanding of terms.[106] For Ryle, the question of what sort of objects universals are is a "bogus question."[107] Universals such as justice and rationality are not objects in the way in which dogs and tables are objects, and general nouns and adjectives are not proper names that refer to a particular object. It is the grammatical form of such propositions, however, that might tempt us ("us" philosophers, Ryle adds) into thinking, erroneously, that universals denote objects, while in fact they do not. Hence, philosophy is the reformulation of such "systematically misleading expressions." While such a comparison may indeed be used as a hermeneutic tool to recognize and tease out the philosophical relevance of ideas of a humanist such as Nizolio, it is obvious that Ryle's analysis in terms of categories and category mistakes is fundamentally different from Nizolio's antirealist argument, which focuses on universal terms as collective terms, and on the correct understanding of synecdoche.

A philosopher who did see himself as a sort of ally of Nizolio was Leibniz, the editor of the humanist's work. Leibniz regarded Nizolio as a nominalist, and for this reason "all the more appropriate for our times," since "nothing is truer" than the "rule" of the nominalists "that everything in the world can be explained without any reference to universals and real forms."[108] However, Nizolio also made "many and great errors," and a very serious one concerns precisely the central idea of universals as nothing more than all singulars taken simultaneously and collectively.[109] According to Leibniz, the universal is not an aggregate or a "collective whole," but a "distributive" whole or logical whole: "when we say every man is an animal or all men are animals, the acceptation is distributive; if you take

[106] Copenhaver and Schmitt 1992, 355: "When Ryle claimed that the doctrine of universals arises from a grammatical mistake, his real ally in heresy was not Erasmus but the Ciceronian Nizolio, for whom synecdoche was the most misleading of all expressions."

[107] See Ryle 1932. [108] Leibniz 1969, 128; Leibniz 1966, 428.

[109] For what follows, see Leibniz 1969, 128–130; Leibniz 1966, 430–431.

that man (Titius) or this man (Caius), you will discover him to be an animal."[110] For if the collective whole of all human beings is the same as the genus man, we would get absurd propositions such as "the whole genus is an animal," or "for if they are the same, we may substitute the whole genus man in the proposition that all men are animals or every man is an animal." The concept of man as being a rational animal is independent from the number of instances that we find in the world. Even if there were no human beings on earth, it would still be true to say that man is a rational animal.[111] For the young Leibniz of the 1670 preface to his Nizolio edition, the meaning of a concept is not the same as its extension.[112]

Moreover, Nizolio's position does not leave much independent work for the mind to do: the mind simply grasps a collective whole, and in arguing and proving adds and subtracts classes in arithmetical fashion. But Leibniz wants to assign a much more active role to the mind: it adds its own universal propositions to inductively gained data so that we can arrive at truly universal knowledge. From Nizolio's position on universals, "it would follow that we could attain no knowledge through demonstration – a conclusion which Nizolio actually draws – but only through collecting individuals or by induction."[113] But induction can never result in "true universality." Without discussing Leibniz's position in more detail, one might see these early remarks, provoked by the reading of Nizolio, as early anticipations of his more mature view of the *Discours de métaphysique* from 1686, in which concepts are said to be "so complete that it is sufficient to contain and allow us to deduce from it all the predicates of the subject to which this notion is attributed."[114] Nizolio – among many other thinkers, of course – was important in order for Leibniz to develop his own thoughts about concepts and predication.

Leibniz was not only critical of Nizolio. In the same preface he praises him for having recognized the importance of a clear, nontechnical style in philosophy, and he defends the principle that "whatever cannot be

[110] This is more or less what medieval logicians called "confused supposition": in "every man is an animal," "man" supposes confusedly and distributively (*confuse et distributive*) because it is used for any man, as Peter of Spain 1972, 83 / 2014, 249.

[111] Cf. n. 83 above.

[112] For Leibniz's criticism of Nizolio on this point, see Cassirer 1906–1957, 1:151 and 2:133–135; Tillmann 1912, 58–63. What Ong 1958, 204 said about Ramus may apply to Nizolio as well: "This view makes it necessary for him [Ramus] to overlook the elemental difference between the comprehension and extension of a term, and to view increase in comprehension by the addition of specifying notes . . . as quite the same thing as grouping of individuals . . .within a genus." The meaning of a term seems to be defined here by its extension.

[113] Leibniz 1969, 129; Leibniz 1966, 430–431.

[114] Leibniz 1989, 41.

explained in popular terms is nothing and should be exorcised from philosophy as if by an incantation, unless it can be known by immediate sense experience."[115] Like Nizolio, Leibniz thinks that the "passion for devising abstract words has almost obfuscated philosophy for us entirely," though Leibniz was not entirely immune to such criticism himself.[116] But while sharing Nizolio's plea for a common language in philosophizing, Leibniz has omitted elegance from the three praiseworthy marks of speech (clarity, truth, and elegance), "since our discussion concerns philosophical discourse and the style that befits it." Not surprisingly, he considered Nizolio's principles of correct philosophizing, which included knowledge of classical languages and their literature as well as grammar and rhetoric, "principles of speech rather than of thought."[117] Thus, although he presented Nizolio as an excellent guide toward a "sober, proper, natural, and truly philosophical way of speaking," his omission of elegance from philosophical style suggests that the Ciceronian link between *verba* and *res*, style and content, elegance and clarity-truth, was no longer felt as intimate and intrinsic in the way it had been to humanists such as Nizolio.[118]

Nizolio's project clearly had its philosophical limitations. But, as this chapter has suggested, in stressing observation and sense perception while rejecting what he considered to be the essentialist and fixed categories of the Aristotelian-scholastic system, Nizolio aimed to make room for the inquisitive human mind to categorize the world with flexible classes. And it is these classes, as real universals, that should be the true subject matter of general statements to be qualified and modified as our knowledge advances.

[115] For this and the following quotations see Leibniz 1969, 124, 126, 121–122; Leibniz 1966, 414, 417, 409–410. See also Leibniz 1966, 423 (not in Leibniz 1969): "But I have not found anyone who has so penetrated the essence of scholastic terms [or: who has cut back scholastic terms; *resecuerit*] in other areas of philosophy as Nizolio has done in logic. Though he has hitherto been little known, I think he deserves all the more to stand as a model for the reform of philosophical terminology."

[116] Cf. Leibniz's use, for example, of "*ubiety*" while also stating that "we know, too, that it is abstractions which cause the most problems when one tries to get to the bottom of them. Anyone knows this who is conversant with the intricacies of scholastic thought: their thorniest brambles disappear in a flash if one is willing to banish abstract entities, to resolve that in speaking one will ordinarily use only concrete terms and will allow no terms into learned demonstrations except ones which stand for substantial subjects"; Leibniz 1981, 217 and 221 ("ubiety") (*Nouveaux Essais* II, xxiii).

[117] Leibniz in Nizolio 1956, 1:30 (1.1): "loquendi potius quam sentiendi principia."

[118] For Leibniz 1969, 122, elegance is only useful for "securing attention, in moving minds, and in impressing things more deeply on the memory." Cf. Wels 2000, 87 n. 146; Fenves 2001, 13–79, esp. 13–27; Laerke 2009.

CHAPTER 6

Skepticism and the Critique of Language in Francisco Sanches

Humanism and Skepticism

A central aspect of the critique of scholastic language that we have studied in the previous chapters is the abstract terminology that humanists found not only ungrammatical and ugly but also dangerous, because it invited philosophers to populate the world with abstract entities to which that terminology was supposed to refer. The idea could easily arise that this terminology was a window to a world of stable essences, which, once grasped by a process of abstraction and deductive reasoning, could form the basis of certain, true knowledge. Whatever the difficulty of achieving truth and certainty, Aristotelian science (which is much broader than our modern notion of science) was wholly geared toward arriving at true and necessary conclusions.[1] Starting from true, necessary, and indemonstrable axioms, further truths can be derived by way of valid syllogisms. Aristotle himself had stated that scientific knowledge must be universal and cannot explain particular events or things.[2] His medieval followers in general endorsed the Aristotelian ideal of demonstrative science, though there was much disagreement about crucial notions such as truth, certitude, evidentness, necessity, demonstration, and the scope of true, necessary knowledge.[3]

[1] Barnes 1969; Taylor 1990; Pasnau 2017, 3–6 and 142–143 for a recent discussion, arguing that it is misleading to characterize Aristotle's *Posterior Analytics* as a theory of science or scientific knowledge. Greek *episteme* in the *Posterior Analytics* is best translated as understanding; cf. Burnyeat 1981.

[2] Aristotle 1984, 122 (*Posterior Analytics* 1.8, 75b21). In *Metaphysics* 13.4, 1078b24 he states that "the essence is the starting-point of deductions" (1984, 1705).

[3] For an extensive discussion see Pasnau 2017, who reads much of the history of epistemology as a history of the quest for an epistemic ideal (and a rejection of the feasibility of such a quest), starting with Aristotle's *Posterior Analytics*, which consequently should be interpreted as a description of such an ideal, that is, a kind of normative ideal that delineates the limits of human inquiry.

Without being much concerned about the details of the various positions defended by the scholastics, humanists began to view the Aristotelian model as a bookish and abstract exercise in expounding demonstrative syllogisms based on definitions that supposedly give the essential structure of things. But in criticizing the language of Aristotelian science, they also seemed, from time to time, to put a question mark over the notions of truth and demonstrative certainty. If it is possible to find them at all, truth and certainty are not to be found by the kind of logic set out by Aristotle in his *Posterior Analytics*. Observation rather than syllogistics is the key to making any progress. Things, rather than logical concepts, are what the philosopher should be concerned about. Rejecting the outdated historiographical claim that humanism had done nothing but retard scientific progress, scholarship over the last fifty years has shown the multiple ways in which humanists, in particular in the later Renaissance, contributed to a wide spectrum of natural philosophical and medicinal disciplines.[4] This is not to say that the earlier humanists, studied in the previous chapters, were much concerned about the natural world or that they replaced the Aristotelian framework by another method; the rhetoric of "observing the facts" was often part of a critique of what they considered to be the abstract nature of scholastic thought rather than an attempt to formulate an alternative to the demonstrative ideal of Aristotelian science. Yet, their critique of the Aristotelian paradigm may be said to have prepared for a climate in which alternative approaches could be envisaged.[5]

Because their critique often entailed a certain skepticism about the aims of truth and certainty which they thought were embedded in scholastic Aristotelianism, it is not surprising that humanists have often been branded as skeptics. This started even in their own time, though the accusation of skepticism did not always concern a skeptical attitude toward Aristotelian science. In the sixteenth century in particular, when

[4] Blair and Grafton 1992, and Grafton and Siraisi 1999 for a resumé of the historiographical debates, with further bibliography; Blair 2006.

[5] Schmitt 1972, 11 n. 23. Cf. Pasnau 2017, 31: "Yet it is clear enough that the sixteenth and seventeenth centuries display a growing concern over whether the traditional epistemic ideal of certainty is achievable. Sometimes these doubts amount to an attack on philosophy itself – which means, for that time, also an attack on science itself." Cf. Menn 1998. Before the seventeenth-century critics, Renaissance Aristotelians such as Nifo and Zabarella had already tried to make room for observation, experience, and the utilization of signs within a demonstrative model – a method called *regressus*; these thinkers believed many theories about nature to be provisional and hypothetical; for a clear case see Martin 2011 on Renaissance meteorology: "This does not mean, however, that they were anticipating or applying the modern scientific method or Baconian induction" (23). On the other hand, the ideal of demonstrative certainty remained strong throughout the seventeenth century; see Serjeantson 2006, 164.

confessional strife became rampant in Europe, "Skeptic" became a term of abuse alongside "Epicurean" or "Lucianist" (after the satirist Lucian). The humanist preference for open-ended genres such as dialogues, rhetorical declamations, the argument from both sides (*in utramque partem*), poetry, a philological-grammatical approach to religious texts, and so on, reflected, in the eyes of their opponents, a multi-perspective approach that destabilized tradition and dogma.[6] In modern times, scholars have often associated humanism with skepticism,[7] finding support in the fact that the sixteenth century witnessed the slow rediscovery and use of ancient skeptical texts such as Cicero's *Academica* and, later in the century, Sextus Empiricus's *Outlines of Pyrrhonism* and *Against the Professors*.[8] Thus, because of his critique of scholastic logic and his interest in forms of argumentation that seem to rely on verisimilitude rather than on certainty, Valla has sometimes been regarded as an Academic skeptic. Juan Luis Vives, as discussed in Chapter 4, followed Rudolph Agricola in maintaining that there are many things about which we do not have certainty: "What knowledge we have gained can only be reckoned as probable and not assumed as absolutely true."[9] Erasmus has been called a skeptic for his anti-intellectualism and dislike of rational theology. Already Petrarch had said that he had become a "proselyte of the Academy," who does "not affirm anything, and doubt every single thing."[10] And many more examples could be found.

The polemical use of the term shows that "skepticism," like all "-isms," is a slippery one. Someone who criticizes established dogmas does not, of course, necessarily accept the tenets of ancient skepticism. A philosopher who doubts whether we can know the essences of things, and here we may think of Vives, is not automatically a skeptic – many medieval philosophers would then count as skeptics.[11] And someone who cautiously tries to steer a middle course, as Erasmus did in the debate on free will, is not

[6] Rummel 2000, 51, quoting the Louvain theologian Jacques Masson, in a chapter entitled "No Room for Skeptics."

[7] Kahn 1985; Copenhaver and Schmitt 1992, ch. 4; Rummel 1995 and 2000; Jardine 1977 and 1983; Panizza 1978; Patey 1984, 13–19; Casini 2009.

[8] Information about Academic skepticism could be derived from the writings not only of Cicero but also Plutarch, Galen, Diogenes Laertius, Lactantius, Augustine, and others. On the circulation of Sextus Empiricus before the editions of Henri Estienne (1562) and Gentien Hervet (1569) see Floridi 2002. The classic study is Popkin 2003 (first ed. 1960); understandably not all conclusions have been accepted by later scholars; see for example Ayers 2004; Perler 2004; Backus 2009; Pasnau 2017, 319.

[9] See Chapter 4, n. 69. For a critique of the idea that Valla had endorsed a form of philosophical skepticism, see Nauta 2006a.

[10] Quoted in Cassirer, Kristeller and Randall 1948, 34–35, from Petrarch's letter to Francesco Bruni.

[11] On widely held views that essences cannot be known, see Pasnau 2011.

automatically a skeptic.[12] Also, the use of skeptical arguments or tactics does not automatically turn one into a skeptic, nor is pessimism about the possibility of certain knowledge the same as skepticism. Further, skepticism can range from the local to the global, from religion and science to everyday life, from theory to practice, from explicit endorsement to a merely methodological use. Skeptical arguments may be used to serve a nonskeptical outcome as well as a skeptical one; they may be employed as an expression of one's religious faith (as Montaigne famously did in his *Apology for Raymond Sebond*) or as a preparation for faith (as can be seen in Gianfrancesco Pico della Mirandola's *Examen vanitatis*).[13] It is not surprising therefore that scholars disagree about the importance of skepticism in the history of philosophy.[14] In our application of this label we must therefore be careful, distinguishing between intention, unintended effect, aim, argument, and technique, and also between belief and religious faith. It would perhaps be advisable to restrict the label only to the explicit endorsement of the tenets of philosophical skepticism (of whatever form), but this would go against other, common uses of the term.

Francisco Sanches's *That Nothing Is Known*

Skepticism in whatever form, however, plays a considerable role in the critique of Aristotelian thought if only because it questioned the epistemological ideals of "dogmatic" philosophers, in particular the scholastics. An interesting case is presented by the Portuguese philosopher and medical writer Francisco Sanches (1551–1623), whose *That Nothing Is Known* (*Quod nihil scitur*), published in 1581, is widely regarded as one of the most systematic expositions of philosophical skepticism produced in the sixteenth century, though whether it is closer to Academic skepticism or to Pyrrhonism is a moot point.[15] His main target is scholastic Aristotelianism,

[12] Backus 2009 shows that Erasmus and Castellio cannot be called skeptics, and more generally that Richard Popkin's thesis that "the Reformation debates about the rule of faith instanced the more general problem confronted by Scepticism, that of justifying the criterion of truth" (63) is unfounded. As she concludes: "Thus early modern scepticism has nothing to do with Reformation debates which focus on the status of reason in relation to faith . . . If Pyrrhonism did revive in the 16th c., it did so independently of the confessional debates of the period" (87). See Shapiro 1983, 75–76; Pasnau 2017, 204.

[13] Schmitt 1967 on Pico's critique of Aristotelianism. In general, Penelhum 1983.

[14] See Pasnau 2017 and Perler 2006 for two different evaluations of the role of skepticism in the history of philosophy. On the similarity between late-medieval and early-modern debates on knowledge and perception and the role of skeptical arguments, see Adriaenssen 2017.

[15] Sanches never mentions Sextus Empiricus's works, and his position seems to come closer to Academic skepticism with its emphasis on verisimilitude and probability (Popkin 2003; Limbrick

and in particular the claims to truth and certainty that he thought were intrinsic features of Aristotelian demonstrative science and logic. His diagnosis of scholastic language as wordy and abstract connects him with humanists such as Valla and in particular Vives, to whom he might have been indebted.[16] Like Vives, Sanches had been exposed to late-medieval scholastic logic, which he found wanting in all respects, and like Vives he developed, though in a much stronger way, a position that emphasizes the limits of human knowledge. As an alternative to the Aristotelian demonstrative model, both authors stressed empirical observation, experience, and judgment, elements they saw present in the art of medicine. As a physician Sanches was quite familiar with the writings of Galen, but how far he developed the latter's ideas on method remains difficult to assess since Sanches's own work on method, announced as forthcoming in *That Nothing Is Known*, was probably not written.[17]

This has not hindered scholars from seeing in Sanches's text an adumbration of modern scientific method. Popkin argued that "Sanches was the first Renaissance sceptic to conceive of science in its modern form, as the fruitful activity about the study of nature that remained after one had given up the search for absolutely certain knowledge of the nature of things."[18] Another scholar sees Sanches inaugurating "that (intrinsically anti-humanistic) resetting pattern, so to speak, of philosophical reflection which was to characterize the Cartesian or 'modern' approach to philosophy in the seventeenth century."[19] These judgments have been qualified,

in Sanches 1988; Paganini 2008; Lojacono 2011; Buccolini 2017) than to Pyrrhonism (De Carvalho in Sanches 1955; Naya 2003; Howald in Sanches 2007; Caluori 2007 and 2018). But as Schmitt (1972, 7–8) has already shown, in the Renaissance Pyrrhonism and Academic skepticism were not distinguished from each other. Sanches's main sources for his knowledge of ancient skepticism are Cicero (esp. *Academica*), Diogenes Laertius's *Lives of Eminent Philosophers*, Plutarch's *Adversus Colotem*, and Galen's medical works. In a letter to Christopher Clavius he calls himself *Carneades Philosophus*, after the leading figure of the Academic skeptics in antiquity; in Sanches 1955, 146 and 153.

[16] On Sanches's possible debt to Vives see Comparot 1983; Limbrick in Sanches 1988, 28–33; Howald in Sanches 2007, ciii is more cautious ("kaum mit Sicherheit zu sagen"). Sanches 1988, 273: "scarcely past boyhood, I was being initiated into dialectics." I will give references to Limbrick's English translation; the 1581 Latin text is reproduced by her on pp. 91–164, with the original page numbers in the margins.

[17] "[T]he goal of my proposed journey is the art of medicine, which I profess, and the first principles of which lie entirely within the realm of philosophical contemplation" (Sanches 1988, 171). On his critical engagement with Galen, see Limbrick in Sanches 1988, 50–76, and most recently Buccolini 2017.

[18] Popkin 2003, 41; cf. Limbrick in Sanches 1988, 53: "embryonic form of scientific method based on experimentation and a weighing of the facts by the faculty of judgment in which experience, too, was to play a decisive role." See Serjeantson 2006 for some good remarks on the new discourse of "fact" as opposed to the characteristic scholastic assumptions about proof and persuasion in the early-modern period.

[19] Lupoli 2009, 151.

for striking as the parallels between Sanches's prologue to *That Nothing Is Known* and the beginning of Descartes's *Discours de la méthode* seem to be at first reading, the differences in their approach to the theory of knowledge are perhaps more significant.[20] Nevertheless, Descartes might have had Sanches in mind when he stated that he "was not copying the sceptics, who doubt only for the sake of doubting and pretend to be always undecided."[21] Sanches thus occupies an interesting position between humanists such as Valla and Vives on the one hand, and early modern philosophers such as Descartes, Mersenne, Gassendi, and Leibniz on the other. In view of the theme of this study, the linguistic aspect of his critique will be highlighted in what follows, but this cannot of course be separated from an examination of the structure and arguments of *That Nothing Is Known*.

"The Endless Uncertainty of Names"

A central feature of Sanches's critique is the verbal nature of Aristotelian science; in fact right from the start he suggests that any attempt to state something about science and knowledge is precarious because of language:[22]

> how are we to assign names to something we do not understand? I do not see how – yet names they are. Hence there is an endless uncertainty concerning names, and a great deal of confusion and deceitfulness in the matter of words, perhaps even in everything I have just asserted.

The skeptic too cannot do without words, and Sanches himself never wants to say anything dogmatic, not only because – as he frequently states – he is as ignorant as anyone else but also because his words too might already suggest too much fixity.[23] This is what he loathes in Aristotelian science: its concepts, definitions, and demonstrations try to reveal the nature of things while in fact they are mere layers of words. Of course, his opponent, always presented as an imaginary interlocutor, will say: when I define man as

[20] Howald in Sanches 2007, lxiii–lxiv; Carvalho in Sanches 1955, 188. "Theory of knowledge" is a problematic term when applied to early-modern thinkers. For a critique see Pasnau 2017, for example, 24: "if epistemology is conceived of in its usual modern guise, then Descartes cannot be said to have a theory of knowledge at all. What he has is an idealized epistemology, a theory of *Scientia*."

[21] Descartes 1984–1991, 1:125 (*Discourse on method* III); cf. Limbrick in Sanches 1988, 84.

[22] Sanches 1988, 174; cf. 185: "all human activities are suspect, including the very words I am writing at the moment."

[23] Potential miscommunication and misunderstanding led Galen, some of whose works Sanches knew well, to say that "I wish I could both learn and teach things without the names for them"; quoted by Morison 2008, 140. It is an age-old sentiment. See also Chiaradonna 2019, 325 and Reinhardt 2011 on Galen's views on the limits of language.

a rational and mortal animal, I define a thing, not a word, but this, Sanches says, will not do, for what, for example, is rational?[24] This requires further explanation, which means further verbal explication, till we end up, in this case, with the highly general concept of Being, which, as the opponent admits, cannot be defined "for it has no higher genus to which it belongs." All these words that we use while descending the categorical ladder from being via substance, body, living, animal, man to the individual Socrates, are just words. And if these words, Sanches continues, refer to one and the same Socrates, they are "too many words"; if not, then Socrates is not a single thing with a fixed identity. This is of course a very strange assumption, as if the number of words should match that of things (or aspects of the world), and his interlocutor is quick to defend the plurality of words: they point to qualities or attributes of one and the same thing, "attributes to which I give, severally, their appropriate names."[25] This gives Sanches the opportunity to introduce a theme that will run as a basso continuo throughout his treatise: the opposition of words and things, or more generally the opposition between a kind of armchair philosophy and an empirical approach based on experimental observation:[26]

> Not only do you fail to comprehend the man as a whole, who is something large, solid, and perceptible by the senses; you divide him into portions so small as to escape the senses, which are the most reliable of all means of judging – portions that have to be sought for by means of the reason, which is deceitful and obscure.

In due course Sanches will also put a question mark over the reliability of the senses, while reason will be judged to be essential when it comes to passing sound judgment on the information derived from the senses. But at this stage Sanches focuses on the verbal nature of the Aristotelian enterprise, starting in typically skeptical manner, from the position of his opponents, though these opponents would of course not accept his polemical description of metaphysical concepts as portions too small to see.

The next step for Sanches is to question the need for technical terminology. The Aristotelians have recourse to their great master, but Sanches – for the sake of argument – says that he might cite Cicero as an authority. And if his opponents object that Cicero's language is less exact than

[24] The interlocutor plays several roles in Sanches's text (opponent, pupil, colleague); this gives the text a dialogical nature, actively inviting the reader to participate in the dialogue. It has some similarities with the ancient genre of diatribe, made popular in the sixteenth century. See Howald in Sanches 2007, xlv–xlvii.

[25] Sanches 1988, 175.

[26] Ibid.; an important theme also for Galen; see Morison 2008, 139; Chiaradonna 2019, 325.

Aristotle's, Sanches will simply deny this, saying that it was Cicero's business "to show the meanings of words."[27] This does not mean, however, that he wants to defend Ciceronian language as opposed to Aristotelian terminology. Already in the prologue, Sanches had said to his readers not to expect an elegant, polished style from him:[28]

> Truth slips away while we substitute one word for another and employ circumlocutions – for this is verbal trickery. If that is what you want, seek it from Cicero, whose function it is; I shall speak prettily enough if I speak truly enough.

His aim in setting Cicero against Aristotle is simply to make a general point about authors twisting words to serve their own purpose: "there is no agreement among them, no fixity or stability or set of guidelines. Each of them mutilates words as he pleases, and distorts their meaning in this way or that, adapting them to his own purpose." Sanches thus rejects the elegant language of the Ciceronians as much as the technical terminology of the dialecticians and philosophers. In what seems to be an attack on the arts of the trivium, he denounces the practitioners of grammar, rhetoric, and poetry for their "useless loquacity," and the logicians for their fixation on order, rules, and constraints. "Which of them will you prefer to trust?" Sanches pretends not to know of course, but he suggests, much in line with Vives, that "the meanings of words appear to depend, for the most part or wholly, on popular usage; and here, accordingly, is where we must look for them; for who but the populace (*vulgus*) taught us how to speak?"[29] The basis for discussion should therefore perhaps be "what most people say." So when we start discussing what knowledge or health is, we should start with "the common sayings of mankind" – a Galenic point that Sanches could have learned from Galen's *Methods of Healing* in Thomas Linacre's translation.[30] For Galen, ordinary language should be the starting point in any inquiry.[31]

[27] Ibid., 176. [28] Ibid., 171 for this and the following quotation.

[29] Sanches 1988, 176–177. He seems to allude to the famous line from Horace, often quoted by humanists in this connection: "if Usage so will it, in whose hands lies the judgement, the right and the rule of speech" (Horace 1926, 457; *Ars Poetica* 71–72).

[30] See Galen, *Methods of Healing*, X 40–2, quoted by Hankinson 2008, 167. Cf. Morison 2008, 146. But Sanches would probably find the other aspects of Galenic method, such as the deliverance of element-theory, and the search for causes, definitions, and so on, too dogmatic and rationalist.

[31] Hankinson 2008, 180; Morison 2008; Chiaradonna 2019, 325–326: "Yet Galen also suggests that the analysis of meanings of words in ordinary language *is* necessary for scientific research, since those meanings are connected to our common notions, which are by no means misleading or stipulative. Rather, common notions are a basic set of concepts shared by all human beings that provide a pre-theoretical knowledge of things . . . Such pre-scientific knowledge should be taken as a starting-point for appropriate knowledge (as is the case with dialectical premises)."

Sanches realizes, however, that there is no fixity and stability in the common language of the people either. As he repeatedly says, every question, every issue depends on words,[32] and words do not have fixed meanings: whatever meaning we give to words, these words will never be able to disclose the nature of things. In an allusion to the notion of the first name-giver (*impositor*) who was supposed to have assigned a name to a thing for the first time, Sanches says that it is fruitless to enquire what meaning was assigned by the first person who bestowed this word.[33]

In his attempt to checkmate his opponent, Sanches has arrived at the conclusion that language, whether technical or common, is an utterly unreliable guide in philosophy and science. But perhaps he has also checkmated himself, for in what follows we find him defending common usage but also, as a physician, acknowledging the need for some technical terminology. Let us begin with this last point. We saw Sanches alluding to Cicero, and because he was discussing "quality," it is clear that he had the following passage from Cicero's *Academica* in mind, where the interlocutor Varro defends his choice of the word *qualitates* as a translation of the technical Greek term *poietetas*:[34]

> I have therefore given the name of "qualities" to the things that the Greeks call *poiotētes*; even among the Greeks it is not a word in ordinary use, but belongs to the philosophers, and this is the case with many terms. But the dialecticians' vocabulary is none of it the popular language, they use words of their own; and indeed this is a feature shared by almost all the sciences: either new names have to be coined for new things, or names taken from other things have to be used metaphorically. This being the practice of the Greeks, who have now been engaged in these studies for so many generations, how much more ought it to be allowed to us, who are now attempting to handle these subjects for the first time!

As it was Cicero's project to render Greek philosophy and terminology into Latin, making it accessible to the common public, he grants this to Varro, of course: "I think you will actually be doing a service to your fellow-countrymen if you not only enlarge their store of facts, as you have done, but of words also."[35] This defense of new words and technical terminology might seem inconsistent with Cicero's appeal to common linguistic usage –

[32] Sanches 1988, 101 ("almost every enquiry is about a name"); cf. 95–96; 97, and elsewhere.

[33] Ibid., 177. On the notion of *impositor* see Cameron 2012.

[34] Cicero 1951, 435–437; *Academica* 1.7.25.

[35] Ibid., 437 (1.7.26). Cf. Cicero 1951, 11 (*De natura deorum* 1.4.8) on his defense of Latin as an equally resourceful language as Greek for philosophy – a position warmly endorsed, as we have seen, by humanists such as Bruni (see Chapter 1, n. 64).

"the orator should not weigh his words in the goldsmith's balance, but rather in a sort of popular scale"[36] – but an orator is not a philosopher or a scientist. Like Vives before him, Sanches seems to vacillate somewhat on this point. We must start, he says, with the common sayings of mankind: "But here too we must accept the universally approved principle that all men think themselves healthy when, etc." The "etc." becomes clear in what follows.[37] In his marginal annotations he refers the reader to Aristotle's *Physics* and Galen's *De differentiis morborum*. In his commentary on the latter work Sanches remarks that "Galen was right in striving to take the meaning of health and sickness from common linguistic usage; for linguistic usage as well as the will of people gives speech its signification."[38] This, however, also represents a serious problem for the sciences,

> since the populace does not use words appropriately nor does it understand the things referred to by those words, for while it speaks of health, it does not know at all what it is. Hence medical doctors, who understand or nearly understand the matter, are forced to use words in a different way than the populace does, or to use words with a different meaning (*ad alia significata transferre*) or, even, impose new meanings (*nova imponere*) after consultation of Galen, Cicero and other writers.[39]

But while inventing new words or using words in a different way than common people do is allowed to the medical doctors and practitioners of other crafts and professions in the sciences, it is apparently forbidden to philosophers, for in *That Nothing Is Known* Sanches's target are the dialecticians and philosophers who he accuses, in terms similar to Vives's, of abusing words, for example, even such a simple word as "is":[40]

> They distort words from their proper meanings, and corrupt them in order to have another language of their own, quite different from their mother-tongue, yet the same. And when you go to them in order to learn something, they change the meanings of the words you had hitherto employed, in such a way that these no longer denote the same objects – that is, objects in the natural world – but instead the objects that they themselves have invented.

They do so, Sanches continues, to make a big impression on their audience, effectively silencing them in awe. Like the critics before him, Sanches polemically contrasts the philosophers, who spent so much time and

[36] *De oratore* 2.38.159; Cicero 1942, 1:313. Interestingly, Cicero criticized Epicurus for being inconsistent in his appeal to ordinary language while at the same time using words such as "pleasure" and "morality" in his own, idiosyncratic way; see Taylor 2016.

[37] Sanches 1988, 177. [38] Passage cited by the editors of Sanches 1988, 177 n. 34; my translation.

[39] Ibid.; my translation. The phrases echo Cicero's words from the passage in the *Academica*.

[40] Sanches 1988, 119, translation with one emendation.

energy on such a clear and familiar word as "is," with the common people: "Children are better scholars than philosophers. If you ask them whether papa is at home, then (if he should in fact be there) they answer, 'He is.'"[41] Philosophers, however, think that we can express truths about things that do not even exist. "Man is an animal" was true even before any person existed. The "is" in this proposition, they say, signifies essence. But how can a man be an animal if man does not exist, Sanches asks rhetorically, concluding without much argumentation that all this philosophizing about being, existence, and essence is a mere game of words, and not a harmless game at that, since with the introduction of new words they invent new things: "whereas they ought to investigate the natures of things and their causes, and do in fact claim to do so, they invent *new* things."[42] Not that Sanches thinks that such an investigation will lead to any positive result.

Furthermore, he rejects the idea of some philosophers – without mentioning any names – that "philosophy can be taught in no language but Greek or Latin, because, they claim, there are no words available for us to translate a great many expressions that are in those tongues."[43] As examples Sanches gives the usual suspects such as *entelecheia*, *essentia*, *quidditas*, and *corporeitas*, and "similarly artificial creations of the philosophers, which, having no meaning at all, can be neither understood nor explained by anyone – much less rendered into everyday speech (*sermo vulgaris*), which is accustomed to assign only to *real* things (but not to invented things) names of their own."[44] Sanches probably does not want to say that everyday speech cannot be used to refer to fictions or dreams, but the message is clear: While our common language refers to the world of things, the jargon of the philosophers refers only to their own fictions. Again, the contrast is between (mere) words and things. Similar tactics were used later by Hobbes and Leibniz to show the artificiality of words: ask for a translation of such a word into the vernacular or in the language of common people and you will see how nonsensical such a word is.[45]

The idea behind such an alleged exclusivity of Latin or Greek, Sanches maintains, is that they are believed to have a particular efficacy in expressing the nature of things. This is nonsense, he says, deriding etymologies that purport to show that words have been assigned in accordance with the nature of the thing signified, such as "*la-pis*" (stone) from "*laedat pes*"

[41] Sanches 1988, 217. [42] Ibid., 180. [43] Ibid., 217. [44] Ibid., 119.
[45] See below Chapter 7, n. 24.

(hurts the foot).[46] Moreover, the same etymology does not work in other languages that have different words for the same object. Perhaps then, only in the first language, that of Adam, who assigned names to things on the basis of his knowledge of the natures of things? Well, "in that case it were much to be desired that Adam had committed to writing either his own philosophy or a version, in his own language, of the philosophy we have."[47] But now we have many languages, and neither Greek nor Latin nor any other language directly reflects the nature of things. They also change through continual use, so that for example, "ancient spoken Latin and Greek" have died out altogether, and mutual borrowings have resulted in languages that cannot be considered "wholly regular and uncorrupted": "Therefore there lies in words no power to explain the nature of things, except that which they derive from the arbitrary decision of him who applies them; and the same word, *canis* (dog), may mean 'bread' (*panis*) just as much as 'dog,' if he so pleases." Arbitrary decisions would spill over into linguistic anarchy if this would be true, and elsewhere Sanches champions common usage as the arbiter of meaning, however flexible and mutable this usage is. Sanches's strategy is therefore to undermine the confidence that his opponents put in their Aristotelian terminology, as if their words provide us with a clear window on the nature of things. Words cannot do that; in fact, they have nothing in common with things, and even onomatopoeic words only resemble things in their sounds. Sanches's conventionalism goes hand in hand with his rejection of essences, or at least with giving up the hope that we can ever have knowledge of the inner essences of things.

A Critique of Aristotelian Definitions of Knowledge

Without much argumentation, Sanches repeats his critique of the focus on words rather than on things throughout his treatise. He first critically reviews two Aristotelian definitions of knowledge. The first definition states that knowledge is a mental disposition, acquired by demonstration –

[46] Here, and in many other places, Sanches makes use of infinite regress to suggest that we remain at the level of mere words. To explain a word (in etymology, in definition, and so on), we need another word, and then another word, and so ad infinitum. On Galen's rather skeptic approach toward etymologies, see Morison 2008, 123–127 and 132–137. Sanches's frequent appeal to infinite regress might have been inspired by Diogenes Laertius's account of Agrippa's modes: "The mode which involves extension ad infinitum refuses to admit that what is sought to be proved is firmly established, because one thing furnishes the ground for belief in another, and so on ad infinitum"; Diogenes Laertius 1925, 1:501.

[47] Sanches 1988, 219 for this and the following quotation.

a definition that defines the obscure by the more obscure, Sanches thinks. He critically questions his fictive interlocutor about the latter's attempt to give substance to this definition of knowledge (and some of its reformulations), leading to a critique of the predicables (genus, species, differentiae, and so on), the notion of abstraction (including the active intellect), a whole range of notions explained by Aristotle in his *Categories*, demonstration and, unsurprisingly, the syllogism. Like his predecessors, Sanches finds "the science of syllogisms" totally uninformative – a maze of words, a *labirynthum*, "word-chains" (*verborum concetationes*), useless, and indeed "most harmful inasmuch as it distracts me from the observation of facts and keeps me engaged in the study of itself."[48] Sciences are not created by syllogisms, and usually "we are satisfied with a direct relation of antecedent and consequent."[49] Sanches's tactic is simply never to accept a clarification or a sort of proof, but to constantly ask for further clarification, though it is, of course, not part of his brief to make his opponent's case as strong as possible; we are hardly ever told what the function and purpose of a particular concept or doctrine is or why it had been introduced in the first place. And so the Aristotelians, in piling up words upon words, sink further down in their verbal swamp: "everything in Aristotle's *Metaphysics* and his other works is a definition of terms. Hence, almost every enquiry is about a name." And even if we decide to assign a word afresh so that we know that this particular word has this meaning, it does not help you: "You do not know what 'word' is, what 'this' is, what 'meaning' is."

Sanches is careful not to seem dogmatic about knowledge himself, though he does not always succeed in doing so, and at times he has to restrain himself "for I have said more than might have appeared suitable to one who knows nothing!"[50] His forthright rejection of his opponents' positions is often thinly disguised as skeptical questioning, and he often introduces his own ideas and theses, perhaps only for the sake of (counter) argument, as strategic moves in an argumentative game. After all, the treatise is presented as his own quest, his own pursuit of "a definition of knowledge," establishing "as far as I am able, a kind of scientific knowledge that is both sound and as easy as possible to obtain."[51] For instance, against his opponents' view that knowledge is "an acquired disposition which is an accumulation of many syllogistic inferences," Sanches entertains the idea that knowledge "can be only of one each individual thing, taken by itself, not of many things at once, just as a single act of seeing relates only to one

[48] Sanches 1988, 188 and 186; cf. Serjeantson 2006, 152, and see Chapter 8, n. 11 on Locke.
[49] Ibid., 186; 183 and 184 for the next two quotations. [50] Ibid., 199. [51] Ibid., 189 and 290.

particular object."[52] This suggestion too, however, will fall prey to skeptical doubts, since each thing in itself is so complicated that we will never know it entirely. Yet, Sanches develops this position a bit more, arguing that knowledge is an active mental gazing at the images of the things stored in the memory:[53]

> It is not, therefore, things or images of them existing within us that produce or constitute knowledge; rather, the memory is filled up by them and the intellect subsequently reflects on them. Hence I can now draw the inference that it is quite wrong for knowledge to be described as an "acquired disposition"; for an "acquired disposition" is a *quality*, and cannot easily be transferred, whereas knowledge is not a quality, unless you were willing to describe seeing as a quality; rather it is a single action of the mind, which can be entirely perfect even at the first glance and lasts no longer than the mind is engaged in – and this is also true of seeing.

Only when the mind directly "contemplates" the images of the things we can speak of knowledge; just recalling them is remembering, not knowledge as such.

If Sanches really means to say here that only when the mind contemplates (*contemplari*) its pictures can we speak of knowledge, this would be quite an innovative thesis, perhaps anticipating Descartes's position according to which ideas are objects of thought or perception; as a rule, scholastics did not treat species as inner objects of perception.[54] As Sanches says elsewhere: "knowledge is nothing but inward seeing."[55] But it is difficult to see in this a momentous step in the history of epistemology. The context, again, is polemical; in refuting the Aristotelian thesis that knowledge is a kind of acquired disposition, Sanches wants to stress the momentary and active nature of the mind in contrast to the passive storage of images in the mind that would be enough to count as knowledge on his opponents' account:[56]

[52] Ibid., 189 and 190. [53] Ibid., 192.

[54] Pasnau 2017, 73; Pasnau quotes another passage from Sanches on p. 259, concluding that it "would not have been credible to say that we *see* images, because this is something that no one at the time accepted." However, the passages quoted by me might be read as saying precisely this, at least if Sanches's contemplation of images can be interpreted as perception.

[55] Sanches 1988, 189.

[56] Sanches 1988, 191. In emphasizing the mind's active role in gaining knowledge, Sanches might be seen as tacitly taking a position in medieval debates on the passive or active nature of the soul (as Howald in Sanches 2007, clii does) but if at all, he does so only at a very general level; the text hardly presents any evidence for a critical engagement on Sanches's part with particular scholastic positions.

> I do admit that these things must *exist* in someone's mind in order to be known by him; this, however, is not knowledge but memory, just as seeing is not an accumulation of visual presentations within the eye (suppose that this is how seeing occurs), even though seeing cannot occur *without* those visual presentations.

Yet, it is interesting to see Sanches arguing, as far as his skeptic stance allows him of course, for a turn inward, or introspection as an argument against what he presents as the standard Aristotelian account.

The distinction between knowledge and remembrance leads Sanches to digress on Plato's theory of knowledge as recollection. Without going into detail, we may note again Sanches's linguistic perspective: "our enquiry is about a name,"[57] and in the course of his digression he appeals to ordinary usage ("what we say") to make clear that knowledge is not recollection; why else should we use different words? "They do not mean the same thing."

Without signaling that he now turns to discussing a second, Aristotelian definition of knowledge, he critically examines the definition of knowledge as understanding something by means of its causes.[58] Using his favorite tactic, he attempts to show that the opponent's position leads to an infinite regress (to know me, you must know my father, and then his father, and so on).[59] The word "cause" is not very clear either, and which of the four Aristotelian causes are we talking about? Moreover, Aristotle himself had acknowledged that knowledge of something depends on its first principles, which however cannot be demonstrated and hence are unknown. But perhaps more importantly, Sanches's opponents have perverted (*deflectentes*) "realities into words and syllogisms," identifying first principles with the primary propositions of each particular science, causes with intermediate propositions, and elements with subject, copula, and other terms of which a syllogism consists. Again, in the hands of the Aristotelians the search for things soon becomes a game of words.

The doctrines discussed so far, he says, appear to him as false while his own ideas, which he will discuss in an equally critical manner, appear to him as true (*vera*), but this of course is not to say that they *are* true: in fact, the upshot is that "we completely lack knowledge," and "that nothing can be known." Sanches's alternative formulation, which reminds us of

[57] Ibid., 195.

[58] Scholars often comment on Sanches's well-ordered and systematic discussion, but he frequently says "let's go back to our topic," "Now I return to my theme," "I will turn to something else" (195; 201; 211, 220; 224), and he does not guide the reader clearly through the discussion.

[59] Sanches 1988, 196. Causal understanding is part and parcel of the Aristotelian epistemic ideal, see Wallace 1972–1974; for a survey see Pasnau 2017, 153–155.

Aquinas and other scholastics, of knowledge being "perfect understanding of a thing," is liable to the same critique: "we attempt to demonstrate the natures of things in words, and these words again in other words, which is both hard and impossible."[60] We lack a criterion to arbitrate our dispute.[61] Yet, the fierce opposition to the Aristotelian account with its focus on universals, definitions, demonstrations, and syllogisms, reveals Sanches's own preference: ideally, perfect knowledge is of particulars, including their accidents, and should be based on empirical observation: "it is only of individuals that knowledge can be possessed . . . I cannot see anything that is 'universal'; everything in them is particular."[62] Here he sounds like a strict nominalist, but unlike a nominalist such as William of Ockham who had located generality in thought and language, founding the meanings of written and spoken language on mental language, Sanches considers such universals such as man and horse as fictions of the philosopher:[63]

> You will maintain that you are not considering particular things, which as such are not the objects of knowledge, but universals such as "man," "horse," and so on. But in fact, as I said before, your "knowledge" is knowledge not of the real man but of the "man" whom you invent for yourself accordingly, you *know* nothing.

At an early stage in his career Ockham had indeed defended the position that universals were mental constructs (*ficta*), that is, pure "intentional objects" that do not exist in any of the Aristotelian categories – a position he later replaced by the view that universals are mental acts: the universal concept dog is the act of thinking about several dogs at once.[64] It might be that Sanches refers here to this early theory of Ockham, but since he considers universals also on the same footing as "Democritus's Atoms, Plato's Ideas, Pythagoras's Numbers, and Aristotle's Universals, Active Intellect, and Intelligences" as being all "non-existent things,"[65] it is doubtful whether he has such a specific position in mind. It seems that he does not use the word "fiction" in a technical sense (as Ockham did) but rather as a general word of abuse to contrast the world of concrete things to the fictions of the philosopher's imagination.[66] Moreover, if he has an Ockhamist in mind, which the interpretation of *ficta* in terms of Ockham's

[60] Sanches 1988, 200. For some illustrative quotations from Aquinas, Duns Scotus, and other scholastics, see Pasnau 2017, 144.

[61] Ibid., 201. [62] Ibid., 213; cf. the preface, 168. [63] Ibid., 196. [64] Adams 1987, 1:71–107.

[65] Sanches 1988, 168.

[66] Howald in Sanches 2007, cxxvi–cxxxvi sees in Sanches clear allusions to the nominalist position, and even in more detail to the *ficta*-theory of Ockham. However, Sanches uses the term in general to refer to the philosopher's "fictions" (*fictio*, *figmentum*); see for example 1988, 290.

earlier theory supposes, the reply he puts in the mouth of his interlocutor does not fit a nominalist such as Ockham, for the latter did consider the possibility of intellectual knowledge of individuals while in general endorsing the Aristotelian ideal of scientific demonstration.[67] Sanches's criticisms that science should be about things rather than about mental fictions might reflect a common objection, already stated by Duns Scotus, against the nominalist position, according to which science, properly speaking, is about mental concepts that stand for (*supposit*) things in the outside world rather than being about these things directly;[68] but, again, it might equally well be directed at Aristotelians in general, for example, Thomas Aquinas, according to whom the intellect knows only universals while the senses perceive the individuals. In other words, Sanches's seemingly nominalist statements are argumentative moves in his anti-Aristotelian polemic rather than an explicit engagement with a particular nominalist position.

As a skeptic, Sanches cannot endorse the view he seems to favor, namely that knowledge is the perfect understanding of a thing. Not only does an explanation of the parts of this definition easily lead to an infinite regress ("the doubt about names would go on forever"[69]), Sanches's discussion of the three elements – thing, understanding, and perfection – aims at showing how difficult the attainment of this ideal is and how great our ignorance is; he diagnoses the human predicament as pretty hopeless and incurable.[70] The variety of things is endless, both in individuals and in species (if there are such things as kinds, but Sanches is skeptical); they are all in some way connected;[71] each thing down to the most humble creature is a vastly complex system; there are things we cannot perceive (too big or too small), their accidents are perhaps nothing in themselves but dependent on the perceiver; there might even be a plurality of worlds; our categorization of the living world into species is changing with the finding of new organisms in the new world. Such findings might be interpreted as an increase of our knowledge, of course, but Sanches always draws the opposite conclusion: that we are ignorant and do not know anything. Seemingly accepting the traditional assumption that knowledge can be had

67 Serene 1982; Moody 1935, 220–280.

68 For Duns Scotus's criticisms see Duns Scotus 1997–1998, 215; cf. Adams 1987, 1:71–107. Howald in Sanches 2007, cxxxi n. 16.

69 Sanches 1988, 200.

70 This feature of an incurable human predicament is emphasized by Lupoli 2009.

71 Sanches 1988, 204–206, and on his skepticism about kinds see 213–215. Cf. perhaps Diogenes Laertius on one of Agrippa's modes: "The mode derived from relativity declares that a thing can never be apprehended in and by itself, but only in connexion with something else. Hence all things are unknowable"; Diogenes Laertius 1925, 1:501.

only of things that remain identical over time, he asks how we as corruptible and finite beings can claim to know things that are incorruptible, infinite and eternal.[72] Things are generated and corrupted in many different ways, and some miraculous examples of generation are recounted by Sanches without compunction. In this bewildering proliferation of phenomena our mind, "vacillating this way and that, can never come to rest";[73] Sanches apparently does not expect any Pyrrhonian tranquillity of the mind (*ataraxia*) to set in, since the mind is "tortured incessantly by grief, in despair of being able to know anything completely." Moreover, the mind has to work with the material – images of the outward appearance of things – that the senses provide, and this material often misleads us and, even if reliable, can never provide knowledge of the essences of things, only of their accidents.[74]

The examination of the two other elements in the definition of knowledge as the perfect understanding of a thing, namely understanding (*cognitio*) and the perfection of knowledge, leads, predictably, to the same conclusion that nothing can be known. The understanding has three aspects: the thing that is apprehended, the apprehending subject, and the apprehension itself. To understand apprehension we need to study the soul, but this is extremely difficult and obscure, as Vives, to whom Sanches refers, had already said. Sanches defends Vives against Julius Caesar Scaliger's criticism: if Vives's opinion is "absurd," as Scaliger had said, then Sanches is "inclined to be the most absurd of all."[75] In discussing this issue Sanches repeats points already made, namely that scientific knowledge or knowledge which occurs as a result of argumentation "is *not* that which is gained by syllogisms and divisions and categories and other mental operations of a similar sort," and that we can never go beyond

[72] One influential formulation about *scientia* in its most strict form (of four ways in which we can speak of *scientia*) as being comprehension of immutable things is by Robert Grosseteste in his commentary on Aristotle's *Posterior Analytics*; Grosseteste 1981, 99; cf. Pasnau 2017, 146.

[73] Sanches 1988, 233 for this and the following quotation. The other points just mentioned can be found on p. 225 (dependence on perceiver), 222 (plurality of worlds), 222 (new organisms), and 228 (corruptible beings).

[74] Howald in Sanches 2007, cxxxvi–cxliv and Paganini 2007, 74–77 read Sanches's discussion of the mind's dependency on images received from the senses as an engagement with the Thomistic species-theory, but there is hardly anything in the text that justifies such a reading, not least because Sanches does speak here of "*simulacra*" and "*imagines*," not of "*species*" (236–237); he uses the term "species" elsewhere but apparently in the more general sense of impression as, for example a dog has of its environment (241). Sanches's discussion is brief and general, without alluding to scholastic epistemological debates on the role and status of sensible species, intelligible species, and so on; which is not to say that he was not familiar with the general outlines of these debates, but his goal is simply to undermine both the reliability of both the senses and reason.

[75] Sanches 1988, 240.

the accidents of things to know the thing's essence.[76] The steps in sense perception are obscure and full of uncertainty: we never know what the ideal circumstances are, or which medium we can trust. External media and internal media (sight, hearing, taste, and so on) all affect our perception of things, and Sanches could build on a long tradition of skeptical arguments that aimed at showing the uncertainty of human perception.

In later sections he discusses the human body, arguing that perfect understanding requires a perfect body, a condition that is never met of course. His opponent might want to claim that understanding is not dependent on the body, but according to Sanches, whose medical profession is evident in these pages, "it is futile to say that the mind understands, just as it is to say that the mind hears. It is the *human being* who does both, using body *and* mind in both instances."[77] Neither perfect bodies nor perfect minds exist, and hence neither "perfect understanding and consequently not scientific knowledge either – which is the same thing" exist. Again, the conclusion is "that nothing is known."

The student who wants to pursue a scholarly career has to overcome not only the limits of bodily and mental powers, but also the current educational and didactic practices. The educational system encourages membership of a sect rather than critical thinking of one's own, something a skeptic, inspired by Cicero's defense of the freedom to philosophize, wants to champion.[78] The focus is always on texts rather than on things; the scholarly community thrives on disputations and disagreements, but for all its members' differences of opinion they form a closed-off community that only recognizes its own way of philosophizing with its emphasis on syllogisms, verbal explications, commentaries, epitomes, list of headings, and other forms of instructions. The alternative is experience combined with judgment, but while this is the way to go, Sanches ends his treatise by emphasizing, once again, the limits of these "methods." Experience never reveals the natures of things, while judgment reveals

[76] The thesis that we know substances only through qualities was defended by a number of scholastic authors, for example Richard of Mediavilla, Vital du Four, Duns Scotus, Ockham, and Nicholas of Autrecourt; see Robert 2006 and Perler 2006, 255; Pasnau 2011, 115–134. It was repeated by many later authors; see, for example, Gassendi as quoted by Pasnau 2011, 116: "nothing beyond qualities is perceived by the senses," and Descartes (Pasnau 2011, 136). Cf. Introduction, n. 12.

[77] Sanches 1988, 262 and 263.

[78] In many of his works Cicero defends the orator's eclectic freedom to use arguments from whatever provenance (*De oratore*, *Academica*, *De Fato*, *De natura deorum*, *De finibus*, etc.); on his Academic skepticism in which this *libertas disserendi* plays an essential role, see Seigel 1968, 16–30; Görler 1995; Glucker 1995; Inwood and Mansfeld (eds.) 1997. On the theme of philosophical freedom see also Sutton 1953; Stewart 1994; Maclean 2006, 260–272.

them "only by speculation" (278). And while "much experience makes a man both learned and wise," "what good does it to *me*," Sanches asks, "that another person has had a particular set of experiences, unless I should have the same experiences for myself? They [i.e. other people's experiences] will produce belief, not scientific knowledge, in me."[79] Sanches seems to advise the young scholar not to draw his inferences from merely bookish learning but always "to compare this information experimentally with *facts* by observing things, up to the very end of his life"; but he immediately goes on to draw a gloomy picture of such a scholarly life, marked as it is by melancholy and despair. Even if the scholar has a strong mental and physical health as well as the right attitude and so on, he or she will never transcend the level of belief. Raising the bar for scientific knowledge to an unrealistically high level, he concludes: "But even if he were to observe a huge number of facts, yet even so he would not be able to observe *all* the facts, as anyone possessing true scientific knowledge must do."[80]

Coming to the end of the treatise, the reader might wonder how strong and convincing Sanches has presented his skeptical case. Often, his questioning and doubting slides over into polemical and rhetorical outbursts, without developing arguments and counterarguments with the aid of the arsenal developed by the ancient skeptics; his use of skeptical tropes is limited, and so is his knowledge of ancient skepticism in general.[81] His target is an ideal that his opponents would be quick to recognize as such: an ideal – an ideal of infallible, certain, and all-inclusive knowledge that remains far out of sight.[82] His opponents would also agree that essences are an elusive category, only approachable, if at all, via accidents. Sanches never seems willing to say: "Okay, we do not know the thing perfectly, but at least we have made some progress." Relaxing the criteria of the epistemic ideal of certainty or embracing lower levels of knowledge is, of course, not part of Sanches's agenda. Nor is he interested in the finer details of the adjustments – if he knew of them at all – that his scholastic opponents had proposed to the Aristotelian notion of knowledge. Sanches's response would probably be: I only question the claims of my opponents: "by your account, scientific knowledge ought to be certain, infallible, and

[79] Sanches 1988, 282 for this and the following quotation. [80] Ibid., 287.

[81] Caluori 2007, 37 n. 23 refers to § 33, 39, 60 and 93f; Limbrick in Sanches 1988, 78: "Compared to his predecessors his knowledge of ancient sceptical sources was very limited."

[82] According to Pasnau 2017, the epistemic ideal was treated as ideal by Aristotle and many later traditions. The basic assumption that runs through Sanches's argument seems to be that his Aristotelian opponents thought this ideal had already been attained, or could be attained by following their procedures.

everlasting."[83] To present a viable, plausible alternative was apparently not part of Sanches's skeptical attack.

As noticed, there are clues in the text that hints at such an alternative, namely, fallible, conjectural, or probabilistic knowledge of particular things via their outward appearances, gathered from observation and corrected by fallible reason. This is confirmed by his medical writings, in which the Ciceronian vocabulary of the Academic skeptic occurs frequently: the likely, the verisimilar, the probable, the reasonable, and the legitimacy of one's own judgement.[84] The admonition to study things rather than "words" (or logical concepts) can be read on almost every page. It is an alternative that might have governed his practice as a physician, for how would Sanches have been able to cure his patients if his skeptical doubts about knowledge, method, and everything else had left him paralyzed? He might have found an example in the ancient school of Empirical doctors, who had close affinities with the Pyrrhonists. While Sanches never referred to the *Outlines of Pyrrhonism* by the empirical doctor Sextus Empiricus, he could have known about the medical schools in antiquity from Galen, who himself was highly critical not only of the Empirical and Rationalist doctors, but also of the Skeptics.[85] Among the Pyrrhonists listed by Diogenes Laertius are several Empirical doctors.[86] The Empiricists relied on personal observation and confirmed testimony (*historia*) as well as some forms of common reasoning, for example analogical reasoning (though this was a matter of controversy). They opposed the Rationalists, who emphasized the need for theory and the postulation of purely rational entities such as atoms and elements. Like the Empiricists, Sanches questioned such entities and anything that goes beyond daily observation and experience. As already quoted above: "For who could understand nonexistent things? From this source come Democritus's Atoms, Plato's Ideas, Pythagoras's Numbers, and Aristotle's Universals, Active Intellect, and

[83] Sanches 1988, 288. Scholastic authors debated "whether or not *scientia* demands that one grasp *all* of a thing's causes" (Pasnau 2017, 182–183). Sanches is mentioned by Pasnau as part of a tradition of critics, from Nicholas of Cusa to Marin Mersenne, who cast doubt on the Aristotelian framework, "on the grounds that to have *any* such knowledge would require knowledge about *everything*."

[84] See Buccolini 2017, 4. These terms were borrowed from the (Greek) rhetorical tradition; see Glucker 1995, 136. On the connection between skepticism and rhetoric see below.

[85] Hankinson 2008, 165: "it is indeed important for Galen that medical knowledge, of both a theoretical and a practical kind, is capable of being exhibited in demonstrative form – that is, as a deductive inference of a secure conclusion from properly founded first principles." Galen himself was highly critical of the skeptics, dismissing standard skeptical arguments. While Sanches called Galen his *antiquissimus praeceptor*, he did not share these basic convictions of Galen: "I doubt many things that were very clear to him" (Sanches quoted by Buccolini 2017, 9).

[86] Hankinson 2008, 226; for the affinities between Empiricism and skepticism, see ibid. 225–236.

Intelligences."[87] Although in his more polemical moments he questions the reliability even of the senses, he also confirms their importance:[88]

> We have to submit our judgment to the senses. But even if sense-perception functioned perfectly, and could distinguish their qualities, it would not for that cause *know*, but merely "(re)cognise," just as a peasant can tell his donkey apart from a neighbour's (or his own) ox. As things stand, however, sense-perception cannot offer even as much as this . . . Yet this kind of understanding is better than any other we have.

This of course requires trust in our senses, and at some places in *That Nothing Is Known*, Sanches makes clear that we would be better advised to trust people with much experience in certain fields such as commerce, agriculture, and navigation (and probably also medicine which he does not mention here) than the so-called learned people relying on theoretical concepts and methods.[89] As a physician Sanches would therefore not claim to possess any knowledge, yet he could practice his art by making observations, listening to other experts, and accepting in a noncommittal way what sense perception tells him. The ancient skeptic's observance of life, as Sextus had formulated, consists in "guidance by nature, necessitation by feelings, handing down of laws and custom, and teaching of kinds of expertise."[90] Likewise, Sanches could practice his art as a skeptic, though the text of *That Nothing Is Known* does not present a program for that, as his remarks on method are scanty, nor do his medical works constitute an idea of a new medical science or scientific methodology. Though he frequently stresses conjecture, probability, verisimilitude, and judgment based on observation and experience, these remarks are not developed into a coherent alternative to Aristotelian demonstrative knowledge.

Sanches Between Humanism and Early-Modern Philosophy

Sanches's position between, on the one hand, the linguistically inspired attacks on Aristotelian logic and scientific demonstration by the humanists and, on the other hand, the development of early-modern philosophy, is therefore somewhat complicated. As a skeptic who had shown the difficulties of reaching certainty and truth in science, he was known to readers in the early modern period, and, as noted, Descartes (and also Mersenne) were probably among his readers. Bayle called him a great Pyrrhonist and Gabriel Naudé recommended his work, while Dutch and German

[87] Sanches 1988, 168. [88] Ibid., 254. [89] Ibid., 287.
[90] Sextus Empiricus 2000, 9 (*Outlines of Scepticism* 1.23).

theologians often thought him dangerous enough to honor him with – sometimes book-length – refutations.[91] For some modern scholars skepticism "with its contrasting of the pros and cons for any hypothesis" contributed to the demise of Aristotelianism, and hence Sanches can even be seen, in the words of Popkin already quoted above, as "the first Renaissance sceptic to conceive of science in its modern form."[92] This is to give Sanches perhaps too much credit. The emphasis on observation, experience, and conjecture might seem "modern" enough but, as argued above, was not developed into anything systematic. Such an interpretation also seems to be based on a rather crude dichotomy between a supposedly scholastic emphasis on absolute truth and demonstrative certainty versus an early-modern recovery of experience, observation, and probability. But the quest for certainty was, of course, still very much alive in the seventeenth century, while not a few scholastics had argued that probable knowledge was perhaps the highest attainable goal. Also, to argue that Sanches had "demonstrated convincingly that true knowledge in the Aristotelian sense of knowing a thing in terms of its causes was a logical impossibility" is to read too much into his somewhat rambling discourse, if only because his skeptical questioning does not amount to a convincing demonstration.[93]

If he was not a precursor of modern science, perhaps he was a belated humanist? Here too we must be cautious. To some extent his work exhibits some humanistic features such as a classical style (at least in conformance to classical Latin), literary examples, and a (modest) display of classical learning. But more importantly, his skeptical undermining of the Aristotelian ideal of demonstrative science seems to place *That Nothing Is Known* squarely in the tradition of the humanist critique of Aristotelianism. As seen, Sanches criticizes everything of which the scholastics were accused by the humanists: a technical language, an arrogant attitude, self-importance, armchair philosophy, slavish obedience to their master, and so on. In a way similar to that of Valla and Vives, he appeals to common language, common linguistic usage, and the common people to ridicule the esoteric and outlandish nature of scholastic language. His defense of the freedom to philosophize without following any sect, inspired by the Academic skepticism favored by Cicero, was a sentiment shared by

[91] Limbrick 1988, 82–88.

[92] Popkin 2003, 41; cf. Limbrick 1988, 77, and 53: "embryonic form of scientific method based on experimentation and a weighing of the facts by the faculty of judgment in which experience, too, was to play a decisive role." For a balanced view see Schmitt 1972, 11 n. 23.

[93] Limbrick 1988, 78.

many humanists and was repeated in later times, and explicitly defended, for instance, by Gassendi.[94] And yet, Sanches himself does not present his skeptical probing as a humanist project, let alone suggest that he wants to return to classical Latin as the only viable language in which philosophy and science should be conducted. In fact, he is highly critical of the prestige of classical Latin in humanist circles, characterizing his own style as plain and simple, without any rhetorical decor, nor does he share the belief in a marriage between rhetoric and philosophy as defended by many humanists from the time of Petrarch onwards. As we have seen, Sanches does not aim, he says, at speaking elegantly and beautifully, but only truthfully, and he rejects the trivial arts, including rhetoric as full of "useless loquacity."[95]

This negative attitude toward rhetoric might seem perfectly understandable for a medical doctor, but for a skeptic it is less straightforward than it seems at first sight. From his reading of Cicero's works, Sanches certainly knew of the close connection between rhetoric and skepticism in ancient times. As one of the interlocutors says in Cicero's *De Fato*: "there is a close alliance between the orator and the kind of philosophy of which I am a follower, since the orator borrows subtly from the Academy and repays the loan by giving to it a copious and flowing style and rhetorical ornament."[96] And the other interlocutor too brings them into close harmony when he answers: "I am acquainted with the rhetorical discourses of your school (*rhetorica vestra*), and have often heard and also often shall hear you in them; moreover your *Tusculan Disputations* show that you have adopted this Academic practice against a thesis advanced."[97] In defining itself as speech and counterspeech, as *in utramque partem disserere* (to argue on both sides) rhetoric looks uncannily close to skepticism, for skepticism is, to quote Sextus's canonical description, "an ability to set out oppositions among things which appear and are thought of in any way at all," followed by suspension of judgement (*epoche*) and freedom from worry (*ataraxia*).[98]

Moreover, in opposing different sides of the matter, both rhetoric and skepticism do not aim at teaching any positive doctrines. As a method of discourse, rhetoric has strong affinities with the way skepticism works. Indeed, it has been said that skepticism comes close to a discourse strategy, and one may even speak of a "sceptic rhetoric as long as its status as useful

[94] Gassendi 1972, 18. Cf. Murr 1992. [95] Sanches 1988, 176.

[96] Cicero 1942, 2:195 (slightly adapted) (*De Fato* 3). The next three paragraphs are taken from Nauta 2006a, 392–393.

[97] Cicero 1982, 197 (*De Fato* 4).

[98] Sextus Empiricus 2000, 4 (*Outlines of Scepticism* 1.8). For the following I am indebted to Sluiter 2000, 93–123, esp. 106–113.

practical guidelines without epistemological claims is acknowledged."[99] This suggests another resemblance between the two. Both concern our linguistic representation of the appearances rather than the appearances themselves. This is evident in the case of rhetoric, but also the skeptics "say what is apparent to themselves and report their own feelings without holding opinions, affirming nothing about external objects": "When we investigate," Sextus writes, "whether existing things are such as they appear, we grant that they appear, and what we investigate is not what is apparent but what is said about what is apparent – and this is different from investigating what is apparent itself."[100]

It is interesting to notice that Sextus himself found the proximity between rhetoric and skepticism so disturbing that he sought to refute it, hardly convincingly, by redefining rhetoric as the production of useless and incomprehensible speech.[101] For the same reason Sanches may have wanted to distance himself from rhetoric in view of the undeniably close proximity between the discourse strategy of the skeptic and that of the orator, but it must be admitted that his own style of undermining the position of his philosophical interlocutor does not come close to arguing the case from both sides. Indeed, there is an obvious difference between the two: the orator argues one side of the case in order to win, while the skeptic only opposes the dogmatist in order to balance the case. Oratory does not thrive on doubt but on credibility, that is, on the ability to put forward arguments as persuasive and strong as possible in order to render doubtful things credible.[102]

Sanches did quite the opposite: he rendered all things doubtful. If he had recognized the historical proximity between the discourse tactics of the skeptic and the orator at all, he would not have been worried about it. His negative view of rhetoric and his distrust of words was sincere, which separates him from humanists such as Valla, Vives, and Nizolio. Sanches's skeptical quest is different from their attack on Aristotelian dialectic and terminology. He shared their utter disdain for what they thought was an abstract wordplay, but while their critique of Aristotelian dialectic was part of an educational, didactic project that aimed to transform the traditional trivial arts, bringing dialectic more in line with how

[99] Sluiter 2000, 120 n. 6; she adds that Sextus himself speaks about "speaking skeptically" (*skeptikoos legein*) in *Against the Mathematicians* 11.19.

[100] Sextus Empiricus 2000, 7 and 8 (*Outlines of Scepticism* 1.15 and 1.19).

[101] Sluiter 2000, 110.

[102] Within the forensic setting of oratory, only cases about which opinions divide – which may be termed *dubia materia* – are to be discussed and settled; but it is precisely the settling of doubtful matters by rendering doubtful things credible that is the orator's aim.

people actually speak and argue, Sanches's goal was to undermine certainty and absolute truth; the attack on the language and dialectics of his opponents was an important element in it but, unlike his humanist predecessors, he did not seek the solution in a reform of dialectic or language. While he, like they, contrasted ordinary language to the technical language of the scholastics, he did not dream of reclaiming classical Latin as the common language, arguing that ordinary language provided an unstable foundation on which to build scientific knowledge.

It would be unfair to downplay Sanches's attempt to undermine the goals and ideals of Aristotelian science. These ideals were real enough, but many scholastic authors often treated them as such: ideals, which helped to regulate the scope and nature of our knowledge-claims. With a biased and partial reading of this tradition, it was easy to project onto them the belief that these scholastic authors claimed to possess the key to certainty and knowledge, as if the Aristotelian paradigm held the holy grail to absolute knowledge. As a biased reading, it certainly did an injustice to the advanced and nuanced distinctions and qualifications of the scholastics, but to criticize a paradigm required somewhat stronger than subtle argumentation. For Sanches, and with him other critics of the Aristotelian paradigm, it required a less subtle but perhaps polemically more effective attack on the Aristotelian edifice with its "foundation made of fragile materials"[103] than trying to emend an argument here and there. As such, Sanches's skeptical attack was an interestingly idiosyncratic voice in the rising choir of critics of Aristotelian thought and language.

[103] Sanches 1988, 275.

CHAPTER 7

Thomas Hobbes and the Rhetoric of Common Language

Introduction

A brilliant stylist himself and a staunch critic of scholastic-Aristotelian philosophy, Hobbes had every reason to contrast the common language with the technical terminology of his opponents. While "the common sort of men seldom speak insignificantly," the scholastics had invented an abstruse, incomprehensible jargon full of "Latin and Greek words."[1] Hobbes's examples of this "insignificant speech" include neologisms such as "entity," "essence," and "essentiality," which we have met in the works of his humanist predecessors.[2] But Hobbes's list also includes words that humanists such as Valla and Vives would not have found abstruse or absurd at all, such as "free will" and "immaterial or incorporeal substance." Hobbes's attack on such terminology was an essential part of his mechanization of scholastic natural philosophy. His thorough materialism, according to which everything was ultimately to be reduced to (and explained by) matter in motion, was the fruit of a critical engagement with the Aristotelian scholastics, but it was a fruit that earlier critics of the philosophy of the schools would have considered as dangerous and heretical – just as many of his contemporaries did. Thus while Hobbes's critique stands in

[1] *Leviathan* 8.27. All references in the text are to Curley's edition (Hobbes 1994b). "L 8.27: 46" means *Leviathan*, chapter 8, paragraph 27, on p. 46. This edition also gives the pagination of the Head edition of 1651 and that of the Molesworth edition in *The English Works* (London, 1839, reprint Aalen 1966), which makes comparison to other editions, such as Malcolm's critical edition, easy (Hobbes 2012). Unless otherwise stated, for other works I refer to OL = Opera Latina, EW = the English Works. Other abbreviations used: L = *Leviathan*; EL = *Elements of Law*; DCv = *De Cive*; DCo = *De Corpore*; DHo = *De Homine*; EEMH = *Examinatio et Emendatio Mathematicae Hodiernae*; PPG = *Principia et Problemata Aliquot Geometrica*; SL = *Six Lessons to the Savilian Professors of Mathematics*.

[2] L 46.17: 459–460; the invention of new words could lead to the invention of new things; see for example Hobbes's comment on "velleity": "The expression of vain glory is that we call a wish, which some of the Schoolmen, mistaking for some appetite distinct from all the rest, have called velleity, making a new word, as they made a new passion which was not before" (Hobbes 1994a; EL 1.9).

some way in the tradition of humanist polemics against scholastic language, its motivation and final result are different and much more radical.

In this chapter we will study Hobbes's use of common language not only in his attacks on the "insignificant speech" of the scholastics, but also in the definitions of his own philosophy. As is well known, Hobbes was a careful observer of linguistic usage, and it is not surprising to find him frequently appealing to "what we are used to say" or common linguistic usage. This does not mean that he accepts that usage in any simple way. Like so many of his contemporaries, Hobbes was ambivalent about common language. As a move in his polemical invectives against the "cant of the schoolmen" (L 5.15: 25), it was tempting to choose the side of the people, who used language in a so-called normal, natural, and common way. But common language also reflected patterns of thinking that Hobbes found deeply disturbing, and throughout his writings "the vulgar" are often characterized as superstitious, ignorant, and irrational.[3] In rhetorically highly charged debates on politics, morality and religion, ordinary language was a pliable tool, and in particular in the hands of demagogues, rhetoricians, and politicians it was a dangerous weapon that could stir up the minds of the people, even leading to sedition and revolts. In the sometimes no-less-heated domain of natural philosophy, common language was thought to be too variable to provide a stable instrument of scholarly and scientific discourse: "How fallacious it is to judge of the nature of things by the ordinary and inconstant use of words" (L 25.1: 165). As is well known, Hobbes seeks a solution for this "inconstancy" of language in the "apt imposing of names" and in clearly defining one's own terms (5.17: 25). Using geometry as his great source of inspiration, he emphasizes the importance of definition as the starting point for demonstrations and deductions.[4] But definitions must be based on the common understanding of terms. To define, as Hobbes says in his geometrical works, is to observe "how the word to be defined is most constantly used in common speech."[5] Our prescientific consensus, reflected in ordinary language, is the basis for the definitions of our basic philosophical concepts, and although the deductions and conclusions within the sciences are not necessarily couched

[3] See, for example, L 30.14: 225–226. Indeed, the distinction between the people ("the vulgar") and the enlightened "was a demonstrable feature of Hobbes's mentality" (Collins 2005, 33).

[4] Pécharman 2016, 38 points out that Hobbes's ideal method is exemplified by geometry but can be attained by other parts of philosophy: "Demonstration is *more logico*, geometers are simply the first to have applied logical method." As Hobbes says in *De Motu* (often but erroneously called *Anti-White* by modern scholars): "there is no other demonstration than logical" (*De Motu*, XXXIX.7, cited by Pécharman 2016, 37).

[5] Hobbes 1845a, 229 (SL 2); cf. Hobbes 1845b, 26 (EEMH 1).

in ordinary language – in fact, revision of ordinary language is only to be expected given its "inconstant" nature – they cannot go against them either. So the status of ordinary language seems complicated: we should avoid its ambiguity by clearly defining our terms, yet these definitions cannot stray too far from it either (and are ultimately based on definitions of our basic concepts which reflect a prescientific consensus).

Good definitions are crucial in the establishment of civil science as well. Hobbes claims that his "definitions (of such words as are essential to all political reasoning) [are] universally agreed on" (32.1: 245). For someone like Hobbes who has a difficult message to preach – give undivided, absolute power to the sovereign – this is a striking claim to make. Does Hobbes really think that everybody agrees with his definitions? He probably means to say that everybody should agree with his definitions given the aim each of us has to live a secure, peaceful life. The seemingly descriptive language hides a barely concealed prescriptive force. A similar challenge Hobbes faces in the domain of natural philosophy: how to convince his readers of his radical materialism with no place whatsoever for immaterial, spiritual entities? Without attempting to give a comprehensive answer, this chapter identifies one particular strategy – one among others – that Hobbes employs, even though perhaps not always in a deliberate or explicit manner. At the risk of oversimplification we may put it like this: Hobbes seems at times to convey the impression that his views are not so radical after all but rather in line with common sense and ordinary language. Compared to "the cant" of the scholastics, Hobbes might indeed think that his philosophy is couched in ordinary language. This is, however, not to say that he accepts ordinary language unconditionally; for reasons just mentioned he clearly does not. Nor does he use linguistic usage to arrive at his philosophical views and commitments; these commitments, expressed in his definitions, are primary and not the result of an examination of linguistic usage. Still, for Hobbes the expression is important, since everything in his view hinges on the right understanding of words and well-explained definitions. It is here that description ("this is how this word is used") and prescription ("this is how we should use it") become somewhat intertwined; ordinary language is appealed to but at the same time subtly revised to match Hobbes's own philosophical views – or so this chapter will argue.

In what follows we will concentrate on only those aspects of his philosophy that shed light on the theme just sketched, ignoring many other interesting topics. We will start looking at his critique of scholastic language, followed by a discussion of his defense of common usage as an alternative to the "absurd speech" of the schoolmen, particularly in his debates with Bishop Bramhall and the mathematicians from Oxford. But as said, the notion of common usage is far from straightforward, and in the next sections we will study how Hobbes suggests that his definitions and the meaning he assigns to words are compatible with common usage ("what we are used to say") while at the same time revising that common usage in line with his philosophical aims. In the last section we will zoom out a bit, suggesting that the revision of common usage is part of Hobbes's wider tactic to persuade the people that his civil science comes close to what every reasonable person should endorse.

The Critique of Scholastic Language

Because Hobbes does not view classical Latin as alpha and omega in the way many Renaissance humanists had done, his criticisms of the language of the schools go beyond the level of (alleged) mistakes in the Latin grammar and vocabulary, though at this level too Hobbes, as we will see, knew how to hold his ground. If it were only a matter of grammar, a tone of mockery and haughty derision would perhaps be enough. But for Hobbes scholastic terminology was the expression of what he considered a religiously and politically dangerous picture of the world. Abstract terminology had populated the world with abstract entities, such as separate souls that were believed to survive bodily death. The notion of a separate soul had been an important instrument to instill fear in people, inducing them to obey the Church that had set itself up as guardian and authority over this shady world. It was the doctrine of separated essences in particular that had led people to believe in souls separated from their bodies, from which "many other absurdities" followed (L 46.19: 460).

In several places Hobbes subjects the language of the schools to a withering critique. In the chapter on speech in the *Leviathan*, he divides "insignificant sounds" into two sorts (L 4.20–21): "One when they are new, and yet their meaning not explained by definition; whereof there have been abundance coined by schoolmen, and puzzled philosophers. Another, when men make a name of two names, whose significations are contradictory and inconsistent." To coin new words in itself is not wrong as long as one clearly explains their meaning.[6] Examples of this latter kind are "incorporeal body," or "incorporeal substance." As he continues:

[6] Hobbes has nothing against terms of art; cf. Pécharman 2016, 25 n. 20. She also points out, *pace* Feingold 1997, that Hobbes's criticism of scholastic philosophy as "insignificant speech" does not include scholastic logic. This is true but it does not mean that Hobbes was not critical of aspects of Aristotelian logic. Against the background of an official restoration of Aristotelian logic in Oxford (Sgarbi 2013, 41; McConica 1979, 296–297), pruned from its late-medieval accretions, it is not surprising to find Hobbes greatly simplifying it, omitting, reducing, and skipping over elements

> For whensoever any affirmation is false, the two names of which it is composed, put together and made one, signify nothing at all. For example, if it be a false affirmation to say *a quadrangle is round*, the word *round quadrangle* signifies nothing, but is a mere sound. So likewise, if it be false to say that virtue can be poured, or blown up and down, the words *in-poured virtue*, *in-blown virtue*, are as absurd and insignificant as *a round quadrangle*.

In the next chapter, on reason and science, he develops this point by explaining how absurdities arise when we mix up words that belong to different categories. The diversity of words may be reduced, Hobbes says, "to four general headings": names of (i) bodies ("living," "sensible," "hot," "cold"), (ii) of accidents and properties ("being moved" or "motion," "being hot" or "heat"), (iii) of "our fancies," that is ideas as sensed by us (that is anything seen, heard, felt, etc.), and (iv) of names and speeches ("general," "universal," "affirmation," "syllogism," "oration").[7] He then argues that the application of a word of one category to another results in absurdities, for example when we give names of bodies to accidents, or vice versa ("faith is infused or inspired," "extension is body," "phantasms are spirits"); or when we give names of bodies to names or speeches ("there be things universal," "a living creature is genus, or a general thing"); or names of accidents to names and speeches ("a man's command is his will").[8] Another cause of "absurd conclusions" is "the use of metaphors, tropes, and other rhetorical figures, instead of words proper," which – though lawful in common speech – should not be admitted in the "reckoning and seeking of truth," that is in science and philosophy.[9] A last source mentioned by Hobbes is the use of names "that signify nothing, but are taken up, and learned by rote from the schools, as *hypostatical*, *transubstantiate*, *consubstantiate*, *eternal-now*, and the like canting of schoolmen" (L 5.8–15: 24–25).

Hobbes's analysis of "those we call absurd, insignificant, and nonsense" seems to comprise more than one notion of inconsistency: "a round

he did not find useful or philosophically relevant such as the Aristotelian categories and the moods of the syllogism. It is a "pared-down neo-Aristotelian account of syllogistic reasoning," "a minimalist, Renaissance Aristotelian logic" (Raylor 2018, 193–194; Pécharman 1995 and 2016, 30). And yet, Hobbes also considers natural reasoning more important than logical rules, praxis more important than theory; Hobbes 1999a, 49 and 56 (DCo 1.4.13 and 1.5.56). Mersenne defends the creation of neologisms in his *La verité des sciences*: though barbarous and crude, they are useful because "they express better or more briefly what we want to say" (quoted by Burchell 2007, 67).

[7] L 4.14: 20; cf. L 46.16: 459, where (ii) is omitted; also Hobbes 1999a, 52 (DCo 1.5.2).

[8] L 5.10–14; Hobbes 1999a, 51–52 (DCo 1.5.2) for a similar list.

[9] Hobbes had nothing against rhetoric itself but believed it should never enter the fabric of science, that is in the construction of knowledge, though of course it could help, if needed, to adorn the truth or to open the understanding. Hobbes's position remained basically the same from the mid-1630s onwards. See Schuhmann 1998, Nauta 2002a, and in particular Raylor 2018.

quadrangle" seems to be a different kind of inconsistency than "free will" or "incorporeal body" (unless body is already defined in terms of something corporeal). Further, some of Hobbes's examples of absurd propositions such as "whiteness is a white thing" and "extension is a body" are not self-evidently absurd. In addition, Hobbes frequently rejects this terminology as empty talk ("mere words," or "words without meaning") in the sense that these words do not refer to or stand for the thoughts or ideas of the speaker.[10] But the absence of a referent of the word seems to be another sort of emptiness than talking about a round quadrangle ("round" and "quadrangle" having meaning, but not their combination).

By the standards of his own materialistic philosophy, however, many terms turn out to be absurd, such as "incorporeal substance" or "incorporeal body," and his inclusion of terms just quoted (including "free will," since, as he argues elsewhere, a person can be free, but not his will) clearly reveals Hobbes's ultimate aim, namely to criticize a number of philosophical and theological doctrines that he finds dangerous for the stability of the commonwealth, which rests on people obeying their sovereign. This critique forms the basso continuo of Part IV of the *Leviathan.* In his rhetorically superb chapter "Of Darkness From Vain Philosophy and Fabulous Traditions," Hobbes puts his own language critique into the framework of his materialist philosophy: "For the interpreting of which *jargon* there is need of somewhat more than ordinary attention in this place" (L 46.15: 458). He first presents us. therefore. with the barest outline of his materialist philosophy: the world consists of matter in motion; hence spirits too "have dimensions, and are, therefore really bodies (though that name in common speech be given to such bodies only as are visible or palpable, that is, that have some degree of opacity)" (L 46.15: 459). He then summarizes some of his views on language in order "to know now upon what grounds they say there be *essences abstract*, or *substantial forms.*" One source of abstract language is the copula, "is (*est*)," that has given rise to words such as "entity, essence, essential, essentiality."[11] But as Hobbes points out, the copula *est* does not have a separate meaning itself. There might even be languages that do not have such a copula, yet those people "would be not a jot the less capable of inferring, concluding, and all kind of

[10] L 5.5: 24; L 46.19: 460–461. Hobbes seems to be rather cavalier about the distinction between falsity and absurdity, using these words interchangeably; see Soles 1996, 111. On Hobbes's table of absurdity see Morris Engel 1961; Martinich in Hobbes 1981; Soles 1996; Duncan 2016 (who argues that we see no notion of Rylean category mistake in Hobbes).

[11] A similar list in Hobbes 1999a, 34 (DCo 1.3.4). On the absence of the copula *est* in Hebrew, see the Latin Appendix to Latin *Leviathan*, I (Hobbes 1994b, 499).

reasoning than were the Greeks and Latins." This sort of terminology is not only philosophically insignificant but it has also proven to be politically pernicious.

It is, of course, not that abstraction in itself is wrong. In fact, it is an important feature of philosophizing, reflected in our use of so-called concrete and abstract names. If we want to consider heat or motion in itself – as is common in reasoning and science – we abstract from the heat or movement of this or that body and consider the accident by itself. "Heat" and "motion" are called abstract names that, as Hobbes explains in *De Corpore*, denote the "cause" of their corresponding concrete names.[12] The "abuse of abstract names" arises when we abstract those accidents such as heat from the bodies and postulate abstract entities as referents of these abstract names, of which "separated essences" are the most pernicious creatures. This doctrine of separated essences, "built on the vain philosophy of Aristotle," has been exploited by the Church to frighten people and let them believe in ghosts (souls) walking around churchyards, and in the doctrine of transubstantiation (in which accidents are abstracted and reified), and in virtues being "poured or blown" into man from heaven. All these and other doctrines, such as the place where souls dwell after leaving their bodies, have lessened the dependence of people on the sovereign power, for who "will not obey a priest, that can make God, rather than his sovereign, nay than God himself? Or who, that is in fear of ghosts, will not bear great respect to those that can make the holy water, that drives them from him?" (L 46.18: 460). But if this "superstitious fear of spirits were taken away, and with it, prognostics from dreams, false prophecies, and many other things depending thereon, by which crafty ambitious persons abuse the simple people, men would be much more fitted than they are for civil obedience" (L 2.8: 11).[13] Hobbes's materialism exorcizes spiritual, incorporeal, immaterial entities (substantial forms, essences, souls, separate accidents, etc.), and an important aspect of his method in doing so is to lay bare the mechanisms of linguistic abstraction. Hobbes's analysis of forms of absurd speeches was therefore meant as a further confirmation of his materialistic philosophy, and his division of words into four classes as well as the resulting forms of absurd speeches clearly reflect the materialist ontology he defends. Linguistic analysis is not a goal in itself but serves to lend support to his philosophical views.[14]

[12] Hobbes 1999a, 34 (DCo 1.3.4). Cf. Appendix to Latin *Leviathan* I (Hobbes 1994b, 514).

[13] Cf. Hobbes 1998, 80 (DCv 6.11).

[14] Such a conclusion was reached by Morris Engel as early as 1961; cf. Duncan 2016, 73; Leijenhorst 2002b.

Just as there is a close connection between what Hobbes calls absurd, insignificant speech and the immaterialist, spiritual side of scholastic Aristotelianism, there is a correspondingly close connection between significant speech and materialism. One of the main functions of language – next to counseling, teaching, showing our wills and purposes to others, and pleasing ourselves and others – is to register our thoughts and transfer this "mental discourse" into words (L 4.3: 16–17). As known, Hobbes distinguishes between marks and signs, that is, words employed for our own use in calling to mind a thing previously conceived, and words for communicating our ideas to others. But the important point to stress here is that thoughts – brought to our own mind or communicated to others – have nothing spiritual to them. They are the effects of motions exerted by external bodies. The details need not detain us here, but the important consequence is that for Hobbes thoughts are not pictorial representations of the world outside us, but physical effects in the form of local motions in our body. Our thoughts (or images, ideas, or concepts, terms that Hobbes uses interchangeably) do not reflect things as they are. It is the way the world appears to us, as an effect of mechanistically explained motion outside and inside our body, that tells us how the world is. It is a moot point whether Hobbes can account for the objective world of matter, when its existence is inferred from the effects the world exerts in us. Nor does his reductionist program seem to leave any room for intentionality and for our feeling that sense perception, memory, imagination, and thinking are not the same – processes that on Hobbes's materialist, mechanistic picture become pretty much the same.[15] Leaving these problematic aspects aside, the consequence for his view of language is that words must refer, in order to be meaningful, to our thoughts, which are material processes. Though Hobbes occasionally speaks of imposing names on external things (or things being signified by words[16]), he always means to say that words stand for our concepts; these concepts do not mirror things as they are, as if they were independent of our understanding of them: "but seeing names ordered in speech (as is defined) are signs of our conceptions, it is manifest they are not signs of the things themselves."[17] Words signify thoughts, not things. Hobbes consciously distances himself from late-Aristotelian authors who often argued that words signified concepts primarily and things secondarily (via those concepts, which were believed to

[15] Leijenhorst 2002a, 79 and 88; Leijenhorst 2007, 94; Sorell 1986, 79.
[16] For example Hobbes 1998, 237 (DCv 18.4).
[17] Hobbes 1999, 21 (DCo 1.2.5), quoted by Leijenhorst 2002a, 40, with further discussion; cf. also Leijenhorst 2002b, 351; Nuchelmans 1983, 131; Ashworth 1981.

be natural signs that signify external things as they are). For him they can only signify our thoughts. Thoughts, then, are the *sine qua non* for significant speech; without corresponding thoughts, words become meaningless, empty jargon. This was, of course, a traditional idea, but in Hobbes's case this emptiness can almost be taken in a literal sense of having no foundation in his materialistic ontology.

"The Common Sort of Men Seldom Speak Insignificantly"

Hobbes's analysis of the insignificant speech of the scholastics might suggest that the alternative is common language – a modern language such as English or French or an international language such as (a form of) classical Latin. This impression is confirmed by Hobbes's own practice, but of course scientific discourse requires more than just the use of one's mother tongue or classical Latin. Putting aside for the moment the question of what these requirements are, Hobbes's own practice shows that philosophizing is not limited to one particular language. Depending on the audience and immediate context, he expounds his philosophical ideas in Latin or English, often recycling and revising passages between several works. His technical work on logic and geometry was published mainly in Latin but translated into English, and Hobbes's polemics with Ward and Wallis were carried out both in Latin and English. He translated his *Leviathan* into Latin for an international audience; his *De Cive* from 1642 was translated into English some years after its publication.[18] Hence, for Hobbes there are no intrinsic features of a language that would make it more suitable for philosophy than another language. This is of course not to say that the Latin vocabulary effortlessly finds its equivalent in English. Sensitive to the several meanings of a word and its connotations in Latin and Greek, he had to choose from that variety a translation that suited his own purposes. Good examples are the renditions of *imaginatio*, *sensus*, *phantasma*, Greek *phantasia*, and *forma*.[19]

Obviously, Hobbes acknowledges the status of Latin and Greek as "languages of the sciences," useful to learn "because of science," and

[18] See Malcolm 2002, 234–258 for conclusive evidence that the poet Charles Cotton stands behind "C. C." as translator.

[19] Sacksteder 1978, 40: "Hobbes is teaching Philosophy to speak English in a special way using a prototype from the vernacular ... Linguistically, he is maneuvering rather than translating; and philosophically, he is creating rather than transmitting," though he also writes that "Philosophy is not so much taught to speak English; it is admonished to attend to its Latin, or to one rich vein therein" (41).

elsewhere he says that they "are become immutable, which none of the modern tongues are like to be."[20] As a translator from Greek and Latin himself, he realizes that for some Latin words such as *pulchritudo* and *turpitudo* ("signs of goodness and evil"), "we have no words precisely answerable."[21] But in *Behemoth* he has one of the interlocutors say that knowledge of the three holy languages was necessary "to the detection of Roman fraud, and to the election of the Romish power," "but now that's done, and we have the Scripture in English, and preaching in English, I see no great need of Greek, Latine, and Hebrew."[22]

Even though his first and last major works are translations of Thucydides and Homer, the classical languages did not hold a special privilege for him when it comes to philosophy and science. In fact, much that had been written in these languages through the ages, including classical antiquity itself, had led to seditious ideas and bloodshed to the extent that "there was never anything so dearly bought as these western parts have bought the learning of the Greek and Latin tongues."[23] And much of post-classical Latin had developed into the language of the papacy, "not commonly used by any nation now in the world," the papacy being famously characterized by Hobbes as "the ghost of the old Roman language" (L 47.22: 483).

Indeed, the aura of Latin as a special language has all too long been used to mystify the people. We can easily shatter that illusion by translating "a Schoolman" into "any of the modern tongues, so as to make the same intelligible; or into any tolerable Latin, such as they were acquainted withal, that lived when the Latin tongue was vulgar" (L 8.27: 46). If the result does not make sense, as Hobbes tries to show by quoting Suárez, the original Latin did not make sense either. The purpose of such language is to mystify, "to hide the truth, but also to make men think they have it, and desist from further search," points frequently made by critics of scholasticism.[24]

But if we decide to choose to use Latin we should follow classical usage, though Hobbes does not seem to specify the point. In his polemics with Wallis, accusations of poor Latin were traded, for example on the use of the

[20] Hobbes 1839, 100 (DHo 11.10); Hobbes 1840c, 456 ("Answer to Davenant").

[21] Hobbes 1994b, 44 (EL 7.3); and L 6.8: 29. [22] Hobbes 2010, 225–226 (*Behemoth*, Dialogue 2).

[23] L 21.9: 141. In *Behemoth* "the democraticall principles of Aristotle and Cicero" through the study of "Greek and Latine" are identified as one of the causes of the Civil War; Hobbes 2010, 164, 322 (cited Raylor 2018, 28, who concludes that for Hobbes "Humanism undermines the foundations of monarchy").

[24] L 46.40: 467; often remarked on also in *Behemoth*, for example Hobbes 2010, 134–135, 176–177, 180–181.

Latin verb *adduco* or the meaning of *problematice*.[25] For modern languages the question of what linguistic usage or custom is does not seem to bother Hobbes, but one does not need to be a sociolinguist to know that different groups or layers of society – court, university, parliament, pulpit, market, and so on – often have their own sociolect.[26] Given his own movements through different societal strata, Hobbes must have been aware of different sociolects. But when he talks about "the ordinary person" who speaks as "significantly as any scholar" or about "the people who seldom speak insignificantly" he does not have anything more specific in mind.[27]

In his disputes and polemics with others, most notably Bishop Bramhall on free will and liberty, and with Wallis and Ward on science and geometry, he frequently appeals to the natural good sense and understanding of the common people, who understand words equally as well as the "learned men" do, or even better. Against Bishop Bramhall, who thinks that "the true natures of things are not to be judged by the private ideas or conceptions of men but by their causes and formal reasons," Hobbes defends "the ordinary person," who would be at a loss if words were *not* to signify the idea or conception of that thing.[28] The bishop seems to think that common or "unlearned" people do not know what "empty," "body," or "upward" mean because they do not know what the scientist knows about such topics. But this is nonsense, says Hobbes. "Ordinary men" understand these words as well as "learned men": "When they hear named an empty vessel, the learned as well as the unlearned mean and understand the same thing, namely, that there is nothing in it that can be seen; and whether it be truly empty, the ploughman and the Schoolman know alike." (The same example of talking about emptiness was used, as we have seen, by humanists such as Valla and Vives; the example goes back to Cicero's *De Fato*.) In opposition to the bishop, Hobbes defends the common person: "Nor do I think that any man is so simple, as not to find that to be good which he loveth . . . Or is there any unlearned man so stupid, as to think eternity is this present instant of time standing still, and the same eternity to be

[25] Hobbes 1845a, 322 and 324 (SL 5); Jesseph 1999, 328–333; Isermann 1991, 128 n. 58.

[26] In cataloguing Hobbes's use of bad language, Wallis's explanation for Hobbes's switch from the Latin of *De Corpore* to the English of the *Six Lessons* was that "when ever you have thought it convenient to repaire to Billingsgate [location of fish markets in London], to learn the art of Well-speaking, for the perfecting of your naturall Rhetorick; you have not found that any of the Oister-women could teach you to raile in Latin, and therefore it was requisite that you apply your selfe to such language as they could teach you" (*Due Correction* 2, quoted by Jesseph 1999, 331).

[27] Hobbes 1841, 398 (QLNC); L 8.27: 46.

[28] Hobbes 1841, 397 (QLNC).

the very next instant after . . . ?"[29] And in his reply to Bramhall's criticisms of Hobbes's distinction of command and counsel, Hobbes writes:[30]

> His Lordship, I think, to seem a perfect understander of the unintelligible language of the Schoolmen, pretends an ignorance of his mother-tongue. He talks here of *command* and *counsel,* as if he were no Englishman, nor knew any difference between their significations. What Englishman, when he commandeth, says more than, *Do this*; yet he looks to be obeyed, if obedience be due unto him. But when he says, *Do this, and thou shalt have such or such reward,* he encourages him, or advises him, or bargains with him; but commands him not. Oh the understanding of a schoolman!

Hobbes in particular objects to Bishop Bramhall's authoritative tone and what he considers to be an arrogant attitude in the bishop when it comes to the language and understanding of the common people: "Or how can an unlearned man be brought to think the words he speaks, ought to signify, when he speaks sincerely, anything else but that which himself meant by them?"[31] – that is to say, of course the common people use words as sense and experience have taught them, conforming themselves to the consensus of their linguistic community. What Bramhall wants, Hobbes implies, is obedience to Church authorities by way of "the enchantments of words not understood":[32]

> But he that hath lighted on deceiving or deceived masters, that teach for truth all that hath been dictated to them by their own interest, or hath been cried up by other such teachers before them, have for the most part their own natural reason, as far as concerneth the truth of doctrine, quite defaced or very much weakened, becoming changelings through the enchantments of words not understood.

Hobbes makes a similar appeal to "common speech" in his protracted and for him ill-fated polemics against Wallis, whom he accuses of departing from common language. Here the context is geometry and the role of definitions.[33] In his discussion of proportion, for example, he defends his

[29] Hobbes 1841, 399–400 (QLNC). [30] Hobbes 1840b, 343 ("Answer to Bishop Bramhall").

[31] Hobbes 1840b, 399 ("Answer to Bishop Bramhall"); cf. L 8.27: 46. For a similar position see the next chapter, on Locke.

[32] Hobbes 1841, 399 (QLNC). Cf. Isermann 1991, 121.

[33] On this role see Jesseph 1999, 140–142, and 198–206, and Jesseph 2018. For Hobbes, proper definitions reveal the causes of the things defined; hence one definition can be better than another one. It is unclear how many of Hobbes's own definitions can meet this requirement. For the ambiguity of Hobbes's notion of "cause" see the pertinent observations by Malcolm: "The idea of uniting the knowledge of necessary truths [geometry] with the knowledge of causes [natural philosophy] was in the end a snare and a delusion" and hence "his own theoretical writings on

definition by appealing to our common way of speaking about proportion:[34]

> When a geometrician prefixeth before his demonstrations a *definition*, he doth it not as a part of his geometry, but of natural evidence, not to be demonstrated by argument, but to be understood in understanding the language wherein it is set down ... But when there is no significant definition prefixed, as in this case, where Euclid's definition of proportion, that it is a *whatshicalt habitude of two quantities, etc.*, is insignificant, and you allege no other, every one that will learn geometry, must gather the definition from observing how the word to be defined is most constantly used in common speech.

Hobbes proceeds to briefly examine how proportion is used "in common speech."[35] And clarifying his definition of equality, attacked by Wallis, Hobbes remarks: "All which is common speech, as well as amongst mathematicians, as amongst common people; and though improper, cannot be altered nor needeth to be altered by intelligent men."[36] More generally, Hobbes argues here that "all definitions proceed from common understanding."[37]Accurate definitions depend "on the understanding of words, from observing how their meanings vary as the circumstances differ and what is common in all this variety of meaning; for the precise meaning of a word is that which is everywhere understood by it."[38] And in *Principia et Problemata Aliquot Geometrica* he writes: "There cannot be doubt concerning the truth of a legitimate definition, because it has its truth from the consensus and choice of the people (*a consensu et arbitrio hominum*) that have imposed words freely on things."[39] Now most of these statements refer to the definitions of the most basic philosophical concepts,

the nature of scientific knowledge became more and more misleading as guides to his actual practice" (2002, 155).

[34] Hobbes 1845a, 229 (SL II). On Hobbes's idiosyncratic approach to the doctrine of ratios, see Jesseph 1999, 85–94, in a chapter devoted to Hobbes's "thoroughly materialistic conception of mathematics" (111).

[35] Hobbes 1845a, 229 (SL II); cf. Hobbes 1998, 236–237 (DCv 18.4).

[36] Hobbes 1845a, 227 (SL II). [37] Hobbes 1845a, 226 (SL II). [38] Hobbes 1845b, 26 (EEMH I).

[39] Hobbes 1845c, 157 (PPG I). Cf. also Hobbes 1998, 215 (DCv 17.12); Isermann 1991, 119–120. On deserved qualifications of various aspects of Hobbes's so-called conventionalist or arbitrary theory of scientific truth (based on definitions of terms that make up propositions) see Bertman 1978, 546–547; Sorell 1986, 45–49; Jesseph 1999, 198–200 ("those names are most aptly imposed when they designate causes, or at least possible causes"); Leijenhorst 2002b, 362 ("the choice of labels may be arbitrary, but what these labels signify, viz. our concepts, is not"); Malcolm 2002, 152: "our use of the same word [blue] to describe them [blue objects] is not a mere freak of human will or fancy. Indeed, his mechanistic theory of sense-perception ensures this, since the nature of the conception in our brains which we connote with the word 'blue' is *caused* directly by the motion of the object which we see." Cf. Gert 2001.

which is the domain of the *prima philosophia*. More specialized concepts in geometry and the individual sciences might not need to meet this requirement, and certainly the deductions derived from the definitions need not be expressed in common language of course. Natural philosophers and mathematicians have the freedom, even the obligation, to define their terms in the way they deem fit, and to correct those of others if necessary: it is necessary "for any man that aspires to true knowledge, to examine the definitions of former authors, and either to correct them where they are negligently set down, or to make them himself."[40] But the example of proportion, quoted above, suggests that geometers in making their own definitions must observe "how the word to be defined is most constantly used in common speech." As Cees Leijenhorst writes: "scientists are able to reach a *communis opinio* simply because ordinary language is based upon a pre-scientific consensus. In this respect, Hobbes's theory of definition is based on common sense ... This, however, does not mean that ordinary language is a holy cow, for it is inherently subject to ambiguity and confusion."[41] Indeed, ordinary language is not a holy cow, and yet Hobbes defines the truth of a definition in terms of "the consensus and choice of the people," so that we may wonder how Hobbes thinks we can find a common core of meaning that a word has in different circumstances. The implicit assumption here – and elsewhere Hobbes states this explicitly – is that, because the whole point of communication is to make oneself understood, linguistic usage is based on consensus and convention.[42]

Hobbes realizes, however, how difficult it is to reach consensus. As he writes in the *De Cive*:[43]

> It sometimes happens that though words have fixed meanings defined by decision (*ex constituto*), they are so distorted in popular usage from their proper meanings by a particular passion for ornament or even deception, that it is very difficult to recall to memory the concepts for the sake of which they were attached to things, and it needs a keen judgement and intense labour to overcome the difficulty.

In the *Elements of Law*, he had expressed the same thought: "there is scarce any word that is not made equivocal by divers contextures of speech, or by

[40] L 4.13: 19; cf. L 7.5: 36: "When a man's discourse beginneth not at definitions ...." See also Hobbes 1999, 21 (DCo 1.2.4). See above n. 33 and 34; cf. Pécharman 2016.

[41] Leijenhorst 2002a, 51. Cf. already Schuhmann 1985, 168. We may add that Hobbes's concept of science as a unified whole with several parts also make it unlikely that there is a big difference in the status of definitions in the *prima philosophia* and the other more specialized parts.

[42] Leijenhorst 2002b, 363; Sorell 1986; Isermann 1991.

[43] Hobbes 1998, 237–238 (DCv 18.4).

diversity of pronunciation and gesture."[44] This equivocation of names makes it difficult to

> recover those conceptions for which the name was ordained; and that not only in the language of other men, wherein we are to consider the drift, and occasion, and contexture of the speech, as well as the words themselves; but also in our own discourse, which being derived from the custom and common use of speech, representeth not unto us our own conceptions.

If we want to deliver ourselves from such equivocations we must find out the "true meaning of what is said: and this is it we call understanding." The suggestion of finding the original meaning of the word, however, does not seem to go easily with Hobbes's idea, just quoted from his geometrical work, that the "precise meaning of a word is that which is everywhere understood by it." "Custom and common use of speech" seem responsible for equivocations, while they also need to be carefully examined in order to distill "what is common in all this variety of meaning."

Hobbes does not explain how he thinks we can arrive at the so-called original meaning. He does not believe "that men once came together to take counsel to constitute by decree what all words and all connections of words would mean."[45] Nor does he of course believe that the original meaning is to be equated with a meaning that would reflect the thing's essence, for words are conventional, not naturally significative. The story of Adam's giving names to the animals in Paradise, told in slightly different versions by Hobbes, does not support such an idea either. It seems, then, that Hobbes's idea that we can "recover those conceptions for which the name was ordained" must remain somewhat wishful thinking; it is indeed something that requires "a great ability." He might think that by simply settling on an "apt imposition of names" (5.17: 25) or "the right definition of names" (4.13: 19) we have tied the meaning to the original conception (if we can agree on the identity of the latter at all), but someone like Hobbes, who is unusually sensitive to the multiple ways in which language is used and to the ways in which words come and go and are ever finding new meanings and nuances,[46] must realize that this is a procedure that does not seem to work in daily practice, perhaps not even among a selective group of mathematicians, as his own battles over the right definition of terms with the Oxford professors must have taught him.[47] As we will see in the next

[44] Hobbes 1994a, 37 (EL 5.8) for this and the following quotations.

[45] Hobbes 1991, 38 (DHo 10.2; OL II, 89). [46] Cf. Hobbes 1999, 21 (DCo 1.2.4).

[47] Even if they do have the same concept in mind, for instance of a straight line, they may give different definitions of it. See Hobbes 1845c, 395 (PPG IV).

two sections, Hobbes thinks, however, that he can recover the true meaning of words, meanings that he assigns to words in such a way that they express his philosophical views.

Revising Ordinary Speech: A Balancing Act

While scientists are free to emend the definitions of others or invent new definitions, they have to adapt themselves to the linguistic customs and conventions of their community. But these conventions are not static. The task, therefore, is to present one's definitions in terms that are comprehensible to one's audience (whether a small scientific community of specialists or the wider public) while at the same time revising these terms so that they capture one's philosophical assumptions and commitments or, as Hobbes sometimes says, one's own "principles."[48]

To convince the audience of the correctness of our definitions it might therefore be tempting to present our terms and theories built out of these terms as actually conforming to common usage, or at least reflecting what should be counted as the "proper" use of language. This means revising ordinary language while playing down the revising act itself: The revision has to be done without giving the impression that one has widely departed from common usage. It is a balancing act we find Hobbes practicing all the time. The mechanization of Aristotelian natural philosophy means redefining central concepts such as substance, quality, essence, body, cause, necessity, metaphysics, science, reason, sense, imagination, and a host of other terms. The development of a moral science and political theory that aim at radically changing our ideas about power, sovereignty, freedom, and so on, requires redefinitions of terms such as justice, law, right, freedom, liberty, contract, person, and many more, based also on definitions of the passions and desires and other ingredients of human psychology. And to support this political theory (and ultimately his materialist ontology), biblical passages in which, for example, angel, eternal torment, consecration, second death, hell, salvation, kingdom, and many other terms had been used by the Church to claim power over the people, have to be reinterpreted, with a view to the wider context and the intentions of the original authors.[49]

To be sure, it would be difficult for Hobbes to present all this revision of older and current ideas, theories, and practices as a return to common sense and common language, or as being in line with them. He clearly realizes

[48] Hobbes 1999, 7 (DCo, Ad Lectorem). [49] See, for example, L 44.37: 434.

that his materialist ontology, the interpretations of many items of dogma or biblical passages that spring from his ontological commitments, and the idea of the absolute power of the sovereign, would not be greeted with much enthusiasm, to say the least.[50] This makes it all the more expedient for him to work on his conviction strategy. How should he convince his readers that his theories, which are perhaps quite radically different from what they think, teach, or have been taught, are the right ones?[51] Apart from the wide array of rhetorical devices that Hobbes used, including examples, analogies, metaphors, stories, and anecdotes, there is another strategy, aimed at showing that much of what he says is not too far from what his readers might say or think themselves, certainly after a moment's reflection.[52] Part of this strategy is the frequent use of phrases such as "men call," "it is called," "we generally call," "commonly called," which can be found on virtually every page of the first part of the *Leviathan*. In this part, Hobbes transforms many concepts from Aristotelian natural philosophy into a mechanistic picture of human perception and cognition. Treatment of almost all concepts is introduced or accompanied by a statement about or examination of the terms in use, and some chapters make this explicit in the title, for example the chapter on the passions "and the Speeches By Which They Are Expressed." Does Hobbes use ordinary language to strengthen his case or does he revise it; or does he somehow do both at the same time? Let us look at some examples.

The first part starts with chapters in which Hobbes mechanizes sense, imagination, memory, understanding, and so on. After having developed the crucial point that our sense perceptions are the result of a mechanical process of motion including an internal counter-pressure directed outward toward the sense organs, Hobbes concludes: "And this *seeming*, or *fancy*, is that which men call *sense*" (L 1.4: 6). Hobbes then contrasts his account with the "insignificant speech" of the scholastics, who invoke visible and intelligible species to explain processes of perception and knowledge. In the

[50] See, for example, the Letter Dedicatory to *Leviathan* (Hobbes 1994b, 2): "That which perhaps may most offend are certain texts of Holy Scripture, alleged by me to other purpose than ordinarily they use to be by others." For the reception of Hobbes's work, see Collins 2005; Parkin 2007; Malcolm 2002, 457–545.

[51] In addition to the wider public or readership Hobbes also hoped his work would be read and its lessons put into practice by rulers. Cf. Collins 2005, 33.

[52] On Hobbes's use of rhetoric see above n. 9. Sorell 1990a lists four strategies: the brief, confirming summary rule; an appeal to inner experience common to all men; clear, simple definitions; and the interpreted piece of scripture to show that his conclusions are compatible with the divine law and the Scriptures; cf. also his 1990b. A less positive judgment on Hobbes's use of devices of rhetorical persuasion was given by Hobbes's erstwhile friend Edward Hyde, Earl of Clarendon (briefly summarized by Raylor 2018, 2).

next chapter imagination is defined: "This *decaying sense*, when we would express the thing itself (I mean *fancy* itself), we call *imagination* . . ., but when we could express the *decay*, and signify that the sense is fading, old and past, it is called *memory*. So that *imagination* and *memory*, are but one thing, which for diverse considerations hath diverse names" (L 2.3: 8–9). These (quasi)descriptive phrases like "men call" and "it is called," here and elsewhere, might suggest that Hobbes claims that people talk about these processes in the way in which he describes them. This is, however, not his claim. Hobbes's point is that people use various words – "sense," "imagination," "memory," "remembrance," "understanding," and so on – which on Hobbes's account are only different names for what is essentially one and the same physical process, seen from various perspectives. Hobbes does not criticize the fact that we use a variety of such (common) words "for diverse considerations," as long as we do not consider them as standing for separate, immaterial processes and immaterial entities like species and faculties of an immaterial soul. But even though he does not claim that ordinary usage confirms his own understanding of the terms, he clearly links these ordinary words to aspects of the mechanical processes he describes, with the implication that his own account is after all compatible with ordinary language. In a way, he revises ordinary language by suggesting that what we call sense (or any concept) is what, on his account, it actually is, but he does not stress the distance between his account and how we ordinarily use the terms in question. By concluding that (to paraphrase) "and *this* is what we all call sense," he maps ordinary language onto his account. He thereby revises it, but the revision is subtly defused by the kind of identification suggested by "and this *is* what we all call sense," enhanced by the frequent sneers at the absurd and insignificant speech of the scholastics in these chapters.

Similar observations can be made regarding the chapter "Of the Passions and the Speeches By Which They Are Expressed," the title of which already indicates the importance of examining current usage. In this chapter and in similar discussions of the passions in for example *The Elements of Law*, *De Corpore*, and *De Homine*, Hobbes aims at reducing the variety of passions to a only a few simple types such as appetite, desire, aversion, hate, joy, and grief, analyzed in terms of bodily motions as part of his mechanical theory of nature.[53] Hence, we might consider it as a venture in empirical reconstruction rather than "an extended piece of descriptive semantics":[54] "He

[53] Hobbes 1994a, 43–64 (EL 7–10); Hobbes 1999, 279–280 (DCo 4.25.13).

[54] Sorell 1986, 90 for this and the next quotation.

does not seem to be recovering the ordinary senses of the terms 'hope', 'kindness', 'lust' and the rest." This is true, and yet by constantly using, also here, phrases such as "commonly called," "we call," "generally called," "it is called," and the like, Hobbes at least wants to show how common terms referring to our emotions can be projected onto his empirical picture. Again, some examples.

Having distinguished between vital and animal motions, Hobbes states that "imagination is the first internal beginning of all voluntary motion" (L 6.1: 27). These motions are too small to be seen, hence "unstudied men do not conceive any motion at all to be there, where the thing moved is invisible." These small first beginnings of motion "are commonly called endeavour." "Commonly" might mean here "in English" rather than "nontechnical"; the two senses are of course not identical. "Endeavour" is the English translation of the technical term *conatus*, which Aristotelians had used to refer to the inner strivings of things, an idea foreign to Hobbes's mechanical picture. Hence, the word "commonly" cannot include the Aristotelians, who had not used the word with Hobbes's meaning; they are explicitly criticized in this section for their "absurd speech." But neither can it include the common people ("unstudied men"), who have no use for such a technical term.[55] Hobbes continues to write as if he describes common usage: "This endeavour, when it is toward something which causes it, is called appetite or desire, the latter being the general name .... And when the endeavour is fromward something, it is generally called aversion. These words, appetite and aversion, we have from the *Latins*" (L 6.2: 28). Again, Hobbes's claim is not that his usage follows ordinary usage directly but he links it with his account. The "we" is presumably not a royal we, but refers to the English users of common terms such as "desire" and "appetite" (and perhaps "endeavour" but then not in the sense of these small first beginnings of motion).

Another tricky case are Hobbes's definitions of "good" and "evil": "But whatsoever is the object of any man's appetite or desire that is it which he for his part calleth good .... For these words of good, evil, and contemptible are ever used with relation to the person that useth them, there being nothing simply and absolutely so ..." (L 6.7: 28–29). Hobbes surely does not derive his conviction that there is no absolute good or *summum bonum* from an examination of common linguistic usage; it follows from his metaphysical commitments. But he seems to find confirmation from linguistic usage all the same when he uses a descriptive phrase like "are

[55] It may include Galileo; see Leijenhorst 2007, 88.

ever used." We may question this of course: Are they really always used in this way? Words of good and evil might also be used *not* in relation to the person who uses them but indeed to an objective notion. The meaning of good is subtly revised, then, though again the revision is defused by phrases like "are ever used."[56] And when he defines felicity he uses the phrase "men call," immediately adding his own view on what it actually is: "Continual success in obtaining those things which a man from time to time desireth, that is to say, continual prospering, is that men call felicity; I mean the felicity of this life. For there is no such thing as perpetual tranquillity of mind, while we live here" (L 6.58: 34). What "men" call felicity might precisely the thing Hobbes rejects, but the tenor of such passages suggests otherwise; an impression enhanced by the contrast Hobbes draws, once again, with the insignificant speech of the scholastics: "the word of schoolmen *beatifical vision* is unintelligible" (L 6.58: 35).

In some cases the prescription to use a word with the meaning Hobbes assigns to it is quite explicit, for example when he defines the will: "in deliberation, the last appetite or aversion immediately adhering to the action, or to the omission thereof, is that we call the will, the act (not the faculty) of *willing*."[57] Hobbes rejects the scholastic definition of the will as rational appetite, but also points out that "common discourse" might give us the wrong idea that the will is something autonomous: "And though we say in common discourse, a man had a will once to do a thing, that nevertheless he forbore to do, yet that is properly an inclination, which makes no action voluntary; because the action depends not of it, but of the last inclination or appetite." Later we will see Hobbes basing his account of free will on what "we are use to say."

Also in the next chapter, entitled "Of the Ends, or Resolutions of Discourse," we find Hobbes using "it is called" in presenting his own definitions of will, judgment, doubt, conclusion, science, conscience, belief, and faith, implying that these definitions somehow capture what we mean by these terms. For instance, the long definition of science, comprising all the characteristic elements of his view of science (e.g.

[56] In the same passage on good and evil, Hobbes compares the Latin, which has two general words (*pulchrum* and *turpe*) with the wider array of more specific words in English (fair, beautiful, handsome, etc.), used "as the subject shall require." All these words "in their proper places," "signify nothing else but the *mien*, or countenance, that promiseth good and evil. So that of good there be three kinds . . . " (L 6.8: 29). Again, Hobbes's own philosophical position requires some revision of ordinary language: the richness of expression is not rejected and might even be applauded, yet properly speaking they mean much the same.

[57] L 6.53: 33 for this and the next quotation; the phrase "we call" becomes "is called" in the next chapter, L 7.2: 35.

"knowledge of the consequence of words"), ends in a relative clause "which is commonly called science." In the next section Hobbes discusses conscience, which he reduces elsewhere to one's own judgment: "For a man's conscience and his judgment is the same thing" (L 29.7: 212). His philosophical commitments lead him to downplay the authoritative, almost divine status of conscience, to which people had appealed as an independent authority, in the belief that it is a sin to act against one's conscience. So the term receives a somewhat deflationary account that subtly suggests a commonly shared understanding of the term rather than an idiosyncratic usage by Hobbes. In his *Elements of Law* Hobbes had already defined conscience as follows: "So that conscience, as men commonly use the word, signifieth an opinion, not so much of the truth of the proposition, as of their own knowledge of it, to which the truth of the proposition is consequent. Conscience therefore I define to be opinion of evidence." In *Leviathan* he elaborates on this by giving an etymology that traces a shift from conscience as External Witness to conscience as Internal Lawgiver.[58] At first the term had denoted the sharing of knowledge: "when two or more men know of one and the same fact, they are said to be conscious of it one to another."[59] Later, Hobbes observes, the term came also to stand for one's own "secret facts and secret thoughts," and "therefore it is rhetorically said that the conscience is a thousand witnesses" – a "striking and revisionary" use of this proverb, as Raylor states, concluding that Hobbes's "history of the term empties it of theological or epistemological authority, removing both the '*con*' – the sense of shared, public witnessing – and the '*-scientia*' – the sense that such belief constitutes certain knowledge, or *scientia*. Small wonder that it outraged traditional moralists like Clarendon."[60] The important point for our purpose to notice here is that Hobbes anticipated such outrage by trying to suggest – often too opportunistically and unconvincingly perhaps – that his understanding of the terms is in line with common usage (also sometimes presented as "proper" usage, as we will see in the next section).

In the next section Hobbes discusses the terms belief and faith. His definitions are accompanied by remarks on how we use these terms (and their equivalents in Latin and Greek). It is the "singularity" of ecclesiastical use of these words that is abnormal: "*I believe in*, as also the Latin *credo in* and the Greek *pisteuo eis*, are never used but in the writings of divines.

[58] See Raylor 2018, 234, who argues that Hobbes's discussion of conscience is an example of his analysis of "the problem of the systematic abuse of metaphor" (233, with references to other discussions of Hobbes's treatment of conscience).

[59] L 7.4: 36 and 29.7: 212.

[60] Raylor 2018, 237–238.

Instead of them, in other writings are put: *I believe him, I trust him, I have faith in him, I rely on him* . . .; and [that] this singularity of the ecclesiastic use of the word hath raised many disputes about the right object of the Christian faith."[61] In this ecclesiastical context, "believing in" means "not trust in the person, but confession and acknowledgement of the doctrine." The singularity of ecclesiastical usage stands in opposition to common use. Without going into the argumentative context of Hobbes's remarks here, we may note again that he supports his philosophical views by an examination of common usage, sometimes subtly revising it to make it accord with these views.

When we come to the core of Hobbes's moral and political philosophy, in which key terms such as natural law, right, peace, war, covenant, contract, duty, justice, merit, civil law, person, sovereign, and commonwealth must be defined, we see him less concerned with mapping his definitions onto ordinary language. This is not surprising, given his view that this whole field had suffered from bad definitions or a lack of definitions, and that up to his own time there have been, as he claims, no science worthy of the name. Key concepts such as right and law have been confounded; civil law and civil right have been "promiscuously used for the same thing, even in the most learned authors," and "likewise *laws* and *charters* are taken promiscuously for the same thing."[62] Liberty has been misunderstood and misused from ancient times onward as if it meant something that sanctions resistance to the sovereign power. All these terms require precise definitions, discriminating between the various meanings and disambiguating equivocal words; from these definitions Hobbes can then erect his edifice. We do not need to quote in full his famous definitions of the laws of nature (let alone discuss them) to notice their style of presentation: the right of nature *is* liberty, and so on; the law of nature *is* a precept, and so on; to lay down one's right to anything *is* to divest oneself, and so on; a person *is* he whose words or actions, and so on; the civil law *is*, to every subject, those rules, and so on.[63] Hobbes clearly lays down his definitions without apparently taking care to give them the sanction of common usage ("we say," "commonly called," etc.) But even

[61] L 7.5: 36–37; cf. Hobbes 1998, 238 (DCv 18.4); cf. Appendix to Latin *Leviathan*, I (Hobbes 1994b, 498).

[62] L 14.3: 79, L 26.4: 173 and L 26.45: 189; cf. Hobbes 1994a, 81 and 19 (EL 15.1 and Epistle Dedicatory); Hobbes 1998, 32–33 (DCv 2.1); Hobbes 2005, 34–35 (*Dialogue*) criticizing Coke.

[63] But in giving his definition of war Hobbes gives the impression that he is relating a commonly understood meaning of the term, comparing the definition of war with the homely example of "foul weather": "they are in that condition which is called war" (L 13.8: 76). What he means is: "called war by me," but he conveniently leaves out that qualification.

in these cases where the definitions are not explicitly backed up by common usage, Hobbes probably thinks that they proceed from common understanding, which would be a vitally important requirement for his whole project: if the deduction of the natural laws and everything that follows from them were a philosophical exercise that went beyond the understanding of the common people, Hobbes's project of reform would be a failure; the principles of his science cannot be too difficult, and must "put men in mind what they know already, or may know by their own experience."[64] We will come back to this aspect below.

"Improper" and "Proper Speech"

In addition to phrases such as "we call" and "generally called," there is another term that serves a similar function: the "proper" meaning of a term is meant to denote what Hobbes sees as the right use of the term to be distinguished from other meanings or connotations that it has received through the ages.[65] A famous, and intensively discussed example is liberty: "By liberty is understood, according to the proper signification of the word, the absence of external impediments . . . ."[66] Hobbes realizes that his definition according to which liberty is consistent with necessity must go against what most people would understand by it, and perhaps for that reason he appeals to "what we use to say" in explaining this notion. If someone or something is held back from moving by external impediments, we are used to say it is not at liberty to move (L 21.1: 136):

> And so of all living creatures, whilst they are imprisoned, or restrained, with walls, or chains; and of the water whilst it is kept in by banks, or vessels, that otherwise would spread itself into a larger space, we use to say, they are not at liberty, to move in such manner, as without those external impediments they would. But when the impediment of motion, is in the constitution of the thing itself, we use not to say, it wants the liberty; but the power to move; as when a stone lieth still, or a man is fastened to his bed by sickness.

Hobbes's appeal to common usage does not look very convincing: do we really say that the water is "not at liberty" to flow outside the banks?

[64] Hobbes 1994a, 21 (EL 1.2).

[65] The term "proper speech" could also be used to denote the perspicuous and concise style that was the model for scientific writing in the Mersenne circle. Throughout his career Hobbes stressed the importance of a clear, perspicuous, and concise style, and never mentioned that cornerstone of Ciceronian-humanistic rhetoric: elegance; see Burchell 2007 and Raylor 2018.

[66] L 14.2: 79; Latin *Leviathan*: "id quod ea vox proprie significat" (Hobbes 2012, II, 199). On liberty see Skinner 1998 and 2008.

Though he omits the example later from his Latin translation, here he seems to suggest that this is normal usage, because he speaks about it as "this proper and generally received meaning of the word," and at the end of his discussion he sums up: "And this shall suffice (as to the matter in hand) of that natural *liberty*, which only is properly called *liberty*" (L 21.4: 137). By using the notion of "proper signification" Hobbes seems to suggest that this is the right (or "original") meaning of the term in spite of the way in which it is often used in common discourse; hence he calls all applications of "free" and "liberty" to things that are not subject to motion an abuse of the term; yet, to defend his controversial definition he also claims that it is "the generally received meaning of the word" and in line with what "we use to say."

Similarly, in his discussion with Bishop Bramhall, Hobbes defends his definitions of free will, liberty, and related notions such as external impediment, by frequently appealing to common language: it is the bishop who does "not understand sufficiently the English tongue." Hobbes himself does not find "in anything that I have written any impropriety in the use of these or any other English words. Nor do I doubt but an English reader, who has not lost himself in School-divinity, will very easily conceive what I have said."[67] Because there do not seem to be facts on the basis of which we can decide the matter in one way or the other, the issue is often a verbal one in the nonpejorative sense of the word, and throughout the dispute we find references to how we describe such and such, what we say in such and such a circumstance, whether we can properly say this or that, and so on. On one occasion, when the notion of compulsion is discussed, Hobbes is confident enough to claim that "of this dispute the English and well-bred reader is the proper judge," as he thinks that his usage conforms to common, English usage as opposed to the "absurd speech" of the bishop.[68] And when he defends his application of the word "liberty" to animals and rivers he appeals to what "men that speak English use to say" in this or that situation, identifying it with proper language.[69]

But to claim support from the so-called common usage of "English and well-bred speakers" or the "common people, on whose arbitration depends the signification of words in common use," is a tricky tactic, for this very concept of liberty (just as is the case of conscience and many other

[67] Hobbes 1841, 352 and 353 (QLNC).

[68] Hobbes 1841, 260 (QLNC). Whether Hobbes, here and elsewhere, is right to claim to have ordinary usage on his side is a question that would require an extensive survey of contemporary usages.

[69] Hobbes 1841, 403–404 (QLNC).

concepts) has been grossly misunderstood by many people, "well-bred" or not:[70]

> For if we take liberty in the proper sense, for corporal liberty; that is to say, freedom from chains, and prison, it were very absurd for men to clamour as they do, for the liberty they so manifestly enjoy. Again, if we take liberty, for an exemption from laws, it is no less absurd, for men to demand as they do, that liberty, by which all other men may be masters of their lives. And yet as absurd as it is, this is it they demand.

In spite of the impression Hobbes frequently wants to convey, namely that his usage complies with common speech, he also concedes that revision of common speech is necessary, but when and how and to what extent often remains somewhat implicit. As before, it seems that Hobbes wants to have it both ways: to revise common usage and then presenting the result as, in fact, being in line with common usage;[71] description (what an English speaker would say in such and such a case) goes hand in hand with prescription (this is the way we should use the term), and the term "proper signification" sometimes seems to bridge these two levels: it is how the term should be used but also how it is (supposedly) used.

Another example of properly and improperly speaking is the law of nature. As Hobbes famously concludes his discussion: "These dictates of reason men use to call by the name of laws, but improperly ... [L]aw, properly, is the word of him that by right hath command over others. But yet if we consider the same theorems, as delivered in the word of God, that by right commandeth all things, then are they properly called laws."[72] The proper signification must therefore capture what Hobbes thinks the concept implies, and hopefully this comes close to common usage, as the example of liberty must suggest.[73] That the concept of a law implies a lawgiver is something everybody can understand, as Hobbes makes clear in a comment on his definition of civil law (L 26.3–4: 173):

[70] Hobbes 1841, 92 (QLNC).

[71] Sometimes the word "common" can also refer to what is in common use in the schools, for example, L 14.1: 79: "The right of nature, which writers commonly call *jus naturale*." Cf. L 15.14: 94: "Justice of actions is by writers divided into *commutative* and *distributive*"; with Curley's note referring to Aristotle and Aquinas.

[72] L 15.41: 100; cf. Hobbes 1998, 56 (DCv 3.33); cf. L 26.8: 174: "not properly laws, but qualities that dispose men to peace and to obedience."

[73] Cf. his discussion of command and counsel: "To avoid which mistakes, and render to those terms of commanding, counselling, and exhorting, their proper and distinct significations, I define them thus ... " (L 25.1: 165). Having explained the concepts, he concludes: "As the difference of counsel from command hath now been deduced from the nature of counsel ... " (L 25.11: 168), smoothly proceeding from defining a term to talking about the nature of the concept.

> Civil Law is, to every subject, those rules which the commonwealth hath commanded him ... to make use of, for the distinction of right and wrong .... In which definition there is nothing that is not at first sight evident. For every man seeth that some laws are addressed to all subjects in general, some to particular provinces ..., and are therefore laws to every of those to whom the command is directed, and to none else.

Every person can see the truth of this definition, and hence can (that is, must) follow Hobbes in his deductions: "And therefore, whatsoever can from this definition by necessary consequence be deduced ought to be acknowledged for truth (ibid.)."[74]

One such consequence is that the sovereign power cannot act unjustly, for injustice in its "proper" signification is the breaking of the covenant. Since we as subjects have authorized the sovereign to act on our behalf and because "to do injury to one's self, is impossible," we cannot complain of injury perpetrated by the sovereign power; we are all "authors" of everything the sovereign power does, nor can the latter act unjustly: "It is true that they that have sovereign power, may commit iniquity; but not injustice, or injury in the proper signification."[75] Again, though the term "proper" may suggest otherwise (namely that it has been settled in a way independent of how Hobbes chooses to use the term), it is Hobbes who defines what is the proper meaning of the term.[76]

We find a similar use of the word "proper" in Hobbes's discussions of terms such as spirit, inspiration, angel, kingdom of God, holy, word of God, miracles, martyrs, Antichrist, and images (or idols); and the titles of several chapters announce that the discussions are about the "significations" of these terms (e.g. chapters 34, 35, and 36). Hobbes's own interpretations of these terms are an important part of his critique of religion and the Church. Hobbes redefines these terms in such a way that they are in line with his materialist philosophy or his ideas about the Church–state relations. But while this is a deliberate and explicit act of interpretation (something Hobbes was well aware of[77]), the use of phrases such as "proper

[74] In this case, Hobbes even bends the definition as used in the schools to suit his own case: "And this is also to be gathered out of the ordinary definition of justice in the Schools; for they say that *justice is the constant will of giving to every man his own*. And therefore where there is no *own*, that is, no propriety, there is no injustice ..." (L 15.3: 89, with Curley's note ad loc.).

[75] L 18.6: 113; cf. L 17.13: 109.

[76] Cf. Hobbes 1998, 139 (DCv 12.12) on a good kind of eloquence, partly based on "an understanding of words taken in their proper meanings as defined." For another example, see his revision of the scholastic definitions of commutative and distributive justice: "To speak properly, commutative justice is the justice of the contractor ... " (L 15.14: 95).

[77] See the Letter Dedicatory to *Leviathan* already quoted above n. 50.

signification" must also suggest that these meanings are not entirely of Hobbes's own making but independently support his views. Without going into detail, we may give the following examples to illustrate this point.

For instance, inspiration, "properly" speaking is "nothing but the blowing into a man some thin and subtle air or wind" (L 34.25: 270). If spirits are "not corporeal, but have their existence only in the fancy, then it is nothing but the blowing in of a phantasm (which is improper to say, and impossible; for phantasms are not, but only seem to be somewhat) (ibid.)." Hobbes supports his interpretation by claiming that "the most common acceptation of the word spirit is in the signification of a man's intention, mind, or disposition," thereby rejecting the idea that a spirit is something noncorporeal (L 36.15: 288). A spirit is "either properly a real substance, or metaphorically some extraordinary ability or affection of the mind or of the body" (L 34.14: 265). Hence there can be no images of noncorporeal things (God, the soul, spirits) but only of "bodies visible" (L 45.15: 444):

> an image (in the most strict signification of the word) is the resemblance of something visible. In which sense the phantastical forms, apparitions, or seemings of visible bodies to the sight, are only images ... And these are the images which are originally and most properly called ideas and *idols*, and derived from the language of the Graecians ... But in a larger use of the word *image* is contained also any representation of one thing by another.

Another example where the proper signification that Hobbes assigns to the term is motivated by his wider views is the Kingdom of God. In criticizing what he calls the "greatest, and main abuse of Scripture" namely that the Kingdom of God is "the present Church," Hobbes defines the Kingdom of God as "a kingdom properly so named, constituted by the votes of the people of Israel," and "properly meant a commonwealth."[78] In similar vein, the word "holy" is interpreted in the light of Hobbes's view that God was the king of the Jews ("his peculiar people by covenant"), and that "the kingdom of God is a civil kingdom." "By *holy* is always understood, either God himself or that which is God's in propriety ... And wheresoever the word Holy is taken properly, there is still something signified of propriety, gotten by consent."[79] Similarly, Hobbes's discussion of the meaning of the phrase the "Word of God," understood "properly, as the words he hath spoken to his prophets," serves to underscore his idea that it is the sovereign who determines what is to be considered as the Word of God (L 36.3: 280).

[78] L 44.4: 412; L 35.2: 272; L 35.7: 274. [79] L 30.5: 221; L 35.13: 276; L 35.15–16: 277.

A last example: Hobbes's proper (here: "true") definition of martyr as a witness of the resurrection of Christ must resolve the problem of martyrdom; on Hobbes's view one can outwardly obey an iniquitous sovereign or an infidel without incurring Christ's punishment, so that there is no need to become a martyr at all.[80]

Hobbes thus uses the notion of proper signification to give meaning to terms that are compatible with, or rather underscore, his philosophical views. In many cases, for example liberty, law, and image, he seems to mean by "proper" a literal, nonmetaphorical meaning (in line with how "proper" was often used, "improper" standing for metaphorical), often claiming to have common usage on his side or (as in the case of his biblical interpretation) support from scriptural passages. In due course, terms could receive metaphorical, "improper" meanings or showed "larger uses," but this was often, so Hobbes suggests, for politically or religiously dubious reasons.

Thus Hobbes's strategy in defining terms and claiming what words "properly" mean seems to involve minimizing or downplaying his own role as definer in order to persuade people to accept his interpretations and definitions. But of course the result of all this defining work is to lend credit to Hobbes's own philosophical views. He therefore has to walk a fine line between invoking "common speech" and giving his own revisionary definitions. As we have seen, there need not be a tension between the two. In rejecting the language of the schools and the Church as absurd speech that aims at confounding and mystifying people, it is tempting to come to the side of the people and emphasize the viability of common language as an alternative. Yet common language must always be critically approached and surveyed to smooth out the ambiguities, inadequacies, and "inconstancies" it contains. Hobbes claims that the result of this revision – for example, his definitions of freedom, liberty, servitude, law, and many other terms – is in fact how we commonly use these terms, but what he means is that this is the way in which we should use these terms.

Critics of Hobbes have not been slow to point out that Hobbes's strategy of redefinition serves his own purposes. Thus John Wallis wrote to Robert Boyle:[81]

[80] L 42.12: 340. A less clear example is his application of Person to the Trinity ("personated thrice"): in view of his own definition of person God may "properly enough be said to be three persons" but he adds that "neither the word Person, nor Trinity, be ascribed to him in the Bible" (L 42.3: 334). A slightly different meaning of "proper" is "correct," for example when Hobbes asks "Can it be properly said that God hath voice and language" (L 36.9: 284) where it means something like "correctly" or "rightfully" or "Does it make sense to ask . . . ?"

[81] Quoted in Shapin and Schaffer 1985, 118. Similar judgements in Sommerville 1992, 2; Pettit 2008, 53–54 and 67. Clarendon also complained that Hobbes relied on tendentious definitions; see Raylor 2018, 2.

> Mr Hobs is very dexterous in confuting others by putting a new sense on their words rehearsed by himself: different from what the words signifie with other men. And therefore if you shall have occasion to speak of chalk, he'll tell you that by chalk he means cheese: and then if he can prove that what you say of chalk is not true of cheese, he reckons himself to have gotten a great victory.

Hobbes's reply to such an accusation would be (and we have already had occasion to quote him on this), that it is everybody's right and obligation to define one's own terms in line with one's own chosen "principles," and to check and revise other scholars' definitions. This might also be Hobbes's reply to a modern critic who could point out that Hobbes's strategy of redefinition comes close to the tactic of rhetorical paradiastole or redescription that he himself condemns.[82] It is rather Hobbes's claim that his own redefinitions are supported by – or compatible with or even written in – common language that makes his position vulnerable to criticism.

A Civil Science for Everyone

It is therefore not surprising to find Hobbes claiming, at the beginning of Part III of *Leviathan*, that his civil science is based on definitions "universally agreed on" (32.1: 245). The rhetoric of common language might thus also be seen as an expression of something more fundamental, namely, the suggestion that his civil science is not a theoretical construct that requires deep philosophical skills to understand but rather an ordering and systematization of prescientific, common-sense moral and civic knowledge. Hobbes's civil science cannot be too complicated, nor can it claim to produce completely new knowledge.[83] Otherwise his main goal would be in vain, namely to persuade people to endorse his principles and definitions because these principles lead people to accept the sovereign power in exchange for protection "from the invasion of foreigners and the injuries of one another."[84] He hopes to convince the reader that in spite of much

[82] Pettit 2008, 54: "The strategy of redefinition is not very different from rhetorical paradiastole or redescription of the kind that Hobbes so expressly condemned. For he used it, again and again, to outmaneuver his opponents by switching from the meanings they gave their terms to the meanings that suited his purposes better." On the ancient practice of rhetorical paradiastole see Skinner 1996, 138–153.

[83] Cf. Sorell 1986, 12, 26 and 142; Isermann 1991, 119; Brockdorff 1919, 52 quoted by Isermann 1991, 122 n. 49; Leijenhorst 2002b, 363.

[84] L 17.13: 109. Cf. Hobbes 1839, xii (*Concerning Body*, Epistle to the Reader): "Think not, Courteous Reader, that the philosophy, the elements whereof I am going to set in order, is that ... which is found in the metaphysic codes .... Philosophy, therefore, the child of the world and your own mind, is within yourself."

complaint and grievance throughout the ages, the distribution of duties and rights between sovereign and the citizens that inevitably follows from Hobbes's definitions of law, right, liberty, and justice is the right one, since it is the only one that is in everybody's interest, namely to have a stable commonwealth in which each of us can live a "commodious life." Undivided power vested in the sovereign might not seem to correspond with one's own personal interest, but it does not require much intellectual work to follow Hobbes through his arguments that distinguish between the real and apparent good and real and apparent justice. Therefore, when the argument might ring too artificial or perhaps too complicated, Hobbes reminds the reader that his argument can be followed by everyone, unless blinded by "notable multiplying glasses (that is their passions and self-love), through which every little payment appeareth a great grievance" (L 18.20: 118); for though everyone "by nature" has these glasses, everyone also possesses an inborn power to reason by which they can discover or at least understand the dictates of reason, improperly called laws, that show the road to peace. If readers for instance find the warlike state of nature strange, and so distrust "this inference made from the passions," let them consult their own "experience": everyone locks their door and chests, and nobody goes on a journey unarmed, and so on. And whoever finds the deduction of the laws of nature "too subtle," will find them "very reasonable" when thinking of its contraction "into one easy sum, intelligible even to the meanest capacity, and that is *Do not that to another, which thou wouldst not have done to thyself.*"[85] As he says in the opening chapter of *The Elements of Law*: his aim is "only to put men in mind what they know already, or may know by their own experience."[86]

This last claim seriously underestimates the corrective or revisionary dimension of Hobbes's moral and civil science: it is Hobbes's aim to substitute the "magnifying glasses" for "prospective glasses (namely moral and civil science)";[87] his project offers of course not only an articulation, ordering, and systematization of what people already know but also a correction of their biased and "passionate" ideas of what just, good, and free is, their ideas about liberty and about rights and duties and of those of the sovereign. We have already seen Hobbes mocking people who wrongly crave freedom that they in fact already enjoy, and in various places (e.g. in chapters 29 and 30) he lists common but wrong opinions that weaken the

[85] L 13.10: 77; cf. L 15.35: 99. [86] Hobbes 1994a (EL 1.2).

[87] L 18.20: 118. But as Sorell 1986, 143 comments on this statement by Hobbes: "But this is a remark about principles or starting points, not about what is deduced from them." See also his discussion, esp. 7–13, and 133–144.

commonwealth such as "that every private man is judge of good and evil actions" (L 29.6: 212) and that "whatsoever a man does against his conscience is sin" (L 29.7: 212). Hobbes would not have started to write about politics in the first place if he thought people in general thought correctly about power, freedom, and sovereignty. As the political situation had made abundantly clear, they evidently did not. Hobbes's moral and civic science is presented as a timely and necessary correction of such views, and he hopes it will be taught in the universities.[88]

The reason to stress this obvious point is the analogy it offers with Hobbes's rhetoric of common language. Just as he appeals to common usage while at the same time revising it (and often implying that the revision is in accordance with common usage as well), so he presents his whole project of establishing a moral and civil science sometimes as a mere articulation of what people already know and sometimes (and more prominently) as a revision and correction of their beliefs. His project may be defined in terms of this revision resulting in a moral *science*, yet he also frequently stresses that we all can arrive at his conclusions by simply looking into our own minds and observing our own passionate nature ("*nosce teipsum*, read thy self").[89] We do not need to grasp the physical basis of our emotional life in order to understand what is required to curb these passions so that we may live in peace, something we all desire. Nor do moral and civil science require an understanding of the principles of the other two parts of Hobbes's trilogy, physics and geometry, even though they are connected and somehow based on these other parts in the sense that "the principles of the politics consist in the knowledge of the motions of the mind, and the knowledge of these motions from the knowledge of sense and imagination."[90] Referring to moral philosophy as the study of the motions of the mind, that is, the passions, Hobbes states in the chapter on method in *De Corpore* that "*civil* and *moral philosophy* do not so adhere to one another, but that they may be severed. For the causes of the motions of the mind are known, not only by ratiocination, but also by the experience of every man that takes the pains to observe those motions within himself."[91] These people, untrained in geometry and physics and without a scientific understanding of the motions of the mind, will nevertheless be

[88] L 30.14: 225–226 and "A Review and Conclusion": 496; cf. Hobbes 1998, 13–14 (DCv, preface to the Readers). Tuck calls it therefore "the greatest of the English revolutionary utopias" (Tuck 1993, 135, and Tuck in Hobbes 1991, xliii).

[89] L Intro.3: 4.

[90] Hobbes 1839, 74 (*Concerning Body* 1.6.7); cf. Hobbes 1998, 13 (DCv, preface to the Readers).

[91] Ibid.

able to arrive at the conclusions of Hobbes's civil philosophy, when they realize that to live in peace requires the establishment of a coercive power; otherwise men "will always be making war upon one another, which may be known to be so by any man's experience, that will but examine his own mind."[92] And "all men easily recognize that this state is evil when they are in it; and consequently that peace is good."[93] In short, to persuade people that they should endorse his definitions, principles, and the conclusions derived from them, Hobbes often appeals to common language, common understanding, and people's own experience and observations in an attempt to bridge the distance that they might feel between their own views and Hobbes's.

We might even go a step further. Perhaps we might say that Hobbes tries to convince people that his ideas about obedience and sovereignty are in fact their own (or should become their own), for have they not authorized the sovereign to protect them? In a way, the people *are* the state: "This is more than consent, or concord; it is a real unity of them all, in one and the same person, made by covenant of every man with every man ... This done, the multitude so united in one person is called the Commonwealth."[94] Hence, we cannot accuse the sovereign of injustice, for "to do injury to one's self, is impossible," something which Hobbes elsewhere compares with the absurdities in "the disputations of scholars" (L 14.7: 81). From this point of view, the iconography of the great Leviathan, consisting of its individual subjects, is a perfect illustration of Hobbes's persuasive tactic.[95] It is we who have established this "artificial man," "of whose acts a great multitude, by mutual covenants one with another, have made themselves every one the author" (ibid.). But at the same time, it is also something bigger than the sum of its parts. This "Mortal God" should also be feared and kept in awe.[96] The parallel with

[92] The context is a discussion of the analytical method (proceeding from observed phenomena to first principles) and synthetical method in philosophy (starting with principles). For discussion see Jesseph 1999, 228–246.

[93] Hobbes 1998, 55 (DCv 3.31). But Hobbes is also often more pessimistic: "Common people know nothing of Right and Wrong by their own meditation; they must therefore be taught the grounds of their duty," referring to the rebels who were taught publicly "Rebellion in the pulpits" (Hobbes 2010, 302; *Behemoth*, Dialogue 3).

[94] L 17.13: 109. For discussion of the ambiguity of the word "the people" in Hobbes's argument see Malcolm 2002, 37, citing *De Cive*: "The *People* rules in all Governments, for even in *Monarchies* the *People* Commands." See also Raylor 2018, 224–225.

[95] On the iconography and the dioptric device that probably inspired it, see Malcolm 2002, 200–228.

[96] Both reason and fear are dependent on each other; as Malcolm 2002, 228 writes: "Rather, as Hobbes's whole complex argument about the conditional covenant underlying the institution of sovereignty suggests, they are entirely interdependent: the logic of authorization will come into play only when it implies the existence of a power sufficient to bind the passions. It is a curious structure

Hobbes's rhetoric of common language looks perhaps a bit far-fetched, but in all these cases – Hobbes's appeal to common language, people's own experience, and their collective "authorship" of the state – the impression he gives is that his theory is an extension and development of a shared basis; just as scientific knowledge is based on prescientific, common experience and prudence, and its linguistic expression based on common language and shared definitions, so the civil state is based on consent and agreement. At one point Hobbes even draws a parallel between definitions and laws: "names imposed by Statutes are equivalent to Definitions," but the big difference is of course that the sciences do not have a sovereign power as the Great Definer.[97]

This, however, raises the following question. Hobbes's presentation of his ideas as an extension and development of a shared basis in experience and in language might seem to put a constraint on the role of the sovereign; for it is a crucial part of Hobbes's theory that the sovereign has absolute power that includes the power of defining terms by which social-political life is regulated:[98]

> it is the responsibility of the same sovereign power to come up with rules or measures that will be common to all, and to publish them openly, so that each man may know by them what he should call his own and what another's, what he should call just and unjust, honourable and dishonourable, good and bad; in summary, what he should do and what he should avoid doing in social life.

If we do not set up a common measure, we will remain in the state of nature, "where every man is his own judge, and differeth from other concerning the names and appellations of things, and from those differences arise quarrels, and breach of peace."[99] But this constitutive power of the sovereign will probably define the meaning of terms in a way that does not coincide with what people mean by these terms; in fact, the necessity of setting up a common measure shows that they will not coincide; people

of argument that requires two different ways of seeing the relation between the individual and the state to be entertained at one and the same time."

97 Hobbes 2005, 97 (*Dialogue*). Isermann 1991, 121 concludes that promise rather than command is the analogue of law, since in science no one can command how to use terms, though we can promise to use terms as agreed upon.

98 Hobbes 1998, 79 (DCv 6.9); and also what human life is: the sovereign (through the laws) decides whether "some strange and deformed birth . . . be a man or no"; Hobbes 1994a, 181 (EL 29.8).

99 Hobbes 1994a, 181 (EL 29.8). Isermann 1991, 121 n. 44 mentioning scholars such as S. S. Wolin, P.-F. Moreau, and K. Schuhmann, who all see a parallel between laying down one's natural right in the state of nature with laying down one's linguistic "natural right" when we transfer the right of defining terms such as "good," "bad," "just," and "unjust" to the sovereign as the Great Definer.

usually think only about their short-term self-interest. So is the institution of property and morality just a question of stipulation, a purely arbitrary affair?[100] As one scholar puts it: the sovereign's legislation "will not draw on preexisting terms to describe the sorts of behavior that are mandatory or forbidden for the populace. It will first introduce new terms or concepts, and so new possibilities of behavior, and then regulate for how these should materialize in social life."[101] The sovereign is thus said to give "people new categories by which to orient themselves," and "new concepts by which to navigate."[102] So the constitutive role of the sovereign in establishing a range of social-political terms might seem incompatible with the claim of common language made by Hobbes in defining – on behalf of the sovereign, so to speak – the same range of terms.

But the answer might be this: though the sovereign is indeed free in defining terms, these terms cannot be defined arbitrarily or whimsically but must be defined in a way that makes clear how peace and commodious living are to be ensured. If the sovereign takes Hobbes's account seriously, as Hobbes hopes they will do, people will see that the definitions of good, bad, just, unjust, and so on, constitute a juridical framework that serves their common goal, namely protection and commodious living. This juridical framework is based on the laws of nature, which become part of the civil laws once the civil state has been established. And the laws of nature are of course guides of moral behavior and virtuous actions, which, as Hobbes claim, are "immutable and eternal": "for injustice, ingratitude, arrogance, pride, iniquity, acception of persons, and the rest, can never be made lawful. For it can never be that war shall preserve life, and peace destroy it" (15.38: 99–100). No sovereign power can define justice in a way that goes against the laws of nature. Of course, the civil laws comprise much more than the laws of nature, but they too must ultimately be directed to the goal for which the people have installed and authorized a sovereign power in the first place.[103] It would therefore be unwise policy on the sovereign's part if they were to draw on completely new terms to regulate and constitute social life in the civil state. As Hobbes's theory prescribes, it will require correcting the biased, subjective, untutored, and "passionate" opinions that come natural to us – "the magnifying glasses"

[100] Cf. Cassirer 1906–1957, 2:56. [101] Pettit 2008, 130. [102] Ibid., 131.

[103] For a correction of the widespread view that the law of nature is whatever the sovereign wills it to be, see the excellent discussion by Malcolm 2002, 437; "morality remains an objective standard, by which the laws or actions of the sovereign can still be judged," pointing out that "Hobbes carefully manages the transition in his argument from the psychological level to the moral, and again from the moral to the jural."

mentioned above – but as suggested in this chapter, Hobbes does not think that a wholly new vocabulary is required to rectify and canalize these beliefs into an enlightened view of what it takes to live peacefully in a commonwealth. His persuasive strategy in setting out his civil science tries to present it as something we all should naturally endorse and rationally support, given this common aim of living a peaceful, commodious life.

CHAPTER 8

Between Private Signification and Common Use: Locke on Ideas, Words, and the Social Dimension of Language

Introduction

As much as it was the starting point for many new developments in the eighteenth century, Locke's *Essay Concerning Human Understanding*, first published in 1690, can also be viewed as a final step in the critique of Aristotelian-scholastic language and thought that had started more than 300 years earlier.[1] Locke took an apparently drastic step in arguing that whatever order we discern in the world is of our own making; it is the human mind – rather than a supposedly objective, mind-independent order of things – that is responsible for the categorizations of the world. Hence, language can no longer be regarded as a mirror of the world; it is an expression of our thoughts about the world, not of the world itself.[2] Though drastic and innovative in many respects, it was a step that had been prepared for by centuries of various forms of critique of Aristotelian thought and language, some of which we have studied in the previous chapters.[3] These centuries had seen a gradual move away from an essentialist conception of the world expressed in an equally essentialist language toward a view that emphasized the creative role of the human mind, and one in which demonstrative certainty and absolute truth had to make place for probability, verisimilitude, and even uncertainty. But a move away is not a linear process, and the early-modern period is no less marked by the resilience of the Aristotelian tradition and various attempts to find room for certainty, truth, forms, and essences in a world full of change.

Yet, it might also be found strange to find Locke, within the covers of one book, somehow connected with earlier stages of this critique in Renaissance

[1] According to Kretzmann, the *Essay* is "the first modern treatise devoted specifically to philosophy of language" (Kretzmann 1967, 379); cf. Losonsky 2006, 3.

[2] This is a simplistic way of putting it, which will be qualified in what follows, but the idea is that, according to Locke, words primarily and immediately signify ideas, not things.

[3] This is, of course, not to say that Locke's step was *directly* indebted to earlier traditions of critique; developments in the New Science, in which Boyle was an important source for Locke, played a major role as well.

humanism. By the time Locke had started working on his *Essay*, the humanist ideal of a revival of classical Latin as essential for clear, precise thinking and as a storehouse of erudition and learning had lost much of its appeal. True, humanist scholarship had given people what we nowadays would call transferable skills, and these skills were used to good effect, also by Locke, in many diverse domains, but classical Latin as the sole vehicle for clear thinking had found serious competitors in the national languages, or, in some circles, in the search for an Adamic language. But here, too, there is a sense in which Locke can be seen as a distant heir to humanist reflection on language, and it is a sense connected to a certain anti-essentialist strand running through these centuries. In earlier chapters we have frequently seen how humanists, but also Hobbes, had appealed to common linguistic usage in their fight against what they considered to be the unduly abstract and esoteric language of the scholastics. When it suited their purpose, humanists such as Valla and Vives could even come to the defense of the so-called common people who, as members of a linguistic community, used language in accordance with custom and convention. A possibly elitist project (as classical Latin was of course far from being a common language) was presented and genuinely felt as a democratization of thought and language, at least when compared to the so-called abstruse questions and terminology of the schools.

Three hundred years later Locke still felt the need to break the spell that philosophical language had cast on the minds of people. Not only his rejection of innate ideas, but also his critique of essences and concomitant language can be seen as serving the goal of a democratization of knowledge, learning, and language. In confronting the self-appointed guardians of established doctrines and dogmas, Locke felt it necessary at times – as we will see below – to appeal to common linguistic usage and common language, however unstable in itself, praising, just as Robert Boyle but also humanists such as Agricola and Vives had done, workmen and other professionals for their practical knowledge and corresponding terminology. The jargon of the schools was not a harmless game that could simply be laughed off, since it served to secure one's authority and position, and to impress, overpower, and dominate others. Of course, times had changed, and Locke's targets now included Anglican clergy, religious fanatics (Enthusiasts), mystical thinkers, and political absolutists, but the underlying critique of the "learned gibberish" as a means to claim authority and power had resonated through the previous centuries.[4]

[4] Cf. 3.10.13: 497. All references in the text are to Nidditch's edition (Locke 1975); "3.10.13: 497" means Book III, chapter 10, paragraph 13, on p. 497. Italics in the quotations from Locke's text are always Locke's. See Goldie 1983 on Locke's political and religious targets.

Compared to these earlier critics, Locke went further in his critique of language, opening up new perspectives in the study of language, such as we see in Condillac; for Locke's target was not just scholastic language but language in general – its power, its potential, and in particular its dangers and all the obstacles that successful communication faces. Such an analysis had never been absent from critical reflection, but it became an urgent task with the rise of the New Science and corresponding ideas about knowledge, methods, and language. Ambiguity – the perennial charge against language – had to be avoided and preferably removed forever. Two widely explored options did not appeal to Locke. For obvious reasons the Ciceronian ideal of a fusion of rhetoric and philosophy was no longer a viable option for his generation; rhetoric in the constructing of science was anathema for this Royal Society member. But neither did Locke believe in the construction of an artificial language, for the very reason that such a tool was totally infeasible (3.11.2: 509; 3.11.25: 522).[5]

A better strategy to avoid ambiguity was an appeal to the geometrical ideal of strict definitions and deductions. To define one's terms rigorously had always been considered an important requirement, but in order to find wide acceptance such definitions, as Hobbes had argued, had to be based on common language or at least shared linguistic practices, but this was generally felt to be building an edifice on quicksand; there is nothing so unstable as common language. As part of his Way of Ideas Locke sought, as will be explained below, to stabilize language by tying it closely to our ideas: as long as we have clear ideas of the matter, and use words, chosen to stand for these ideas, in a consistent way, we should be able, in principle, to successfully communicate and perhaps reach mutual agreement to the benefit of ourselves and society. Locke sought thereby to counter the intuition that words signify things or their inner essences. This widespread intuition had its philosophical justification in scholastic thought, or so Locke believed: words should ultimately be able to disclose the inner essences or substantial forms of things. It was therefore this doctrine he had to attack; but absent this order, a new order as referent of our language had to be described: the mental world of our ideas. The problem of stabilization was thereby just pushed one level further up. Locke's task can thus be seen as offering a way between, on the one hand, the Scylla of inner and

[5] The Lockean skepsis on the feasibility of schemes such as Wilkins's is well expressed by Thomas Baker in his *Reflections upon Learning*: "For this Language being design'd not to express words but things, we must first be agreed about the nature of things, before we can fix Marks and Characters to represent them, and I very much despair of such an agreement"; quoted in Colie 1965, 41.

unknown essences of things as supposed referents of words and, on the other hand, the Charybdis of an unruly social and linguistic practice where common usage is "a very uncertain rule" (3.11.25: 522).

In the context of this study we will focus on Locke's critique of language, but as this can only be understood against his broader epistemological and metaphysical views, we will also have to pay considerable attention to these views, without however entering into all the intricacies of his arguments or the scholarly debates that they have provoked since the *Essay* was published. In what follows we will start with a brief look at Locke's critique of scholastic language, but since this "learned gibberish" is, for Locke, only one form of insignificant speech, we will then proceed to discuss his views about the requirements for significant speech and the remedies proposed in case these requirements are not met. Locke's answer contains elements that, at first sight, cannot be reconciled with each other so easily: his linguistic thesis according to which words as arbitrary signs are imposed by the mind on its ideas has a mentalistic and even solipsistic ring to it, yet communication is a social activity, governed by rules, customs, and conventions. We will end, therefore, by looking in more detail at the social dimension of language to see how the social world shapes our apparently private minds.

The "Gibberish" of the Philosophers

As already indicated, Locke's criticisms of language went beyond those of his predecessors. First, he did not limit himself to the so-called jargon of "Peripatetick Philosophy" (3.10.14: 497), but considered the language of all philosophical sects as prone to linguistic misbehavior. Second, living at the time he did, Locke thought it no longer necessary to spend too much time on refuting the details of scholastic terminology or the technicalities of late-medieval logic. Third, he saw philosophical abuse as an example of a much wider phenomenon among people: an endemic and even virtually unavoidable inclination to use words in all kinds of inconsistent and incorrect ways.

Locke's observations on philosophical language are shaped by his distrust of systems. His own philosophy might now be called a system, but what Locke himself had in mind was the kind of edifice that had been erected not to inspire but to impress, show off, and overpower others. Philosophers become so wedded to their inventions that they can no longer tell the difference between the system and the world it purports to explain, believing that their terms directly reflect the nature of things. As the leading paradigm, the Aristotelian-scholastic system offers plenty of examples:

> Who is there, that has been bred up in the Peripatetick philosophy, who does not think the Ten Names, under which are ranked the Ten Predicaments, to be exactly conformable to the Nature of Things? Who is there, of that school, that is not persuaded, that *substantial Forms, vegetative Souls, abhorrence of a Vacuum, intentional Species*, etc. are something real? These Words Men have learned from their very entrance upon Knowledge, and have found their Masters and Systems lay great Stress upon them: and therefore they cannot quit the Opinion, that they are conformable to Nature, and are the Representations of something that really exists. (3.10.14: 497)

The Aristotelian sect, however, is not the only one, and Locke goes on to mention the Platonists with their World Soul and the Epicureans with their atomic swerve. Modern philosophers, too, have often failed to define their notions properly: "Nor have the Modern Philosophers, who have endeavoured to throw off the jargon of the schools, and speak intelligibly, much better succeeded in defining simple *ideas*" (3.4.9: 423). They have not only failed to define their simple ideas properly but they have introduced obscure terms and assigned new and unusual meanings to words: "Though the Peripatetick Philosophy has been most eminent in this way, yet other sects have not been wholly clear of it," including the Cartesians, to whom Locke clearly alludes (3.10.6: 493). And elsewhere Locke includes under "the Mint-Masters of these kind of terms" also "the disputing natural and moral philosophers of these latter ages" (3.10.3: 491). Indeed, "scarce any sect in philosophy has not a distinct set of terms that others understand not" (ibid.).[6] Examples of philosophical "gibberish," mentioned here and there in the *Essay*, are substantial form, prime matter (3.10.15: 499), motion being defined as "the act of a being in power, as far forth as in power" (2.4.8: 422), "the act of perspicuous, as far forth as perspicuous" (ibid.), and the *ubi* (where) of immaterial spirits (2.23.21: 307). These terms are devoid of any explanatory value, but if one thinks otherwise, as for instance in the case of the distinction between *in loco* (in place) and *ubi* (where), one is invited to put it into "intelligible *English*" (2.2.3.21: 307). Apparently, the term "velleity" (meaning the lowest degree of desire) had passed such a test, but many other such abstract nouns, especially in the case of substances,

[6] As did many of his contemporaries, Locke distinguished Aristotle from his followers, calling Aristotle "one of the greatest Men amongst the Antients; whose large Views, acuteness and penetration of Thought, and strength of Judgment, few have equalled" (4.17.4: 671). Cf. Mercer 1993, 41 on this distinction and the search for the "real Aristotle" (61).

such as *aurietas* (gold-ness), *saxietas* (stone-ness), or *lignietas* (wood-ness) had never found any acceptance.[7]

In his more optimistic moments Locke believed that his own age had begun to see through this kind of jargon – an age, "that is not much disposed to admire, or suffer themselves to be deceived by such unintelligible ways of speaking" (2.4.8: 422).[8] Yet, jargon remained a serious threat to emancipation and toleration, to religion and morality; it was its air of authority and power more than its being an affront against grammar or linguistic propriety that worried Locke. Though governments owe their peace and liberty to "unscholastick Statesmen," to craftsmen, men of business, and so on, they have let themselves come under the sway of philosophers with their verbal chicaneries:

> Nevertheless, this artificial Ignorance, and *learned Gibberish*, prevailed mightily in these last Ages, by the Interest and Artifice of those, who found no easier way to that pitch of Authority and Dominion they have attained, than by amusing the Men of Business, and Ignorant, with hard Words, or Imploying the Ingenious and Idle in intricate Disputes, about unintelligible Terms, and holding them perpetually entangled in that endless Labyrinth. Besides, there is no such way to gain admittance, or give defence to strange and absurd Doctrines, as to guard them round about with Legions of obscure, doubtful, and undefined Words. (3.10.9: 495)[9]

Jargon creates insiders and outsiders. It keeps common people, says Locke, from "true Knowledge" (ibid.). Running through these passages is an opposition in various forms between common people and philosophers/ scholars, or perhaps in more general terms, nonphilosophers versus philosophers or even nonacademic versus academic, reflecting a distinction Locke frequently draws between philosophical and public (or vulgar) discourse, to which we will come back later. "Unlearned" people understand words such as "white" and "black" well enough, whereas

[7] In his very brief chapter on abstract and concrete terms, Locke argues that grammatical difference reflects difference between ideas: simple ideas have abstract and concrete names (e.g. redness and red), while names of substances hardly have any abstract names, also because people feel they do not know the essence of, for example, gold-ness, hence they have no need for such a word (*aurietas*). "Humanity" (*humanitas*) seems one of the few exceptions, but Locke points out that this noun derives from the adjective human (*humanus*), not from *homo* (3.9.2: 475) – a traditional point; see for example Valla (2012, 1:60; *DD* 1.4.12).

[8] Ironically but perhaps also inevitably, contemporaries criticized Locke for his own terminological innovations. Henry Lee wrote that the *Essay* was "writ in a kind of new Language" (quoted by Yolton 1956, 87). Many readers, including Leibniz (1981, 293), complained about Locke's idiosyncratic use of terms such as "idea" and "real and nominal essence," stating that his use is contrary to ordinary language or common speech (ibid., 87–90).

[9] Cf. 3.11.10: 514.

philosophers confound such understanding by their "art and subtlety" (3.10.10: 495); people of "ordinary capacity" initially understand a text or law well enough until they consult an "expositor" (3.9.9: 480; 3.10.12: 496); country people can read the signs of coming rain very well without making use of syllogisms (4.17.4: 672); jewelers and smiths have better ideas about the objects of their crafts than philosophers (2.23.3: 296); and so on. This is not to say that we should always follow the common people; indeed, their ideas and language, as we will see, stand in need of improvement and correction, but the solution Locke suggests is not the kind of elucidation that a philosopher, parson, reverend doctor, or schoolmaster offers (3.10.16: 499).[10] The opposition between the common people and the philosopher is of course an age-old topos, but, as noticed in the previous chapters, it became a fixed element in the weaponry during the Renaissance and early-modern period, when opposition against scholastic-Aristotelian thought as a bulwark of the so-called establishment mounted.

Locke seems a distant heir to humanism also in his critique of the syllogism, though his focus on ideas and their connections gives a new twist to the traditional complaints.[11] The syllogism is limited in use, if useful at all; it is artificial and unnatural (e.g. in the place of the middle term), not reflecting the way our "native rustick Reason" works (4.17.6: 679); it does not add to our stock of knowledge; the requirement that it must consist of at least one general proposition goes against the idea that we usually reason about particulars; its use in discovering fallacies is relevant only in the highly artificial setting of rhetorical and dialectical disputations in the schools. Our "native faculty" rather than the rules of logic helps us "to perceive the Coherence, or Incoherence of its *Ideas*," and "range them right" (4.17.4: 671).[12] Very often, the syllogism clouds our native, natural way of seeing how things hang together. Moreover, translation into syllogistic form presupposes seeing the connections between our

[10] Locke could also be critical of people; they are often swayed by their passions, indifferent to and incapable of critical thinking and sound reasoning, unable to follow the Law of Nature, and so on; for discussion see White 1978, 23–36; cf. Pasnau 2013, 85–86.

[11] Syllogistic was scorned by Bacon, Descartes, and many others; see Passmore 1953; Gaukroger 1989; Barnes 2001, who concludes that Locke "had little understanding of logic" (132). While much less negative about syllogistic and Aristotelian logic in general than Locke, Hobbes too, after his brief exposition of syllogistic, emphasizes the importance of practice and natural reasoning over formal rules of syllogistic. Going through the demonstrations of geometers is much more profitable for learning "true logic" than reading the precepts of logicians (Hobbes 1999a, 49; *De Corpore* I.IV.13). See Chapter 7, n. 6. For Valla's critique see Nauta 2009, 239–252.

[12] D'Alembert and many others in the eighteenth century followed Locke in this (De Gandt 2001, 134). On Lockean "logic" and its direct influence on later handbooks see Winkler 2003; Schuurman 2004; Poggi 2018.

ideas, so that such a translation becomes superfluous (4.17.4: 675): "A man knows first, and then he is able to prove syllogistically. So that *Syllogism* comes after Knowledge, and then Man has little or no need of it" (4.17.6: 679). Locke does not reject syllogisms entirely; whoever finds them useful may as well use them, as long as one realizes that the syllogism is not the only way of reasoning, nor the best one (4.17.4: 671).

Perhaps more strongly than earlier critics of syllogistic, Locke seems in particular suspicious about its air of systematization and authoritarianism. Modern philosophers might think that such a suspicion does gross injustice to the whole enterprise of logic and the intentions of its practitioners, yet the feeling was that the syllogism puts a "native," "natural" skill that everybody to a greater or lesser extent possesses into a straightjacket, established and declared binding by a group of self-appointed judges about something so fundamental as reasoning and thinking; hence the opposition in Locke's text between native/natural versus artificial, and between the common person ("a Country Gentlewoman" or "a man unskilful in Syllogism") and the logician. If rationality is to be identified with mastery of the logician's art, only "one of Ten Thousand" can be declared rational, but God, as Locke famously said, "has not been so sparing to Men to make them barely two-legged Creatures, and left it to *Aristotle* to make them Rational . . . . He has given them a Mind that can reason without being instructed in Methods of Syllogizing: The Understanding is not taught to reason by these Rules" (4.17.4: 671).[13]

This does of course not mean that this "native faculty" works fine, and that the perspective of the common person is sacrosanct. In criticizing the jargon of the schools and the "artificial" methods of the logicians, this "native" perspective might strategically offer a good antidote against the pretensions of the philosophers, but as soon as that perspective itself comes under scrutiny, Locke finds much that stands in need of correction. At this point, then, we must turn to his critique of language in general, not just of the jargon of the scholastics, and consider how he thinks we can emend and rectify our speech and thinking. It is here that Locke transcends the traditional critique of scholastic language, though the starting point of his own solution is a direct response to what he sees as a fundamental tenet of scholastic thought, namely the idea that there is an order of essences

[13] Likewise, Locke is skeptical about the rule that we must use genus and *differentia* in defining something: "little necessity there is of such a Rule, or advantage in the strict observing of it . . . Languages are not always so made, according to the Rules of Logick, that every term can have its signification, exactly and clearly expressed by two others" (3.3.10: 413).

independent of human thinking, one that our thinking can get to know and language can capture in words. Locke's answer, as is well known, is to stress "the workmanship of our understanding": words do not reach out to the inner essences of things; they can only stand for our ideas; hence, we must make sure that our ideas are as distinct, adequate, real and true as possible, and that we use words to refer to these ideas in a consistent way as far as possible; words without corresponding ideas are "insignificant noise" (3.2.7: 408); "little more than bare Sounds" (3.9.9: 480).

This strategy, however, as has also long been recognized, seems to create a tension in Locke's overall position. On the one hand his emphasis on the individual mind and its "inviolable right" to impose its own words on its ideas gives his theory an air of solipsism; the individual mind is in charge of letting words stand for its private individual ideas (semantic individualism); on the other hand, communication presupposes a common public space, a shared ground, shared linguistic practices ruled by customs and conventions so that we can fruitfully realize the goal that Locke ascribes to language: to make known our ideas to one another in the easiest and shortest possible way, and "thereby to convey the knowledge of things" (3.10.23: 504; cf. "the chief end of language"; 3.5.7: 432; 3.6.33: 460; 2.22.5: 290). A private mind in a social world seems to be the Lockean predicament – small wonder, then, that communication becomes such a problematic and risky affair. We seem far removed from the humanist emphasis on the social world of communication. Yet, Locke also speaks of language as the "great Instrument, and common Tye of Society" and "the great Bond that holds Society together, and the common Conduit, whereby the Improvements of Knowledge are conveyed from one Man, and one Generation to another" (3.11.1: 509), so these Lockean minds cannot be regarded as isolated monads, with closed windows and without any mutual influence. But unless Locke can show us a way out of this solipsistic picture, these praises of the social dimension of language may sound hollow. As we will see, Locke's answer is not a philosophical knockdown argument but a general insistence on the social embeddedness of our thinking and language as its expression.

Signification and Classification: Locke's Anti-Essentialism

Locke's critique of language, though a permanent feature of his treatment of language throughout Book III, follows on his analysis of signification, which is meant to support his anti-essentialist program.[14] To understand his discussion of the imperfections and abuses of languages as well as his recommendations for remedying these abuses, it is necessary first to discuss these earlier chapters on signification and classification.

Notwithstanding scholarly controversies about its individual theses, the outlines of Locke's philosophy of language are fairly straightforward. We build up our knowledge by way of ideas – our representations of the world in our mind – starting from the simple ideas derived directly from sense perception, leading on to the more abstract and complex ideas that are the result of the working of the mind (see e.g. 2.22.9: 292). As "immediate objects of perception, thought or understanding" (2.8.8: 134) ideas are what we are directly and immediately aware of. We know the world therefore indirectly via our ideas: "Tis evident, the Mind knows not Things immediately, but only by the intervention of the *Ideas* it has of them" (4.4.3: 563).[15]

In communicating our ideas, we cannot but make use of words to express them; as marks or signs, these words are said to stand for ideas or signify them: "*Words in their primary or immediate Signification, stand for nothing, but the* Ideas *in the mind of him that uses them*, how imperfectly soever, or carelessly those *Ideas* are collected from the Things, which they are supposed to represent" (3.2.2: 405). Because I am the only one with direct access to my ideas, my words can signify immediately only my ideas: "their signification, in his use of them, is limited to his *Ideas*, and they can be Signs of nothing else" (3.2.8: 408). The criterion seems epistemological: "Words being voluntary Signs, they cannot be voluntary Signs imposed by him on Things he knows not" (3.2.2: 405). I cannot let them stand for your ideas, which are unknown and inaccessible to me, nor can I let them stand for the things themselves. Locke realizes that it is very natural for me to think that my word "dog" stands fora dog and also for your idea of dog. He insists however that these presuppositions are "abuses of language": to presuppose that my word signifies something other than my own idea only brings "unavoidable Obscurity and Confusion into their Signification" (3.2.5: 407).

[14] Scholars disagree about the connection between Locke's metaphysical/epistemological discussion and his philosophy of language. Jolley 1999, 144: "can be traced independently of the role of language" (cf. 162); Atherton 2007, 278 ("close connection"); Losonsky 2006, 8 ("tied to his epistemology" and "to his psychology and philosophy of mind"); Schuurman 2004 ("side show"); Dawson 2007, 256 n. 112. Romanell 1984 attempts to tie it to Locke's medical background.

[15] Is the idea really distinct from the object it represents or is it the object that it represents as it appears to the mind? On the ongoing debate on what Locke meant by representation and therefore by idea, see Lennon 2007.

Why would Locke insist on this point? If by things he means the true nature or essence of things, it is plausible for him to suggest that our words cannot stand for them, because he thinks these essences are utterly unknown to us. But what about things in their ordinary appearances? If I talk of this dog here right in front of me, can I not be said to *know* this dog? And if so, why can my word, which immediately signifies my idea of dog, not be somehow also about the dog? Scholars have given different answers to this question, but on one plausible reading Locke's worry is not so much that words are taken to stand *also* for things, but that they are taken to stand *only* for things without the intervention of ideas.[16] On this view, words indirectly stand for things by standing directly and immediately for ideas. Though Locke never says that words signify things "secondarily," "indirectly," or "mediately," he is fully aware that our intention in communicating our ideas is to speak about the things of which our ideas are expressions; I want to tell you something about the dog, not about my idea of the dog.[17] As Locke puts it, we want "to be understood" to speak of things (3.9.15: 484; cf. 3.11.11: 514), and he often speaks about our "discourse of things" (3.6.33: 460), about words that have "application to things" (3.2.2: 409) and "ultimately represent things" so as to agree "with the Truth of Things" (3.11.24: 520), and about words that "intimate also some real Existence" (3.4.2: 421).[18] We must "regulate the signification of their Names by the Things themselves, if we will have our Names to be the signs of them, and stand for them" (3.9.11: 481). So we intend to speak about things in the world, even though the immediate signification of our words can only be our ideas; one of the ends of language is "*to convey* the *Knowledge* of Things" (3.10.23: 504).

It is true that Locke never says that words signify things "secondarily," but passages such as these suggest that communicating ideas is communicating one's ideas about things with the intention to say something about those things. The presence of the idea of dog in my mind enables me to

[16] Winkler 2009; Kretzmann 1967; Ayers 1991; Atherton 2007, 278–279. For a different view, see Ott 2004 with a good reply by Winkler 2009. For the late-scholastic background see Ashworth 1981 and Lenz 2010, 104–157.

[17] In spite of such statements, Locke's view about signification has led many readers, from John Stuart Mill onward, to find fault with Locke's insistence on ideas as the immediate signification of words: it is my intention to tell you something about the dog rather than about my idea of the dog (unless this idea is the topic of our discussion). Cf. Guyer 1994, 121. Locke's "intentionalism" – briefly, that we have the intention to be understood and that in interpreting speakers or writers we aim at recovering their intentions or intended meanings – is stressed by Winkler 2009.

[18] Lenz 2010, 115 suggests that Locke's term "ultimate" may echo the Scotist distinction between thought as the immediate significate of a word, and thing (or rather substance) as the "ultimate" significate (*ultimum significatum*).

speak of dogs; I can call a dog "a dog" only insofar as the animal conforms to my general idea of dog (which on Locke's account, as we will see, is the species). The word "dog" stands for the dog *by immediately signifying my idea*. If I did not have a general idea of dog, I would not be able to determine whether this animal here can be categorized as a dog. My idea therefore stands "between the thing that exists, and the Name that is given to it; it is in our *Ideas*, that both the Rightness of our Knowledge, and the Propriety or Intelligibleness of our Speaking consists" (2.32.8: 386). Thanks to the intervention of my idea of dog I can speak about dogs: "There is no Knowledge of Things conveyed by Men's Words, when their *Ideas* agree not to the Reality of Things" (3.10.24: 505).

Also, given Locke's empiricism it would be strange if words were cut loose from things. To put it simply, since my ideas are a representation of the world, my words by which I express these ideas also stand for things in the world. Locke is sometimes quite explicit about this. Ideas, at least certain kinds of ideas, "agree with Things" (4.4.3: 563) so that "we cannot but be infallibly certain, that all the Knowledge we attain concerning these *Ideas* is real, and reaches Things themselves" (4.4.5: 564).[19] This strongly suggests that the Lockean mind is not locked up in its own world. Obviously, it lives in a world shared with others who perceive things in much the same way; my idea of an apple will be like yours, since such an idea is a collection of qualities (producing simple ideas in me) that both you and I see going together most of the time: "the sensible *Ideas*, produced by any Object in different Men's Minds, are most commonly very near and undiscernibly alike" (2.32.15: 389). There is enough overlap in our ideas of common objects to achieve mutual understanding: "we come to have the Ideas of particular sorts of Substances, by collecting such Combinations of simple Ideas, as are by Experience and Observation of Men's Senses taken notice of to exist together" (2.23.3: 296).[20]

[19] Locke refers here to simple ideas, being "the natural and regular productions of Things" (4.4.4: 564) and complex ideas that "cannot want any conformity necessary to real Knowledge" (4.4.5: 564). Our ideas of substances are of course a much trickier category, and his complaint in 3.2.5 about words standing for things is therefore addressed "particularly to Substances, and their Names." But these too are "not put barely for our *Ideas* but being made use of ultimately to represent Things . . . ." And "their Names should stand for such Collections of simple Ideas, as do really exist in Things themselves, as well as for the complex *Idea* in other Men's Minds" (3.11.24: 520–521). Via the simple ideas we get to know the thing, though of course not its inner essence. (2.23.3: 296). For discussion see Winkler 2009.

[20] This shared ground is emphasized, for example, by Ayers: "Locke's whole philosophy is founded, not only on the principle that the content or material of our thought, even thought about thought itself, is drawn from our own experience of the world, but on the assumption of shared experience and, in general, a shared psychology" (Ayers 2013, 69).

One reason perhaps why Locke does not want to say in a straightforward way that words signify things is to counter the view, still popular in his time, that words are not purely conventional but have a natural relationship, however distant, to the things they name. After the immediate signification of words, this is the second aspect of his linguistic thesis we must discuss. In line with a well-established and age-old tradition, Locke argues that words as such are arbitrary and voluntary signs.[21] There are no natural constraints on the choice of a particular sound to stand for a particular idea: "not by any natural connexion, that there is between particular articulate Sounds and certain *Ideas*" (3.2.1: 405). Locke applies these words "arbitrary" and "voluntary" both to the words themselves and the act of "imposition" by which I apply an arbitrary sign to my idea ("voluntary Imposition, whereby such a Word is made arbitrarily the Mark of such an *Idea*"; ibid.). Following Hobbes, Locke distinguishes two functions of a word: it can function as a mark of my own idea and as a sign for expressing my idea to others.[22] Closely connected to their arbitrary nature is my liberty in assigning words to my ideas: each of us "has so inviolable a Liberty, to make Words stand for what *Ideas* he pleases, that no one hath the Power to make others have the same *Ideas* in their Minds, that he has, when they use the same Words, that he does" (3.2.8: 408).

For the internal recording of my ideas this view is plausible: I am free to use whatever sign I choose to stand for my own idea in my own interior monologue, but am I free to use whatever word I like when communicating my ideas? I had better conform to the common use of my linguistic society. We are born within a society, and common use limits our freedom in this respect: common use, "by a tacit Consent, appropriates certain Sounds to certain *Ideas*" (3.2.8: 408).[23] Before I was born the Dutch word *hond* already signified the idea of a dog, so on learning to use this word I almost automatically and perhaps unconsciously accepted this sound to

[21] Aarsleff 1964 put Locke's argument against the background of the still-popular view that sounds are not (merely) conventional but have natural origins, being somehow pictures of things.

[22] Guyer 1994, 145 n. 3 notes that, unlike Hobbes, Locke uses the terms "mark" and "sign" interchangeably; cf. Ott 2004, 22 n. 68.

[23] 3.6.51: 471: We have the same liberty as Adam had, who gave names to his ideas at the beginning of language, only with this difference that we already live in a society with an established language. Locke distinguishes between "the beginning of languages" versus "languages made" (3.5.15: 437; cf. also 3.9.7: 478), which corresponds – we might say – with two forms of conventionalism: in the first case it means that there are no natural constraints on what rules may be established when a word is introduced, in the second case it means that the correct use of a word depends on linguistic custom and conventions.

stand for my idea of a dog (granted the notion that words stand for ideas). Yet, Locke insists on our freedom in assigning words to our ideas, because he wants to underscore the essentially arbitrary and voluntary nature of signs. Just the fact that we often do not understand each other, he says, shows that I have a different idea in mind (i.e. have assigned a different idea to the word) than you in spite of our using that same word.

There are clearly two issues here: what my word signifies (namely my idea) is one thing, its "common acceptation" (or meaning) in a language is something else.[24] Locke uses strikingly similar terminology in both cases: I am said to "assign," "annex," or "apply" words to my ideas, and so common use is said to "appropriate," "apply," or "annex" words to ideas.[25] Common use thereby limits my freedom insofar as it had already assigned significations to words before I started using them. But now we might wonder what is left of the picture of a mind that has an "inviolable right" to use "arbitrary" signs in an act of "voluntary imposition." Perhaps we should not read too much into this talk of common use *doing* this or that.[26] What Locke probably means to say is that we all stand in a long tradition going back to a moment when people began to use certain (arbitrarily chosen) sounds to stand for certain ideas. In taking over this word (*hond*, "dog") to stand for this type of idea (dog) I am conforming myself to that longstanding custom, but this does not mean that the word is no longer an arbitrary sign, nor does it mean that it does not stand for my idea. Still, such a reply seems to evade the question: Is Locke defining signification in terms of a relationship between word and idea or in terms of its common public usage? The long-established relationship between an idea and the word that is commonly used to stand for it is not the same as the immediate relationship between my use of the word and my (individual, subjective) idea. As suggested, what might have led Locke to insist on the model of a mind imposing arbitrary words on its own ideas, even if he

[24] The issue has been intensively debated over the years. Fregean distinctions between idea, reference, and sense have been projected onto Locke (and onto Hobbes and other pre-Fregean philosophers) to see if and how they match. A classic statement that Locke confused a theory of meaning (common acceptation) and signification is Bennett 1971, to which Hacking 1975, 43–53 responded that Locke and other early-modern philosophers were simply not interested in a theory of meaning (that is, a theory of common acceptation). The debate includes Kretzmann 1968; Ashworth 1984; Ayers 1991; Guyer 1994; Losonsky 1994; Jolley 1999, 162–168; Ott 2004; Dawson 2007; Winkler 2009; Lenz 2010, 382–391 (arguing for a complementarity between what other scholars usually see as an incompatibility or inconsistency in Locke).

[25] For example 2.21.20, 3.2.8; 3.6.51; 3.9.8; 3.10.23; 3.11.12.

[26] Perhaps we should also not read too much into Locke's talk of the person who imposes words on ideas almost in a deliberate act. My word stands for my idea, but how exactly that relation has been established is, arguably, no part of the signification.

had to accept the limits posed by common use on that model, was his aim to counter any naturalist intuition (the word has a natural connection with the thing) and also to counter any essentialist intuition (the word refers to the supposed essence of the thing rather than to my idea).

This anti-essentialist aspect becomes very prominent in Locke's application of his account of signification to general terms such as "horse" and "gold," but also other abstract terms such as "murder" and "sacrilege." The vast majority of words are general terms, and hence they stand for general ideas, that is, ideas that represent many distinct individuals: "Words become general, by being made the signs of general *Ideas*" (3.3.6: 411).[27] Generality is something of words and ideas, not of nature: "all things that exist are only particulars" (3.3.6: 410). There is nothing general or universal in nature. The essence of horse is not a universal or form that exists in individual horses; it is an abstract idea in my mind, arrived at by abstracting from the individual features of this or that horse.[28] What we call essences or species are constructions of the mind – "the Worksmanship of the Understanding" as Locke famously calls it (3.3.12–13: 415) – rather than being essences existing in individual things: "this whole mystery of genera and species, which make such a noise in the schools . . . is nothing else but abstract ideas, more or less comprehensive, with names annexed to them." As we have already briefly seen in this chapter, these words signify ideas, but via these ideas they reach out to the things themselves (3.3.13: 416):

> And what are the Essences of those Species, set out and marked by Names, but those abstract *Ideas* in the mind; which are, as it were, the bonds between particular Things that exist and the Names they are to be ranked under? And when general Names have any connexion with particular Beings, these abstract *Ideas* are the *Medium* that unites them.

To belong to the species horse is nothing other than to be ranked under the abstract idea of horse, and to "have the right" to that name.

In order to distinguish essence as abstract idea, made by the mind, from essence as traditionally understood as the ultimate reality of a thing, Locke introduces his famous distinction between nominal and real essence, one of the most discussed parts of his philosophy.[29] Things have "a real, but

[27] Ayers 1991, II, 65–77 on Locke's nominalism.

[28] Locke gives two accounts of abstraction; for discussion see Jolley 1999, 49–50; Chappell 1994, 39–42. Constructions of the mind or not, Locke also holds, rather inconsistently, that such abstract ideas "are all ingenerable, and incorruptable" (3.3.19: 419); see Jolley 1999, 153; Aaron 1967, 32; Newman 2007, 343–346.

[29] This is not the place to go into this hugely debated topic. For a comprehensive discussion see Ayers 1991, II, Part 1. Useful introductory treatments include Atherton 2007; Jolley 1999, 143–168; Jones

unknown Constitution of their insensible Parts, from which flow those sensible Qualities, which serve us to distinguish them from one another, according as we have Occasion to rank them into sorts, under common Denominations" (3.3.17: 418). But "the sorts" into which we categorize things are of our own making, and these abstract ideas are called nominal essences. Even though the similarities between things are real enough – "Nature in the Production of Things, makes several of them alike" (3.3.13: 415) – it is "the Workmanship of the Understanding" that makes "patterns" (general ideas, the nominal essences), based on the observation of these similarities.

Locke's discussion is complex and has been subject to different interpretations; for example, it is unclear whether Locke thinks there is a mind-independent world of essences that "can be identified as containing just those qualities responsible for ideas of the nominal essence."[30] For our purposes we may leave these issues aside and just emphasize the ultimate effect of a de-essentialization of the world: individual things have no essences in the traditional, scholastic sense of the word. There are no substantial forms – "forms or molds" – that carve up reality independent of us. There are collections of insensible parts of matter that somehow give rise to qualities which we can perceive, but in the absence of any knowledge of these corpuscular structures it is the human mind that has to choose which features go into the formation of an abstract idea (the nominal essence).[31] Classification is thus an open-ended process: we would be wise

2012. One of the issues that is much discussed is whether Locke's theory of classification follows from considerations of the microscopic constitution of things (the corpuscularian hypothesis, or the idea of a great chain of being according to which there are no clear boundaries between species) – a position argued for by, among others, Michael Ayers – or follows from his theory of ideas and language – a position defended by, among others, Paul Guyer: "Locke's thesis is not that we must draw arbitrary lines between species because they naturally form a continuum; his position is rather that just because nature contains only many particulars resembling each other in many ways we must decide which differences between individual objects, whether grossly salient or barely noticeable, to include in our abstract ideas of them and thus in our definitions of general terms" (Guyer 1994, 145 n. 4). Cf. Atherton 2007, 266–278.

[30] Atherton 2007, 263; Ayers 2013, 72: "The 'real essence' of a kind is simply whatever it is in the physical structure of members of the kind that explains the presence in them of the properties marked off by the nominal essence of the kind."

[31] Later Locke suggests that spirits, in a way utterly unknown to us, may have as clear an idea of a substance, for example, gold, as we have of a triangle. Their ideas may perfectly capture the "radical Constitution of Substances" from which "all their Properties and Operations flow" (3.11.23: 520). It is doubtful, however, whether Locke means to say that things can be categorized objectively after all, based on their ontological structures, but that our finite minds simply cannot reach that fundamental level; the spirits' ideas must be direct mirrors of these (atomic) structures (the existence of spirits can be accepted only on faith; see 4.11.12: 637). Leibniz makes a similar point in response to Locke: "If we had the acuity of the Higher Spirits . . . " (Leibniz 1981, 310). The thrust of Locke's account is that the boundaries of species are drawn by us, not by nature.

to select those features of a thing that invariably go together, but as our knowledge of things advances we will have to modify our abstract essences and hence our classification.[32]

One further aspect must be briefly introduced here, since this too will recur in Locke's critique of language. In the case of substances, the real essence cannot be the same as the nominal essence; at least it is difficult to see how they could be: We do not know the real essence, while we do know of course the nominal essence, being a product of our own mind. But at least we have a certain "pattern" or "archetype," namely the thing in front of us that we try to capture in our definition or abstract idea (3.6.43: 466; 3.6.51: 470; 3.9.11: 481). Locke makes it clear, however, that even if we come to discover more about the internal constitution, we will never be able to exchange our nominal essence (the abstract idea) for the real essence: it is the human mind that decides which features form the basis of our classification.[33] In the case of mixed modes – a broad class of ideas that include triangle, gratitude, and murder (Locke's examples in 2.12.4: 165) – nominal and real essences are the same. In such cases the mind does not usually seek "patterns in nature": "the Mind in mixed Modes arbitrarily unites into complex *Ideas*, such as it finds convenient ... 'Tis evident then, that the Mind, by its free choice, gives a connexion to a certain number of *Ideas*; which in Nature have no more union with one another, than others that it leaves out" (3.5.6: 431). We make up our own abstract idea, for instance, of incest, combining simple ideas (3.5.3: 429); hence real and nominal essence coincide in the case of mixed modes: whatever we put in the definition, so to speak, *is* the thing (3.5.14: 436; cf. 3.10.19: 501; 3.11.15: 516). Also in simple ideas the two coincide but for a different reason: unlike in the case of incest, where there is no causal basis of the abstract idea in nature (on Locke's account), in the case of my experience of red there is a causal basis, even though I do not know what causes this experience, and how. I take my idea of red to

[32] The going-together rule presupposes a real union of qualities in a substance, of which we have only a confound notion (3.6.21: 450). Atherton 2007, 284 suggests that this provides us with a norm: "It tells us that we ought to include within our idea of any substance whatever ideas are found to co-occur with those ideas that have already been found to go together, and that we ought to exclude ideas that do not recur. We have, that is, a way to identify a real horse or real gold. The particular thing in front of me is a real horse or real gold if it presents me with those ideas that have been found to go together. We also have a standard we can use in altering our existing ideas."

[33] Jolley 1999, 160–161; Guyer 1994, 133–134 and cf. 138: "No facts about nature can free us from the necessity of choosing our criteria for the differentiation of species by a 'voluntary imposition' of sense on our general terms"; Atherton 2007.

be that particular aspect of the world that has caused this idea in me (2.32.15: 389).[34]

Leaving aside the many problems that scholars have diagnosed in Locke's account, what is important to stress here, again, is its deflationary nature: essences are not out there; they are of our own making. Of course we will let ourselves be guided, as far as possible, by nature and the similarities we discover between things, but classification always remains a human affair.[35] And this is even more palpable with the huge number of abstract ideas that we make up ourselves without an "archetype" or "pattern" to go by.[36] The deflationary account has thus also an "inflationary" dimension: the human mind takes center stage on Locke's account; it is passive in sense perception, but after this initial stage it becomes an active force, and is ultimately responsible for the way we categorize the world.[37] It is the mind "that combines several scattered independent *Ideas*, into one complex one; and by the common name it gives them, makes them the Essence of a certain Species, without regulating it self by any connexion they have in Nature" (3.5.6: 430).

But it is not only the mind that has gained more importance in Locke's account, but also words as signs of our ideas. In assigning a word to several ideas, the mind uses this word as a "knot" that ties these ideas together:

> *The near relation* that there is *between Species, Essences, and* their *general Names*, at least in *mixed Modes*, will further appear, when we consider, that it is the Name that seems to preserve those *Essences*, and give them their lasting duration. For the connexion between the loose parts of those complex *Ideas*, being made by the Mind, this union, which has no particular foundation in Nature, would cease again, were there not something that did, as it were, hold it together, and keep the parts from scattering. Though therefore it be the Mind that makes the Collection, 'tis the Name which is, as it were the Knot, that ties them fast together. (3.5.10: 434)

34 See Atherton 1998, 209; Guyer 1994, 132; Winkler 2009, 491–492.

35 There is nothing essential to a thing; what we deem to be essential is up to us, and will differ between people: it is in reference to the complex idea or nominal essence that a quality is said to be essential (see 3.6.4: 440–441). For an analysis see Ayers 1991, II, 39–90; Atherton 2007, 258–285; Pasnau 2011, 655–661 who thinks this is one of the best arguments in the entire period (1274–1671) covered by his study.

36 Locke's claim that nominal essences of mixed modes differ from those of substances in having no "archetype" to frame them has been criticized by Leibniz; they are on a par in that the human mind is responsible for the framing, also in the case of substances; see Leibniz 1981, 321 (*New Essays* 3.6); Jolley 1999, 160–161; Atherton 2007, 265. But Locke would insist (unconvincingly) that "we have not the liberty, as in mixed Modes, to frame what Combinations we think fit" (3.9.11: 481).

37 Locke's use of the age-old metaphor of the mind as a *tabula rasa* – and empiricism in general – has led to the erroneous idea that the Lockean mind is essentially passive; see, for example, Seuren 2013, 119 n. 6. For a defense of Locke's views see Mackie 1976, 210; Jolley 1984, 180; Jolley 1999, 27.

A word (or name) stabilizes the collection of ideas the mind has formed: in the case of mixed modes where there is no "pattern" that ensures that everybody combines the same set of simple ideas to form the abstract idea, the right use of words is of course vitally important. But also in the case of words of substances, where we do have patterns or standards in nature, it is the human mind that frames a nominal essence, assigning a word that, as a knot, unites a collection of simple ideas together, thereby forming the boundaries of this species. Since nature does not set the boundaries for us, the standards do not unambiguously prescribe which ideas have to go into one's abstract idea of, for instance, gold (see 3.9.13: 482):

> For in all these, and the like Qualities, one has as good a right to be put into the complex *Idea* of that Substance, wherein they are all join'd, as another. And therefore *different Men* leaving out, or putting in several simple *Ideas*, which others do not, according to their various Examination, Skill, or Observation of that subject, *have different Essences of Gold*; which must therefore be of their own, and not of Nature's making. (3.6.31: 458–459; cf. 3.9.13: 483)

This obviously can give rise to misunderstanding and miscommunication, for as my words signify my ideas, and my ideas are framed by my mind without any external necessity, the chances that we talk at cross purposes are substantial. Locke's anti-essentialism goes hand in hand with a constructive role for the mind in framing ideas and assigning names to them, but it has seemingly robbed Locke of a stable foundation for mutual understanding and communication. With some key ideas in place, we can therefore now look at his critique of language, which is a direct consequence of his larger philosophical project.

The Critique of Language

Given Locke's linguistic thesis, one would expect him to lay the responsibility of miscommunication at the level of ideas. If words are just arbitrarily chosen signs, with no natural connection to their ideas, there can be nothing wrong in them as such: as sounds "they are all equally perfect" (3.9.4: 477). But in practice words can hardly be separated from the ideas for which they stand, and this is the reason, as Locke explains, why he decided to devote an entire book to words after having laid out his theory of ideas (2.33.19: 401; 3.9.21: 488). The imperfections of language are intrinsically bound up with the nature, composition, and framing of ideas, and though the source of misunderstanding and miscommunication ultimately lies in ideas (3.10.25: 505), the expression of them in language carries its own responsibility, something which people as a rule do not sufficiently realize.[38]

Locke lists three main imperfections, of which the first two apply to ideas of mixed modes:

i) Abstract ideas are assemblages of ideas put together by the mind, so it is highly likely that, for example, my idea of democracy is not (exactly) the same as yours, even though we use the same word.

ii) Moreover, nature does not provide us with a standard or archetype in the case of mixed modes, so our significations cannot be rectified or adjusted by pointing to something in nature. We often start just copying words from our parents and teachers, and only gradually fill them with content, but such words, for example, honor, faith, or grace, will often remain poorly defined and understood.

iii) And if nature does provide us with standards, as in the case of substances like gold and horse, our words will be very uncertain since we do not know the ideas they are supposed to stand for. I do not know the real essence of gold, so what I take gold to be (that is, what I have put in my nominal essence of gold) is likely to be different from yours.[39]

Obscurity, confusion, and misunderstanding are therefore natural and inevitable outcomes of the natural workings of the mind. Of course, we can be asked to explain our terms or we can consult experts or commentaries (in the case of law or Scripture) but history shows that such attempts have usually led only to further disagreements and controversies. And yet, this, as Locke sometimes suggests, is the best we can do: even though there is no language police, we should consult experts and accept their well-informed ideas and corresponding words. Another type of authority is common use that, as Locke says, "*regulates the meaning of Words* pretty well for common Conversation" (3.9.8: 479; also 3.9.15: 484), but this is insufficient for philosophy and science, where a much more exact understanding of ideas and their words is required.[40] We will come back to the role of common use later in this chapter.

So far Locke has dealt with "the imperfections of words," which are "natural" (3.11.1: 509) and to a large extent unavoidable. Imperfections

[38] Put in a positive way, Locke elsewhere confirms the central role of ideas: "it is in our *Ideas*, that both the Rightness of our Knowledge, and the Propriety or Intelligibleness of our Speaking consists" (2.32.8: 386).

[39] Later Locke adds another imperfection on the part of language: sometimes we lack words to express our complex ideas (3.10.27: 505; 3.10.33: 507), though it seems that this too is a matter of fact rather than an imperfection that can be corrected; cf. 3.11.27: 523: "provision of Words so scanty in respect of that infinite variety of Thoughts."

[40] Locke sometimes uses "meaning" instead of "signification" (e.g. 3.10.22: 503).

become "abuses" when people deliberately use words outside "their ordinary meaning," or use words without carefully defining the ideas which they signify, or use words deliberately in an inconsistent way, and so on.[41] The abuses result from laziness; sloppiness or willful negligence; or from a deliberate obscurity, so typical of philosophers, used in order to impress others. This "affected obscurity" arises when philosophers introduce new words without clear definition, or assign new meanings to existing words, thereby "confounding their ordinary meaning" (3.10.6: 493). As we have seen above, Locke has harsh words to say about philosophers' jargon, style of argumentation, and disputation, "their empty Speculations" that have brought "Confusion, Disorder, and Uncertainty into the Affairs of Mankind; and if not destroyed, yet in great measure rendred useless, these two great Rules, Religion and Justice" (3.10.12: 496). Also, the next abuse on Locke's list has been mentioned in the section "The Gibberish of the Philosophers" above, because it is a vice typically found among philosophers, who are so wedded to their own terms of art that they no longer can tell the difference between words and things, or rather they believe their words perfectly correspond to the real nature of things. Aristotle's ten categories – substance, quality, quantity, relation, and so on – are a good example of such reification: Aristotelians believe these terms to be "Representations of something that really exists" (3.10.14: 497). Another example is the concept of matter, which philosophers have sometimes identified with body. But if words stand directly for things, and these things were really the same, then, Locke argues, these two words could be used interchangeably. However, linguistic propriety strongly suggests that body and matter are not the same: it is proper to say "there is one matter of all bodies," but it would go against linguistic propriety to say that "one matter is bigger than another" (3.10.15: 498). For Locke, body and matter are two different conceptions, hence philosophers should realize that they are talking and arguing about their ideas, not about the things themselves: "if Men would tell, what *Ideas* they make their Words stand for, there could not be half that Obscurity or Wrangling, in the search or support of Truth, that there is" (ibid.: 499).

The next, fifth abuse is one that runs as a basso continuo throughout Locke's discussion: to let words stand for things we do not know, in particular the so-called real essences of things. Even though he calls it an

[41] The demarcation between imperfection and abuse is not always very clear: the first abuse (using words without clear ideas) is basically a repetition of the corresponding imperfection; cf. Locke's own use of "imperfection" where he was talking about "abuses" (3.10.18: 500), and he couples the two as if more or less equivalent: "imperfection or abuse" (3.10.15: 499).

"abuse," Locke thinks this is almost unavoidable: in saying "gold is malleable" I want to be understood to be saying more than just "what I call Gold is malleable," namely that what has the real essence of gold is malleable (3.10.17: 499–500). But since we do not know the real essence, we compensate for our lack of knowledge by letting the word stand for it: "And therefore the Mind, to remove that Imperfection as much as it can, makes them, by a secret Supposition, to stand for a Thing, having that real Essence, as if thereby it made some nearer approaches to it" (3.10.18: 500). This presupposition comes very naturally to us, Locke explains, because the regularity we see in nature including the boundaries of species, we feel, cannot be an accidental thing or something we make up. I take the word "horse" to stand for the real nature of horse rather than for my idea (the nominal essence or the species). This is not a harmless mistake, of course. It is the expression of an essentialist doctrine according to which there are precise essences by which nature is carved up into species, that we have ideas of these essences, and that our words refer to these essences. This is making words the signs of nothing, causing "great Disorder in Discourses and Reasonings about them, and [is] a great inconvenience in our Communication by Words" (3.10.21: 503).

The last abuse is to think that words hardly need any explanation, since we often presuppose that they, by long and familiar use, will trigger the same ideas in speaker and hearer; they both take words "to be the constant regular marks of agreed Notions, which in truth are no more but the voluntary and unsteady signs of their own *Ideas*" (3.10.22: 503). Locke's point is by now the familiar one that complex ideas are collections of simple ideas, and that my idea, for example, of life will be different than yours, even though we use the same (very common) word "life" and think we understand the same by it.[42]

In a later recapitulation Locke adds the use of rhetoric as an abuse of language, at least where truth and knowledge are concerned. He has harsh words to say about rhetoric, "that powerful instrument of Error and Deceit." Figurative speech and eloquence have their place in popular speeches and harangues when our speech is aimed at delight and pleasure, moving the emotions, and trying to bring the audience over to our position, but as soon we aim at imparting information and conveying

[42] Guyer 1994, 145 n. 7 rightly observes that only the last two abuses follow from Locke's theoretical arguments; the other abuses "may be avoided by any careful speaker even without comprehension of Locke's theory of language."

our thoughts, thereby contributing to knowledge and public well-being, any use of the "Arts of Deceiving" is out of the question.

Locke's strict demarcation of truth, knowledge, information, and improvement on the one hand and pleasure, delight, emotional appeal, literary effect, and rhetorical persuasion on the other was a view widely shared by his Royal Society fellows and other proponents of the New Science. Hobbes, for instance, had banned "metaphors and tropes of speech" from true reasoning that aims at producing knowledge and constructing science, though he allowed for the possibility that they might be helpful in "opening up" the understanding.[43] But at times Locke's position looks even more rigid than Hobbes's (and perhaps Bacon's): whereas Hobbes allows for a coexistence of rhetoric and science, Locke seems to ban rhetoric even from the domain of common conversation since this domain too is (or should be) all about the communication of thought. In the *Essay* Locke frequently distinguishes a civil use from a philosophical use of language: "By their *civil Use*, I mean such a communication of Thoughts and *Ideas* by Words, as may serve for the upholding common Conversation and Commerce, about the ordinary Affairs and Conveniences of civil Life, in the Societies of Men, one amongst another . . . ." The philosophical use serves "the precise Notions of Things, and to express, in general Propositions, certain and undoubted Truths . . . " (3.9.3: 476). The two uses are said to be "very distinct" in that philosophical use requires much more precision in ideas and corresponding language than common conversation, yet the goal of both is the same: understanding, which can only succeed if words excite the same idea in the hearer as in the mind of the speaker.[44] Hence, the mechanism whereby ideas are communicated in "common and civil conversation" cannot be different from that used in philosophy and science, even though there is much more precision required in the latter domain.

Locke's distinction between philosophical and civil use is therefore one of degree rather than one of kind, and this implies that rhetoric must be banned even from civil and common conversation: "all the artificial and figurative application of Words Eloquence hath invented . . . are certainly, in all Discourses that pretend to inform or instruct, wholly to be avoided" (3.10.34: 508).[45] It is perhaps hard to see how language as "the great

[43] Hobbes 1994b, 39 (*Leviathan* 8.8); moral terms, because they are so liable to different interpretations, "can never be true grounds of any ratiocination" (ibid. 21–22; *Lev.* 4.24). See Chapter 7, n. 9.

[44] If common conversation is taken broadly so as to include "gossipings" (3.11.3: 509), it will not always reach out to the higher goals of communication Locke routinely lists.

[45] Cf. Shapiro 1983, 240: "it is the philosophical use of words, with its emphasis on precision and truth, which established the proper standard for *all* communication." This would indeed be the ideal standard, but Locke also frequently states that common language, with all its looseness and imprecision, usually serves its purpose very well, with the implication that it does not need to be

instrument and common tie of society" and "the great Bond that holds Society together" (3.11.1: 509; cf. 3.10.10: 495) should be wholly devoid of any emotional appeal and rhetorical effect, and Locke of course realizes how conversation – both philosophical and civil conversation – often falls way short of the ideal of an emotionless and utterly dispassionate conversation between rational people disclosing their minds to each other in a perfectly transparent way, pruned of any kind of ambiguity and confusion. Still, the practical shortcomings are no reason to forgo this ideal.

Having discussed the natural imperfections and deliberate abuses of language, Locke briefly discusses some remedies, repeating many of the points already made (3.11). In brief, we should avoid using words without corresponding ideas; we should try to have clear and distinct ideas and, in the case of complex ideas, "determinate" ideas, that is, precise collections of the simple ideas contained in them. Consistency is of course important as well, even though nobody, including Locke, as he admits himself, will succeed in always using words in exactly the same way. In case of things known and distinguished by their outward shapes, it might be helpful to compile a dictionary containing "a natural history" of things, that is, little pictures or drawings, as in the books of the naturalists, which show the thing much better than a long verbal description, but Locke is skeptical about the feasibility of such a project.[46]

Common Use and the Social Dimension of Language

One remedy on Locke's list requires special attention in the light of our initial question about the social dimension of what seems an essentially mentalist conception of language. It is all very well to restrict the signification of words to ideas in the speaker's mind, but as soon as words are spoken we enter a common space where words already have a meaning, hence we must apply words "as near as may be, *to such* Ideas *as common use has annexed them to*" (3.11.11: 514). As already discussed, the freedom to assign words to ideas is an important notion for Locke to block any naturalist idea about language and also to counter essentialist intuitions, but from a societal perspective such a semantic individualism looks irrelevant: I am free to impose words on my ideas, but as soon as I want to communicate my ideas I have to adapt myself to the rules and conventions

much more precise (nor is it likely it will ever attain such level of precision: "scarce to be expected," 3.11.10: 514).

[46] See above n. 5.

of my linguistic community. As the great tie and bond that keeps societies together, language is of course a vital part of the human predicament, and Locke acknowledges this obvious fact in many places, yet his remedy of following common use as far as possible is qualified in various ways, which reflects his wavering attitude toward common use and language in general.

We must follow common use as far as possible, yet it is not precise enough for philosophy and science. If Locke were to restrict his advice to following common use in public speech and common conversation, while accepting revising common use in the more exact domains, this would not create a tension. But in fact his advice is not limited to common conversation but presented as general advice, seemingly covering all the areas in which people communicate their ideas: "But in Communication with others, it is necessary, that we conform the *Ideas* we make the vulgar Words of any Language stand for, to their known proper Significations, . . . or else to make known that new Signification, we apply them to" (3.6.51: 471). While frequently making the distinction between philosophical and public use of language, Locke does not seem to have any hard criteria to distinguish between the two. And the fact that common use cannot be tampered with on pain of miscommunication is relevant for philosophical language as well. Though we might want to revise language whenever "Men in the Improvement of their Knowledge, come to have *Ideas* different from the vulgar and ordinary received one," linguistic innovations must be introduced, as Locke frequently says, only "very warily and sparingly" (3.7.51: 471; cf. 3.11.12: 515 on "making new words," something "men seldom venture to do"). All that seems to remain is to be as clear and explicit as possible about the meaning we have assigned to our ideas, but how far we may stray from common use remains unclear. As already noted, Locke duly suggests that we should learn words by consulting experts or people "versed in physical Enquiries," but if no one has the authority, as Locke also says, "to change the Stamp they are current in; nor alter the *Ideas* they are fixed to" (3.11.11: 514),[47] it is unclear how we shall ever reach an agreement, the more so in light of the imperfections naturally built in the use of language. Moreover, while authorities in natural philosophy are perhaps not so difficult to identify – though

[47] "The proper signification and use of Terms is best to be learned from those, who in their Writings and Discourses, appear to have had the clearest Notions, and apply'd to them their Terms with the exactest choice and fitness" (3.11.11: 514). On uses of the comparison between money and language, the value of both which is established by common use, in the seventeenth century, see Dascal 1976, who also discusses its classical origins; for Valla, see Chapter 2, n. 9; for Vives, Chapter 4, n. 14.

Locke's own discussion leads to a certain skepticism here too – self-proclaimed authorities in morality and religion, precisely those areas where disagreements are rampant, must be treated with suspicion. Indeed, their disagreements often lead only to confusion among common people, who thought they understood terms "very well," and in fact did so (3.10.12: 496). Centuries of scholarship piling up commentaries on commentaries on commentaries do not inspire much confidence that we can leave it to the authorities, in spite of Locke's recommendation that the "proper signification and use of Terms is best to be learned from those, who in their Writings and Discourses, appear to have had the clearest Notions, and apply'd to them their Terms with the exactest choice and fitness" (3.11.11: 514).[48]

Authorities or experts are therefore unlikely to give us much stability in our meanings of words, but neither will common use provide a stable foundation, since it is itself a source of much disagreement: "the rule and measure of Propriety it self being no where established, it is often matter of dispute, whether this or that way of using a Word, be propriety of Speech or no" (3.9.8: 479). But this looks worse than it is, for we have seen Locke frequently claiming that common use regulates the meaning of words pretty well for common conversation, and even in scientific discourse we should be very wary of straying from common use.

It might seem, then, that Locke does not offer a way out of the rather pessimistic picture he has painted. If the imperfections are natural, intrinsically bound up with the way in which words stand for ideas, remedies can only reach so far, and the hope that people can agree on the interpretation of their words is likely to be wishful thinking, even though Locke ends on a positive note: a charitable way of interpreting each other's words with a focus on the intentions of what the other wants to say will "sufficiently lead candid and intelligent Readers, into the true meaning" of each other's words, and we can ask for explanation (3.11.27: 524). Locke seems to be caught between a certain optimism and a rather poignant pessimism and skepticism about the possibility of transcending the human linguistic predicament: it would perhaps be ideal if people could just, "quitting terms, think upon Things" (3.10.22: 504) without having "to spend their Lives in talking about them" (3.10.13: 497), but this is not for us human beings.

[48] "We have nothing else to refer these our *Ideas* of mixed Modes to as a Standard, to which we would conform them, but the *Ideas* of those, who are thought to use those Names in their most proper Signification" (2.32.12: 388).

We do spend our lives talking about things, expressing our views of the world, our ideas and beliefs. This "great Instrument, and common Tye of Society" (3.1.1: 402) is all we have, and as an expression of our human condition it shares all its imperfections and possibilities. Rather than saying that Locke does not offer a solution to the problem of language in that he does not bridge the gap in any theoretically satisfying way between private minds and the essentially social dimension of language use, we might say that there is hardly anything to be *solved*; the human linguistic predicament is not a "problem" to be "solved." No remedy will be sufficient to repair the natural imperfections, but of course we must do our best, as Locke advises us, to improve our situation along the lines he has sketched. Common use has a key role to play here in assigning words to ideas and ideas to words, in authorizing our use of words, and regulating their meaning. Common use, however, is never sacrosanct, certainly not for a proponent of the new science as Locke was; it embodies enough erroneous ideas and beliefs, collected over the centuries, to make revision necessary, but revision, as Locke's whole stance implies, has to be conducted gradually without drastic ruptures in our linguistic practices; no artificial system will ever be accepted by the people as an alternative to common language.

The history of common linguistic usage is thus a history of successes and opportunities, no less than of failures. As the great bond that holds society together, language offers an entry not only into the minds of people and how they frame their ideas, giving words as "knots" to tie them together and express them, but also into society at large.[49] Language thus tracks the development of society – a humanist theme that resonates in some of Locke's observations on the social dimension of language. At the beginning of time, people used words in particular to refer to things that they saw or felt with their senses, and only later started to apply such words to refer to insensible things or processes, for example, to "imagine," "apprehend," "comprehend," "adhere," "conceive," "instill," "disgust," "disturbance," and "tranquillity" – "all Words taken from the Operations of sensible Things, and applied to certain Modes of Thinking" (3.1.5: 403).[50] At those early stages, abstract considerations and hence abstract terminology were lacking:

[49] "The ordinary Words of Language, and our common use of them, would have given us light into the nature of our *Ideas*, if they had been but considered with attention" (3.8.1: 474).

[50] Aarsleff 1964, 186 quotes Clauberg, whose work was known to Leibniz and Locke, but the observation can be found much earlier, for example in Pontano; see above Chapter 3.

> Mankind have fitted their Notions and Words to the use of common Life, and not to the truth and extent of things . . . Where they had no philosophical Notions, there they had no Terms to express them: And 'tis no wonder Men should have framed no Names for those Things, they found no occasion to discourse of. From whence it is easy to imagine, why, as in some Countries, they may have not so much as the Name for a Horse; and in others, where they are more careful of the Pedigrees of their Horses, than of their own, that there they may have not only Names for particular Horses, but also of their several Relations of Kindred one to another. (2.28.2: 349–350)

With the development of societies, different range of words and expressions were introduced to reflect the widening experience, interests, and beliefs of the people, and small wonder therefore that different cultures developed different languages, which will not always correspond one-to-one to each other, "it being so obvious to observe great store of *Words in one* Language, *which have not any that answer them in another.* Which plainly shews, that those of one Country, by their customs and manner of Life, have found occasions to make several complex *Ideas*, and give names to them, which others never collected into specifick *Ideas*" (3.5.8: 432–433; cf. 2.22.6: 290). Locke uses this idea to support his central claim that categorizations are a product of the human mind, giving as examples words of law, words of measurement, and words standing for complex notions, concluding that "if we look a little more nearly into this matter, and exactly compare different Languages, we shall find that, though they have Words, which in Translations and Dictionaries, are supposed to answer one another; yet there is scarce one of ten, amongst the names of complex *Ideas*, especially of mixed Modes, that stands for the same precise *Idea*, which the Word does that in Dictionaries it is rendered by" (3.5.8: 432–433; cf. 2.22.6: 290).

Such statements have led some scholars to view Locke as a precursor of linguistic relativism, also called the Sapir–Whorf hypothesis, named after the American linguists Edward Sapir and Benjamin Lee Whorf.[51] According to this hypothesis, different structures of languages lead to

[51] The suggestion was frequently made at a time that the Sapir–Whorf thesis was still highly influential; see for example Colie 1965, 45 n. 61; Christmann 1966; Penn 1972. For some critical remarks see Elffers 1996, with a brief remark on Locke on p. 76, and Nauta 2006b on the application of linguistic relativism to Renaissance humanist thought in the works of Michael Baxandall and by Ronald G. Witt, with a brief remark on Moss 2003, which argues for a close correspondence between the turn to humanist Latin and changes in modes of thinking as reflected in rhetoric, dialectic, grammar, literary studies, and theological discourse; Moss does not, however, locate these changes in the grammatical structure of classical Latin (or Neo-Latin) vis-à-vis medieval Latin, but in the entire constellation of cultural and historical phenomena during the Renaissance. Linguists are still very

different worldviews, though as one critic once complained: "an enterprising Ph.D. candidate would have no trouble in producing at least 108 versions of Whorfianism," not least because of different formulations by Whorf himself.[52] On taking a closer look, however, we do not find in Locke the central idea of linguistic relativism, namely that different languages are formative in shaping different worldviews; Locke does not argue for a correlation between thought differences and language differences. His point is rather that different nations collect ideas in different ways (or lack particular ideas at all), depending on (as he explains elsewhere) "Fashions, Customs, and Manners of one Nation, making several Combinations of *Ideas* familiar and necessary in one, which another people have had never any occasion to make . . ." (2.22.6: 290). This makes translation sometimes very difficult, in particular across time, for example, the Greek word for ostracism is difficult to translate into the language of a nation that has no such custom. This does not mean however that Locke thinks that languages are incommensurable, let alone that different grammatical and/or syntactical structures of one language are responsible for different worldviews *because of* those structures. He does not speak about differences in grammar or syntactical features such as number, gender, mood, and case tense, but about differences in ideas that are then expressed in words; nor does he suggest that the grammar of a particular language shapes the framing of an idea.[53]

Even though the framing of ideas seems primary and the expression in language secondary, the close interrelationship between the two, often remarked upon by Locke, makes thinking up to a certain point a social affair. My ideas derive not only from my privately felt sensations and reflections, but are also the result of social practices and bodily constitution. In fact, as we have frequently observed, Locke stresses the power of words over ideas in the sense that we often first learn the words and then gradually (and often imperfectly or sometimes not at all) form the ideas for which these words stand. As a "knot" a word gathers a collection of ideas together into one complex idea, and without the unifying word, "the several parts of that, would no more be thought to make one thing, than

much divided about the whole cluster of ideas captured by the term "linguistic relativism"; see Lucy 1992; Evans and Levinson 2009; Werlen 2002; Seuren 2013.

[52] Black 1969, 30; cf. Robins 1976, 101. Whorf seemed to endorse a strong form of linguistic relativism, often termed linguistic determinism, according to which language causally shapes and determines our though patterns. But it is a moot point whether this is what Whorf had in mind. He might just have meant a weak form: language influences thought. See Hill 1988, 14–36, on 15–16.

[53] Hence, there is no ground for Dawson's claim that Locke develops "the grammatical claim that languages are not intertranslatable" (2007, 227).

any other shew, which having never been made but once, had never been united into one complex *Idea*, under one denomination" (3.5.10: 434). It is the mind that brings the ideas together into one complex idea, but "the continuation and fixing of that Unity, depends on the Name in common use annexed to it" (ibid.). Common use is an essential tool in stabilizing our ideas. While not determining directly the contents of my ideas, the label seems to do more than just naming its contents: It actually unifies and brings order to that content.

This process of collecting ideas and naming them is of course subject to social mechanisms such as upbringing, education, customs, and so on:

> This strong combination of *Ideas*, not ally'd by Nature, the Mind makes in it self either voluntarily, or by chance, and hence it comes in different Men to be very different, according to their different Inclinations, Educations, Interests, *etc.* Custom settles habits of Thinking in the Understanding, as well as of Determining in the Will, and of Motions in the Body; all which seems to be but Trains of Motions in the Animal Spirits. (2.33.6: 396)

While the association and habitual trains of ideas, which is Locke's topic here, take place in my body, they are the result of the interaction between the world and me; thinking takes place in a social context, and is shaped by it, as terms such as "fashion," "education," "customs," and "manners of life" obviously suggest. And because these associations of ideas, worn down by social practices and the environment, become such strong habitual trains, it is often very difficult to loosen or untie their connections in the case that "wrong connexions" have been formed. Custom and conventions – both social and linguistic – have always this double edge to them: they provide a norm for propriety and can be appealed to whenever something is deemed to be outlandish, but at the same time they are also the expression of some established traditions and ways of thinking we had better get rid of.

In spite of the solipsistic overtones of Locke's account, then, Lockean minds are not – or not only – private theaters where we freely and voluntarily frame ideas and assign names to them in a voluntary act of imposition – but ours are social minds, embedded in social and linguistic practices that shape our views of the world and give expression to them. The social world is built on the ideas we receive and construct, and common linguistic usage, for all its imperfections, is essential in framing and conveying these ideas.

Conclusion

Though this book has studied only a limited set of authors and texts in considerable detail, some general conclusions may be drawn. First, we may note the historical continuity of the critique of scholastic language from the early days of humanism to the end of the seventeenth century. When Leibniz, for instance, praised Nizolio for his rejection of abstract terminology, he quoted an old dictum that had been made popular by his humanist sources: "Der Gebrauch ist der Meister" (linguistic usage is the master/rule), endorsing the humanistic point that philosophical language should follow the common language of the people: the "passion for devising abstract words has almost obfuscated philosophy for us entirely."[1] Similarly, Gassendi was quite explicit about his debt to humanists, mentioning Vives, Charron, Ramus, and Gianfrancesco Pico, and referring to Valla's program of ontological reduction in his own rejection of what he considered to be the useless superstructure of the scholastic conceptual armory: scholars should use "the common and accepted manner of speaking (*communis et protritus loquendi usus*)."[2] Like Valla and Vives, he thinks that the so-called "rigor" of the philosophers can only be defined in terms of the common and accepted manner of speaking.[3] When Hobbes contrasted "the common sort of men" who "seldom speak insignificantly" with "the schoolmen" and their "insignificant speech," he continued and deepened the humanist polemics. And though with Locke we enter a new phase in the philosophy and critique of language, he also stands with one foot in this earlier tradition of humanist and early-modern critique of the "jargon of the schools," with the "Peripatetick Philosophy" as being "most eminent in this way."[4] As we have seen, it was the humanist idiom of "common language" (and related expressions) and "the people"

[1] Leibniz 1969, 126; see Chapter 5, n. 116. Cf. Laerke 2009, 942 n. 25.
[2] Gassendi 1658, 3:151B (*Exercitationes paradoxicae adversus Aristoteleos*). Cf. Nauta 2016, 69–71.
[3] Ibid., 110B. [4] Locke 1975, 423 and 493 (*Essay* 3.4.9 and 3.10.6); see above Chapter 8.

that was repeated and put to new use by early-modern philosophers in their critique of scholastic language. Here then is a clear line of continuity between the Renaissance and early-modern philosophy.

Historical influence however is one thing, philosophical importance is another, and this brings us to a second point: How philosophically sound and interesting were the accusations thrown out at the scholastics? This is a difficult question to answer since what is philosophically sound is not the same for every historian of philosophy. What for one historian seems to be a liberation from the supposedly abstract, dogmatic, orthodox, rigid, and futile enterprise of the scholastics is for another historian a lapse from "good philosophy." Some make their sympathy quite explicit, for example Robert Pasnau: "the Scholastics had the great virtue of being relatively uninterested in rhetoric and utterly unconcerned with compromising philosophical rigor for the sake of popular accessibility. They shared the view of the contemporary analytic tradition that the best philosophy will often be technical, difficult, and perhaps comprehensible only to specialists."[5] This view has a long history behind it. In both German idealism and Anglophone analytical philosophy, the philosophical "superficiality" or "emptiness" of humanism became a topos. Hegel, for example, believed that humanism was incapable of purely conceptual and rational thinking. Heidegger thought that humanism had neglected "das Wesen des Menschen." Bertrand Russell wrote that the Renaissance brought "nothing original in philosophy," while for D. W. Hamlyn it is a period "in which philosophy was at a low ebb."[6] Such a view was supported, ironically perhaps, by scholars of humanism such as P. O. Kristeller, for whom "the Italian humanists on the whole were neither good nor bad philosophers, but no philosophers at all."[7] It is therefore not surprising to find Renaissance humanism often being neglected in histories of philosophy,[8] a neglect defended by Pasnau in his impressive study of metaphysical thought between the thirteenth and the late seventeenth century:[9]

> in terms of *historical* influence, the most prominent philosophical trends during this period are scholastic Aristotelianism and the rise of the mechanical philosophy ... In my view, these two trends are also the most *philosophically* interesting developments during this period ... Readers whose interests lie elsewhere – aficionados of humanism, or the wild and wooly

[5] Pasnau 1997, 8.

[6] See the references in Frank 1995, 38–40; Copenhaver and Schmitt 1992, 344; Monfasani 2006.

[7] Kristeller 1979, 90–91. [8] See the observations by Hankins 2007, 338–345.

[9] Pasnau 2011, 4 (italics in the original).

> ideas of Renaissance Platonism – will want to find another guide to these centuries.

In view of the influence – of course via a myriad of routes – of the humanists on early-modern philosophers in their critique of scholastic language and thought – we might want to qualify the first part of this claim, without denying of course the central role of Aristotelianism throughout this period.[10]

The second part – about what is *philosophically* most relevant – is dependent, as said, on one's view of what "good" philosophy is. If defined, first and foremost, in terms of rigorous argumentation, semantic precision, conceptual clarification, and a technical approach, it is certainly true that anyone coming to Renaissance humanism in the expectation of finding such features will be disappointed. If defined in a broader sense that also includes a critical approach toward these very features, the complaints by humanists and early-modern philosophers alike might be seen as containing a philosophically relevant, perhaps even important message, namely that language is not a neutral instrument but shapes the way in which we categorize the world: abstract terminology invites us to populate the world with all kinds of abstract entities, from *ubicatio* and *haeceitas* to the immaterial essences such as souls that Hobbes found so pernicious. Such language easily becomes a self-sufficient universe with no clear connection to the world that people observe and experience, that is the world of concrete things (*res*). In accordance with such a view, the study of language as primarily an instrument of communication should start with an empirical study of words, grammar, and so on, rather than treating it as a formal system that can be studied apart from its particular uses. In a similar vein, argumentation is not something to be studied apart from the practice of arguing but should be approached as a practice in which usefulness, persuasion, and plausibility are more relevant than logical form or deductive validity. Beyond the field of the language arts, similar complaints were voiced about scholastic treatments of moral and natural philosophical themes. Whether all these claims are justified may reasonably be doubted of course, but the dangers of abstraction, essentialism, formalism, technicality, systematism, and idealization were felt to be real. The suspicion did not necessarily lead to a rejection of any kind of abstraction or technical

[10] Cf. Bianchi 2007, 49: "To say that Aristotelianism was the predominant philosophical tradition is not to say that it was the most original, the most innovative, or even the most important (whatever such terms might signify), but only that it exercised an influence quantitatively greater than that of any other tradition."

vocabulary *tout court*, but the widespread feeling was that scholasticism had developed, partly due to institutional, religious and societal factors, a mode of philosophizing that was out of tune with a description and analysis of morality, knowledge, faith, language, human beings, society, and the world either as commonly experienced or as explored by the new science (which, of course, introduced its own terms of art). It would be difficult to deny the philosophical relevance of this kind of critique, also in view of its recurrent presence throughout the history of philosophy – a point to which we will return.

So the destructive part can be considered to be philosophically interesting or at least relevant, but what about the constructive part? How well developed are the alternatives to what was considered to be the "insignificant speech" of the scholastics? This brings us to a third point. We have not found much philosophical reflection about the nature of common language, while this is obviously far from a precise or clear notion. As our discussion has suggested, common language could mean different things to different authors during this period. When it served their argument, humanists, for instance, could fuse their critique of scholastic Latin as being ungrammatical and not following classical rules with their critique of scholastic language and logic as being "unnatural," that is, a far cry from how ordinary people speak, write, and argue. Other authors rejected the "insignificant speech" for similar reasons (vague, abstract, devoid of explanatory power, politically dangerous, pretentious, defending one's authority, suggesting expertise, creating group identity, and so on), defending common speech or common linguistic usage and sometimes taking side with the common people, but the question of precisely *whose* so-called common speech was being spoken of remained unclear. What are the scope and methods of this speech? Who is its arbiter? What are the criteria for possible acceptance of a technical term (e.g. in a particular science)? Neither do we find much discussion about the extent to which a word may be used outside the so-called normal or natural context from which it was supposed to have derived its meaning. For instance, Valla claimed that it is an abuse of words to say that the senses are "being acted upon (*pati*) by an object," that the soul is moved or is self-moving, that inanimate things have a final cause, or to apply the matter/form distinction to God, but, again, who or what determines the borders of the rightful application of a term is not discussed nor, of course, could Valla himself avoid such uses.[11] Similarly, Leibniz criticized the scholastics, because

[11] See Nauta 2016, 63–64.

"strange though this sounds, their speech abounds with figures. What else are such terms as *to depend, to inhere, to emanate* and *to inflow*?"[12] But why this is such a sin he does not say, nor are such terms wholly absent from his own philosophical *oeuvre*.

But though the exact scope and nature of common language remained an unexplored topic, the search for an alternative to scholastic language – however gradual, difficult, groping, and half-hearted the process often turned out to be – was premised on a philosophically relevant conviction, namely that philosophy is an activity that should be conducted in a language comprehensible to a broader range of people than "the specialists," because it raises fundamental questions about people's lives, their beliefs and knowledge about the world, and about the world itself. Again, one need not share this conviction to appreciate the point that a turn to common language (or what was presented as such) is a philosophically important feature of the period.

This leads to the next point. The humanist approach toward Latin as a common, natural language – whatever one may think of the internal (in) consistency of the attempt to present a language soon to be regarded as "dead" as a living, natural, common language – raised questions that transcended the humanist focus on Latin. One example is the reflection on the art of translation. A full recognition of the assumptions about translation, which are anything but philosophically neutral, would explicitly try to answer questions such as: What is the locus of the correspondence between two languages: words? meanings? textual structure (*ratio*)? content (*res*)? What does it mean if a word turns out to be impossible to translate? What exactly makes for a good translator of a (philosophical) text? How much knowledge of the literary, historical, and cultural background of an author is required in order to give an adequate translation? What does it mean to say that one language is "richer" in semantical resources than another? Do differences in vocabulary and syntax tell us something about differences in thinking? Are grammatical categories (nouns, adjectives, verbs, etc.) direct reflections of an ontological order (substances, qualities, actions, etc.)? If so, does the use of a particular language result in a different ontology? While Leonardo Bruni was not interested in such theoretical questions, we have seen that his own critique of medieval translations led him to reflect at least on some of these questions.

[12] Leibniz 1969, 126.

Another example of the philosophical relevance of the turn to common language has been highlighted in the chapter on Pontano (Chapter 3): his positive evaluation of language as the natural expression of man's social nature. Inspired by the literary and philosophical heritage of classical antiquity and bound by their own linguistic, moral, and religious agendas, humanists such as Pontano began to explore – often tentatively and unsystematically, to be sure – the social, emotive, and active functions of language. Focusing on language as a tool for communication, persuasion, practical deliberation, and argumentation rather than as an object of theoretical speculation to be studied in splendid isolation from the actual use of language, humanists underscored the intimate connection between language and sociability. It is an aspect that has often been connected to the Enlightenment when, according to some historians, a new conception of language emerged. The story then goes something like this. After an age in which the power of the word had been treated with suspicion, Enlightenment thinkers such as Condillac, David Hume, and Adam Smith began to underscore the constructive role of language in the formation of thought and culture. Communication was no longer seen as a risky affair that negatively interfered with the contemplation of ideas by an isolated individual thinker, but as the natural expression of man's social nature, the natural vehicle by which people give vent to feelings, emotions, and beliefs. Reflection on the origin of language stressed this affective and emotional dimension of language. Compared to the paradigm of the solipsistic Cartesian thinker, silently gazing at his or her clear and distinct ideas, this new focus on the social dimension of language looks fresh and important. It is therefore not surprising that scholars have detected here "an altogether new understanding of the nature of language."[13] Whatever the historical plausibility of the claim that the dominant paradigm in the seventeenth century was "largely Augustinian and orthodox," the relevant point to stress here is that these insights were not completely new with the Enlightenment, and that they may well be seen as a development of inchoate ideas on language as human action that we find in humanist thought.

In drawing these conclusions, we have almost unnoticeably moved from the issue of which language to use in philosophy to the issue of how to study language, but the two aspects are of course closely related: the defense of common language in philosophy was inspired by an empirical study of

[13] Aarsleff 2001, xii–xiv. On the Cartesian heritage, see Ricken 1994, 3–50. See above Chapter 3, n. 37.

what was felt to be a natural language, and vice versa. The critique of scholastic language was also a critique of the scholastic study of language. This divide between the scholastic study of language as a systematic rule-governed system and the humanist study of language as a human activity has been a major theme of this study, but it is important to note by way of conclusion that this divide is a paradigmatic example of a recurrent tension between a formal and empirical approach that has marked the study of language in the modern period. As Michael Losonsky has observed: "The divide between the Renaissance humanist perspective on language as human action and the Scholastic perspectives on language as a formal system – a divide that modern philosophy unsuccessfully tried to overcome – seems to be an enduring and prominent landmark of the study of human language."[14] To put it simply, the richness and complexity of natural languages defy categorization; actual linguistic performance resists theory. This was basically Valla's point when he ridiculed the attempt by medieval grammarians to offer a general theory of grammar without studying the differences between individual languages: "We can no more give a theory for grammar . . . than for the different words that different peoples use."[15] Zooming out from the specific humanist-scholastic context, we see the two perspectives on language as human activity and language as a formal system recurring in various guises at various stages in the ages that followed up to our own times. It has proven to be very difficult to unite the two approaches: "This distinction has the paradoxical consequence that the empirical basis of the study of language tends to undermine the very idea that language is a system that can be represented by a theory."[16] Seen in this wider historical perspective, the humanist and early-modern critique of scholastic language was not only a crucial element in the gradual erosion of the Aristotelian-scholastic paradigm, but also an early articulation of a fundamental position in the philosophical debate on language.

[14] Losonsky 2006, 252.

[15] Valla 2012, 2:85 (*Dialectical Disputations* 2.11.7); see above Chapter 2, n. 14.

[16] Losonsky 2006, xiv. On the basis of discussions of several "linguistic turns" (located in the works of Locke, Leibniz, Condillac, Wilhelm von Humboldt, J. S. Mill, Frege, and twentieth-century philosophers such as Wittgenstein, Carnap, Quine, Davidson, J. L. Austin, and Derrida), he concludes that attempts to unite the two approaches have (so far) been unsuccessful.

Bibliography

Aaron, R. I. (1967). *The Theory of Universals*. Oxford.

Aarsleff, H. (1964). "Leibniz on Locke on Language." *American Philosophical Quarterly* 1: 165–188.

(2001). "Introduction." In Condillac 2001, xi–xxxviii.

Adams, M. M. (1987). *William of Ockham*. 2 vols. Notre Dame, IN.

Adriaenssen, H. T. (2017). *Representation and Scepticism from Aquinas to Descartes*. Cambridge.

Adriaenssen, H. T., and L. Georgescu (eds.). (forthcoming). *Navigating the Old and the New: The Philosophy of Kenelm Digby*. Berlin.

Aertsen, J. A. (1996). *Medieval Philosophy and the Transcendentals: The Case of Thomas Aquinas*. Leiden.

Agricola, R. (1539). *De inventione dialectica: Lucubrationes*. Ed. Alard of Amsterdam. Cologne. (Repr. by Nieuwkoop 1967).

(2002). *Letters*. Ed. and trans. A. van der Laan and F. Akkerman. Assen.

Apel, K. O. (1975). *Die Idee der Sprache in der Tradition von Dante bis Vico*. 2nd revised ed. Bonn.

Aristotle. (1984). *The Complete Works of Aristotle: The Revised Oxford Translation*. Ed. J. Barnes. 2 vols. Princeton.

(1993). *Posterior Analytics*. Trans. J. Barnes. Oxford.

Arnauld, A., and P. Nicole. (1992). *Logique ou l'art de penser*. Paris.

Ashworth, E. J. (1981). "'Do Words Signify Ideas or Things?' The Scholastic Sources of Locke's Theory of Language." *Journal of the History of Philosophy* 19: 299–326. [Repr. in her *Studies in Post-Medieval Semantics*. London 1985, no. VII.]

(1984). "Locke on Language." *Canadian Journal of Philosophy* 14: 45–73. [Repr. in *Locke*, ed. V. Chappell, Oxford 1998, 175–198.]

Atherton, M. (1998). "The Inessentiality of Lockean Essences." In *Locke*. Ed. V. Chappell, 199–213. Oxford.

(2007). "Locke on Essences and Classification." In *The Cambridge Companion to Locke's "Essay concerning Human Understanding."* Ed. L. Newman, 258–285. Cambridge.

Ayers, M. (1991). *Locke: Epistemology and Ontology*. 2 vols. London.

(2004). "Popkin's Revised Scepticism." *British Journal for the History of Philosophy* 12: 319–332.

(2013). "Essences and Signification: Response to Martin Lenz." In *Continuity and Innovation in Medieval and Modern Philosophy. Knowledge, Mind, and Language*. Ed. J. Marenbon, 69–79. Oxford.

Backus, I. (2009). "The Issue of Reformation Scepticism Revisited: What Erasmus and Sebastian Castellio Did or Did Not Know." In *Renaissance Scepticisms*. Ed. G. Paganini and J. R. Maia Neto, 63–89. Dordrecht.

Bacon, F. (1857–1874). *The Works*. Ed. J. Spedding, R. L. Ellis, and D. D. Heath. 14 vols. London.

(2000). *The New Organon* [1620]. Ed. L. Jardine and M. Silverthorne. Cambridge.

Barnes, J. (1969). "Aristotle's Theory of Demonstration." *Phronesis* 14: 123–152.

(1993). "Introduction." In Aristotle 1993, xi–xxv.

(2001). "Locke and the Syllogism." In *Whose Aristotle? Whose Aristotelianism?* Ed. R. W. Sharples, 105–132. Aldershot.

Baron, H. (1928). *Leonardo Bruni Aretino. Humanistisch-philosophische Schriften, mit einer Chronologie seiner Werke und Briefe*. Wiesbaden.

Bennett, J. (1971). *Locke, Berkeley, Hume: Central Themes*. Oxford.

Bertman, M. (1978). "Hobbes on Language and Reality." *Revue internationale de philosophie* 32: 536–550.

Bianchi, L. (2007). "Continuity and Change in the Aristotelian Tradition." In *The Cambridge Companion to Renaissance Philosophy*. Ed. J. Hankins, 49–71. Cambridge.

Bird, O. (1962). "The Tradition of the Logical Topics: Aristotle to Ockham." *Journal of the History of Ideas* 23: 307–323.

Birkenmajer, A. (1922). "Der Streit des Alonso von Cartagena mit Leonardo Bruni Aretino." *Vermischte Untersuchungen zur Geschichte der mittelalterlichen Philosophie, Beiträge zur Geschichte der Philosophie des Mittelalters* 20: 129–210.

Birkhead, T. (2018). *The Wonderful Mr Willughby: The First True Ornithologist*. London.

Black, M. (1969). "Some Troubles with Whorfianism." In *Language and Philosophy*. Ed. S. Hook, 30–35. New York.

1972. *The Labyrinth of Language*. London.

Blair, A. (2006). "Natural Philosophy." In *The Cambridge History of Science*, Vol. 3: *Early Modern Science*. Ed. K. Park and L. Daston, 365–406. Cambridge.

Blair, A., and A. Grafton. (1992). "Reassessing Humanism and Science." *Journal of the History of Ideas* 53: 529–540.

Boethius, A. M. S. (1978). *De topicis differentiis*. Trans. E. Stump. Ithaca, NY.

(1988). *In Ciceronis Topica*. Trans. E. Stump. Ithaca, NY.

Botley, P. (2004). *Latin Translation in the Renaissance: The Theory and Practice of Leonardo Bruni, Giannozzo Manetti and Desiderius Erasmus*. Cambridge.

Breen, Q. (1952). "Giovanni Pico della Mirandola on the Conflict of Philosophy and Rhetoric." *Journal of the History of Ideas* 13: 384–412.

(1956). "Introduction." In Nizolio 1956.

(1958). "The *Antiparadoxon* of Marcantonius Majoragius or, A Humanist Becomes a Critic of Cicero as a Philosopher." *Studies in the Renaissance* 5: 37–48.

(1968). *Christianity and Humanism. Studies in the History of Ideas*. Ed. N. P. Ros. Grand Rapids, MI.

Brekle, H. E. (1985). *Einführung in die Geschichte der Sprachwissenschaft*. Darmstadt.

Broadie, A. (1993). *Introduction to Medieval Logic*. 2nd revised ed. Oxford.

Brockdorff, C. von. (1919). *Hobbes als Philosoph, Pädagoge und Soziologe*. Kiel.

Bruni, L. (1741). *Leonardi Bruni Arretini Epistolarum libri VIII*. Ed. L. Mehus. 2 vols. Florence.

(1928). *Leonardo Bruni Aretino. Humanistisch-philosophische Schriften, mit einer Chronologie seiner Werke und Briefe*. Ed. H. Baron. Wiesbaden.

(1987). *The Humanism of Leonardo Bruni: Selected Texts*. Ed. and trans. G. Griffiths, J. Hankins and D. Thompson. Binghamton, NY.

(2013). *Opere letterarie e politiche*. Ed. P. Viti. Turin.

Buccolini, C. (2017). "The Philosophy of Francisco Sanches: Academic Scepticism and Conjectural Empiricism." In *Academic Scepticism in the Development of Early Modern Philosophy*. Ed. P. Junqueira Smith and S. Charles, 1–23. Berlin.

Burchell, D. (2007). "'A Plain, Blunt Man'. Hobbes, Science, and Rhetoric Revisited." In *Science, Literature and Rhetoric in Early-Modern England*. Ed. J. Cummins and D. Burchell, 53–74. Abingdon.

Burke, P. (1995). "The Jargon of the Schools." In *Languages and Jargons: Contributions to a Social History of Language*. Ed. P. Burke and R. Porter, 2–41. Cambridge.

Burnyeat, M. F. (1981). "Aristotle on Understanding Knowledge." In *Aristotle on Science: The Posterior Analytics*. Ed. E. Berti, 97–139. Padua.

Caluori, D. (2007). "The Scepticism of Francisco Sanches." *Archiv für Geschichte der Philosophie* 89: 30–46.

(2018). "Francisco Sanchez: A Renaissance Pyrrhonist Against Aristotelian Dogmatism." In *Skepticism: From Antiquity to the Present*. Ed. D. E. Machuca and B. Reed, 260–270. London.

Cameron, M. (2012). "Meaning in the Middle Ages: Foundational and Semantic Theories." In *Oxford Handbook of Medieval Philosophy*. Ed. J. Marenbon, 342–362. Oxford.

Camporeale, S. I. 1972. *Lorenzo Valla: Umanesimo e teologia*. Florence.

Casini, L. 2006. *Cognitive and Moral Psychology in Renaissance Philosophy: A Study of Juan Luis Vives' "De anima et vita."* Uppsala.

2009. "Self-Knowledge, Scepticism and the Quest for a New Method: Juan Luis Vives on Cognition and the Impossibility of Perfect Knowledge." In *Renaissance Scepticisms*. Ed. G. Paganini and J. R. Maria Neto, 33–60. Dordrecht.

Cassirer, E. 1906–1957. *Das Erkenntnisproblem in der Philosophie und Wissenschaft der neueren Zeit*. 4 vols. Darmstadt.

Cassirer, E., P. O. Kristeller, and J. H. Randall, Jr. 1948. *The Renaissance Philosophy of Man.* Chicago, Ill.

Casson, D. 2016. "John Locke, Clipped Coins, and the Unstable Currency of Public Reason." In *Etica and Politica / Ethics & Politics* 18: 153–180.

Cave, T. 1979. *The Cornucopian Text. Problems of Writing in the French Renaissance.* Oxford.

Celenza, C. 2018. *The Intellectual World of the Italian Renaissance: Language, Philosophy, and the Search for Meaning.* Cambridge.

Cesarini Martinelli, L. 1980. "Note sulla polemica Poggio-Valla e sulla fortuna delle *Elegantiae*." *Interpres: Rivista di studi quattrocenteschi* 3: 29–79.

Chappell, V. 1994. "Locke's Theory of Ideas." In *The Cambridge Companion to Locke.* Ed. V. Chappell, 26–55. Cambridge.

Chiaradonna, R. 2019. "Galen and Middle Platonists on Dialectic and Knowledge." In *Dialectic after Plato and Aristotle.* Ed. T. Bénatouïl and K. Ierodiakonou, 320–370. Cambridge.

Christmann, H. H. 1966. "Beiträge zur Geschichte vom Weltbild der Sprache." *Abhandlungen der Geistes- und Sozialwissenschaftlichen Klasse der Akademie der Wissenschaften und der Literatur in Mainz* 7: 441–469.

Cicero, M. T. 1913. *De officiis.* Trans. W. Miller. Cambridge, Mass.

1928. *De republica, De legibus.* Trans. C. Walker Keyes. Cambridge, Mass.

1942. *De oratore III, De fato, Paradoxa Stoicorum, De partitione oratoria.* Trans. H. Rackham. 2 vols. Cambridge, Mass.

1949. *De inventione, De optimo genere oratorum, Topica.* Ed. and trans. H. M. Hubbell. Cambridge, Mass.

1951. *De natura deorum, Academica.* Ed. and trans. H. Rackham. Cambridge, Mass.

Codoñer Merino, C. 2010. "Elegantia y gramática." In *Lorenzo Valla: La Riforma della lingua e della logica.* 2 vols. Ed. M. Regoliosi, 1: 67–109. Florence.

Cogan, M. 1984. "Rodolphus Agricola and the Semantic Revolutions of the History of Invention." *Rhetorica* 2: 163–194.

Colie, R. L. 1965. "The Social Language of John Locke: A Study in the History of Ideas." *Journal of British Studies* 4: 29–51.

Collins, J. R. 2005. *The Allegiance of Thomas Hobbes.* Oxford.

Comparot, A. 1983. *Amour et Vérité: Sebon, Vivès et Montaigne.* Paris.

Condillac, E. B. de. 2001. *Essay on the Origin of Human Knowledge.* Trans. H. Aarsleff. Cambridge.

Copenhaver, B. P. 1988. "Translation, Terminology and Style in Philosophical Discourse." In *Cambridge History of Renaissance Philosophy.* Ed. C. Schmitt and Q. Skinner, with E. Kessler and J. Kraye, 77–110. Cambridge.

Copenhaver, B. P., and C. B. Schmitt. 1992. *Renaissance Philosophy.* Oxford.

Coseriu, E. 1971. "Zur Sprachtheorie von Juan Luis Vives." In*Aus der französischen Kultur- und Geistesgeschichte. Festschrift Walter Mönch,* 234–255. Heidelberg.

Cotroneo, G. 1971. *I trattatisti dell' "Ars historica."* Naples.

Crescini, A. 1965. *Le origini del metodo analitico: il cinquecento.* Udine.

Cummings, B. 2002. *The Literary Culture of the Reformation: Grammar and Grace*. Oxford.

Curley, E. "Introduction." In Hobbes 1994b, viii–xlvii.

Dascal, M. 1976. "Language and Money. A Simile and its Meaning in 17th Century Philosophy of Language." *Studia Leibnitiana* 8: 187–218.

Dawson, H. 2007. *Locke, Language and Early-Modern Philosophy*. Cambridge.

Dear, P. 1988. *Mersenne and the Learning of the Schools*. Ithaca, N.Y./London.

De Carvalho, J. 1955. In Sanches 1955.

De Gandt, F. 2001. "Response to Jonathan Barnes." In *Whose Aristotle? Whose Aristotelianism?* Ed. R. W. Sharples, 133–134. Aldershot.

Deitz, L. 2007. "Francesco Patrizi da Cherso's Criticism of Aristotle's Logic." *Vivarium* 45: 113–124.

Del Nero, V. 1991. *Linguaggio e filosofia in Vives. L'organizzazione del sapere nel "De disciplinis" (1531)*. Bologna.

2008. "The *De disciplinis* as a Model of a Humanistic Text." In *A Companion to Juan Luis Vives*. Ed. C. Fantazzi, 177–226. Leiden.

Demonet, M.-L. 1992. *Les Voix du Signe: Nature et origine de langage à la Renaissance*. Paris.

Den Haan, A. 2016. *Giannozzo Manetti's New Testament: Translation Theory and Practice in Fifteenth-Century Italy*. Leiden.

Descartes, R. 1984–1991. *The Philosophical Writings*. Trans. J. Cottingham, R. Stoothoff and D. Murdoch, with A. Kenny. 3 vols. Cambridge.

Digby, K. 1644. *Two Treatises*. Paris.

Diogenes Laertius. 1925. *Lives of Eminent Philosophers*. 2 vols. Ed. R. D. Hicks. Cambridge, Mass.

Dubois, C.-G. 1970. *Mythe et langage au seizième siècle*. Bordeaux.

Duncan, S. 2016. "Hobbes on Language: Propositions, Truth, and Absurdity." In *The Oxford Handbook of Hobbes*. Ed. A. P. Martinich and K. Hoekstra, 60–75. Oxford.

Duns Scotus, J. 1997–1998. *Questions on the Metaphysics of Aristotle*. Trans. G. J. Etzkorn and A. B. Wolter. St Bonaventure, N.Y.

Eamon, W. 1996. *Science and the Secrets of Nature. Books of Secrets in Medieval and Early Modern Culture*. Princeton.

Elffers, E. 1996. "The History of Thought about Language and Thought." In *Linguistics in the Netherlands*. Ed. C. Cremers and M. den Dikken, 73–84. Amsterdam.

Enenkel, K. A. E. and J. Papy (eds.). 2006. *Petrarch and His Readers in the Renaissance*. Leiden.

Evans, N., and S. C. Levinson. 2009. "The Myth of Language Universals: Language Diversity and Its Importance for Cognitive Science." *Behavorial and Brain Sciences* 32: 429–448.

Faithfull, R. Glynn. 1953. "The Concept of 'Living Language' in Cinquecento Vernacular Philology." *Modern Language Review* 48: 278–292.

Fantazzi, C. (ed.). 2008. *A Companion to Juan Luis Vives*. Leiden.

Fantham, E. 2004. *The Roman World of Cicero's "De Oratore."* Oxford.

Feingold, M. 1997. "The Humanities." In *The History of the University of Oxford*. Ed. N. Tyacke. Vol. 4, *Seventeenth-Century Oxford*, 211–358. Oxford.

2001. "English Ramism: A Reinterpretation." In *The Influence of Petrus Ramus: Studies in Sixteenth and Seventeenth Century Philosophy and Sciences*. Ed. M. Feingold, J. S. Freedman and W. Rother, 127–176. Basel.

Fenves, P. 2001. *Arresting Language: From Leibniz to Benjamin*. Stanford, Calif.

Ferraù, G. 1983. *Pontano critico*. Messina.

Floridi, L. 2002. *Sextus Empiricus: The Transmission and Recovery of Pyrrhonism*. Oxford.

France, P. 1972. *Rhetoric and Truth in France. Descartes to Diderot*. Oxford.

Frank, G. 1995. *Die theologische Philosophie Philipp Melanchthons (1497–1560)*. Leipzig.

Friedrich, M. 2002. "'War Rudolf Agricola Nominalist?' Zur Bedeutung der Philosophie Ockhams für den Sprachhumanismus." In: *Res et Verba in der Renaissance*. Ed. E. Kessler and I. Maclean, 369–388. Wiesbaden.

Gaisser, J. H. 2012. "Introduction." In Pontano 2012, vii–xxvii.

Garber, D. 2001. "Semel in Vita: The Scientific Background to Descartes' Meditations." In D. Garber, *Descartes Embodied: Reading Cartesian Philosophy Through Cartesian Science*, 221–256. Cambridge. [Originally published 1986 in *Essays on Descartes' "Meditations."* Ed. A. O. Rorty, Berkeley, Calif., 81–116.]

Garin, E. 1951. "Noterelle sulla filosofia del Rinascimento." *Rinascimento* 2: 319–336.

Gassendi, P. 1658. *Opera Omnia*. Lyon.

1972. *The Selected Works of Pierre Gassendi*. Ed. and trans. C. B. Brush. New York.

1981. *Institutio Logica* (1658). Trans. H. Jones. Assen.

Gaukroger, S. 1989. *Cartesian Logic*. Oxford.

Gavinelli, S. 1991. "Teorie grammaticali nelle *Elegantie* e la tradizione scolastica del tardo umanesimo." *Rinascimento* 31: 155–181.

Gera, D. L. 2003. *Ancient Greek Ideas on Speech, Language and Civilization*. Oxford.

Gerl, H.-B. 1981. *Philosophie und Philologie: Leonardo Brunis Übertragung der nikomachischen Ethik in ihren philosophischen Prämissen*. Munich.

Germano, G. 2005. *Il "De aspiratione" di Giovanni Pontano e la cultura del suo tempo*. Naples.

Gert, B. 2001. "Hobbes on Reason." *Pacific Philosophical Quarterly* 82: 243–257.

Glucker, J. 1995. "*Probabile, Veri Simile,* and Related Terms." In *Cicero the Philosopher. Twelve Papers*. Ed. J. G. F. Powell, 85–113. Oxford.

Goldie, M. 1983. "John Locke and Anglican Royalism." *Political Studies* 31: 61–85.

Gordon, D. 1994. *Citizens without Sovereignty: Equality and Sociability in French Thought, 1670–1789*. Princeton.

Görler, W. 1995. "Silencing the Troublemaker: *De Legibus* I.39 and the Continuity of Cicero's Scepticism." In *Cicero the Philosopher. Twelve Papers*. Ed. J. G. F. Powell, 85–113. Oxford.

Gotti, M. 1996. *Robert Boyle and the Language of Science*. Milan.
Grafton, A. and N. Siraisi. 1999. "Introduction." In *Natural Particulars. Nature and the Disciplines in Renaissance Europe*. Ed. A. Grafton and N. Siraisi, 1–21. Cambridge, Mass.
Green-Pedersen, N. J. 1984. *The Tradition of the Topics in the Middle Ages*. Munich.
Grosseteste, R. 1981. *Commentarius in posteriorum analyticorum libros*. Ed. P. Rossi. Florence.
Guerlac, R. 1979. "Introduction." In Vives 1979, 1–43.
Guyer, P. 1994. "Locke's Philosophy of Language." In *The Cambridge Companion to Locke*. Ed. V. Chappell, 115–145. Cambridge.
Haas, W. 1962. "The Theory of Translation." *Philosophy* 37: 208–228.
Hacking, I. 1975. *Why Does Language Matter to Philosophy?* Cambridge.
Hall, R. A. 1936. "Linguistic Theory in the Italian Renaissance." *Language* 12: 96–107.
Hankins, J. 1987. "The New Language." In Bruni 1987.
2003. "The Ethics Controversy." In *Humanism and Platonism in the Italian Renaissance*. 2 vols. Rome, 1: 193–241.
2006. "The Popularization of Humanism in the Fifteenth Century: The Writings of Leonardo Bruni in Latin and the Vernacular." In *Language and Cultural Change. Aspects of the Study and Use of Language in the Later Middle Ages and the Renaissance*. Ed. L. Nauta, 133–147. Leuven.
2007. "The Significance of Renaissance Philosophy." In *The Cambridge Companion to Renaissance Philosophy*. Ed. J. Hankins, 338–345. Cambridge.
2007–2008. "Petrarch and the Canon of Neo-Latin Literature." In *Petrarca, l'Umanesimo e la civiltà europea. Atti del Convegno Internazionale, Firenze, 5–10 dicembre 2004, II (= Quaderni petrarcheschi*m 17–18). Ed. D. Coppini and M. Feo, 905–922. Florence.
2019. *Virtue Politics: Soulcraft and Statecraft in Renaissance Italy*. Cambridge, Mass.
Hankinson, R. 2008. "Epistemology." In *The Cambridge Companion to Galen*. Ed. R. Hankinson, 157–183. Cambridge.
Harth, D. 1970. *Philologie und praktische Philosophie. Untersuchungen zum Sprach- und Traditionsverständnis des Erasmus von Rotterdam*. Munich.
Harth, H. 1968. "Leonardo's Brunis Selbstverständnis als Übersetzer." *Archiv für Kulturgeschichte* 50: 41–63.
Helmrath, J. 2010. "Streitkultur. Die Invektive bei den italienischen Humanisten." In *Die Kunst des Streitens. Inszenierung, Formen und Funktionen öffentlichen Streits in historischer Perspektive*. Ed. M. Laureys and R. Simons, 261–293. Göttingen.
Hidalgo-Serna, E. 1990. "Metaphorical Language, Rhetoric, and *Comprehensio*: J. L. Vives and M. Nizolio." *Philosophy and Rhetoric* 23: 1–11.
Hill, J. H. 1988. "Language, Culture, and World View." In *Language: The Socio-Cultural Context*. Ed. F. J. Newmeyer, 14–36. Cambridge.

Hobbes, T. 1839–1845. *The English Works of Thomas Hobbes of Malmesbury*. Ed. W. Molesworth. 11 vols. London. [= EW]
1839–1845. *Opera philosophica quae latine scripsit omnia*. Ed. W. Molesworth. London. [= OL]
1839. "Concerning Body." In EW I.
1840a. "Of Liberty and Necessity." In EW IV.
1840b. "Answer to Bramhall." In EW IV.
1840c. "Answer to Davenant." In EW IV.
1841. "Questions concerning Liberty, Necessity and Chance." In EW V.
1845a. "Six Lessons to the Professors of Mathematics." In EW VII.
1845b. "Examinatio et Emendatio Mathematicae Hodiernae." In OL IV.
1845c. "Principa et Problema Aliquot Geometrica." In OL V.
1981. Part I of "De Corpore." Trans. A. P. Martinich. New York.
1991. *Man and Citizen (De homine and De cive)*. Ed. B. Gert. Indianapolis, Ind.
1994a. *The Elements of Law Natural and Politic*. Ed. J. C. A. Gaskin. Oxford.
1994b. *Leviathan, with Selected Variants from the Latin Edition 1668*. Ed. E. Curley. Indianapolis, Ind.
1998. *On the Citizen*. Trans. R. Tuck and M. Silverthorne. Cambridge.
1999a. *De Corpore: Elementorum philosophiae sectio prima*. Ed. K. Schuhmann. Paris.
1999b. *Hobbes and Bramhall on Liberty and Necessity*. Ed. V. Chappell. Cambridge.
2005. *A Dialogue between a Philosopher and a Student, of the Common Laws of England / Questions relative to Hereditary Right*. Ed. A. Cromartie and Q. Skinner. Oxford.
2010. *Behemoth*. Ed. P. Seaward. Oxford.
2012. *Leviathan*. Ed. N. Malcolm. 3 vols. Oxford.
Horace. 1926. *Satires. Epistles. The Art of Poetry*. Trans. H. R. Fairclough. Cambridge, Mass.
Hotson, H. 2007. *Commonplace Learning: Ramism and its German Ramifications, 1543–1630*. Oxford.
Howald, K. 2007. "Einleitung." In Sanches 2007, ix–clxiv.
Hume, D. 1978. *Treatise on Human Nature*. Ed. L. A. Selby-Bigge. Oxford.
Inwood, B., and J. Mansfeld (eds.) 1997. *Assent and Argument: Studies in Cicero's "Academic Books."* Leiden.
Isermann, M. 1991. *Die Sprachtheorie im Werk von Thomas Hobbes*. Münster.
Jardine, L. 1974. *Francis Bacon. Discovery and the Art of Discourse*. London.
1977. "Lorenzo Valla and the Intellectual Origins of Humanist Dialectic." *Journal of the History of Philosophy* 15: 143–164.
1983. "Lorenzo Valla: Academic Scepticism and the New Humanist Dialectic." In *The Skeptical Tradition*. Ed. M. Burnyeat, 253–286. Berkeley, Calif.
1988. "Humanistic Logic." In *The Cambridge History of Renaissance Philosophy*. Ed. C. Schmitt and Q. Skinner, with E. Kessler and J. Kraye, 173–198. Cambridge.

Jesseph, D. M. 1999. *Squaring the Circle: The War between Hobbes and Wallis.* Chicago, Ill.

2018. "Hobbes and the Syllogism." In *The Aftermath of Syllogism Aristotelian Logical Argument from Avicenna to Hegel.* Ed. M. Sgarbi and M. Cosci, 67–82. London.

Johnston, D. 1986. "The Rhetoric of Leviathan." *Thomas Hobbes and the Politics of Cultural Transformation.* Princeton, N.J.

Jolley, N. 1984. *Leibniz and Locke: A Study of the "New Essays on Human Understanding."* Oxford.

1999. *Locke: His Philosophical Thought.* Oxford.

Jones, P. 1982. *Hume's Sentiments: Their Ciceronian and French Context.* Edinburgh.

Jones, J.-E. 2012. "Locke on Real Essence." In *Stanford Encyclopedia of Philosophy.* https://plato.stanford.edu/entries/real-essence/

Kahn, V. 1983. "Giovanni Pontano's Rhetoric and Prudence." *Philosophy and Rhetoric,* 16: 16–34.

1985. *Rhetoric, Prudence, and Skepticism in the Renaissance.* Ithaca, N.Y./London.

Kappl, B. 2006. *Die Poetik des Aristoteles in der Dichtungstheorie des Cinquecento.* Berlin.

Kessler, E. 1979. "Humanismus und Naturwissenschaft bei Rudolf Agricola." In *L'Humanisme allemand (1480–1540). 18e Colloque international de Tours,* 141–157. Munich/Paris.

Kidwell, C. 1991. *Pontano: Poet and Prime Minister.* London.

Kircher, T. 2015. "Petrarch and the Humanists." In *The Cambridge Companion to Petrarch.* Ed. A. R. Ascoli and U. Falkeid, 179–190. Cambridge.

Klein, W. P. 1992. *Am Anfang war das Wort: Theorie- und Wissenschaftsgeschichtliche Elemente frühneuzeitlichen Sprachbewusstseins.* Berlin.

Klima, G. 2005. "The Essentialist Nominalism of John Buridan." *The Review of Metaphysics* 58: 739–754.

Kneale, W., and M. Kneale. 1962. *The Development of Logic.* Oxford.

Knowlson, J. 1975. *Universal Language Schemes in England and France, 1600–1800.* Toronto.

Kondylis, P. 1990. *Die neuzeitliche Metaphysikkritik.* Stuttgart.

Kraye, J. 2001. "Lorenzo Valla and Changing Perspectives of Renaissance Humanism." *Comparative Criticism* 23: 37–55.

2008. "Pico on the Relationship of Rhetoric and Philosophy." In *Pico della Mirandola: New Essays.* Ed. M. Dougherty, 13–36. Cambridge.

Kretzmann, N. 1967. "History of Semantics." In *The Encyclopedia of Philosophy.* Ed. P. Edwards. Vol. 7, 358–406. New York.

1968. "The Main Thesis of Locke's Semantic Theory." *Philosophical Review* 77: 175–196.

Kristeller, P. O. 1979. *Renaissance Thought and Its Sources.* New York.

Krostenko, B. A. 2001. *Cicero, Catullus, and the Language of Social Performance*. Chicago, Ill.
Laerke, M. 2009. "The Problem of *Alloglossia*. Leibniz on Spinoza's Innovative Use of Philosophical Language." *British Journal for the History of Philosophy* 17: 939–953.
2014. "Spinoza's Language." *Journal of the History of Philosophy* 52: 519–547.
Leibniz, G. W. 1966. *Philosophische Schriften*. Berlin.
1969. *Philosophical Papers and Letters*. Trans. L. E. Loemker. Dordrecht.
1981. *New Essays on Human Understanding* (1765). Trans. P. Remnant and J. Bennett. Cambridge.
1989. *Philosophical Essays*. Ed. and trans. R. Ariew and D. Garber. Indianapolis, Ind.
Leijenhorst, C. 2002a. *The Mechanisation of Aristotelianism: The Late Aristotelian Setting of Thomas Hobbes' Natural Philosophy*. Leiden.
2002b. "'Insignificant Speech': Thomas Hobbes and Late Aristotelianism on Words, Concepts and Things." In *Res et Verba in der Renaissance*. Ed. E. Kessler and I. Maclean, 337–367. Wiesbaden.
2007. "Sense and Nonsense about Sense: Hobbes and the Aristotelians on Sense Perception and Imagination." In *The Cambridge Companion to Hobbes's "Leviathan."* Ed. P. Springborg, 82–108. Cambridge.
Lennon, T. 2007. "Locke on Ideas and Representation." In *The Cambridge Companion to Locke's "Essay Concerning Human Understanding."* Ed. L. Newman, 231–257. Cambridge.
Lenz, M. 2010. *Lockes Sprachkonzeption*. Berlin.
Levitin, D. 2015. *Ancient Wisdom in the Age of the New Science: Histories of Philosophy in England, c. 1640–1700*. Cambridge.
Lewis, R. 2012. *Artificial Languages in England from Bacon to Locke*. Cambridge.
Limbrick, E. 1988. "Introduction." In Sanches 1988, 1–88.
Lines, D. 2012. "Aristotle's Ethics in the Renaissance." In *The Reception of Aristotle's "Ethics."* Ed. J. Miller, 171–193. Cambridge.
2015. "Beyond Latin in Renaissance Philosophy: A Plea for New Critical Perspectives." *Intellectual History Review* 25: 373–389.
Locke, J. 1975. *An Essay Concerning Human Understanding*. Ed. P. H. Nidditch. Oxford.
Lojacono, E. 2011. *Spigolature sullo Scetticismo: La sua manifestazione all'inizio della Modernità, prima dell'uso di Sesto Empirico: I sicari di Aristotele*. Padua.
Lo Monaco, F. 2010. "*Vulgus imperitum grammatice professorum*. Lorenzo Valla, *Le Elegantiae* e i *grammatici recentes*." In *Lorenzo Valla: La Riforma della lingua e della logica*. 2 vols. Ed. M. Regoliosi, 1: 51–66. Florence.
Losonsky, M. 1994. "Locke on Meaning and Signification." In *Locke's Philosophy: Content and Context*. Ed. J. Rogers. Oxford.
2006. *Linguistic Turns in Modern Philosophy*. Cambridge.
Luck, G. 1958. "*Vir facetus*: A Renaissance Ideal." *Studies in Philology* 55: 107–121.
Lucretius, 1982. *De rerum natura*. Trans. W. H. D. Rouse and M. F. Smith. Cambridge, Mass.

Lucy, J. A. 1992. *Language Diversity and Thought: A Reformulation of the Linguistic Relativity Hypothesis*. Cambridge.

Lupi, S. 1955. "Il *De sermone* di Gioviano Pontano." *Filologia Romanza* 2: 366–417.

Lupoli, A. 2009. "*Humanus animus nusquam consistit*: Doctor Sanchez's Diagnosis of the Incurable Human Unrest and Ignorance." In *Renaissance Scepticisms*. Ed. G. Paganini and J. R. Maia Neto, 149–181. Dordrecht.

Mack, P. 1993. *Renaissance Argument: Valla and Agricola in the Traditions of Rhetoric and Dialectic*. Leiden.

2005. "Vives's *De arte dicendi*: Structure, Innovations, Problems." *Rhetorica* 23: 65–92.

2008. "Vives's Contributions to Rhetoric and Dialectic." In *A Companion to Juan Luis Vives*. Ed. C. Fantazzi, 227–276. Leiden.

Mackie, J. 1976. *Problems from Locke*. Oxford.

Maclean, I. 1998. "Foucault's Renaissance Episteme Reassessed: An Aristotelian Counterblast." *Journal of the History of Ideas* 59: 149–166.

2006. "The 'Sceptical Crisis' Reconsidered: Galen, Rational Medicine and the *Libertas Philosophandi*." *Early Science and Medicine* 11: 247–274.

MacPhail, E. 2014. *Dancing around the Well: The Circulation of Commonplaces in Renaissance Humanism*. Leiden.

Malcolm, N. 2002. *Aspects of Hobbes*. Oxford.

2012. "Editorial Introduction." In Hobbes 2012, vol. 1.

Marenbon, J. 1997. *The Philosophy of Peter Abelard*. Cambridge.

2003. *Boethius*. Oxford.

Marsh, D. 1979. "Grammar, Method, and Polemic in Lorenzo Valla's *Elegantiae*." *Rinascimento* 19: 91–116.

1980. *The Quattrocento Dialogue: Classical Tradition and Humanist Innovation*. Cambridge, Mass.

2015. "Petrarch's Adversaries: The Invectives." In *The Cambridge Companion to Petrarch*. Ed. A. Ascoli and U. Falkeid, 167–176. Cambridge.

Martin, C. 2011. *Renaissance Meteorology: Pomponazzi to Descartes*. Baltimore, Md.

2014. *Subverting Aristotle. Religion, History, and Philosophy in Early-Modern Science*. Baltimore, Md.

Martinich, A. P. 1981. "Translator's Commentary." In Hobbes 1981.

Maxson, B. 2013. *The Humanist World of Renaissance Florence*. Cambridge.

McConica, J. 1979. "Humanism and Aristotle in Tudor Oxford." *English Historical Review* 94: 291–317.

Melanchthon, Philipp. 1846. "Erotemata dialectices." In *Corpus reformatorum*. Ed. K. G. Bretschneider, 13: 509–752. Halle.

Menn, S. 1998. "The Intellectual Setting." In *The Cambridge History of Seventeenth-Century Philosophy*. 2 vols. Ed. D. Garber and M. Ayers, 1: 33–86. Cambridge.

Mercer, C. 1993. "The Vitality and Importance of Early Modern Aristotelianism." In *The Rise of Modern Philosophy: The Tension Between the New and Traditional Philosophies from Machiavelli to Leibniz*. Ed. T. Sorell, 33–67. Oxford.

Monfasani, J. 1988. "Humanism and Rhetoric." In *Renaissance Humanism: Foundations, Forms and Legacy*. 3 vols. Ed. A. Rabil, Jr., 3: 195–228. Philadelphia.

2006. "The Renaissance as the Concluding Phase of the Middle Ages." *Bulletino dell'Istituto Storico Italiano per il Medio Evo* 108: 165–185.

Monti Sabia, L. 1993. "Echi di scoperte geografiche in opere di Giovanni Pontano." In *Columbeis V*. Ed. S. Pittaluga, 283–303. Genoa.

1995. *Pontano e la storia. Dal De bello Neapolitano all' Actius*. Rome.

Monti Sabia, L., and S. Monti. 2010. *Studi su Pontano*. 2 vols. Messina.

Moody, E. 1935. *The Logic of William of Ockham*. London.

Morison, B. 2008. "Logic." In *The Cambridge Companion to Galen*. Ed. R. Hankinson, 66–115. Cambridge.

Morris Engel, S. 1961. "Hobbes's 'Table of Absurdity.'" *The Philosophical Review* 70: 533–543.

Moss, A. 1996. *Printed Commonplace-Books and the Structuring of Renaissance Thought*. Oxford.

2003. *Renaissance Truth and the Latin Language Turn*. Oxford.

Muratori, C., and G. Paganini (eds.). 2016. *Early Modern Philosophers and the Renaissance Legacy*. Berlin.

Murr, S. 1992. "Foi religieuse et *libertas philosophandi* chez Gassendi." *Revue des sciences philosophique et théologique* 76: 85–100.

Nauta, L. 2002a. "Hobbes the Pessimistic? Continuity of Hobbes's Views on Reason and Eloquence between *The Elements of Law* and *Leviathan*." *British Journal for the History of Philosophy* 10: 31–54.

2002b. "Hobbes's Views on Religion and the Church between *The Elements of Law* and *Leviathan*: A Dramatic Change of Direction?" *Journal of the History of Ideas* 63: 577–598.

2006a. "Lorenzo Valla and Quattrocento Scepticism." *Vivarium* 44: 375–395.

2006b. "Linguistic Relativity and the Humanist Imitation of Classical Latin." In *Language and Cultural Change: Aspects of the Study and Use of Language in the Later Middle Ages and the Renaissance*. Ed. L. Nauta, 173–186. Leuven.

2007. "Lorenzo Valla and the Rise of Humanist Dialectic." In *The Cambridge Companion to Renaissance Philosophy*. Ed. J. Hankins, 193–210. Cambridge.

2009. *In Defense of Common Sense. Lorenzo Valla's Humanist Critique of Scholastic Philosophy*. Cambridge, Mass.

2011. "Philology as Philosophy: Giovanni Pontano on Language, Meaning, and Grammar." *The Journal of the History of Ideas* 72: 481–502.

2012a. "Anti-Essentialism and the Rhetoricization of Knowledge: Mario Nizolio's Humanist Attack on Universals." *Renaissance Quarterly* 65: 31–66.

2012b. "From Universals to Topics: The Realism of Rudolph Agricola, with an Edition of his Reply to a Critic." *Vivarium* 50: 190–224.

2015. "The Order of Knowing: Juan Luis Vives on Language, Thought, and the Topics." *The Journal of the History of Ideas* 76: 325–345.

2016. "The Critique of Scholastic Language in Renaissance Humanism and Early Modern Philosophy." In *Early Modern Philosophers and the Renaissance Legacy*. Ed. C. Muratori and G. Paganini, 59–79. Berlin.

2018. "Latin as a Common Language: The Coherence of Lorenzo Valla's Humanist Program." *Renaissance Quarterly* 71: 1–32.

(forthcoming). "Two Treatises in One Volume: Kenelm Digby Between Body and Soul." In *Navigating the Old and the New: The Philosophy of Kenelm Digby*. Ed. H. T. Adriaenssen and L. Georgescu. Berlin.

Naya, E. 2003. "Francisco Sanches le médecin et le scepticisme expérimental." In *Esculape et Dionysos. Mélanges en l'honneur de Jean Céard*. Ed. J. Dupèbe and F. Giacone, 111–129. Geneva.

Newman, L. 2007. "Locke on Knowledge." In *The Cambridge Companion to Locke's "Essay concerning human understanding."* Ed. L. Newman, 313–351. Cambridge.

Nizolio, M. 1613. *Thesaurus Ciceronianus*. Frankfurt.

1956. *De veris principiis et vera ratione philosophandi contra pseudophilosophos*. Ed. Q. Breen. 2 vols. Rome.

1980. *Vier Bücher über die Wahren Prinzipien und die wahre philosophische Methode gegen die Pseudophilosophen*. Trans. K. Thieme. Munich.

Noreña, C. G. 1970. *Juan Luis Vives*. The Hague.

1989. *Juan Luis Vives and the Emotions*. Carbondale, Ill.

Nuchelmans, G. 1983. *Judgment and Proposition: From Descartes to Kant*. Amsterdam.

Ogilvie, B. W. 2006. *The Science of Describing: Natural History in Renaissance Europe*. Chicago, Ill.

Ong, W. J. 1958. *Ramus, Method, and the Decay of Dialogue. From the Art of Discourse to the Art of Reason*. Cambridge, Mass.

O'Rourke Boyle, M. 1977. *Erasmus on Language and Method in Theology*. Toronto.

Ott, W. R. 2004. *Locke's Philosophy of Language*. Cambridge.

Otto, S. 1983. "Rhetorische Techne oder Philosophie sprachlicher Darstellungskraft? Zur Rekonstruktion des Sprachhumanismus der Renaissance." *Zeitschrift für philosophische Forschung* 37: 497–514.

Paganini, G. 2007. "Montaigne, Sanches e la conoscenza attraverso i fenomeni. Gli usi moderni di un paradigma antico." In *Scetticismo. Una vicenda filosofica*. Ed. M. De Caro and E. Spinelli, 67–82. Rome.

2008. *Skepsis: le débat des modernes sur le scepticisme: Montaigne, Le Vayer, Campanella, Hobbes, Descartes, Bayle*. Paris.

Panaccio, C. 2004. *Ockham on Concepts*. Aldershot.

Panizza, L. 1978. "*Lorenzo Valla's* De vero falsoque bono, *Lactantius and Oratorical Scepticism*." *Journal of the Warburg and Courtauld Institutes* 41: 76–107.

Parkin, J. 2007. *Taming the Leviathan: The Reception of the Political and Religious Ideas of Thomas Hobbes in England, 1640–1700*. Cambridge.

Pasnau, R. 1997. *Theories of Cognition in the Later Middle Ages*. Cambridge.

2011. *Metaphysical Themes 1274–1671*. Oxford.

2013. "Divisions of Epistemic Labor: Some Remarks on the History of Fideism and Esotericism." In *Continuity and Innovation in Medieval and Modern Philosophy. Knowledge, Mind, and Language*, 83–117. Ed. J. Marenbon. Oxford.

2017. *After Certainty: A History of our Epistemic Ideals and Illusions*. Oxford.

(ed.) 2014. *The Cambridge History of Medieval Philosophy*. Cambridge.

Passmore, J. 1953. "Descartes, the British Empiricists and Formal Logic." *Philosophical Review* 62: 545–553.

Patey, D. L. 1984. *Probability and Literary Form: Philosophic Theory and Literary Practice in the Augustan Age*. Cambridge.

Pécharman, M. 1995. "La Logique de Hobbes et la 'Tradition Aristotélicienne.'" *Hobbes Studies* 8: 105–124.

2016. "Hobbes on Logic, or How to Deal with Aristotle's Legacy." In *The Oxford Handbook of Hobbes*. Ed. A. P. Martinich and K. Hoekstra, 21–59. Oxford.

Penelhum, T. 1983. "Skepticism and Fideism." In *The Skeptical Tradition*. Ed. M. Burnyeat, 287–318. Berkeley, Calif.

Penn, J. M. 1972. *Linguistic Relativity Versus Innate Ideas: The Origins of the Sapir–Whorf Hypothesis in German Thought*. Berlin.

Percival, W. K. 1976. "Renaissance Grammar: Rebellion or Revolution?" In *Interrogativi dell'umanesimo*. Ed. G. Tarugi, 73–90. Florence. [Repr. in his *Studies in Grammar*, Aldershot 2004, no. IV.]

Perler, D. 2004. "Was there a 'Pyrrhonian Crisis' in Early Modern Philosophy?" *Archiv für Geschichte der Philosophie* 86: 209–220.

2006. *Zweifel und Gewissheit: Skeptische Debatten im Mittelalter*. Frankfurt am Main.

2012. "Scepticism and Metaphysics." In *The Oxford Handbook of Medieval Philosophy*. Ed. J. Marenbon, Oxford, 547–565.

2014. "Skepticism." In *Cambridge History of Medieval Philosophy*. Ed. R. Pasnau. 2nd edition, Cambridge, 384–396.

Peter of Spain. 1972.*Summulae logicales*. Ed. L. M. de Rijk. Assen.

2014. *Summaries of logic*. Ed. and trans. B. P. Copenhaver, with C. G. Normore and T. Parsons. Oxford.

Pettit, P. 2008. *Made with Words: Hobbes on Language, Mind, and Politics*. Princeton, N.J.

Petrarch. 2003. *Invectives*. Trans. D. Marsh. Cambridge, Mass.

2017. *Selected Letters*. Trans. E. Fantham. Cambridge, Mass.

Pico della Mirandola, Gianfrancesco. 1520. *Examen Vanitatis doctrinae gentium*. Mirandola.

Pigman, G. W. 2019. "Introduction." In Pontano 2019, vii–xxvii.

Pinborg, J. 1961. "Interjektionen und Naturlaute. Petrus Heliae und ein Problem der antiken und mittelalterlichen Sprachphilosophie." *Classica et Mediaevalia* 22: 117–138.

Poggi, D. 2018. "Locke and Syllogism: The 'Perception Grounded' Logic of the Way of Ideas." In *The Aftermath of Syllogism. Aristotelian Logical*

Argument from Avicenna to Hegel. Ed. M. Sgarbi and M. Cosci, 105–128. London.

Pontano, G. 1518–1519. *Pontani opera omnia soluta oratione composita*. Venice.

1943. *I dialoghi*. Ed. C. Previtera. Florence.

1953. *De sermone*. Ed. S. Lupi and A. Risicato. Lugano.

2012. *Dialogues. Volume 1: Charon and Antonius*. Ed. and trans. J. H. Gaisser. Cambridge, Mass.

2019. *The Virtues and Vices of Speech*. Ed. and trans. G. W. Pigman III. Cambridge, Mass.

Popkin, R. H. 2003 (1960). *The History of Scepticism from Savanarola to Bayle*. New York.

Porphyry. 1966. *Isagoge: translatio Boethii*. Ed. L. Minio-Paluello. Bruges.

1975. *Porphyry the Phoenician, Isagoge*. Trans. E. W. Warren. Toronto.

Potkay, A. 1994. *The Fate of Eloquence in the Age of Hume*. Ithaca, N.Y.

Priscian. 1855–1859. *Institutiones grammatice*. Ed. M. Herz. Leipzig.

Pseudo-Cicero . 1954. *Ad C. Herennium de ratione dicendi*. Ed. and trans. H. Caplan. Cambridge, MA.

Quintilian, M. F. 2001. *Institutio oratoria*. Ed. and trans. D. A. Russell. 5 vols. Cambridge, Mass.

Rabbie, E. 1986. *Cicero über den Witz. Kommentar zu "De oratore II."* Amsterdam.

Ramus, P. 1543. *Dialecticae institutiones*. Paris. [Repr. Stuttgart, 1964.]

Raven, C. 1942. *John Ray*. Cambridge.

Raylor, T. 2018. *Philosophy, Rhetoric, and Thomas Hobbes*. Oxford.

Regoliosi, M. 2000. "Le *Elegantie* del Valla come 'grammatica' antinormativa." *Studi di grammatica italiana* 19: 315–336.

2010. "*Usus* e *Ratio* in Valla." In *Lorenzo Valla: La Riforma della Lingua e della Logica*. 2 vols. Ed. M. Regoliosi, 1: 111–130. Florence.

Reinhardt, T. 2011. "Galen on Unsayable Properties." *Oxford Studies in Ancient Philosophy* 40: 297–317.

Ricken, U. 1994. *Linguistics, Anthropology and Philosophy in the French Enlightenment: Language Theory and Ideology*. London. [German original 1984, *Sprache, Anthropologie, Philosophie in der französischen Aufklärung*, Berlin.]

Risse, W. 1964. *Die Logik der Neuzeit*. Vol. 1. 1500–1640. Stuttgart.

Rist, J. M. 1994. *Augustine: Ancient Thought Baptized*. Cambridge.

Rizzi, A., and E. Del Soldato. 2013. "Latin and Vernacular in Quattrocento Florence and Beyond: An Introduction." *I Tatti Studies in the Italian Renaissance* 16: 231–242.

Rizzo, S. 2002. *Ricerche sul latino umanistico*. Rome.

Robert, A. 2006. "Jamais Aristote n'a eu de connaissance d'une substance: Nicholas d'Autrécourt en contexte." In *Nicolas d'Autrécourt et la faculté des arts de Paris (1317–1340)*. Ed. S. Caroti and C. Grellard, 113–151. Cesena.

Robins, R. H. 1976. "The Current Relevance of the Sapir-Whorf Hypothesis." In *Universalism versus Relativism in Language and Thought*. Ed. R. Pinxten, 99–108. Berlin.

Roick, M. 2017. *Pontano's Virtues: Aristotelian Moral and Political Thought in the Renaissance*. London.

Romanell, P. 1984. *John Locke and Medicine. A New Key to Locke*. Buffalo, N.Y.

Rossi, P. 1953. "Il 'De principiis' di Mario Nizolio." *Archivio di filosofia* 3: 57–92.

Rotondi Secchi Tarugi, L. (ed.). 1997. *Petrarca e la cultura europea*. Milan.

Rummel, E. 1995. *The Humanist-Scholastic Debate in the Renaissance and Reformation*. Cambridge, Mass.

2000. *The Confessionalization of Humanism in Reformation Germany*. Oxford.

Russell, B. 1959. *My Philosophical Development*. London.

Rutherford, D. 2005. *Early Renaissance Invective and the Controversies of Antonio da Rho*. Tempe, Ariz.

Ryle, G. 1932. "Systematically Misleading Expressions." *Proceedings of the Aristotelian Society* 32: 139–170. [Repr. in his *Collected Papers*, 2:39–62. London, 1971.]

Sacksteder, W. 1978. "Hobbes: Teaching Philosophy to Speak English." *Journal of the History of Philosophy* 16: 33–45.

Salmon, V. 1979. *The Study of Language in Seventeenth-Century England*. Amsterdam.

Sanches. F. 1955. *Opera Philosophica*. Ed. J. de Carvalho. Coimbra.

1988. *That Nothing Is Known*. Ed. E. Limbrick and D. F. S. Thomson. Cambridge.

2007. *Quod nihil scitur / Dass nichts gewusst wird*. Ed. and trans. K. Howald, D. Caluori, and S. Mariev. Hamburg.

Schliesser, E. (ed.). 2015. *Sympathy*. Oxford.

Schmidt, G. 2009. *Thomas More und die Sprachenfrage. Humanistische Sprachtheorie und die "translatio studii" im England der frühen Tudorzeit*. Heidelberg.

Schmitt, C. B. 1967. *Gianfrancesco Pico della Mirandola (1469–1533) and His Critique of Aristotle*. The Hague.

1972. *Cicero Scepticus: A Study of the Influence of the Academica in the Renaissance*. The Hague.

Schuhmann, K. 1985. "Geometrie und Philosophie bei Thomas Hobbes." *Philosophisches Jahrbuch* 92: 161–177.

1998. "Skinner's Hobbes." *British Journal for the History of Philosophy* 6: 115–125.

Schuurman, P. 2004. *Ideas, Mental Faculties and Method: The Logic of Ideas of Descartes and Locke and its Reception in the Dutch Republic, 1630–1750*. Leiden.

Seigel, J. E. 1968. *Rhetoric and Philosophy in Renaissance Humanism. The Union of Eloquence and Wisdom, Petrarch to Valla*. Princeton.

Serene, E. 1982. "Demonstrative Science." In *The Cambridge History of Later Medieval Philosophy*. Ed. N. Kretzmann, A. Kenny, and J. Pinborg, 496–518. Cambridge.

Serjeantson, R. 2006. "Proof and Persuasion." In *The Cambridge History of Science*. Vol. 3. *Early Modern Science*. Ed. K. Park and L. Daston, 132–176. Cambridge.

Seuren, P. 2013. *From Whorf to Montague: Explorations in the Theory of Language.* Oxford.

Sextus Empiricus. 2000. *Outlines of Scepticism.* Trans. J. Annas and J. Barnes. Cambridge.

Sgarbi, M. 2013. *The Aristotelian Tradition and the Rise of British Empiricism: Logic and Epistemology in the British Isles (1570–1689).* Dordrecht.

Shapin, S., and S. Schaffer. 1985. *Leviathan and the Air-Pump: Hobbes, Boyle, and the Experimental Life.* Princeton, N.J.

Shapiro, B. J. 1983. *Probability and Certainty in Seventeenth-Century England: A Study of the Relationships between Natural Science, Religion, History, Law, and Literature.* Princeton, N.J.

Skinner, Q. 1996. *Reason and Rhetoric in the Philosophy of Hobbes.* Cambridge.

1998. *Liberty before Liberalism.* Cambridge.

2008. *Hobbes and Republican Liberty.* Cambridge.

Skouen, T., and R. J. Stark (eds.). 2017. *Rhetoric and the Early Royal Society: A Sourcebook.* Leiden.

Sluiter, I. 2000. "The Rhetoric of Scepticism: Sextus against the Language Specialists." In *Ancient Scepticism and the Sceptical Tradition.* Ed. J. Sihvola, 93–123. Helsinki.

Smith, A. 1982. *The Theory of Moral Sentiments.* Ed. D. D. Raphael and A. L. Macfie. Indianapolis, Ind.

Soles, D. H. 1996. *Strong Wits and Spider Webs.* Aldershot.

Solmsen, F. 1932. "Drei Rekonstruktionen zur antiken Rhetorik und Poetik." *Hermes* 67: 151–154.

Sommerville, J. P. 1992. *Thomas Hobbes: Political Ideas in Historical Context.* London.

Soranzo, M. 2014. *Poetry and Identity in Quattrocento Naples.* Farnham.

Sorell, T. 1986. *Hobbes.* London.

1990a. "Hobbes's UnAristotelian Political Rhetoric." *Philosophy and Rhetoric* 23: 96–108.

1990b. "Hobbes's Persuasive Civil Science." *The Philosophical Quarterly* 40: 342–351.

Spade, P. V. 1982. "The Semantics of Terms." In *The Cambridge History of Later Medieval Philosophy.* Ed. N. Kretzmann, A. Kenny, and J. Pinborg, 188–196. Cambridge.

1994. *Five Texts on the Mediaeval Problem of Universals.* Indianapolis, Ind.

Sprat, T. 1958. *History of the Royal Society.* Ed. J. I. Cope and H. W. Jones. St Louis, Mo.

Stein Kokin, D. 2015. "Polemical Language: Hebrew and Latin in Medieval and Early Modern Jewish-Christian Debate." *Jewish History* 29: 1–38.

Stewart, M. A. 1994. "*Libertas Philosophandi*: From Natural to Speculative Philosophy." *Australian Journal of Politics and History* 40: 29–46.

Stinger, C. B. 1977. *Humanism and the Church Fathers: Ambrogio Traversari (1386–1439) and Christian Antiquity in the Italian Renaissance.* Albany, N.Y.

Stump, E. 1989. *Dialectic and Its Place in the Development of Medieval Logic*. Ithaca, N.Y.

Subbiondo, J. L. 1992. *John Wilkins and 17th-Century British Linguistics*. Amsterdam.

Sutton, R. B. 1953. "The Phrase *Libertas Philosophandi*." *Journal of the History of Ideas* 14: 310–316.

Tateo, F. 1960. *Astrologia e moralità in Giovanni Pontano*. Bari.

Tavoni, M. 1984. *Latino, grammatica, volgare: Storia di una questione umanistica*. Padua.

Taylor, B. 2016. "Definition and Ordinary Language in Cicero's *De Finibus* 2." *Classical Philology* 111: 54–73.

Taylor, C. C. W. 1990. "Aristotle's Epistemology." In *Epistemology*. Ed. S. Everson, 116–142. Cambridge.

Thieme, K. P. 1980. "Nizolius' Auseinandersetzung mit dem Wissenschaftsbegriff der Scholastik." In Nizolio 1980, 7–20.

Tillmann, B. 1912. *Leibniz' Verhältnis zur Renaissance im allgemeinen und zu Nizolius im besonderen*. Bonn.

Trapp, J. B. 2003. *Studies of Petrarch and His Influence*. London.

Trinkaus, C. 1979. *The Poet as Philosopher: Petrarch and the Formation of Renaissance Consciousness*. New Haven, Conn.

1983. "The Question of Truth in Renaissance Rhetoric and Anthropology." In *Renaissance Eloquence*. Ed. J. J. Murphy, 207–220. Berkeley, Calif.

1985. "The Astrological Cosmos and Rhetorical Culture of Giovanni Gioviano Pontano." *Renaissance Quarterly* 38: 446–472.

Tuck, R. 1991. "Introduction." In Hobbes 1991, viii–xxxiii.

1993. "The Civil Religion of Thomas Hobbes." In *Political Discourse in Early Modern Britain*. Ed. N. Phillipson and Q. Skinner, 120–138. Cambridge.

Valla, L. 1962. *Elegantiae Linguae Latinae*. In: Valla 1962, 1: 1–235.

1973. *Gesta Ferdinandi Regis Aragonum*. Ed. O. Besomi. Padua.

1982. *Repastinatio dialectice et philosophie*. Ed. G. Zippel. 2 vols. Padua.

2012. *Dialectical Disputations*. Ed. and trans. B. P. Copenhaver and L. Nauta. 2 vols. Cambridge, Mass.

Vasoli, C. 1968. *La dialettica e la retorica dell'Umanesimo. "Invenzione" e "metodo" nella cultura del XV e XVI secolo*. Milan.

1974. "Intorno al Petrarca ed ai logici 'moderni.'" I: *Antiqui und Moderni: Traditionsbewußtsein und Fortschrittbewußtsein im späten Mittelalter*. Ed. A. Zimmermann, 142–154. Berlin.

Vickers, B. 1968. *Francis Bacon and Renaissance Prose*. Cambridge.

1985. "The Royal Society and English Prose Style: A Reassessment." In *Rhetoric and the Pursuit of Truth: Language Change in the Seventeenth and Eighteenth Centuries*. Ed. B. Vickers and N. Struever, 1–76. Los Angeles, Calif.

1987. *English Science, Bacon to Newton*. Cambridge.

1988. *In Defence of Rhetoric*. Oxford.

1993. "Review of Werner Hüllen, 'Their Manner of Discourse': Nachdenken über Sprache im Umkreis der Royal Society." *Isis* 84: 579–580.

Vives, J. L. 1782–1790. *Opera Omnia*. Ed. Gregorio Mayans y Siscar. 8 vols., Valencia. [Repr. London, 1964.]
1971. *Vives on Education*. Trans. F. Watson. Totowa.
1974. *De anima et vita*. Ed. M. Sancipriano. Padova.
1979. *Against the Pseudodialecticians*. Trans. R. Guerlac. Dordrecht.
1987. *Early Writings*. Ed. and trans. C. Matheeussen, C. Fantazzi and E. George. Leiden.
2000. *De ratione dicendi / Del arte del hablar*. Trans. J. M. Rodriguez Peregrina. Granada.
2011. *L'insegnamento delle discipline*. Trans. V. Del Nero. Florence.
Wallace, W. A. 1972–1974. *Causality and Scientific Explanation*. 2 vols. Ann Arbor, Mich.
Walzer, A. E. 2003. "Quintilian's *Vir Bonus* and the Stoic Wise Man." *Rhetoric Society Quarterly* 33: 25–41.
Warren, E. W. 1975. "Introduction." In Porphyry 1975, 9–23.
Waswo, R. 1979. "The 'Ordinary Language Philosophy' of Lorenzo Valla." *Bibliothèque d'Humanisme et Renaissance* 41: 255–271.
1987. *Language and Meaning in the Renaissance*. Princeton, N.J.
Watson, F. 1971. "Introduction." In Vives 1971, xvii–clvii.
Wels, V. 2000. *Triviale Künste: Die humanistische Reform der grammatischen, dialektischen und rhetorischen Ausbildung an der Wende zum 16. Jahrhundert*. Berlin.
Werlen, I. 2002. *Sprachliche Relativität. Eine problemorientierte Einführung*. Tübingen/Basel.
Wesseler, M. 1974. *Die Einheit von Wort und Sache. Der Entwurf einer rhetorischen Philosophie bei Marius Nizolius*. Munich.
White, M. G. 1978. *The Philosophy of the American Revolution*. New York.
William of Ockham. 1974. *Ockham's Theory of Terms. Part I of the "Summa Logicae."* Trans. M. J. Loux. Notre Dame, IN.
1978. *Expositionis in libros artis logicae prooemium et Expositio in librum Porphyrii de praedicabilibus*. Ed. E. A. Moody. St. Bonaventure, N.Y.
1990. *Philosophical Writings*. Ed. and trans. Ph. Boehner. Revised edition. Indianapolis, Ind.
Winkler, K. 2003. "Lockean Logic." In *The Philosophy of John Locke: New Perspectives*. Ed. P. R. Anstey, 154–178. London.
2009. "Signification, Intention, Projection." *Philosophia* 37: 477–501.
Witt, R. G. 1983. *Hercules at the Crossroads: The Life, Works, and Thought of Coluccio Salutati*. Durham, N.C.
2000. *"In the Footsteps of the Ancients." The Origins of Humanism from Lovato to Bruni*. Leiden.
Wood, N. 1988. *Cicero's Social and Political Thought*. Berkeley, Calif.
Yolton, J. W. 1956. *Locke and the Way of Ideas*. Oxford.
Zak, G. 2015. "Petrarch and the Ancients." In *The Cambridge Companion to Petrarch*. Ed. A. Ascoli and U. Falkeid, 141–153. Cambridge.

Index